CUSANUS TODAY

CUSANUS TODAY

THINKING with **NICHOLAS** of **CUSA**
Between **PHILOSOPHY** and **THEOLOGY**

Foreword by Jean-Luc Marion

Edited by David Albertson

The Catholic University of America Press
Washington, D.C.

Copyright © 2024

The Catholic University of America Press

All rights reserved

The paper used in this publication meets the minimum requirements of American National Standards for Information Science—Permanence of Paper for Printed Library Materials, ANSI Z39.48-1992.

Cataloging-in-Publication Data available from the Library of Congress

ISBN: 978-0-8132-3811-1 | eISBN: 978-0-8132-3812-8

Book design by Burt&Burt
The text is set in Minion Pro and Astoria.

In memoriam

Louis Dupré

1925–2022

List of Illustrations, **x**

Abbreviations, **xi**

Preface, **xiii**

Introduction, **xix**

PART I
THE MODERN GERMAN RECEPTION

1
Cusanus after Idealism: From Hamann to Przywara
John R. Betz
3

2
"Methodic Foundering" or "Methodic Overcoming of Rationality"? Metaphysics of Liberation in Karl Jaspers and Nicholas of Cusa
Tamara Albertini
23

3
Theoria in Cusanus and Gadamer: The Joy of Contemplation
Michael Edward Moore
43

4
Blumenberg Reading Cusanus: The Epochal Threshold as a Liminal Space between the "No Longer" and the "Not Yet"
Elizabeth Brient
59

5
Identifying Difference: Beierwaltes on Cusanus and Hegel
Valentina Zaffino
75

6
The Infinite Sphere from Cusanus to Peter Sloterdijk's Spherology
José González Ríos
89

PART II
NEW DIALOGUES

7
Nicholas of Cusa's Contribution
to the Final Phase of Kitaro Nishida's Philosophy
Kazuhiko Yamaki
107

8
Maurice de Gandillac's Reading of
Nicholas of Cusa and Its Transmission to Gilles Deleuze
Alexia Schmitt
119

9
Jacques Lacan and Learned Ignorance
Jean-Marie Nicolle
131

10
The Wild Science: Michel de Certeau and Cusan Topology
David Albertson
139

11
The Gift in Cusanus: The Neo-Augustinian Humanism of Louis Dupré
Peter Casarella
169

12
A Constant "Re-presenter" of the World's Reality:
Karsten Harries on Cusanus, Art, and Architecture
Il Kim
189

PART III
THINKING WITH CUSANUS

13

The Contemporary Relevance of the Philosophical
Presuppositions of Interreligious Dialogue in Cusanus
João Maria André

203

14

Image or Icon: Phenomenologies of Nicholas of Cusa
Emmanuel Falque

229

15

Cusanus and Heidegger: Multiplying the *Tetractys*
Stephen Gersh

251

16

Nicholas of Cusa on Infinite Desire
David Bentley Hart

265

17

Coincident Unities: Nicholas of Cusa in Radical Orthodox Tradition
John Milbank

281

18

(Con)figuring Cusanus
Cyril O'Regan

313

Bibliography, 331

Contributors, 361

Index, 365

List of Illustrations

Fig. 7-1	Kitaro Nishida in his study. Reproduced with the permission of the Ishikawa Nishida Kitaro Museum of Philosophy.	109
Fig. 7-2	A concave mirror reflecting light toward its focal point.	114
Fig. 12-1	Claude-Nicolas Ledoux, *Maison de gardes agricoles* (1789).	191
Fig. 12-2	Walter Gropius, Gropius House in Lincoln, Massachusetts (1938).	191
Fig. 12-3	Mies van der Rohe, Farnsworth House (1951).	192
Fig. 12-4	Lebbeus Woods, Horizon House (2000).	192
Fig. 12-5	Bamberg Cathedral, Germany (1012).	196
Fig. 12-6	Nicholas of Cusa, *De coniecturis*, I.9. *Unitas* and *alteritas* in *Figura paradigmatica* (Figura P).	199
Fig. 12-7	Leon Battista Alberti, *Della pittura*, Book I: illustration of perspective.	199

Abbreviations

CCCM Corpus Christianorum. Continuatio Mediaevalis. Turnhout: Brepols, 1970–.

CCSL Corpus Christianorum. Series Latina. Turnhout: Brepols, 1954–.

CSEL Corpus Scriptorum Ecclesiasticorum Latinorum. Vienna: Hölder-Pichler-Tempsky, 1866–.

DW Meister Eckhart. *Die deutschen und lateinischen Werke.* Stuttgart & Berlin: W. Kohlhammer, 1936–.

GA Martin Heidegger. *Gesamtausgabe.* Frankfurt am Main: Vittorio Klostermann, 1976–.

LW Meister Eckhart. *Die deutschen und lateinischen Werke.* Stuttgart & Berlin: W. Kohlhammer, 1936–.

MFCG Mitteilungen und Forschungsbeiträge der Cusanus-Gesellschaft

PL Patrologia Cursus Completus, Series Latina. Paris: J. P. Migne, 1844–1864.

Citations of the works of Nicholas of Cusa are abbreviated according to the editions and translations listed in the bibliography.

Preface

Our Anachronistic Predecessor
JEAN-LUC MARION

The legacy of Nicholas of Cusa has been defined as "the presence of one absent."[1] In fact, this presence, long marginal, is no longer in dispute. For almost a century, since the completion of the *Opera omnia* and with the proliferation of bilingual editions in every language, which have given rise to ever more extensive research in all directions, the work of Cusanus has regained a central place. And yet, precisely by virtue of the studies devoted to him, the difference or even divergence among the interpretations of Cusanus that have developed have ended up dissolving the unity of his figure. The present proceedings of the colloquium "Cusanus Today: Thinking with Nicholas of Cusa between Philosophy and Theology" testify to this. We first find in Part 1 a review of the German interpretations of the last two centuries, all governed by the concern to situate the work chronologically, but always hesitating to assign it a role, either as a precursor not yet arrived at the port of modernity, or as a late return to Neoplatonism and

---

1 Stephan Meier-Oeser, *Die Präsenz des Vergessenen: Zur Rezeption der Philosophie des Nicolaus Cusanus vom 15. bis zum 18. Jahrhundert* (Münster: Aschendorff Verlag, 1989).

Augustinianism. Part 2 offers a review of possible but anachronistic relationships of Nicholas of Cusa to recent, if unexpected, thinkers. Finally, in Part 3 comes a series of speculative reworkings of Cusan theses by the most diverse movements in contemporary philosophy. These three orientations all shed some light, but their heterogeneity is surprising and raises a question: Where should one locate the center of Nicholas of Cusa's thought, if indeed there is one?

This eccentricity can probably be explained by a factual observation: his university training was relatively brief (two years in Heidelberg), immediately compensated by an innovative and multidisciplinary training in Padua, yet one that never resulted in an academic chair in either the faculty of theology or that of the arts—he even refused a chair in canon law in Leuven. An outsider to the recently established university system, he never took on its constraints, its language, or its customs. Most of all, his thought could not become the object of teaching or systematized theses; it did not benefit from any institutional reception, whether positive or polemical, which might have included his ideas within the ordinary flow of debates in the recognized schools and publicized them among disciples or through declared adversaries.

Deprived of position and posterity in the university, his thought was really only diffused within local monastic networks through essentially private letters and treatises largely independent of each other. If we add his responsibilities as bishop (often contested in Brixen) and as papal legate (absorbed in ecclesiastical politics), we understand that his work could never be built into a complete architecture, nor handed down as such for reception and scholarship in a conventional academic setting. Nicholas of Cusa thus appears to lack both a point of departure and a posterity within the university, whose lexicon and forms of debate and writing, to make matters worse, he never adopted. Original, perhaps even brilliant, he nevertheless remained entirely on the margins.

It is not surprising, then, that he has long remained on the margins of the dominant historiography of philosophy (Hegel, with whom he has been compared, never cites him in his *Vorlesungen über die Geschichte der Philosophie*). Or at best he is assigned to the cohort of authors whom the "progress of European consciousness" could only leave in an unresolved indeterminacy—in the company, for instance, of Meister Eckhart and Giordano Bruno, Erasmus and Montaigne. Nor is it surprising that the first modern attempt to reevaluate Cusanus consisted, under the influence of the Marburg School and an overly linear reading of the medieval period, in asking whether he might represent one of the last figures of "Scholasticism" (as a "Neoplatonist," a "pantheist," a "mystic," and so on) or a still-confused prefiguration of modernity (given his critique of knowledge as finite, or his reassessment of mathematics in the interpretation of physics). Recent work has definitively shown the fragility of such anachronistic hypotheses.

We do not do justice to Nicholas of Cusa, we do not understand him, by reducing him to a moment of historical transition, confused and still uncertain. Nor do we do him justice, even if it helps us understand him better, by recognizing his relevance in certain contemporary debates, for then we leave undecided the reasons why his concepts can, even today, still make relevant interventions. The fact that we have the impression of finding ourselves in some of his theses is not enough to explain, and surely not to justify, such arbitrary comparisons. It therefore becomes necessary to resort to another hermeneutic, one historically more precise and speculatively more powerful.

Reading through the contributions in this collection, but also spending time in his oeuvre myself, has led me to formulate a clear and simple hypothesis. Nicholas of Cusa, by refusing quite self-consciously and wittingly to participate in the academic turn taken by philosophy *and also by theology* from the thirteenth century onward, without question also refused—one of the very few if not the first to do so—to think within and according to the rules of what was to become in the same period *metaphysica*: beginning at least with the *Quaestiones metaphysicae* of Duns Scotus in the thirteenth century until its culmination in the *Disputiones metaphysicae* of Suárez two centuries later. Cusanus did not so much reactivate philosophical and theological currents that preceded *metaphysica* (he did not return to Augustinianism, to Neoplatonism, etc.), nor did he anticipate the speculative use of mathematics (which he uses to think only divine infinity, not mundane physics). Instead, he confronted medieval thought's indecision in the face of three possible choices, which have been termed "rebellious metaphysics"[2]: either a *philosophia prima* or science of first principles; or a science of the *ens in quantum ens*, which in the seventeenth century would become *ontologia*; or finally what amounted to seizing the title of *metaphysica* and forcing its acceptance, all the way to Hegel. In this

---

2 Olivier Boulnois, *Métaphysiques rebelles: Genèse et structures d'une science au Môyen Age* (Paris: Presses Universitaires de France, 2013).

situation, Nicholas of Cusa made the choice to evade *metaphysica* itself. Hence his anachronism and marginality in his own period; hence his relevance today, when we experience the end of metaphysics and must think without it or beyond it. It is not even enough to read into him a "mystical topology" (Certeau) or the phenomenology of the *Lebenswelt* (Husserl in the *Crisis*). First it is necessary to decipher, if not his overcoming, at least his defusing, bracketing, and destitution of *metaphysica* even before it became established. Coming as he did before it, Nicholas leapt over his epoch and beyond it—right into our situation. His choice to reject *metaphysica* in his time makes him our potential contemporary.

We can only sketch here the ruptures, however clear and sharp, between Nicholas of Cusa and *metaphysica*. Yet a few points are in order. His first intervention is to reject what will become the principle of identity. Far from applying the identity of the thing with itself (A=A) to common beings as well as to God, he starts from the *coincidentia oppositorum*. For in God even the One finds itself taken up and unfolded like the *non aliud*: divine unity is conceived as non-Otherness, which at the same time also defines each creature as "nothing other than itself." Unity does not separate the multiple from the One, but replicates the divine *non aliud* by inscribing it in the other precisely as other. The exteriority of the infinite therefore inhabits and defines all finite creatures. The second intervention challenges what will become the principle of sufficient reason. The relationship of God to creatures no longer passes through the relation of cause and effect and even less through its reduction to efficient causality. God is not reduced to efficient power in opposition to the possibility of the effect; God as the *possest* exercises the effective power of the possible as such. By bracketing the Aristotelian categories of act and potentiality, of *ousia* and accidents as well as relation, Nicholas goes so far as to marginalize the very lexicon of *ens*, such that the latter refers neither to the *conceptus entis*, nor even a pure *actus essendi*, but precisely to the *possest*. Hence the almost-complete extinction of the problematic of the *analogia entis* in Cusanus, both for lack of *ens* and for lack of analogy. For ultimately, we cannot determine a measurable [*mesurable*] relationship—in analogy to the model of mathematical proportionality in four terms—where it is a question of thinking the excess [*démesure*] of the finite by the infinite.

These fundamental theses lead to *docta ignorantia*, which should not be seen as a simple resurgence of ancient Skepticism, but as a recovery and enhancement of the mystical theology (including the *via negativa*) of the

Dionysian tradition. An enhanced recovery, because unlike the immediate successors of Thomas Aquinas, here there is no question of formulating the relationship between cataphasis and apophasis in terms of being-ness (through the *analogia entis*), but of articulating the finite and the infinite *paradoxically*. Only paradoxes, in fact, can first establish a logic different from that of *metaphysica* (categorial, predicative, propositional), and then deal with the infinite as such, without reducing it to a figure of the finite— which is to say that paradoxes think the finite from the infinite, and not the other way around. On this path, Cusanus is directly opposed to Duns Scotus and Suárez, who, like *Schulmetaphysik* and Kant after them, include the infinite and the finite within the *conceptus entis* and the object. It will be necessary to wait for Descartes and perhaps also Pascal to find such an approach to infinity. Among these paradoxes, the most decisive without a doubt concerns the treatment of the impossible: "Hence, since nothing is impossible for God, we should look for him (in whom impossibility is necessity) in those things which are impossible in this world. Just as in this world infinity is actually impossible, so endless magnitude is the necessity which necessitates the existence of not-being, or nothing."[3] While *metaphysica* can only be deployed within the limits of the region of the possible, restricted to self-identity and non-contradiction, *docta ignorantia*, understood as a thought outside of metaphysics, privileges the region proper to God, the region of the impossible, and thinks the finite possible starting from the infinite impossible. This unprecedented reversal will remain without a philosophical echo until at least Schelling, Nietzsche, and the late Husserl. It still remains the frontier of thinking in the epoch of the end of metaphysics. And this is why Nicholas of Cusa can appear not as our contemporary, but as our predecessor.

---

3 "Unde cum deo nihil sit impossibile, oportet per ea quae in hoc mundo sunt impossibilia nos ad ipsum respicere, apud quem impossibilitas est necessitas. Sicut infinitas in hoc mundo actu est impossibilis, sic magnitudo cuius non est finis, est necessitas illa, quae non-ens seu nihil ut sit necessitat." Nicholas of Cusa, *Trialogus de possest*, 59, in *Nicolai de Cusa Opera Omnia*, vol. XI/2, ed. Renata Steiger (Hamburg: Felix Meiner Verlag, 1973), 71; trans. Jasper Hopkins, *A Concise Introduction to the Philosophy of Nicholas of Cusa* (Minneapolis: University of Minnesota Press, 1978), 946.

Introduction

Cusanus Today

DAVID ALBERTSON

"For those wishing to philosophize—which I call the hunt for wisdom—I shall lead them into regions and fields whose place I will describe, which are quite rich, it seems to me, with the bounty that they seek."[1] So wrote Nicholas of Cusa, cardinal bishop, and by this time papal vicar in Rome, during the final years of his life as he looked back on three decades of intellectual expeditions. Here Cusanus promises to lead his readers on a successful hunt through all the best locales, chasing not after foxes or deer, but after treasures of wisdom. His poignant philosophical memoir, *De venatione sapientiae* (*The Hunt for Wisdom*, 1462), gathered together the best insights, strategies, and formulae that he had devised for naming the mystery of God, like a field guide for hunting after the greatest quarry of all.

---

1 "Deinde volenti philosophari, quod venationem sapientiae voco, regiones et in illis loca quaedam describam in camposque ducam, quos praedae, quam quaerunt, apprime puto referas." Nicholas of Cusa, *De venatione sapientiae*, Prol. (1), in *Nicolai de Cusa Opera Omnia*, vol. XII, ed. Raymond Klibansky and Hans Gerhard Senger (Hamburg: Felix Meiner Verlag, 1982), 4.

Yet ironically, despite his efforts to synthesize his abundant writings—which spanned not only theology, philosophy, and countless sermons, but also contemporary painting, cosmology, cartography, optics, mathematics, politics, and interreligious dialogue—Cusanus was only occasionally read in the centuries to follow. His enthusiasm for Pseudo-Dionysius and Boethius impressed the sixteenth-century humanists in the circle of Jacques Lefèvre d'Étaples in Paris, who collected and reprinted his works, works that both enticed and galled Giordano Bruno, who via Schelling may have passed Cusan ideas to Hegel. Descartes and Mersenne mention him a handful of times. Yet as Stephan Meier-Oeser has documented in detail—and Jean-Luc Marion confirms in his preface—Cusanus appears in modern thought not unlike the hidden God of negative theology: the figure of an absence.[2]

Nicholas of Cusa has never fit well into modern categories. Does he belong to the Middle Ages or early modernity? Do his writings commence from faith or from reason? Is his cosmology grounded in mystical traditions or scientific epistemology? In each case, the answer is both, but thinking such divisions together is a difficult challenge for us in the twenty-first century. We can only take his advice to seek out a perspective in which opposites coincide in a simple unity. For Karsten Harries it is just Nicholas's liminal position that remains valuable amid our own plural and fragile modernities. "Precisely because Cusanus straddles that threshold," writes Harries, "he has more to teach us as we try to understand not only the legitimacy, but the limits, of modernity."[3] This coupling together of Nicholas's past and our present proceed in an eminently Cusan dialectic. As postmodern wisdom reveals the shortcomings of modern dualisms, the historical picture of Cusanus grows clearer. The more one considers the exceptional instance of Cusan thought outside such dualisms—the presence of the forgotten, the road not taken—the less compelling those dualisms appear to be. But then how do we name that eccentric status of Nicholas of Cusa in the present?

Access to the Cusan oeuvre has been complicated by the conditions of its retrieval in the late nineteenth century. Neo-Kantians like Hermann Cohen and Ernst Cassirer hailed Nicholas as the first "modern" thinker, anticipating elements of Descartes, Spinoza, Kant, and Hegel in

---

[2] Stephan Meier-Oeser, *Die Präsenz des Vergessenen: Zur Rezeption der Philosophie des Nicolaus Cusanus vom 15. bis zum 18. Jahrhundert* (Münster: Aschendorff Verlag, 1989).

[3] Karsten Harries, *Infinity and Perspective* (Cambridge, MA: MIT Press, 2001), xi.

his speculations. Yet the meaning of "modernity" was itself undergoing a simultaneous reassessment.[4] Since then, Cusanus scholarship has slowly unwound the knot, aided by a healthy skepticism about the "essence" of modernity. The Neo-Kantian enthusiasm for Nicholas of Cusa inspired the founding of the magisterial critical edition of his major works published by Felix Meiner Verlag, first in Leipzig and then Hamburg, from 1927 until its conclusion in 2010. As scholarship on the critical edition progressed, historians gradually learned that Cusanus was more medieval preacher and contemplative than modern philosopher. Yet at the same time, postwar European readers were digging into his works and encountering an exciting, independent voice. So even as Nicholas of Cusa shifted from modern to medieval among historians, he was emerging as a contemporary interlocutor for modern, and even postmodern, authors.

To think with Cusanus today one must begin with the complications of his reception history. Meier-Oeser's early modern retrospective provided an invaluable starting point in 1989. By 2005, Klaus Reinhardt and Harald Schwaetzer published a collection of papers on the reception of Cusanus in the twentieth century, including contributions on Martin Buber, Carl Jung, Jacques Derrida, Jan Patočka, and Niklas Luhmann, along with others revisited in our volume.[5] In 2006, John Milbank issued a second edition of *Theology and Social Theory* furnished with a lengthy preface praising Eckhart and Cusanus as the surest guides for contending with Nietzschean postmodernity.[6] By 2013, another volume, now from Matthias Vollet and Tom Müller, added further points of contact between Cusanus and modern thought, with essays on Friedrich Schleiermacher, Hermann Cohen, Ortega y Gasset, Karl Rahner, and Pavel Florensky, among others.[7] The following year, Emmanuel Falque published the first of several essays on Cusanus, focusing on *De visione Dei* (1453) after the example of Michel de Certeau. After Jean-Luc Marion, in his own essay of 2016, objected to

---

4 See Morimichi Watanabe, "The Origins of Modern Cusanus Research in Germany and the Foundation of the Heidelberg *Opera omnia*," in *Nicholas of Cusa in Search of God and Wisdom: Essays in Honor of Morimichi Watanabe by the American Cusanus Society*, ed. Gerald Christianson and Thomas M. Izbicki (Leiden: Brill, 1991), 17–42.

5 Klaus Reinhardt and Harald Schwaetzer, eds., *Cusanus-Rezeption in der Philosophie des 20. Jahrhunderts* (Regensburg: S. Roderer-Verlag, 2005).

6 John Milbank, "Between Liberalism and Positivism," in *Theology and Social Theory: Beyond Secular Reason*, 2nd ed. (Oxford: Blackwell, 2006), xi–xxxii.

7 Tom Müller and Matthias Vollet, eds., *Die Modernitäten des Nikolaus von Kues: Debatten und Rezeptionen* (Bielefeld: Transcript Verlag, 2013).

Falque's reading, the American Cusanus Society facilitated the translation and publication of both works in English.[8] Most recently, Enrico Peroli and Marco Moschini have revived the question posed by Hans Urs von Balthasar in his own estimate of the German cardinal in 1964, the five-hundredth anniversary of his death: *Warum wir Cusanus brauchen*.[9] The book invites Cusanus scholars to identify which Cusan concepts have the most potential to inform thinking today.

Why do we need Cusanus? We find ourselves in something of a Cusan "moment." Like us, Nicholas was fascinated with vision and visuality, with technology and the power of the mind, with the difference between nature and artifice, with human plasticity. He pursued perhaps the deepest encounter with Islam of any Christian humanist in his day. If the negative theology of Pseudo-Dionysius and Eckhart resonated with deconstruction in the 1980s, Cusanus is attuned to the passage through negation, as he himself transitioned from an austere apophasis in his early writings toward a more complicated cataphasis in later works. Cusan concepts even anticipate current topics in the continental philosophy of religion: on alterity (Levinas), invisibility (Merleau-Ponty), or the icon (Marion); on the interweaving of philosophy and theology at the phenomenological threshold (Falque); on the infinite and the application of mathematics to theory (Lautman, Deleuze, Badiou). Nicholas's promise to lead philosophers toward wisdom has been kept, with a slight delay. "I shall lead them into regions and fields rich with the bounty that they seek": it has never been truer than it is today.

The present volume proceeds in three parts. In Part 1, the first six chapters study the sustained reception of Nicholas of Cusa in twentieth-century German thought, from Erich Przywara and Karl Jaspers up through contemporaries like Peter Sloterdijk. Famous scholars of Cusanus, including Hans Blumenberg and Werner Beierwaltes, are examined not only as guides to the cardinal's writings but as members of this rich tradition of reception, a group that includes philosophers influenced by the cardinal, like Hans Georg Gadamer. In Part 2, the next six chapters look to subsequent waves of reception outside of Germany: first in Japanese philosophy, then shortly thereafter in France with Maurice de Gandillac and Jacques Lacan, followed

---

[8] Falque responds to Marion in his contribution to the present volume, where the reader can find pertinent references concerning this controversy.

[9] Enrico Peroli and Marco Moschini, eds., *Why We Need Cusanus / Warum wir Cusanus brauchen* (Münster: Aschendorff Verlag, 2022).

by post-1968 writers like the Jesuit cultural theorist, Michel de Certeau. Beyond Europe we find new dialogues spiraling outward, not only in Japan but among the American scholars Karsten Harries and Louis Dupré—who in their own *translatio studii* were both born in western Europe but separately found their way to Yale University by the early 1970s, where they inspired another generation of Cusanus readers, including at least four of our contributors. Part 3 sets out from the present by inviting leading Christian thinkers to engage Cusanus as a contemporary dialogue partner, whether in philosophy with Emmanuel Falque and Stephen Gersh, in theology with David Bentley Hart and John Milbank, or in interreligious dialogue with João Maria André. Finally, Cyril O'Regan completes the volume by meditating on the unique promise of Cusan thought. In the guise of a conclusion, O'Regan considers the figure of Cusanus in our present, even peering beyond it, a challenge achieved not by referencing the past (nor through the footnotes that verify such retrospection) but by evoking possible "Cusan futures" in dialogue with the scholarship found in the present volume—a better introduction than I could hope to offer here.

This collection of essays is the fruit of an international conference held at the University of Notre Dame on September 19–21, 2019, which I had the good fortune to co-organize with my friend and colleague Peter Casarella (now at Duke Divinity School), whose energetic ministrations at Notre Dame made the event possible. Little did we appreciate the conveniences of international travel and face-to-face presence in those final months before the global pandemic! We are grateful to our hosts at the Department of Theology and to all of our financial sponsors, especially the Medieval Institute at Notre Dame, the Henkels Lecture Fund at the Institute for Scholarship in the Liberal Arts, and the American Cusanus Society. Heartfelt thanks are due to the Watanabe Family and the Morimichi Watanabe Fund at Long Island University for their ongoing generous support. At Notre Dame we thank Christopher Rios, Kristen Garvin-Podell, Thomas Burman, Duncan Stroik, C. J. Jones, Sarah Mustillo, Denis Robichaud, and in particular John Betz, who suggested the volume's title, as well as long-time friends of the American Cusanus Society, Garth Green, Nancy van Deusen, and Stephen Lewis. John Martino at The Catholic University of America Press has been an exemplar of patience throughout all manner of pandemic disruptions.

During the long preparation of the volume, we mourned the passing of Louis Dupré on January 11, 2022, a teacher to many, whether personally or through his many influential works; on this point see Peter Casarella's tribute in this volume. Our common efforts are dedicated to his memory, with profound gratitude.

Pentecost 2023

PART I
The Modern German Reception

1

Cusanus after Idealism

From Hamann to Przywara

JOHN R. BETZ

The two principles for which Nicholas of Cusa is most known, and which have received the most scholarly attention, are assuredly those of learned ignorance (*docta ignorantia*) and the coincidence of opposites (*coincidentia oppositorum*). Indeed, they more or less define Cusanus in textbook accounts of his place in the history of ideas. What is less understood, however, is the historical reception of these principles and their *Wirkungsgeschichte*. A complete historical account of this nature would be an enormous undertaking; a whole book could be written on the principle of the *coincidentia oppositorum* in German Idealism alone.[1] In what follows, therefore, I will limit myself to two important but historically neglected figures of the German intellectual tradition, who uniquely deployed these Cusan principles in order to defend and clarify the nature of Christianity with respect to various forms of

---

1 See Stephan Meier-Oeser, *Die Präsenz des Vergessenen: Zur Rezeption der Philosophie des Nicolaus Cusanus vom 15. bis zum 18. Jahrhundert* (Münster: Aschendorff Verlag, 1989).

modern rationalism: the eighteenth-century Lutheran author and man of letters, Johann Georg Hamann (1730–1788), and the twentieth-century Jesuit, Erich Przywara (1889–1972).

No doubt, Hamann and Przywara are very different—they would seem to have little if anything in common other than being Christian thinkers of note. Yet they are curiously united by their assimilation of the cardinal's ideas (or in Hamann's case, what he knew of his ideas second-hand). Indeed, Nicholas of Cusa's ideas were influential enough that one could with justification call both Hamann and Przywara distinctive heirs of his thought. Hamann, for example, invokes both principles against the dualisms of Immanuel Kant's philosophy and what he perceived as the presumption of modern rationalism; and Przywara similarly invokes them. Indeed, one could argue that the *coincidentia oppositorum*, and the apophaticism it implies, is the lynchpin of Przywara's understanding of the analogy of being.

Cusanus in Hamann

Turning first to Hamann, one might legitimately wonder what the German Lutheran literary critic writing in the northeastern Prussian port city of Königsberg during the last half of the eighteenth century has to do with the Bishop of Brixen. And the question is all the more acute given that Hamann may never have read Cusanus in the first place, as a result of the lack of extant editions of his work. Moreover, Hamann mistakenly attributed the principle of the coincidence of opposites to Giordano Bruno. We cannot, therefore, speak of any direct influence or lineage. But we can nevertheless speak of a *Wirkungsgeschichte*, inasmuch as Cusanus mediated two ideas—learned ignorance and the coincidence of opposites—that would profoundly shape Hamann's response to Kant and the Enlightenment in general.

Learned Ignorance

Let us begin with the idea of learned ignorance, which Hamann deploys in the first of his pseudonymous publications, the *Socratic Memorabilia*, in 1759, which was dedicated to an anonymous pair of friends identified simply as "the two," but whom we know to be Christoph Berens and Immanuel Kant. While the anonymous public would have been in the dark about the dedication, Berens and Kant would have understood its significance, because after Hamann's dramatic conversion in London the year before, "the two" had conspired to win Hamann back to the common cause, which later became conventionally known as the Enlightenment.[2]

By the time Hamann returned from London, however, he was a changed man, and his response to their attempt to reconvert him was as impassioned and wry as it was erudite. Whereas Hamann's contemporaries were wont to regard Socrates as a champion of reason, Hamann presents him instead as profoundly affected by his ignorance: "Socrates seems to have talked as much about his ignorance as a hypochondriac about his imagined illness."[3] But Socrates's ignorance was not simply a personal affectation, much less a doctrine acknowledging an evident fact or, still less, a grudging admission; rather, it was something profoundly felt. And in this regard, Hamann criticizes ancient and modern accounts of Socratic ignorance that, he thinks, barely scratch the surface of it:

> The ignorance of Socrates was a feeling [*Empfindung*]. Between a feeling and a doctrine, however, there is a greater difference than that between a living animal and its anatomical skeleton. However much the ancient and modern skeptics wrap themselves in the lion's skin of Socratic ignorance, they nevertheless betray themselves by their voice and their ears. If they know nothing, why does the world need a learned demonstration of it? Their hypocrisy is ludicrous and shameless. Whoever has need of so much acumen and eloquence to convince himself of his ignorance must harbor within his heart a powerful antipathy toward the truth of it.[4]

We might wonder what Hamann might have made of Cusanus's *De docta ignorantia*, if he had known it, given what he says here about "learned demonstrations" of ignorance (though we can be fairly certain that he would have had little patience for purely intellectual accounts of negative theology). His point here, in any event, is that Socratic ignorance is *toto coelo* different from what skeptics might make of it, who vainly imagine that it amounts to rational skepticism of, say, popular religion. On the contrary,

---

[2] See John R. Betz, *After Enlightenment: The Post-Secular Vision of J. G. Hamann* (Oxford: Wiley-Blackwell, 2009), 34–35.
[3] Johann Georg Hamann, *Sämtliche Werke*, ed. Josef Nadler, 6 vols. (Vienna: Herder, 1949–57), 2:70. Unless otherwise noted, all translations are my own.
[4] Hamann, *Sämtliche Werke*, 2:73.

Hamann says, Socrates's ignorance was a kind of feeling, which cannot be communicated like a doctrine or, as he elsewhere says of faith, "like merchandise."⁵ Rather, it can be understood only by a similar, empathetic feeling: "Just as one must know this malady [i.e., hypochondria] in order to understand a hypochondriac and make sense of him, so too a sympathy with ignorance would seem to be required in order to have a conception of Socratic ignorance."⁶ And for Hamann, such feelings, like faith, can be communicated at best only indirectly.

And so it was, Hamann avers, with Socrates. He did not try to communicate his wisdom, that is, his ignorance, directly, but indirectly in a way that was initially confounding:

> The opinion of Socrates can be reduced to [what] he said to the Sophists, the intellectuals of his time: I know nothing. Thus it came about that these words were a thorn in their eyes and a scourge on their backs. All Socrates's intuitions, which were nothing but the expectorations and secretions of his ignorance, seemed as frightening to them as the hair on the head of the Medusa, as the navel of the Aegis.⁷

In other words, far from being the historical champion of rationalism the *Aufklärer* made him out to be, Hamann alleges, few would have been more dreadful to them, the modern-day Sophists, than Socrates. Moreover, he points out what his contemporaries should presumably have remembered, given their learning, but seem to have forgotten: namely, that it was Socrates's professed ignorance, and not any encyclopedic knowledge, that made him wise in the eyes of the oracle of Apollo at Delphi:

> The god doubtless laughed behind his golden beard when, during the time of Socrates, the ticklish [question] was put to him as to who among all those living at the time was the wisest. *Sophocles* and *Euripides* would never have become such great models for the theater were it not for their art of analyzing the human heart. But *Socrates* surpassed

---

5 See Johann Georg Hamann, *Briefwechsel*, ed. Walther Ziesemer and Arthur Henkel, 7 vols. (Wiesbaden: Insel-Verlag, 1955–75), 7:176.
6 Hamann, *Sämtliche Werke*, 2:70.
7 Hamann, *Sämtliche Werke*, 2:73.

them both in wisdom since he had come further in self-knowledge than they had, and knew that he knew nothing.[8]

In other words, according to Hamann, the wise know that they know nothing—or if not nothing, then at least nothing compared to God. Such is the divine joke, as Hamann saw it, which is as old as Western philosophy itself, and in light of which the philosophical presumption of his own age looked comical—as comical as Adam covering up his nakedness with fig leaves.

But what seems to be nothing but a not-knowing or an unknowing is at the same time, paradoxically, the beginning of a different kind of knowing. And in this respect, for Hamann, as for Cusanus, learned ignorance has a positive mystagogical function, for it is by means of it, indeed "by means of it alone," Cusanus says, that "we can draw near the maximum and triune God of infinite goodness."[9] The only notable difference here is that Hamann correlates Socratic ignorance with what Paul says in 1 Corinthians 8:1–3, where, after contrasting knowledge that puffs up with love that builds up, the Apostle reverses conventional wisdom, suggesting that true knowledge is not about actively knowing anything, but rather about being known by God. Thus Hamann observes:

> For the testimony that Socrates gave of his ignorance I know of no more honorable seal and at the same time no better key than the oracle of the great *teacher of the Gentiles*: εἴ τις δοκεῖ ἐγνωκέναι τι, οὔπω ἔγνω καθὼς δεῖ γνῶναι · εἰ δέ τις ἀγαπᾷ τὸν θεόν, οὗτος ἔγνωσται ὑπ' αὐτοῦ. "*If anyone thinks that he knows something, he does not yet know as he ought to know. But if a man loves God, he is known by him*"—just as Socrates was known by Apollo to be a *wise man*. But as the seed of all our natural wisdom must decay and perish into ignorance, and as from this *death*, from this *nothing*, the *life* and *nature* of a higher knowledge must spring forth newly created—thus far the *nose* of a Sophist does not reach.[10]

---

8 Hamann, *Sämtliche Werke*, 2:71.
9 Nicholas of Cusa, *De docta ignorantia*, I.26 (89), in *Nikolaus von Kues: Philosophisch-Theologische Werke*, vol. 1, edited by Paul Wilpert and Hans Gerhard Senger, rev. ed. (Hamburg: Felix Meiner Verlag, 2002), 112; trans. H. Lawrence Bond, *Nicholas of Cusa: Selected Spiritual Writings* (New York: Paulist Press, 1997), 127.
10 Hamann, *Sämtliche Werke*, 2:74.

The point here, in any event, is not to equate Hamann's understanding of learned ignorance with that of Cusanus, but simply to offer a point of comparison and, more importantly, to show how the idea of learned ignorance lived on into the eighteenth century and was ironically deployed in the middle of the Enlightenment.

Coincidentia oppositorum

Let us now turn to the concept of the *coincidentia oppositorum*, which Hamann cites in a letter to Johann Gottfried Herder on November 18, 1782, the year after the publication of Kant's *Critique of Pure Reason*.[11] Although we now know the principle to originate with Cusanus, Hamann attributes it to Giordano Bruno, owing to the lack of editions of Cusan writings at the time. As he puts it to Herder: "*Jordani Bruni Principium coincidentiae oppositorum* is worth more to me than all Kantian criticism."[12] Given Hamann's importance to post-Kantian philosophy—considering his influence on Herder, Jacobi, Schelling, and Hegel, not to mention later figures such as Kierkegaard and Wilhelm Dilthey—this is a remarkable statement, which makes the Cusan principle, via Hamann, fundamental to all of the attempts to come to terms with the divisions left by Kant's philosophy, such as those between reason and experience (or revelation), concept and sensibility, form and matter, truth and history, reason and tradition, reason and language, logic and rhetoric, thought and words, thought and signs: in short, between what is thought (the noumenal) and what appears (the phenomenal). As Hamann puts it in his *Metacritique of the Purism of Reason* in 1784,

> Are not *ideae matrices* and *ideae innatae* the children of one spirit? Do not sensibility and understanding, the two branches of human knowledge, spring from a common, but unrecognized root, so that by means of the former objects are given, and by means of the latter, they are thought (understood and comprehended): what is the purpose of so violent and unauthorized a separation of what nature has joined

---

[11] As it happens, Hamann was the first to read and review the first *Critique*, having mediated its publication and read the initial proofs. See Betz, *After Enlightenment*, 220.
[12] Hamann, *Briefwechsel*, 4:462.

together? Will not this dichotomy or division cause both branches to break off from their transcendental root and wither?[13]

That, at least, is Hamann's prophetic contention—and not just because he sees no justification for unnaturally separating what nature has joined together, but because *all of these pairs*, which Kant has alchemically separated in a quixotic quest for the "philosopher's stone," are naturally given and united in language. In other words, according to Hamann, everyday language mysteriously does what no amount of philosophizing can do, uniting the sensible and the intelligible, and so forth, making it a marvelous sign of the Logos, who unites all things, God and humanity, heaven and earth, Jews and Gentile, male and female, in himself.[14]

Thus, for Hamann, as for Cusanus, philosophy at some point becomes Christology, inasmuch as Christ is the one in whom apparent opposites coincide. This much, however, is nothing new. Maximus the Confessor, for instance, also speaks of Christ in terms of a cosmic reconciliation of opposites. What is genuinely new in Hamann is that the principle of the *coincidentia oppositorum* becomes the formal root of his "linguistic turn." For, to put it simply, whereas Kant divided concept and sensible intuition, Hamann understands them as always already united in language, making language itself a proto-Christological reality, indeed, a kind of *admirabile commercium* of the sensible and the intelligible. And in general, based on his Christological reading of language, Hamann moves away from an abstract, timeless rationality toward an incarnate one, and thus toward a linguistic conception of reason whereby reason is not so much a transcendental as a hermeneutical faculty always already immersed in language, history, and

---

13 Hamann, *Sämtliche Werke*, 3:278. Hamann is therefore wont to compare epistemological problems with marital problems. See Hamann, *Briefwechsel*, 7:158: "What God has joined together, no philosophy can separate; just as little unite, what nature has separated." As Oswald Bayer notes, "Hamann's contemporaries are 'adulterers' first and foremost as *'Scheidekünstler.'* They understand themselves ... to be following a method similar to that of chemistry, namely, a method that 'separates the empirical from the rational,' the *a priori* from the *a posteriori*, the separation of accidental historical truths from the necessary truths of reason, the separation of Jesus from the Christ, the separation of the human from the divine quality of the Bible." See Oswald Bayer, "Die Geschichten der Vernunft sind die Kritik ihrer Reinheit: Hamanns Weg zur Metakritik Kants," in *Hamann—Kant—Herder: Acta des vierten Internationalen Hamann-Kolloquiums*, ed. Bernhard Gajek (Frankfurt am Main: Peter Lang, 1987), 60–61.

14 Hamann, *Sämtliche Werke*, 3:284. See James C. O'Flaherty, *Unity and Language: A Study in the Philosophy of Johann Georg Hamann* (Chapel Hill: University of North Carolina Press, 1952).

culture—a faculty whose proper function therefore lies not in abstracting from these realities, in search of a *logos asarkos*, but in the interpretation of the Logos as communicated in and through them.

Although Hamann's only explicit mention of the *coincidentia oppositorum* is found in the aforementioned letter and in the context of his metacritical writings, the basic idea of it can also be found twenty years earlier in his *Aesthetica in nuce* (1762), where it implicitly informs his theological aesthetics. As he did with language, Hamann is wont to see creation in general in terms of a coincidence of opposites. As he puts it, in a central passage: "The unity of the author is reflected in the dialect of his works;—in all one tone of immeasurable height and depth! A proof of the most glorious majesty and of the most complete self-emptying!"[15] And the same Christological uniting of opposites shows up in his later debate with Moses Mendelssohn, who in his *Jerusalem* had proposed a similarly strict separation of Church and state. The circumstances motivating Mendelssohn's work are complicated, and cannot help but evoke sympathies, but Hamann found his friend's divisions unwarranted and ultimately inimical not just to Church and state, but to Judaism itself. He therefore responded with a prophetic little work entitled *Golgotha and Scheblimini*—the latter term signifying the elevation of Christ to the right hand of the Father—by which he meant a final Christological coincidence of cross and resurrection, glory and kenosis.[16] Again, my point here is not to establish any direct line of influence of Cusanus on Hamann, but simply to show how Hamann picked up Cusanus's two most famous principles, deploying them in the middle of the Enlightenment in the name of a *greater* enlightenment—an enlightenment found through the suffering of the knowledge of one's ignorance as the prerequisite of faith in the incarnate Logos, whose hypostatic union is beyond rational comprehension.

Let us turn now briefly to post-Kantian philosophy. While Hamann's emphasis on learned ignorance seems to have had little effect, his use of the principle of the coincidence of opposites paved the way for Schelling and Hegel.[17] To be sure, any influence Hamann may have had on Schelling and

---

15 Hamann, *Sämtliche Werke*, 2:204.
16 See Betz, *After Enlightenment*, 258ff.
17 This is already evident from Schelling's early philosophy of nature and subsequent philosophy of identity as an identity in difference of subject and object, the ideal and the real, the conscious and the unconscious, and so forth.

Hegel was initially indirect, because of the pseudonymous and occasional nature of his writings, which were not collected into an edition until 1821 (Schelling, for instance, did not encounter Hamann's works until 1806, when Jacobi provided him with a selection of his writings).[18] It is clear, however, that Schelling and Hegel both admired Hamann, especially for his forceful objection to any philosophical halving of reality and for his corresponding attempt to unite what Kant had divided. Indeed, seeing Hamann himself as a kind of embodiment of the principle of the *coincidentia oppositorum*, Schelling called him "a true πᾶν of harmony and discord, light and darkness, spiritualism and materialism."[19] And Hegel, while more critical of Hamann's idiosyncracy and unwillingness to write for the public at large, was similarly impressed: "It is wonderful to see how in Hamann the concrete Idea ferments and turns itself against the divisions of reflection."[20]

Cusanus in Przywara

Having shown how Cusanus lived on in surprising ways in the eighteenth century, I turn now to his twentieth-century reception in the work of the Jesuit, Erich Przywara. Admittedly, the selection of Przywara as a second major heir of Cusanus's thought may seem *prima facie* as peculiar as the selection of Hamann. For, though Przywara was arguably the most brilliant and prolific philosopher-theologian writing between the World Wars and exercised a profound influence on Edith Stein, Karl Rahner, and Hans Urs von Balthasar, today he is virtually unknown and few have studied his works. And yet, just as Hamann embodied the Cusan principles of learned ignorance and the coincidence of opposites, Przywara's philosophical theology is similarly informed by them, especially by the principle of the *coincidentia oppositorum*, which stands in the background of Przywara's understanding and development of the Thomistic *analogia entis*.

---

18 For a fuller treatment of Hamann's reception, see John R. Betz, "Reading Sibylline Leaves: Hamann in the History of Ideas," *Journal of the History of Ideas* 70 (January 2009): 93–118, and Lisa Marie Anderson, ed., *Hamann and the Tradition* (Evanston, Ill.: Northwestern University Press, 2012).
19 F. W. J. Schelling, *Sämtliche Werke*, ed. K. F. A. Schelling (Stuttgart/Augsburg: J. G. Cotta'scher Verlag, 1856–61), I/10: 171.
20 G. W. F. Hegel, *Werke*, vol. 11, *Berliner Schriften 1818–1831*, ed. Eva Moldenhauer and Karl Markus Michel (Frankfurt am Main: Suhrkamp Verlag, 1970), 326.

This is not to say that Cusanus himself figures as prominently in Przywara's writings as Augustine or Thomas or, for that matter, Pseudo-Dionysius. He clearly does not; compared to these three, Cusanus appears almost nowhere. There is also the problem that Przywara's thought is a genuine synthesis of the tradition. Indeed, far from being a partisan of any one school or religious order, he draws freely from all, which problematizes any prioritization of one influence over another.[21] Nevertheless, it is notable that Przywara speaks of Cusanus as a culminating figure and appeals to him as an obvious ancestor of his thought. So, leaving aside a number of Przywara's reviews of works on Cusanus,[22] let us begin with a brief survey of some passages in which he explicitly discusses him.

Przywara as a Disciple of Cusanus?

In *Gottgeheimnis der Welt*, an early work from 1923, Przywara speaks of Cusanus as "that strangely beautiful evening star of the fading Middle Ages."[23] Years later, in 1952, he calls him "the great heir of Augustine."[24] In 1958, he describes Cusanus as "the most brilliant disciple of Augustine," "the great heir of German mysticism," and the "bold culmination" of a tradition of "thinkers of oppositions" from Heraclitus to Augustine.[25] Moreover, in 1959, in a letter to the Swiss scholar-statesman Carl Jacob Burckhardt Przywara calls Cusanus one of the "profoundest philosophers and greatest diplomats."[26] And, perhaps most tellingly, in an interview on the occasion

---

[21] In this regard, Karl Rahner spoke of Przywara's "lifelong dialogue with the past and the present, with the entirety of Western intellectual history from Heraclitus to Nietzsche," and of "his openness to all in order to give to all." See Karl Rahner, *Gnade als Freiheit: Kleine theologische Beiträge* (Freiburg: Herder, 1968), 268.

[22] See, for example, his review of Rudolf Odebrecht's *Nicholas von Cues und der deutsche Geist*, in *Deutsche Literaturzeitung* 55 (1934): 680–82; "Plotin und Nikolaus von Cues," in *Stimmen der Zeit* 134 (1938): 263–265; his review of K. H. Volkmann, *Nicolaus Cusanus*, in *Les Études philosophiques* 12 (1957): 432; and his review of Heinz-Joachim Heydorn, *Eine Untersuchung zur Vorgeschichte der modernen Existenz* (1952), which appeared under the title, "Der späte Jünger des Nikolaus von Kues," in *Die Österreichische Furche* 11 (1955).

[23] Erich Przywara, *Schriften*, 3 vols. (Einsiedeln: Johannes Verlag, 1962), 2:207.

[24] See Erich Przywara, *Humanitas: Der Mensch Gestern und Morgen* (Nuremberg: Glock und Lutz, 1952), 640.

[25] See Erich Przywara, *Analogia Entis*, trans. John R. Betz and David Bentley Hart (Grand Rapids, MI: Eerdmans, 2014), 515; and idem, "Philosophisches Denken," *Die Furche* 14 (1958).

[26] Letter to Carl Jacob Burckhardt, January 22, 1959 (from Przywara's *Nachlass* in the Archive of the German Province of the Society of Jesus).

of his sixty-fifth birthday, in which the interviewer notes that people have called him, among other things, a disciple of Augustine, he gives pride of place to Cusanus: "People have identified Nicholas of Cusa as my great ancestor, which I am rather happy to accept."[27]

Such praise for the great German cardinal is understandable if we consider the similarities between these two great thinkers—surely, two of the most philosophical theologians in the German tradition—and more particularly how, for Przywara, Cusanus perfected Augustine's philosophy of opposition. For, as it happens, the whole of Przywara's doctrine of analogy of being, his *analogia entis*, is structured in terms of relations of opposition, which coincide in God. In order to see in more detail how Cusanus figures in Przywara's *analogia entis*, let us begin with a description of it.

Cusanus and the *analogia entis*

Based upon the teaching of Aquinas and rooted specifically in the "real distinction" between essence and existence, the *analogia entis* has been a mainstay of the Catholic metaphysical tradition ever since Cajetan and John of St. Thomas.[28] While it can be formulated with varying degrees of sophistication and, in Przywara's case, rather mind-boggling complexity, at it simplest it amounts to the doctrine that whereas creaturely being is defined by a non-identity of essence and existence, God is a simple identity of essence and existence by virtue of divine simplicity.[29] In other words, whereas God's essence is to be, the being of creatures is a gift.

---

[27] See Przywara's interview with Stefan Varnhagen in *Ehrung eines grossen Denkers: Zwiegespräch zwischen Autor und Verleger anlässlich des 65. Geburtstags Erich Przywaras am 12. Oktober 1954* (Nuremberg: Glock und Lutz, 1954), 5: "Verleger: ... Wurden Sie nicht gleichzeitig 'Zwillingsbruder Platons' und 'Platon Ihr Ahne,' und jüngst als Schüler Augustins, mit Bernhard von Clairvaux zusammengestellt?! Autor: Solche humorige Elogen hat man schon früher über mich geschrieben. So bezeichnete man besonders Nicholas von Cues als meinen eigentlichen 'hohen Ahnen,' was ich eher annehme."

[28] See Julio Terán-Dutari, "Die Geschichte des Terminus 'Analogia Entis' und das Werk Erich Przywaras," *Philosophisches Jahrbuch der Görres-Gesellschaft* 77 (1970): 164–65. See also John P. Doyle, "Suarez on the Analogy of Being," *The Modern Schoolman* 46 (1969): 219–49; 323–41. For a recent discussion and defense of the Cajetanian tradition—one, however, that uses the same title, but remarkably neglects Przywara's signal contribution to the subject—see Stephen A. Long, *Analogia Entis* (Notre Dame, IN: University of Notre Dame Press, 2011).

[29] See Martin Bieler, "*Analogia Entis* as an Expression of Love according to Ferdinand Ulrich," in *The Analogy of Being: Invention of the Antichrist or the Wisdom of God?*, ed. Thomas Joseph White, O.P. (Grand Rapids, MI: Eerdmans, 2011), 314–37.

Therein, for Przywara, following Thomas, lies the most basic "analogy" between the being of God (as *ipsum esse subsistens*) and the being of creatures, as well as the *philosophical* justification for the doctrine of the Fourth Lateran Council: that for every similarity between Creator and creature, however great, one must always observe the greater dissimilarity between them: *inter creatorem et creaturam non potest tanta similitudo notari, quin inter eos non sit maior dissimilitudo notanda*.[30] In other words, however similar created being may be to God, the being of the Creator, as Being itself, is always *more* dissimilar. Such is the basic point of the *analogia entis*. As Przywara tirelessly explained to critics such as Karl Barth: the *analogia entis* amounts to what every child knows, namely, that God is "always greater"—*semper maior*. But how one understands the *analogia entis* in detail is another matter, and it is here that Cusanus comes into play. So let us now consider how Cusanus figures in it, or, more precisely, what Cusanus *adds* to the *analogia entis*.

But are we not getting ahead of ourselves? Is Cusanus really a thinker of the *analogia entis*? As it happens, this is no idle question. It is not, however, because Nicholas nowhere uses this term; for, as we have already noted, the *analogia entis* did not become a *terminus technicus* until Cajetan. Rather, it has to do with how one understands Cusanus's own doctrine of the *coincidentia oppositorum*, which is not entirely clear. Is God, according to Cusanus, the identity of creation's antitheses, or is God the One who is explicated in the oppositions of creation, but decidedly beyond them? In other words, the *coincidentia oppositorum* could be read in two ways: in more of a pantheist (or at least panentheistic) direction reminiscent of Eriugena, such that God is the fundamental identity of creation and is in some sense bound up with it; or in a more decidedly apophatic, Neoplatonic (essentially Pseudo-Dionysian and Thomistic) direction, which puts God totally beyond creation's oppositions. Or is the *coincidentia oppositorum*, as Przywara seems to have taken it, a kind of veil between God and creation? However one answers these questions, my own view, following Rudolf Haubst, is that there is enough in Cusanus to justify calling him a thinker of the *analogia entis*, since for Cusanus, however much God is explicated *in* creation, God is also *beyond* creation (which is the minimal requirement for

---

[30] See Heinrich Denzinger, *Enchiridion symbolorum definitionum et declarationum de rebus fidei et morum: Compendium of Creeds, Definitions and Declarations on Matters of Faith and Morals*, ed. Peter Hünermann, Robert Fastiggi, and Anne Englund Nash, 43rd ed. (San Francisco: Ignatius Press, 2012), 806.

any *analogia entis*).³¹ For example, in *De docta ignorantia* the great cardinal says: "The whole maximum is most perfectly within all things as simple and indivisible, because it is the infinite center," but it is also "outside every being, inasmuch as it encompasses all things."³² He also criticizes those who fail to see that what of God is unfolded in creation is only an "image" of the truth, and not the truth itself.³³

At the same time, however, it cannot be denied that Cusanus gives the impression of being more of a panentheist in the tradition of Eriugena than a traditional Thomist, as Stephen Gersh, among others, has observed.³⁴ And Przywara himself, notwithstanding his obvious admiration, was not without concerns and reservations. In fact, he worried that the Cusan understanding of God and the world in terms of *complicatio* and *explicatio*, and of God as the being of the world, comes very close to collapsing the analogy of being between God and creation—namely, at the very point at which the cosmic opposites coincide.³⁵ In other words, just when the cosmos begins to adumbrate the divine in a *coincidentia oppositorum*, the cosmos seems to merge with the divine, leading, Przywara observes, "almost directly" to Hegel—with the difference that in Cusanus the *coincidentia oppositorum* ultimately remains a "'veiled, open limit' to a God whose '*explicatio*' in time and space is the world's '*complicatio*.'"³⁶ In other words, the *coincidentia* would seem to

---

31 Rudolf Haubst, *Streifzüge in die cusanische Theologie* (Münster: Aschendorff Verlag, 1991), 232ff. In the words of Vatican I (*Dei Filius*, chapter 1): "[God] is in reality and in essence, distinct from the world, supremely happy in himself and from himself, and inexpressibly loftier than anything besides himself which either exists or can be imagined."

32 Nicholas of Cusa, *De docta ignorantia*, I.21 (64), ed. Wilpert and Senger, 84-86; trans. Bond, 117.

33 Nicholas of Cusa, *De docta ignorantia*, I.25 (84), ed. Wilpert and Senger, 106; trans. Bond, 125.

34 See Stephen Gersh's essay, chapter 15 in this volume. See also Dermot Moran, "Pantheism from John Scottus Eriugena to Nicholas of Cusa," *American Catholic Philosophical Quarterly* 64, no. 1 (1990): 131-52; and Matthew T. Gaetano, "Nicholas of Cusa and Pantheism in Early Modern Catholic Theology," in *Nicholas of Cusa and the Making of the Early Modern World*, ed. Simon J. G. Burton, Joshua Hollmann, and Eric M. Parker (Leiden: Brill, 2019), 199-228.

35 Even when Cusanus uses *complicatio* and *explicatio*, he intends those concepts to have apophatic force that emphasizes the transcendence of God. One can relate unity and plurality as enfolded to unfolded; yet "the manner [*modus*] of enfolding and unfolding exceeds our mind." Nicholas of Cusa, *De docta ignorantia*, II.3 (109), ed. Wilpert and Senger, 26; trans. Bond, 136. I thank David Albertson for this reference.

36 Przywara, "Metaphysics and Christianity," in *Analogia Entis*, 522-23; "Time, Space, Eternity," in *Analogia Entis*, 585-86; See also "Phenomenology, Realogy, Relationology," in *Analogia Entis*, 473.

be ambiguous, confronting us with a dilemma. Either God *is* the coincidence of the world's oppositions, such that God is in some sense immanent to the world as *its* ultimate identity—in which case Cusanus's *coincidentia* would seem to be not much different from Aristotle's prime mover, inasmuch as both function as the onto-theological ground of the world and neither is sufficiently distinct from the world. Or the *coincidentia* is the veil of the God who radically transcends the world, however much he is explicated in it (as the teaching of the Fourth Lateran Council, which Przywara saw as the dogmatic basis of the *analogia entis*, would seem to require).

The matter is not especially clear, owing in part to different emphases in *De docta ignorantia* and *De visione Dei*. In the earlier work God simply is the *coincidentia oppostiorum*; in the latter, God is beyond it.[37] It need not be decided here whether this marks a development in Cusanus's thought, or whether the ambiguity in Cusanus is an indication of the ambiguity of the matter itself (if indeed God is at once *in* creation and *beyond* it, immanent and transcendent). For present purposes it is sufficient to see why Przywara saw Cusanus as a liminal figure in whom "the Middle Ages are crowned and modernity is born."[38] On the one hand, Cusanus looks back to Thomas, whose doctrine of simplicity (Przywara argues) he fills out; on the other hand, he adumbrates Hegel whose own philosophy turns upon a certain unity—or identity—of opposites (being and nothing, eternity and time, universality and particularity, God and world). For Przywara, therefore, everything comes down to whose doctrine of polarity wins out, either his Thomistic version of Cusanus (viz., the *analogia entis*) or Hegel. His 1926 article, "Thomas or Hegel?", makes the choice clear: "The essential thing with regard to 'polarity' is this: does it signify an immanent, self-enclosed 'unity of (creaturely) opposites' or does it signify a 'unity of opposites' that ultimately opens out into what is beyond it, thus signifying the final philosophical formula of the creature's restlessness with respect to God?"[39] In the first case we have Hegel, for whom God is simply the identity of creaturely polarities; in the second case we have Cusanus as Przywara reads him, namely, as a *Gestalt*, a complicated figure, rather a "figure" that could be

---

[37] See Nicholas of Cusa, *De docta ignorantia*, I.4 (11–12), ed. Wilpert and Senger, 16–18; and Nicholas of Cusa, *De visione Dei*, X (38–42), in *Nicolai de Cusa Opera Omnia*, vol. VI, ed. Heide Dorothea Riemann (Hamburg: Felix Meiner Verlag, 2000), 35–38.

[38] Przywara, "Imago Dei: On the Theological Message of Max Picard," in *Analogia Entis*, 557.

[39] See Przywara, "Thomas oder Hegel? Zum Sinn der 'Wende zum Objekt,'" in *Logos: Zeitschrift für systematische Philosophie* 15 (1926): 12–13.

reduced to a single position. For Przywara, therefore, it is crucial that one read Cusanus rightly if one is to avoid seeing him as a precursor to Hegel, and that means reading him not only backward in the direction of Thomas, but also forward toward Franz Xaver von Baader and Johann Joseph von Görres, since all of them underscore, as Przywara does in fidelity to the teaching of Lateran IV, the final difference and *maior dissimilitudo* between Creator and creature.[40]

Cusanus in the *analogia entis*

Whether or not one may speak of a Cusan *analogia entis*, there can be no doubt that Cusanus figures *in* Przywara's updated version of it. To see how this is so, however, we first need to take stock of the fact that Przywara's analogy of being is, in fact, a cruciform analogy *between* analogies: between an analogy proper to creatures qua creatures, which Przywara calls an "immanent analogy," and a "transcendent analogy" between God and creatures. According to the first analogy, creation in its own right is relationally constituted, for instance, between day and night, male and female, and all other natural oppositions, which imply one another; but then, according to the second analogy, this first analogy, taken as a whole, is *itself* an analogy of transcendence. In other words, it is not any one pole, much less any one aspect, of creation that constitutes the analogy of being, but rather the unity-in-difference of one to another. For Przywara, therefore, there is no straightforward analogy, which would allow one to make a direct inference, for instance, from created existence to divine Existence, but in the end only an indirect analogy of proportionality based upon the already mysterious unity-in-difference of essence and existence in creatures; and this is what gives his understanding of the *analogia entis* its apophatic stress.

What is most relevant here, however, is how Cusanus's *coincidentia oppositorum* comes into play in Przywara's *analogia entis*. For what Przywara means by the immanent analogy is that creaturely being is constituted by a correlation of opposites.[41] Indeed, to draw on Aristotle's definition, this is precisely what he means by "analogy" as a proportion of one

---

[40] Compare Nicholas of Cusa's maxim: "No one doubts that there can be no proportion between the infinite and finite." Nicholas of Cusa, *De docta ignorantia*, II.2 (102), ed. Wilpert and Senger, 18; trans. Bond, 133.

[41] See Przywara, *Analogia Entis*, 131 et *passim*.

thing to another (ἄλλο πρὸς ἄλλο).⁴² To say that reality is analogical is thus to say that created reality is a matter of correlated opposites, which resist all philosophical attempts to reduce one to the other. By the same token, it is to say that things go wrong (as they have tended to go wrong in modernity) when one fails to recognize the significance of the opposites and their correlation as an analogy and instead tries, like Descartes, to find a fixed Archimedean point within the rhythmic play of oppositions—oppositions which, according to Cusanus and Przywara, should point us to God. Absent analogy, however, the bane of modernity, from Przywara's perspective, is that it tends to absolutize one pole over another—absolutizing now this pole and now that, doing so always at the expense of the "other" that will in due course take its dialectical revenge.

Of course, once again we are very close to Hegel here. The fundamental difference is that whereas Hegel absolutizes the dialectic as a divine dialectic, more precisely as an identity through dialectic, for Przywara (implicitly following Cusanus) the oppositions that can appear dialectical are more fundamentally analogues. Accordingly, when they are seen for what they are, which is to say, when the world is seen as an analogy, they are at once de-absolutized and relativized. For then they point beyond themselves to their coincidence—not as the immanent identity of the world, but as the mysterious veil separating this world from God, who is expressed *in* the world, but is at the same time decidedly *beyond* the world. As Przywara observes in his lecture series from 1923, *Gottgeheimnis der Welt*, the mystery of the world, as the mystery of its various polarities (e.g., subject-object, being-becoming, person-idea), gives way to a deeper mystery: "The deeper we go in our investigation of the mystery of the world, the more inexorably the mystery of God shines through."⁴³ In other words, the more we penetrate the world's immanence, the more it is seen to be an analogy of transcendence.

---

42 See Aristotle, *Metaphysics*, V.6 (1016b). Of course, Przywara does not mean opposition in the sense of contradiction, for then it would no longer be possible to speak of analogy at all. Rather, he means a correlation of opposites in the way that, metaphysically speaking, being and becoming are correlated, or essence and existence are correlated, or in the way that, epistemologically speaking, subject and object, or consciousness and world, are correlated, or in the way that anthropologically speaking, man and woman, or individual and community, are correlated.

43 Przywara, *Schriften*, 2:157.

But, as Przywara realized, the circumstances of modern culture are such that the *analogia entis* cannot be taken for granted. It is something that has to be seen; and if it is not seen, then it has to be demonstrated and defended. This is what Przywara himself tried to do in a culture that was succumbing more and more to what Charles Taylor has more recently called an "immanent frame"—whether the frame be constructed in the name of ethics (Kant), or logic (Hegel), or, most deceptively of all, in the name of ontological difference (Heidegger). What is worse, the analogy of being can readily fall apart into dialectics, into an immanent agony baptized by Hegel with a divine seal. Thus, keenly aware that the being of the world can degrade into dialectics when seen as immanent totality and not as an analogy, Przywara speaks of the "divine unity of opposites, incarnate in our Catholic 'unity of opposites' as the only possible option for us in this decisive time."[44]

Christological *Coincidentia*

We can now see just how close Przywara is to Cusanus, and how both of them stand vis-à-vis modernity, calling it, so to speak, to a decision for or against dialectics, which at the same time is a decision for or against analogy.[45] For it is really one or the other: either the world's oppositions point beyond themselves or they do not. Either the *coincidentia oppositorum* is the world's veil or the world's seal. If it is the world's seal, then there is finally no mystery, because the world resolves into an identity, albeit in the Hegelian form of an identity through difference; but if it is a veil, then it points beyond itself to the mystery of God, who is veiled in the mystery of the world's differences, as Przywara says, but infinitely transcends them. And so, for Przywara (and Cusanus), by dint of the doctrine of the *coincidentia oppositorum*, we are led into the darkness of faith in which alone God can be found. Thus Przywara speaks with Cusanus in the idiom of learned ignorance and of being "comprehended by" rather than comprehending the God who dwells beyond all our knowing as one "unknown." For "the night unveils its countenance only so far as the light has faded."[46]

---

44 Przywara, *Schriften*, 2:137.
45 In this respect, one could say that Cusanus (prospectively) and Przywara (retrospectively) are contending with the modern immanentizing of God that first occurred in Bruno, so that the choice is essentially between Cusanus-Przywara or Bruno-Hegel. See the conclusion of Hans Blumenberg, *The Legitimacy of the Modern Age* (Cambridge, MA: MIT Press, 1983).
46 See Przywara, *Analogia Entis*, 183.

What makes Cusanus so important to Przywara, however, is not simply what his doctrine of the *coincidentia oppositorum* means for Catholic metaphysics as an antidote to the various forms of modern metaphysics (whether explicitly espoused or not), but how Cusan metaphysics points to Christ as the proper fulfillment of a philosophy of polarity. In other words, both are striving in the same direction: from within metaphysics toward Christ, in whom all the oppositions of creation are finally united. As Przywara put it in an early work: "All the beauty of the cosmos—the majesty of the high mountains, the lovely simplicity of the verdant fields, the splendid concert of birds in the springtime woods, the cracking and thundering of storms at night, the still solitude of the mountain retreat and the rushing confusion of the industrial city—is a manifold image of his unity."[47] And the same lines of thought are developed in Przywara's late work, where the *analogia entis* is configured in increasingly Christological terms, as in his *Christentum gemäß Johannes*.[48]

But let us conclude with an early work on the liturgical calendar from 1923, *Kirchenjahr: Die christliche Spannungseinheit*, which elaborates the same metaphysical-Christological theme of a unity of opposites. On the one hand, naturally enough, the work is about the liturgical calendar and, more particularly, its highs and lows, its feasts and fasts, which mysteriously meet on Holy Saturday (in anticipation of von Balthasar's treatment of the subject some years later).[49] For it is here that the liturgy comes the closest to a kind of *coincidentia oppositorum*, as it looks simultaneously back to Good Friday and forward to Easter. In other words, it is here that we come closest to the meaning of the liturgical calendar as a Christological "unity of opposites" or, more precisely, as the subtitle would suggest, a "unity-in-tension" [*Spannungseinheit*]. At the same time, however, the work's subtitle is a description of the Christian soul that has been formed by the liturgy. Thus Przywara says, "Your Holy Saturday lies between Good Friday and Easter morning, between *miserere* and *alleluia*—it is, as it were, a spanning of one into the other [*Ineinandergespanntsein*]."[50] In other words, the choicest fruit of the liturgical unity of opposites is a spiritual unity of opposites,

---

47 Przywara, *Schriften*, 1:7.
48 Erich Przywara, *Christentum gemäß Johannes* (Nuremberg: Glock und Lutz, 1954).
49 See Hans Urs von Balthasar, *Mysterium Paschale: The Mystery of Easter*, trans. Aidan Nichols (San Francisco: Ignatius Press, 2000).
50 Przywara, *Schriften*, 1:298.

corresponding to what Przywara, following Augustine and Newman, elsewhere calls the "opposite virtues" of love and reverence for God—not one in which the tension is slackened, but one in which the "tension" is preserved undiminished, "so that their unity is not a torpid unity of death, but a unity that is the fruit of the attainment of life."[51]

---

51 Przywara, *Schriften*, 1:306.

2

"Methodic Foundering" or "Methodic Overcoming of Rationality"?

Metaphysics of Liberation in Karl Jaspers and Nicholas of Cusa

TAMARA ALBERTINI

Many prominent twentieth-century philosophers have been inspired by ideas they encountered in Renaissance texts, chiefly in works by Nicholas of Cusa (1401–1464) and Marsilio Ficino (1433–1499).[1] One less-obvious figure to consider is the existential philosopher Karl Jaspers (1883–1969), and yet, as the following will show, by his own admission he may have been the one most dramatically marked by a Renaissance philosopher. In his recollections of Karl and Gertrud Jaspers, Renaissance scholar P. O. Kristeller states that Jaspers's "knowledge of the past philosophers

---

1 Beyond those treated in this volume, these include Ernst Cassirer (1874–1945), Martin Buber (1878–1965), Jean Gebser (1905–1973), Élémire Zolla (1926–2002), and Ioan Petru Culianu (1950–1991). For more philosophers see Klaus Reinhardt and Harald Schwaetzer, eds., *Cusanus-Rezeption in der Philosophie des 20. Jahrhunderts* (Regensburg: S. Roderer-Verlag, 2005).

cited by him was very superficial and in many cases outright wrong."[2] And yet, he also concedes: "I felt that the study with Jaspers and the reading suggested by him gave me an entirely different dimension that goes back to Kierkegaard—the idea of *internal experience* that is not irrational, but is in excess of, is beyond perception, and beyond the reasoning in science and logic."[3] That idea of an internal experience and the contours of what, I think, Karl Jaspers recognized to be a metaphysics of liberation is precisely what drove him toward the philosophy of Nicholas of Cusa.

It would be of little use to list notions or passages in Karl Jaspers's works that contemporary scholars of Nicholas of Cusa might evaluate for whether they reflect Cusanus's ideas accurately. Whether philosophers do justice (or are even able to do justice) to their precursors has often been debated. It suffices to remember the most problematic interpretation of all: Aristotle's rendition of Plato. Moreover, Jaspers made it clear in many of his works that he read the texts of past philosophers primarily to learn how to philosophize. In this respect, he considered himself a student of Kant. There is no archetypal philosophy that one could learn to build or reconstruct; one may only approach it by following those who preceded us on the pathway.[4] As for Nicholas of Cusa, the existential philosopher considered him one of the world's great thinkers.

Karl Jaspers's Affinity with Nicholas of Cusa

It has often been noted that Jaspers did not formally study philosophy. Since he came from a background in medicine and psychology, he ended up reading major philosophers on his own. While one takes for granted that Jaspers studied Plato, Augustine, Descartes, Spinoza, Kant, and Nietzsche, Cusanus experts are pleasantly surprised to discover also the name of Cardinal Nicholas of Cusa amongst the select group. As a matter of fact, Karl Jaspers not only read Cusanus's works but also dedicated an entire book to him, the publication of which, in 1964, he judiciously timed to

---

2 Iryna Mykhailova, "Paul Oskar Kristeller und Karl Jaspers: ein Dialog, der nie stattgefunden hat," *Freiburger Zeitschrift für Philosophie und Theologie* 62 (2015): 346. Unless otherwise indicated, all translations from German are my own.
3 Mykhailova, "Paul Oskar Kristeller und Karl Jaspers," 338.
4 See Thorsten Paprotny, *Karl Jaspers' Philosophie interkulturell gelesen* (Nordhausen: Traugott Bautz, 2006), 65–66.

coincide with the five-hundredth anniversary of the cardinal's death.[5] In that same year, he also gave a radio lecture in which he integrated excerpts of his book to commemorate the anniversary.[6] As could be expected, the book was awaited with great anticipation by Cusanus specialists but then ended up being heavily critiqued. German philosopher and eminent Leibniz scholar Hans Heinz Holz summed up the general sentiment succinctly in his review: "Viel Jaspers—wenig Cusanus."[7] Be that as it may, the more intriguing question is what attracted Jaspers toward Cusan philosophy. This is all the more relevant, considering that the Cusanus book grew out of a chapter Jaspers had hoped to include in his volume on *Die Großen Philosophen* (1957), which indicates that in his perception Nicholas of Cusa was doubtless a major figure of world philosophy.[8]

Indeed, Jaspers was known to be more at ease with past than with contemporary philosophers; the living ones tended to treat him as an outsider to the discipline.[9] However, the understandable desire to avoid the disdain of colleagues was not the sole reason for his academic self-isolation. He thus writes in "On My Philosophy" (1941): "In the voices of Plotinus, Nicholas of Cusa, Bruno, and Schelling I heard as truth the dreams of the

---

5 Karl Jaspers, *Nikolaus Cusanus* (Munich: R. Piper & Co. Verlag, 1964).

6 Karl Jaspers, "Zum 500. Todestag des Nikolaus Cusanus," lecture delivered on Radio Basel, October 8, 1964, available online at Karl-Jaspers-Stiftung, https://jaspers-stiftung.ch/de/karl-jaspers/karl-jaspers-zum-500-todestag-des-nikolaus-cusanus-1964 (accessed November 16, 2020). I am most grateful to the Karl-Jaspers-Stiftung, Basel, for providing this reference.

7 Cited by Richard Wisser, "Nikolaus Cusanus im 'lebendigen Spiegel' der Philosophie von Karl Jaspers," *Zeitschrift für philosophische Forschung* 19 (1965): 529n4. As the above article shows, Wisser himself was much more sympathetic to Jaspers's project. He also corresponded with Jaspers over this issue. See Dominic Kaegi and Reiner Wiehl, eds., *Karl Jaspers Korrespondenzen: Philosophie* (Göttingen: Wallstein Verlag, 2016), 672–76.

8 For the correspondence between Jaspers and his German publisher on this matter, see the appendices in Pavao Žitko, "Karl Jaspers lettore di Cusano: Presupposti Interpretativi ed esiti teoretici" (PhD diss., University of Zagreb and University of Perugia, 2017). Žitko also added the transcription and his translation of a draft for a chapter by Jaspers entitled "Was für Cusanus Wahrheit ist?" (What is truth for Cusanus?) that was not completed and, therefore, remained unpublished (see Žitko, "Karl Jaspers lettore di Cusano, 183–86). Žitko's dissertation is available through the Faculty of Humanities and Social Sciences Institutional Repository, http://darhiv.ffzg.unizg.hr/id/eprint/9984/1/Zitko%2C%20Pavao.pdf (accessed November 16, 2020). The English translation of Jaspers's Cusanus book, however, is included in Jaspers, *The Great Philosophers*, vol. 2, ed. Hannah Arendt, trans. Ralph Manheim (New York: Harcourt, Brace & World, 1962). The same English translation of the Cusanus section is available in a separate publication: Karl Jaspers, *Anselm and Nicholas of Cusa*, ed. Hannah Arendt (New York: Harcourt Brace Jovanovich, 1974).

9 Paprotny, *Karl Jaspers' Philosophie*, 22.

metaphysicians."[10] For Jaspers, there was a timeless quality to Nicholas of Cusa for which he had a particular affinity: "Cusanus is neither old nor new, neither medieval nor modern. Living in time, he is timeless in spirit, one of those who, clad in the raiment of their day and nation, meet as equals over the millennia to discuss the destiny of man [*sich zurufen aus der Erfahrung des Menschenschicksals*]."[11] A strong, if not the strongest, philosophical term in this statement is the one of experience (*Erfahrung*, not reflected in the English translation), suggesting Jaspers found in Nicholas of Cusa a fellow philosopher, whose work affected him through more than mere concepts. Later in life, Jaspers revealed: "I appropriated the magnificence and depth of this philosophy at the end of the First World War and shortly afterward, and have lived with it ever since."[12] In other words, he discovered that Cusan thoughts were transformational. There could be no greater tribute to a predecessor.

Nevertheless, Cusan concepts mattered to Jaspers, too. In Jaspers's *Philosophical Faith and Revelation*, which appeared while Jaspers was working on his Cusanus text, one senses that he identified a treasured endeavor common to him and to the Renaissance philosopher:

> Purely, soberly, simply, Cusanus thinks his way through the world under a speculative empyrean. He does not polemicize against the mystical union that would remove him from the world, but he is factually unready for it. Nor is he ready to think himself into God's nature as if one might set foot there, as if the gulf between the finite and the infinite might be vaulted directly. There is only one possibility of an indirect leap: formal transcending in the pure concepts that rescind their definitions in the *coincidentia oppositorum*. Cusanus thinks in

---

[10] Karl Jaspers, "On My Philosophy (1941)," trans. Felix Kaufmann, in *Existentialism from Dostoyevsky to Sartre*, ed. Walter Kaufmann (Cleveland and New York: Meridian Books, 1956), 137.

[11] Jaspers, *The Great Philosophers*, 2:246. For the original wording, see Jaspers, *Nikolaus Cusanus*, 215–16.

[12] "Die Herrlichkeit und Tiefe dieser Philosophie habe ich mir am Ende des ersten Weltkrieges und kurz danach angeeignet und lebe seitdem mit ihr." Kaegi and Wiehl, *Karl Jaspers Korrespondenzen*, 674; my translation. The quotation is from a letter Jaspers wrote to Richard Wisser in 1964 in response to the latter's review of his Cusanus book.

a direction where nothing is conceivable, definable, imaginable anymore, in the direction of that which really is—and which is nothing as well.[13]

The language of "formal transcending in the pure concepts" conducive to a sort of leap over the Cusan "wall" of the coincidence of opposites does connect to the cardinal's metaphysics. It is not expressed in a manner typical of Nicholas of Cusa, but this is a point of contact worth exploring further.

It would be futile to accuse Jaspers of being ahistorical in his approach, since historical appropriation was not his goal. As Inigo Bocken has stated in response to Kurt Flasch's critique of Jaspers, to blame the twentieth-century philosopher for failing to grasp a Cusan idea in its historic context amounts to an expression of "historic positivism."[14] To quote Richard Wisser, those who use the "historic Cusanus" against the existential philosopher's interpretation ought to do justice to the "historic Jaspers" as well.[15] More importantly, Jaspers did elaborate on the kind of dialogue he was engaged in with past philosophers:

> I philosophize that which matters presently within thoughts from the past. In the knowledge of the past that I appropriate is a *new philosophical present*. As a matter of fact, this knowledge is a basic form of original philosophizing [consisting] in understanding and revealing that which in transmitted tradition and ancient texts presently moves in the depths. What is presently possible is so solely in communication with all that has passed.[16]

---

[13] Karl Jaspers, *Philosophical Faith and Revelation*, translated by E. B. Ashton (London: Collins, 1967), 261. The original German text is *Der philosophische Glaube angesichts der Offenbarung* (Munich: R. Piper Verlag, 1962).

[14] Inigo Bocken, "Der Kampf um Kommunikation. Karl Jaspers' existentielle Cusanus-Lektüre," in Reinhardt and Schwaetzer, *Cusanus-Rezeption in der Philosophie des 20. Jahrhunderts*, 63.

[15] "Wer aber im Namen des 'historischen Cusanus' gegen Jaspers' philosophische Aneignungs- und kritischen Vergegenwärtigungsversuch argumentiert, dem steht es gut zu Gesicht, wenn er auch dem 'historischen Jaspers' Gerechtigkeit widerfahren läßt." Richard Wisser, "Nikolaus Cusanus im 'lebendigen Spiegel' der Philosophie von Karl Jaspers," 530.

[16] "Ich philosophiere im vergangenen Gedanken, was gegenwärtig angeht. Im Wissen vom Vergangenen, das ich aneigne, ist eine neue philosophische Gegenwart. Tatsächlich ist dieses Wissen eine Grundform ursprünglichen Philosophierens, im Zusammenhang mit der Überlieferung, im Studium alter Texte zu begreifen und offenbar zu machen, was gegenwärtig in der Tiefe bewegt. Was jeweils gegenwärtig möglich ist, ist dies nur in der Kommunikation

The statement is quite clear. The dialogue itself is of a philosophical nature, and the purpose of Jaspers's readings was to inject the ideas of his predecessors with new life, not because he deemed them inept but because he adapted them to a contemporary setting, one in which, for instance, the fear of totalitarianism loomed large. Today, in comparative philosophy, this approach is called "fusion."[17]

I propose to examine a single notion in Karl Jaspers's *Psychologie der Weltanschauungen* (*The Psychology of Worldviews*, 1919), an early text written around the time Jaspers says he began to "live with" Nicholas of Cusa's philosophy, and one that has yet to be translated in English.[18] The notion in question is "Gehäuse." I will explain what Jaspers means by this term and show how it connects to Cusanus's philosophy, and how he was able to give a "new philosophical present" to the latter's notion of "infinity," especially as introduced in *De visione Dei* (*On the Vision of God*).

Life within *Gehäuse*

Karl Jaspers seems to have borrowed the term *Gehäuse* from Max Weber (or Georg Simmel) but repurposed it to fit the needs of his own philosophy; it too received a new present.[19] One can tell from Jaspers's usage that he paid close attention to the multiple layers of meanings of *Gehäuse* in appropriating this term. Etymologically speaking, *Gehäuse* is derived

---

zu allem Vergangenen." Quoted in Inigo Bocken, "Der Kampf um Kommunikation," 52; my translation and emphasis.

17 See Tamara Albertini, "'Clarity Is What I Seek First' (Interview with Prof. Tamara Albertini)," by Piotr Pietrzak, *In Statu Nascendi* 3, no. 2 (2020): 29.

18 Karl Jaspers, *Psychologie der Weltanschauungen* (Berlin: Springer Verlag, 1919), 293. Unfortunately, I was unable to consult later editions of this work. Only a few pages of this text are available in English, in *The Worlds of Existentialism: A Critical Reader*, ed. Maurice Friedman (New York: Random House, 1964), 100–102, 148–49, 202. See https://jaspers-stiftung.ch/de/karl-jaspers/werk (accessed November 16, 2020).

19 This term has rarely interested Jaspers scholars. An exception is Paprotny's *Karl Jaspers' Philosophie*. Martin Heidegger's lengthy review of *Psychologie der Weltanschauungen* does not mention the term at all. See his "Anmerkungen zu Karl Jaspers' 'Psychologie der Weltanschauungen' (1919/21)," in *Karl Jaspers in der Diskussion*, ed. Hans Saner (Munich: R. Piper Verlag, 1973), 70–100. It is typically Weber specialists who point out Jaspers's specific use of "Gehäuse." See, for instance, Chris Thornhill, *Karl Jaspers: Politics and Metaphysics* (London: Routledge, 2002), 57–58; and Joshua Derman, "Philosophy Beyond the Bounds of Reason: The Influence of Max Weber on the Development of Karl Jaspers' *Existenzphilosophie*, 1909–1932," in *Max Weber Matters: Interweaving Past and Present*, ed. Daniel Chalcraft et al. (Aldershot: Ashgate, 2008), 55–71; see esp. 61n12.

from late Middle High German *geheus* and *gehiuse* (hut, crate) and is formally a collective noun for *Haus* (house). Its first meaning in contemporary German is "firm, protective enveloping" as in "casing" and "shell."[20] The most common English translation for the technical term *Gehäuse* is "shell." Some Jaspers specialists render it as "objectified cage" or just "cage."[21] However, since the latter is a term also used by Jaspers in German (*Käfig*),[22] it is best to refer to *Gehäuse* as "shell" to avoid any confusion.

At first, "shell" seems an odd translation. However, it turns out that the connotations of this term in English not only help elucidate Jaspers's *Gehäuse* but are even conducive to a better understanding of this notion. Thus one may think of the outer layer of an egg: nurturing on the inside and protective on the outside, it sets a boundary between an "inner" and an "outer." Once the life that it shielded breaks out of it, it loses its function and eventually disintegrates. Jaspers's *Gehäuse*, too, implies a separation between an inside and an outside. Human beings seek protection in a *Gehäuse* and, at the same time, feel an urge to liberate themselves from it. Nevertheless, while a particular *Gehäuse* is ordinarily not permanent, individuals always seek refuge in a *Gehäuse*, unlike oviparous animals that never return to a shell. As much as human beings seek to free themselves from the "shelters" in which they find themselves—whether such shelters were inherited, erected by them, or imposed upon them—human beings merely modify the *Gehäuse* that houses them. Again, what is permanent is not a specific *Gehäuse* but being *in* one. Jaspers uses the example of mussels to illustrate the healthy function of a "shell." Without it, "Man cannot live anymore, as little as a mussel deprived of its shell."[23]

The term's importance in *Psychologie der Weltanschauungen* may be gleaned from its frequent occurrences: Karl Jaspers uses the term over 190 times in that text. Here is how he defines it:

> Under world view [*Weltbild*], we thus understand the totality of all objectival content a human being has. We see the human as a center

---

[20] See https://www.duden.de/rechtschreibung/Gehaeuse (accessed November 16, 2020).

[21] Chris Thornhill and Ronny Miron, "Karl Jaspers," *The Stanford Encyclopedia of Philosophy* (Spring 2022 Edition), ed. Edward N. Zalta, https://plato.stanford.edu/archives/spr2022/entries/jaspers/ (accessed November 16, 2020).

[22] Jaspers, *Psychologie der Weltanschauungen*, 293.

[23] "... der Mensch kann nicht mehr leben, so wenig wie eine Muschel, der man die Schale genommen hat." Jaspers, *Psychologie der Weltanschauungen*, 248.

somewhat within a circle: ... the circumference is the world of objects in which the human is encapsulated in the subject-object-divide. Or we can call the world view the shell in which the soul's life is captured, and which is partly also created by it and put forward outwardly. We live continuously in such a shell. The outermost horizon of our world view we take to be an absolute.[24]

From these lines, one senses that the notion of *Gehäuse* was essential to Jaspers's analysis of any form of totalitarianism. It is common knowledge that the existential philosopher denounced National Socialism as a totalitarian regime both before and after 1945, but that he was critiquing totalitarianism already in 1919 is worth pointing out. Moreover, in his analysis, not only political ideologies become "shells," but also religions and scientific world views once they "ossify" and turn to institutions with dogmatic beliefs and the power to enforce them.[25]

How does one recognize the symptoms of a *Gehäuse*-mentality? "Truth is known and in possession," states Jaspers, and "thinking regarding truth is advocatory, i.e., 'apologetic' and 'aggressive.'"[26] Another symptom is the teleological orientation of the world view in question: its ideologies are filled with promises for a better future. This does not imply that Jaspers's philosophy is free of any *telos*; it is not. However, in his work such ends have no content. They are merely there to help overcome the boundaries of the *Gehäuse*. The only justifiable teleology is the one that has us drop the need for one. Remarkably, Jaspers asserts that Cusanus's *Weltanschauung* is one of mere hinting: it too is without content.[27]

Clearly, "shells" as conceptualized by Karl Jaspers are highly problematic dwellings. They prevent a genuine quest for truth, they generate ideologies,

---

[24] "Unter dem Weltbild verstehen wir also die Gesamtheit der gegenständlichen Inhalte, die ein Mensch hat. Den Menschen als das Zentrum sehen wir gleichsam in einer Kreisperipherie: ... die Peripherie ist diese Welt des Gegenständlichen, in die der Mensch in der Subjekt-Objektspaltung eingeschlossen ist. Oder wir können das Weltbild das Gehäuse nennen, in das das seelische Leben teils eingefangen ist, das es teils auch selbst aus sich zu schaffen und nach außen zu setzen vermag. Wir leben immerfort in einem solchen Gehäuse. Den äußersten Horizont unseres Weltbildes halten wir ganz unwillkürlich für einen absoluten." Jaspers, *Psychologie der Weltanschauungen*, 122; my translation.

[25] Jaspers often uses the terms *verknöchern* (ossify), *versteinern* (fossilize), and *erstarren* (rigidify) for any system or worldview that has become dogmatic.

[26] Quoted in Paprotny, *Karl Jaspers' Philosophie*, 44; my translation.

[27] Jaspers, *Psychologie der Weltanschauungen*, 175.

and they offer pseudo-absolutes. And yet, they are unavoidable. Strictly speaking, Jaspers warns against only the "fertige Gehäuse," that is, the finalized ones that do not undergo further transformation:

> That the human being lives and does not perish is apparent inasmuch as in the process of the disintegration of the old shell he simultaneously builds new shells or prepares to do so. This putting-outward or exteriorization [*Nachaußensetzen*] of life is indeed always a kind of establishing; only in this putting-outward is life recognizable; the process of such putting-outward is life itself.[28]

Human beings could not survive without shells. What, then, prompts the dissolution of a shell? In fact, the breakdown happens to create room for new shells. Ultimately, the disintegration is a "metamorphosis"[29] and a reassuring sign indicating that an individual lives in a shell of his or her own making. The shell grows and changes according to one's relation to reality. It is what Jaspers calls "boundary situations" or "limit-situations" (*Grenzsituationen*), such as struggle, death, chance, and guilt, that induce change. The profound crises these situations trigger become salvific. They invite critical reflection to shed light on and eventually overcome the deficiencies of one's shell. Such catastrophes make human beings aware of their helplessness and the limitations of their shells, and thus reveal the need to make modifications. Nevertheless, not every individual recognizes or acknowledges this need: some use the shell to avoid having to make changes. The fear of freedom keeps them in bondage.

Years later, Jaspers echoes this same thought in his work *Philosophy* by stating that boundary situations "are like a wall we run into, a wall on which we founder. We cannot modify them; all that we can do is to make them lucid, but without explaining or deducing them from something else. They go with existence itself."[30] This suggests another point of contact between

---

[28] "Daß der Mensch lebt und nicht zugrunde geht, ist daran sichtbar, daß er im Auflösungsprozeß des alten Gehäuses gleichzeitig neue Gehäuse oder Ansätze dazu baut. Dieses Nachaußensetzen des Lebens ist ja immer ein irgendwie Festlegen, nur in diesem Nachaußensetzen ist Leben erkennbar, der Prozeß dieses Nachaußensetzens ist das Leben selbst." Jaspers, *Psychologie der Weltanschauungen*, 249; my translation.

[29] Jaspers, *Psychologie der Weltanschauungen*, 249.

[30] Karl Jaspers, *Philosophy*, trans. E. B. Ashton, 3 vols. (Chicago: University of Chicago Press, 1970), 2:178. The original German was first published in 1932.

the existential philosopher and Nicholas of Cusa. However, as the following will clarify, there are walls and there are walls.

Jaspers's Wall and the Cusan Wall of Paradise

In his book on Nicholas of Cusa, Karl Jaspers describes the notion of *coincidentia oppositorum* as a form of not-knowing that spurns rationality (Latin *ratio*, German *Verstand*). It requires a type of thinking that relies on *Verstand* at every stage of the way without the latter's being able to comprehend how opposites could be reconciled. Jaspers recognizes the fundamental challenge of Cusan thinking: it consists in being carried out *through* rationality but only being grasped *by* the intellect (Latin *intellectus*, German *Vernunft*).[31] Despite its grasp, or rather because of it, *Vernunft* finds itself at an infinite distance from the actual coincidence of opposites. In principle, the realm of coincidence beyond the "wall" is inaccessible, and yet it affects the intellect, causing it to hunger for that which it cannot reach. Paradoxically, says Jaspers, the infinite generates nostalgia.[32] Ultimately: "We fail at the wall when we attempt to break through it," writes Jaspers, "but we *experience* the wall as the sign of the deity that holds us."[33]

This is possibly one of the most extraordinary analyses of a Cusan idea in any of Jaspers's works, even though, as the following will show, he discounted an important detail of the wall's description. One senses that the existential philosopher was profoundly moved by what he took to be a description of failure, which for him was the sign of "authentic" thinking, unimpeded by authoritarian boundaries. To "founder" (*scheitern*) or "shipwreck" (*Schiffbruch erleiden*), as Jaspers puts it in his later works, is necessary for breaking out of the *Gehäuse*: with failure comes freedom.

Cusanus's notion of infinity indeed finds a new life in Karl Jaspers's philosophy in that it becomes a remedy for the many "shells" human beings rely on throughout their lives. Not being able to get "there," and yet longing for it, keeps human beings free from dogmatic dwellings. "Infinity itself is

---

31 Jaspers, *The Great Philosophers*, 2:125–26.

32 Jaspers, *The Great Philosophers*, 2:127.

33 My translation closely follows the original German, which speaks of experience, a notion so essential in existential philosophy: "Wir scheitern an der Mauer, wenn wir sie durchbrechen möchten, aber wir *erfahren* die Mauer als das Zeichen der Gottheit, die uns hält" (Jaspers, *Nikolaus Cusanus*, 26; my emphasis). By contrast, Ralph Manheim renders *erfahren* as "recognize" (Jaspers, *The Great Philosophers*, 2:123).

not a world view. Instead, the world view in infinity is unable to crystallize as a shell; the shell is not solid, the thoughts as a system are not fossilized, the contents end everywhere with questions and antinomies."[34]

Karl Jaspers's infinity is conceptualized as a barrier against totalitarianism and a guarantor of intellectual freedom. He believed he had found an ally in Nicholas of Cusa and that the cardinal too had invested his philosophical ingenuity to liberate himself from authoritarian strongholds. At the same time, Jaspers also blamed him for not having dared to break down the *Gehäuse* that is the Christian faith. Although Jaspers had a profound interest in mysticism—especially the "speculative" sort, which he took to be a technique of "transcending through thinking"—he did not truly appreciate mystical *experience*, which is odd considering his reliance on internal experience as a transformative force. For Jaspers, rapture was likely a matter of mere "devotional" mysticism and, therefore, of little philosophical interest.[35] However, before proceeding with an inquiry into what Jaspers may have missed in his reading of Cusan works, especially *De visione Dei*, it is time to hear Nicholas of Cusa himself.

The first time a "wall" is mentioned in *De visione Dei*, it refers to a north wall in the Benedictine Tegernsee monastery on which the brethren are to place the portrait of an "omnivoyant" figure (possibly an icon of Christ) the cardinal had sent them together with the text. The monks are instructed to walk around the painting with their eyes fixated on the portrait's gaze and share their experience with each other: the eyes of the omnivoyant face seem to follow them regardless of the perspectival position they take.[36] Later on, the text clarifies that divine (absolute) vision is to be conceptualized beyond the wall in a "space" where all that exists is perceived at once. Absolute perspective is not bound (the technical term used is "contracted") to one specific angle, but is the sum of all possible perspectives. It is, therefore, best represented by absolute roundness: "the angle of Your eye is a

---

[34] "Das Unendliche ist selbst nicht Weltbild, sondern das Weltbild im Unendlichen ist als Gehäuse nicht kristallisierbar; das Gehäuse ist nicht fest, die Gedanken als System nicht versteinert; die Inhalte endigen überall mit Fragen und mit Antinomien." Jaspers, *Psychologie der Weltanschauungen*, 130; my translation.

[35] I borrow the distinction between speculative and devotional mysticism from Alan M. Olson, "Jaspers's Critique of Mysticism," *Journal of the American Academy of Religion* 51, no. 2 (1983): 253–54.

[36] Nicholas of Cusa, *De visione Dei*, Praef. (3–4), in *Nicolai de Cusa Opera Omnia*, vol. VI, ed. Heide Dorothea Riemann (Hamburg: Felix Meiner Verlag, 2000), 5–6.

circle—or better, an infinite sphere—because Your sight is an eye of sphericity and of infinite perfection. Therefore, Your sight sees—roundabout and above and below—all things at once."[37]

The wall used for the experiment can help us understand the "wall of Paradise" beyond which opposites coincide. Unsurprisingly, it "surrounds" God.[38] Its gate is guarded by the most lofty spirit of rationality (*spiritus altissimus rationis*)—Jaspers speaks of a *Verstandesgeist*[39]—suggesting that one has to overcome *ratio*'s rejection of the idea of coincidence in order to be granted access.[40] On the hither side, the wall separating finite and infinite appears as a "wall of absurdity" (*murus absurditatis*), but it does not present an insurmountable obstacle;[41] it separates as much as it conjoins.[42] Although the intellect too reaches its limit at the wall, its ability to fathom the *coincidentia oppositorum* propels its "eye" to look beyond the wall: "For it is the eye's secret love and hidden treasure, which, having been found, remains hidden. For it is found on the inner side of the wall of the coincidence of the hidden and manifest."[43]

The mystical language evoked by Nicholas of Cusa has only the appearance of speaking, for in fact it speaks of that for which there are no words. Thus, what is the eye? It is that which sees beyond the wall. What does it see? A hidden treasure. How can it see that which is hidden? Because the hidden coincides with the manifest. What is that in which the hidden and manifest coincide? This line of questioning could prove endless: nothing is truly being said of the realm beyond the wall for as long as the process of

---

[37] Nicholas of Cusa, *De visione Dei*, VIII (32), ed. Riemann, 30–31; trans. Jasper Hopkins, *Nicholas of Cusa's Dialectical Mysticism: Text, Translation, and Interpretive Study of "De Visione Dei"*, 2nd ed. (Minneapolis: Arthur J. Banning Press, 1988), 153.

[38] Nicholas of Cusa, *De visione Dei*, XI (46), ed. Riemann, 40–41. In my article "Nicholas of Cusa's Mathematics and Astronomy," in *Introducing Nicholas of Cusa: A Guide to a Renaissance Man*, ed. Christopher M. Bellito, Thomas M. Izbicki, and Gerald Christianson (Mahwah, NJ: Paulist Press, 2004), 373–406, I extracted a figure from *De visione Dei* in which the half-circle used by the monks to walk around the portrait finds its completion on the other "side" of the wall (392). In my reading here, the wall on which the omnivoyant figure is to be placed is a symbolic representation of the wall of Paradise surrounding the divine.

[39] Jaspers, *Nikolaus Cusanus*, 27.

[40] Nicholas of Cusa, *De visione Dei*, IX (37), ed. Riemann, 35. Cusanus speaks of an angel in *De visione Dei*, X (40), ed. Riemann, 36.

[41] Nicholas of Cusa, *De visione Dei*, XII (49), ed. Riemann, 43; trans. Hopkins, 174.

[42] Nicholas of Cusa, *De visione Dei*, XI (46), ed. Riemann, 40–41.

[43] Nicholas of Cusa, *De visione Dei*, XVII (75), ed. Riemann, 61; trans. Hopkins, 211.

understanding is driven solely by rationality. However, as Jaspers emphasizes, the intellect, too, faces challenges when thinking of the absolute:

> It is a kind of thinking that, each time it expresses itself, falls into an essential contradiction, but in such a way that the contradiction itself reveals the truth 'intended.' ... The absolute cannot be adequately conceived of in rational categories, but only in the *coincidentia oppositorum*; and yet the moment the absolute is expressed in words, it is reduced to rational opposites.[44]

Nevertheless, the rational stage of the process is necessary, precisely as it leads to failure, a failure that Jaspers addresses in *Philosophical Faith and Revelation* with reference to Nicholas of Cusa: "if this foundering is carried out methodically, it will touch Transcendence."[45] This insight comes very close to the epistemic strategy developed in *De visione Dei*. What the existential philosopher neglects is that the cardinal's wall has a gate, which is why Jaspers was not accurate when he wrote in his Cusanus book: "We fail at the wall when we attempt to break through it." It is not a matter of "breaking through" but of "passing through"—by applying the right concepts.

Methodic Foundering or Methodic Overcoming of Rationality?

Modern philosophers have grown accustomed to "methodic doubt" as the Cartesian way leading to certainty, but "methodic foundering," as Jaspers distills it out of Cusan philosophy, is a novelty. It is a brilliant proposition and another point of contact between the two figures. Failure, however, is not a goal that the cardinal would have considered worth pursuing—nor is it an ultimate end for Jaspers. So, what does failure achieve? If Descartes's doubt leads to certainty, foundering leads one to overcome the limitations of rationality. That would still not be the purpose of "failing" at the wall: the leap that follows is. To be clear, rationality and intellect are not divorced from each other in the Cusan epistemic apparatus. He thus states: "I see that the intellect is present in reason, as in its own location, so that the intellect

---

[44] Jaspers, *The Great Philosophers*, 2:125.
[45] Jaspers, *Philosophical Faith and Revelation*, 260. Jaspers speaks of a "methodic manner" also in his Cusanus book; see Jaspers, *The Great Philosophers*, 2:123.

is located in a place as a candle [is located] in a room, illumining the room and all the walls and the entire building—according, nevertheless, to its greater or lesser degree of distance [from them]."[46] The intellect does not nullify rationality; it is the faculty that guides it. The underlying analogy is as follows: rationality relates to intellect, as opposites (outside the wall) relate to the coincidence of opposites (inside the wall).

But in what does the method consist? The method that Nicholas of Cusa created was designed to push rationality to its limits. To use Jaspers's shipwreck metaphor, the approach would be similar to piloting the vessel that is *ratio* toward opposites as if they were a ridge of rocks in order to reach the space beyond the ridge, which in *De visione Dei* is represented by the wall of Paradise. An integral part of Cusanus's method is his concept of *coincidentia oppositorum*, which acts as a compass showing north—coincidentally, the cardinal direction used by the Benedictine monks to hang the icon sent with *De visione Dei*.

The extent to which the Renaissance philosopher refined his method emerges when one notices his correlative use of two other concepts: enfolding (*complicatio*) and unfolding (*explicatio*). One important example is the clock: as an eternal concept and as a device built to measure the passage of time. What is present as succession of movements and sounds in the mechanism of a physical clock exists enfolded in the concept of the clock. "So," concludes Cusanus, "let the concept of a clock be, as it were, eternity itself. Then, in the clock, movement is succession. Therefore, eternity enfolds and unfolds succession; for the Concept of a clock—a Concept which *is* eternity—both enfolds and unfolds all things."[47] The challenge in comprehending the notions of *complicatio* and *explicatio* is that they are not perfect opposites. They are not on par, since the former has a metaphysical priority over the latter: for the "*un*folding" of creation to happen, there "first" needs to exist an "*en*folding" of all there is.

---

[46] Nicholas of Cusa, *De visione Dei*, XXII (100), ed. Riemann, 78; trans. Hopkins, 245. In this passage, Nicholas of Cusa uses the term *paries* (interior walls) as opposed to *murus*, which he reserves for the wall of Paradise.

[47] Nicholas of Cusa, *De visione Dei*, XI (44), ed. Riemann, 39–40; trans. Hopkins, 171. See Donald F. Duclow, "Cusanus' Clock: Time and Eternity in *De visione Dei*," in *Akten des Forschungskolloquiums in Freising vom 8. bis 11. November 2012*, MFCG 34, ed. Walter Andreas Euler (Trier: Paulinus Verlag, 2016), 135–46.

Nicholas of Cusa indicates in no uncertain terms that he has mastered the technique of both entering and exiting the space beyond the "wall" by tracing the "folds" leading from *complicatio* to *explicatio* and back:

> Trusting in Your help, O Lord, I turn once again in order to find You beyond the wall of the coincidence of enfolding and unfolding. And when at one and the same time I go in and out through the door of Your Word and Concept, I find most sweet nourishment. When I find You to be a power that enfolds all things, I go in. When I find You to be a power that unfolds, I go out.[48]

We could adapt Plato's charioteer allegory (*Phaedrus*, 246a–254e) to the present context. It is as if Cusanus were riding the concept of coincidence of opposites with one horse in the front and another one in the back of the chariot, that is, one allowing him to pass through the gate (the one guarded by the most lofty spirit of rationality) when the philosopher's mind enfolds, and the other moving him out as a result of the latter's unfolding; unlike in Plato's allegory, there is no bad horse. Nicholas of Cusa again suggests that he was able to simultaneously conceptualize penetrating and emerging from the space within the "wall" surrounding God in the following passage:

> When I find You to be a power that both enfolds and unfolds, I both go in and go out. From creatures I go in unto You, who are Creator—go in from the effects unto the Cause. I go out from You, who are Creator—go out from the Cause unto the effects. I both go in and go out when I see that going out is going in and that, likewise, going in is going out. (By comparison, he who counts unfolds and enfolds, alike: he unfolds the power of oneness, and he enfolds number in oneness.) For creation's going out from You is creation's going in unto You; and unfolding is enfolding.[49]

If Jaspers did not pay sufficient attention to the gate in Cusanus's wall, although he does quote the above passage and speak of "a way in and a way out,"[50] he might have been uncomfortable with the devotional language

---

48 Nicholas of Cusa, *De visione Dei*, XI (45), ed. Riemann, 40; trans. Hopkins, 171.
49 Nicholas of Cusa, *De visione Dei*, XI (45–46), ed. Riemann, 40; trans. Hopkins, 171.
50 Jaspers, *The Great Philosophers*, 2:123–24.

used to describe the "wall of Paradise" and how to move beyond it. That is, Jaspers might have perceived that language as the expression of a *Gehäuse* from which he wished the cardinal to liberate himself.

Yet it is hard to fathom that Cusanus would have considered such a step, not just because he was a Prince of the Church. His Christian faith that God was infinite grounded the metaphysical realm of coincidence of opposites, a teaching that had the potential to transform not only all branches of knowledge, but also how individuals of different world views and religious backgrounds would interact: not as adversaries but as participants in a dialogue using different metaphysical languages in reference to one and the same eternal reality. To be freed from Christian faith would have destroyed Nicholas of Cusa's access to the space beyond the wall—not just for himself but for others too. His ambition was to make the crossing not solely for the loving embrace he may have hoped to experience subjectively after going through the gate. However imperfect he may have found the historical expression of the Christian world view of his day to be, he trusted it could be improved on. In Jaspersian terms, one might say the manner in which Cusanus perceived the *Gehäuse* of historically embodied Christianity is that it could be transformed only by passing through the gate of rationality *and* exiting again. Clearly, in order to revise the dominant world view of one's own time, one needs to return to the hither side of the wall.

That the cardinal had hoped to achieve change is evidenced by his multiple attempts to reorganize the Church and mediate between Eastern and Western Christianity (including Hussites) as well as between Christianity and Islam.[51] As is well known, the cardinal failed utterly at his reformist pursuits. That was his personal foundering, but it was not one that led him to "touch Transcendence," in Jaspers's phrase; rather, silencing rationality is what took him to the absolute. This dimension of Cusan thought is missing in Jaspers's otherwise remarkable dialogue with the cardinal's work. To answer the question posed in the title of the present section, Cusanus's method was designed to overcome the constraints of rationality not through the experience of an existential breakdown, but by pushing this

---

[51] While Nicholas of Cusa's ecumenical vision was remarkable in its historical context, he still filtered his understanding of other religions through the lens of Christianity. For a general assessment, see James E. Biechler, "Interreligious Dialogue," in Bellito, Izbicki, and Christianson, *Introducing Nicholas of Cusa*, 270–96. A critical discussion can be found in Scott F. Aikin and Jason Aleksander, "Nicholas of Cusa's *De pace fidei* and the Meta-exclusivism of Religious Pluralism," *International Journal for Philosophy of Religion* 74 (2013): 219–235.

faculty to its limits. However, when it comes to conceptualizing a metaphysics designed to avert authoritarian teaching, one sees that the two philosophers were driven by a similar concern about the true place of rationality within the overarching endeavor of ideologically unobstructed thinking.

Critiques of Rationalism and Metaphysics of Liberation

There is much overlap between Jaspers's and Cusanus's respective critiques of rationalism, beyond mere points of contact. They both recognized that claims to rationality could become dangerous and could be used for authoritarian purposes if they shut down critical and innovative thinking. Nicholas of Cusa thus made an "idiota," an unschooled layman, the protagonist of a trilogy: *Idiota de sapientia* (*The Layman on Wisdom*), *Idiota de mente* (*The Layman on the Mind*), and *Idiota de staticis experimentis* (*The Layman on Experiments Done with Weight-Scales*). He needed a "free" thinker, someone with a fresh mind who was untainted by established doctrines, in order to demonstrate how "learned" categories are in the way of discoveries, scientific or otherwise. This matter did not escape the attention of Jaspers, who likely identified himself with the position of the Cusan outsider, since he too came to philosophy by way of a detour. He states: "The Layman (*idiota*) becomes the vehicle and discoverer of the truth, who defends it against the book-learning of the theologians. The truth is to be found in the streets and market places, not in the circles of the learned."[52]

For some 1800 years, it seemed rational to the learned to divide the universe into a supralunar and a sublunar world, one presumably unchanging and eternal, the other subjected to generation and destruction. Much ingenuity and reflection went into defending it, although there was nothing truly compelling about that separation. It was but a model until someone called Nicholas of Cusa removed the separation to create a new model: an infinite and center-less universe that rendered the geocentric-versus-heliocentric debate obsolete long before it started.[53] When that debate did flare up after the reception of the Copernican model in the works of Galileo, Giordano Bruno, Tommaso Campanella, and others, many tried to salvage by "rational" means what the learned circles had perpetuated for so long;

---

[52] Jaspers, *The Great Philosophers*, 2:153.
[53] See Albertini, "Nicholas of Cusa's Mathematics and Astronomy," 396–400.

defending the indefensible had no other purpose than the preservation of the unexamined *status quo*.⁵⁴

Karl Jaspers always warned against "rationales" that dispensed with examining historical models and demanded obedient adherence to a religious belief system. He has this in mind when he states:

> Rationalism loses the sense of becoming, the historical that no one is able to resolve rationally. Instead of intuition, it is the law that comes to it. Universally valid doctrines of the spirit arise that become dead in their abstractness, the doctrine of natural law, natural religions, universal human rights, teachings that are taken for granted by our reason, but become [a matter of] rationalism once they are turned into absolutes.⁵⁵

For Jaspers, worshippers of rationality put themselves at risk when they fail to understand that what seems rational depends upon what is conducive to a predetermined aim. Rationality is a means for truth-finding as much as for blocking inquiry; it is not in itself a guarantor of truth. In this respect, Nicholas of Cusa would have been in agreement with the twentieth-century philosopher: When trust in rationality takes a dogmatic turn, it morphs into rationalism.⁵⁶

---

54 In fairness, one can uncover a possible rational aim in that effort directed at maintaining transmitted knowledge against all odds. For example, the brilliant Jesuit astronomer and mathematician Christopher Clavius (1538–1612), who was charged with defending the Aristotelian-Ptolemaic world view, may not have been convinced that geocentrism was backed up by scientific observation and mathematical evidence, but he still opted to support it since it seemed more important to him to protect the Church's doctrinal authority than promote scientific evidence. That, to him, would have been a rational justification. In the end, his defense of the old world view was likely to have been a reflection of his refusal to acknowledge mathematics as a certain science to be placed above theology. For this last comment, see Irving A. Kelter, "The Refusal to Accommodate: Jesuit Exegetes and the Copernican System," *The Sixteenth Century Journal* 26, no. 2 (1995): 273–83.

55 "Dem Rationalismus geht der Sinn für das Werden, das Historische, das keiner rational auflösen kann, verloren. An Stelle der Anschauung tritt ihm das Gesetz. Es entstehen die allgemeingültigen Lehren vom Geiste, die in ihrer Abstraktheit tot werden, die Lehre vom Naturrecht, natürlicher Religionen, allgemeinen Menschenrechten, Lehren, die unvermeidlich für unsere Ratio sind, aber verabsolutiert Rationalismus werden." Jaspers, *Psychologie der Weltanschauungen*, 275; my translation.

56 "Der Verstand hat die Tendenz, sich absolut zu setzen. Er bedarf der Führung durch die Idee und Vernunft. Echte Freiheit ist dort, wo Wahrheit auf dem Wege ist, wo der Mensch die kritische Schwebe zu vollziehen vermag." Karl Jaspers, *Von der Wahrheit* (Munich: R. Piper Verlag, 1947), 806.

However, what Nicholas of Cusa's philosophy cannot accommodate is the existential basis of Jaspers's notion of world view. The latter's work, *Psychologie der Weltanschauungen*, contrasts two kinds of thinkers: the "rationalist," who recommends that one choose from among preexisting rational systems the one that seems the best fit, on the one hand, versus the "living spirit" (*der lebendige Geist*), who grounds his world view existentially in life, feeling, and acting, on the other hand.[57] For the cardinal, life in all its expressions—emotions, actions, sense perceptions, and faculties such as *ratio* and even the intellect—is a matter of "contraction," that is, conditioning. A human being is a different contraction of the absolute (via the world in its totality as the absolute's first contraction)[58] than any other existing being: animal, plant, or stone. Within the same species, there are again manifold, uncountable contractions. In *De visione Dei*, Cusanus points out how eyesight differs from individual to individual, and that emotions and age also account for perceptual contractions:

> ... in those who have sight, sight varies as a result of the variety of its contractedness. For our sight is conditioned by the affections of the organ [i.e., of the eye] and of the mind. Hence, a given individual looks [upon a given thing] now lovingly and gladly, later sadly and angrily, now as does a child, later as does an adult, and, still later, gravely and as does someone elderly.[59]

While the many world views that arise as a result of different individual "contractednesses" are not false—they express each individual's perception and are veridical in that respect—Nicholas of Cusa is not genuinely interested in them. Instead, his goal is to make his readers aware of their multiple contractions so that they may understand the inevitability of different world views and fathom the mode of "uncontractedness," which applies to the divine: a condition unhindered by any limitation. This is what he wished

---

57 Jaspers, *Psychologie der Weltanschauungen*, 277.

58 In *De docta ignorantia*, Cusanus explains: "Contraction means contraction to [i.e., restriction by] something, so as to be this or that. Therefore, God, who is one, is in the one universe. But the universe is contractedly in all things." Nicholas of Cusa, *De docta ignorantia*, II.4 (116), in *Nikolaus von Kues: Philosophisch-Theologische Werke*, vol. 1, ed. Paul Wilpert and Hans Gerhard Senger, rev. ed. (Hamburg: Felix Meiner Verlag, 2002), 36; trans. Jasper Hopkins, *Nicholas of Cusa on Learned Ignorance* (Minneapolis: Arthur J. Banning Press, 1985), 98.

59 Nicholas of Cusa, *De visione Dei*, II (7), ed. Riemann, 11; trans. Hopkins, 121.

the Benedictines from Tegernsee to comprehend when he subjected them to the experiment with the icon of the omnivoyant figure.

For Nicholas of Cusa, the world view one should strive for is one in which everyone understands that differences are the result of individual contractions of the absolute. Each of our senses is a contraction first at the species and again at the individual level. Imagining, remembering, and thinking rationally by applying logical rules or abstracting, the use of the intellect, the experience we bring to everything we do: all these are contractions without which we could neither make sense of our world nor of ourselves. They are not problematic in themselves; turning them into absolutes is. Here lies what I see to be a metaphysics of liberation, one the Cusan was hopeful would change philosophy, theology, and the sciences, basically, all world views that, as Jaspers expressed it, tend to "fossilize" over time. However, Nicholas of Cusa's metaphysics followed a different trajectory from Jaspers's and was also designed to fulfill another purpose.

It is unlikely that Cusanus's contemporaries perceived his philosophy as wanting to liberate them from conventional constraints, whether metaphysical, scientific, or cultural. It appears they paid more attention to his mystical language and, as a result, failed to recognize that Cusanus's mysticism was concept-driven and that his concepts were built to break down unexamined views. What Jaspers neglected to appreciate, they overemphasized. As a matter of fact, the cardinal was both the mystic and the philosopher, but it was his philosophical concepts that took him to mystical heights and back to his practical tasks. His simultaneous entering and exiting of the metaphysical space of *coincidentia oppositorum* reveal a high mastery of conceptual thinking: he had the rare gift of identifying the point of reconciliation for any two opposites.

Every world view is the result of multiple contractions. What matters is not to become hostage to it: therein lies metaphysical freedom.

3

Theoria in Cusanus and Gadamer

The Joy of Contemplation

MICHAEL EDWARD MOORE

Denk nicht, sondern schau!
"Don't think, look!"
—Ludwig Wittgenstein[1]

I recently encountered the modern meaning of theory in a story by Sir Arthur Conan Doyle. Sherlock Holmes insists that he needs more *data* before he can form a *theory* about the strange case of "The Speckled Band."[2] By Conan Doyle's time, theory had come to mean an abstract explanatory understanding regarding an observed set of facts, as in Adam Smith's *Theory of Moral Sentiments* or Darwin's "theory of natural selection." According to Hans Kelsen's *Pure Theory of Law*, first published in 1960, theory

---

[1] Ludwig Wittgenstein, *Philosophical Investigations*, trans. G. E. M. Anscombe, 2nd ed. (Oxford: Basil Blackwell, 1958), Lemma 66, 31. Research for this essay was supported by International Programs and the Stanley-University of Iowa Foundation Support Organization (SUIFSO).

[2] Sir Arthur Conan Doyle, "The Speckled Band," in *The Original Illustrated Sherlock Holmes* (Edison: Castle Books, 1982), 108–23.

wants "to know and to describe its object."³ For the ancient Greeks, however, the term θεωρία (Latin *theoria*) had a different range of meanings: spectacle, beholding, contemplation, speculation, or meditation.⁴ Whereas the modern use of the term indicates a temporary vantage point on the road of scientific inquiry, ancient θεωρία was an open, purposeless state of awareness—a state of mental and spiritual elevation, leading to supreme wisdom.

Theoria has a special place in the *opera omnia* of Cusanus, forming as it does the topic of his last treatise, *De apice theoriae* (*The Pinnacle of Contemplation*), composed just months before his death in 1464.⁵ Hans-Georg Gadamer, who often expressed his indebtedness to the philosophy of Cusanus,⁶ likewise devoted considerable attention to *theoria* and wrote an essay on the same topic five hundred years after the German cardinal entitled *Lob der Theorie* (*Praise of Theory*).⁷ Both thinkers presented theory or contemplation as the purest form of thought, as distinct from the practical concerns of τέχνη, comprising the joy at the heart of philosophy. The following essay explores the transhistorical relationship between Cusanus and Gadamer on the topic of theory. As humanists and philosophers, both men delved into earlier philosophical traditions: Cusanus was admired as a *platonista* by his contemporaries and studied seriously the thought of Augustine, Proclus, and medieval thinkers from Anselm to the School of Chartres to Meister Eckhart. Gadamer's engagement with the history of thought was a key to his philosophical activity, the result of extensive research in the tradition of Western philosophy, including Plato and Aristotle, patristic authors such as Clement of Alexandria and Augustine, Nicholas of Cusa himself, and the German philosophical tradition,

---

3 Hans Kelsen, *Pure Theory of Law*, trans. Max Knight (Clark, NJ: The Lawbook Exchange, 2009), 1. See also Adam Smith, *Theory of Moral Sentiments*, ed. D. D. Raphael and A. L. Macfie (Indianapolis, IN: Liberty Fund, 1982). Darwin regularly called his understanding of natural selection a "theory": see Charles Darwin, *The Origin of Species* (New York: John D. Morris & Co., 1900), 158.

4 See Andrea Wilson Nightingale, *Spectacles of Truth in Classical Greek Philosophy: Theoria in its Cultural Context* (Cambridge: Cambridge University Press, 2004), 72.

5 On the date, see Jasper Hopkins, *Nicholas of Cusa: Metaphysical Speculations* (Minneapolis: The Arthur J. Banning Press, 1998), 1437n1.

6 See Mirela Oliva, "Gadamer and Cusanus on Creation," *Philosophy Today* 55 (2011): 184–91; and Mirela Oliva, "The Metaphysics of Language in Cusanus and Gadamer," *Anuario Filosofico* 49 (2016): 401–22. See also Hans-Georg Gadamer, "Nikolaus von Kues im modernen Denken," in *Nicoló Cusano agli inizi del mondo moderno* (Florence: G. C. Sansoni Editore, 1964), 39–48.

7 Hans-Georg Gadamer, "Praise of Theory," in *Praise of Theory: Speeches and Essays*, trans. Chris Dawson (New Haven, CT: Yale University Press, 1998), 16–36.

including Fichte, Hegel, and Habermas. Certain terms and concepts such as *contemplatio* and *theoria* conveyed ancient ideas and attitudes across time, accompanying the entire history of Western philosophy, which were revived and expanded upon by the late medieval thinker Cusanus and the modern Gadamer. Before turning to Cusanus and Gadamer, therefore, I first sketch out some key moments in the history of *theoria* in ancient and medieval philosophy and theology.

The Emergence of θεωρία

When Solon (640–560 BCE) presented his law code to the city of Athens, the laws were written out on boards set up in the agora.[8] The sage then left the city and set out on a series of travels "in order to see the world."[9] According to the account of the historian Herodotus, the journey of Solon was an act of θεωρία: literally, going to see things for yourself.[10] As King Croesus declared during their famous encounter, Solon deserved to be called a lover of wisdom, a philosopher. As Hannelore Rausch explains, for Herodotus θεωρία, setting forth to see things for yourself, was closely related to the desire for wisdom.[11] These statements of Herodotus lead us to the earliest period of Western philosophy, during the seventh and sixth centuries BCE, for in this text is the very first appearance of the term φιλοσοφία.[12] Solon was reckoned as one of the Seven Sages, associated with the Delphic epigrams: "Know thyself," and "Nothing beyond measure."[13]

---

8 See Philippe Nemo, *A History of Political Ideas from Antiquity to the Middle Ages*, trans. Kenneth Casler (Pittsburgh, PA: Duquesne University Press, 2013), 39–49.

9 See Herodotus, *The Histories*, I.28, trans. George Rawlinson (New York: Alfred A. Knopf, 1997), 18. Jaeger connects Solon's law-giving and his philosophy: see Werner Jaeger, *Paideia: The Ideals of Greek Culture*, trans. Gilbert Highet, 2nd ed., 3 vols. (New York: Oxford University Press, 1945), 1:147.

10 Bruno Snell, *The Discovery of the Mind: The Greek Origins of European Thought*, trans. T. G. Rosenmeyer (New York: Harper Torchbook, 1960), 136–52.

11 Hannelore Rausch, *Theoria von ihrer sakralen zur philosophischen Bedeutung* (Munich: Wilhelm Fink Verlag, 1982), 42. See further the important discussion in Christoph Riedweg, *Pythagoras: His Life, Teaching, and Influence*, trans. Steven Rendall (Ithaca, NY: Cornell University Press, 2005), 96–97.

12 See Pierre Hadot, *What Is Ancient Philosophy?*, trans. Michael Chase (Cambridge, MA: Belknap Press, 2002), 15–16.

13 On Solon and the Seven Sages, see Kathleen Freeman, *Ancilla to the Pre-Socratic Philosophers: A Complete Translation of the Fragments in Diels, "Fragmente der Vorsokratiker"* (Cambridge, MA: Harvard University Press, 1977), 18.

In his realization of a new social order in Athens, Solon hoped to establish the life of the polis upon a foundation of justice, as a commitment to the justice (δίκη) that rules the cosmos.[14] The political order (εὐνομία) was to be based on this justice rather than archaic sacral kingship.[15] "Where there is good law, / There are all human affairs ordered with justice and sense."[16]

As a kind of enlightenment, θεωρία prepared this change. Plato spoke of θεωρία in this way in the parable of the cave, in *Republic* 517.[17] The dialogue *Phaedrus* is a measure of Plato's concern with contemplation:[18] In the cryptic opening scene, Socrates agrees to walk along with Phaedrus as he recounts a discourse on love he has heard and written down. The two men decide to stroll along the holy river Ilissus to cool their feet in the clear water of the stream and to enjoy the shade of a tall plane-tree that grows on the bank.[19] The constant throbbing of cicadas accompanies their discussion and invites careful reflection on the natural setting and reality itself, in contrast to the half-truths of the sophists.[20] A debate about the validity of writing and the nature of love ensues. The gentle landscape embodies the leisure needed for the practice of philosophy. When Phaedrus asks if they were not standing on the very spot where, according to legend, Orithyia was taken hostage by Boreas, Socrates dismisses the question, stating that his precious leisure would be wasted on such vain inquiries. Instead, he wants to live according to the Delphic command: "Know thyself."[21] The dialogue goes on to consider θεωρία as a quality of disinterested love, the highest

---

[14] Solon argued, in terms directly relevant to our own time, that the rich were devoid of sociability and companionship; allowing justice to flourish would end the resulting discord. See Robin Lane Fox, *The Classical World* (New York: Basic Books, 2005), 60–62, and Chester G. Starr, *A History of the Ancient World* (New York: Oxford University Press, 1991), 249–52.

[15] See Jean-Pierre Vernant and Pierre Vidal-Naquet, *Myth and Tragedy in Ancient Greece*, trans. Janet Lloyd (New York: Zone Books, 1990), 125–40.

[16] Hermann Fränkel, *Early Greek Poetry and Philosophy*, trans. Moses Hadas and James Willis (New York: Harcourt Brace Jovanovich, 1975), 221–23.

[17] See Anthony Preus, *Historical Dictionary of Ancient Greek Philosophy* (Lanham, MD: Rowman & Littlefield, 2015), 330.

[18] Plato, *Phaedrus*, in *The Dialogues of Plato*, trans. Benjamin Jowett, 2 vols. (New York: Random House, 1937), 1:233–82.

[19] Plato, *Phaedrus*, in *The Dialogues of Plato*, 235.

[20] See G. R. F. Ferrari, *Listening to the Cicadas: A Study of Plato's "Phaedrus"* (Cambridge: Cambridge University Press, 1987).

[21] Plato, *Phaedrus*, in *The Dialogues of Plato*, 235–36.

form of intelligence, which "rejoices at beholding reality."²² In Plato's philosophy, theory is far from idle wool-gathering, and equally far from the practical solution of worldly problems, or τέχνη.²³

The pure looking of θεωρία is related to the English word *theater* and, indeed, the situation of an audience attending a theater performance. Theater comes from the word θεωρεῖν, "to look at," and leads back to θεωρία.²⁴ Theater was a spectacle, something to be witnessed by the spectators, the θεατής.²⁵ As the audience observed the action on stage, they understood more than the *personae* of the drama: they might feel waves of grief or anger because of the story, but they cannot stop the figures from suffering on stage. In this way they develop a tragic consciousness, and afterward hopefully find themselves in a more meaningful world, in which suffering has been made intelligible.²⁶ Gadamer comments that because of this connection to the theater, an atmosphere of sacral communion, a sensation of joy, adhered to the idea of θεωρία.²⁷ At the same time, the θεωρία of Greek metaphysics sought to bring one into the presence of the real.²⁸ Perhaps encountering presence is one of the constant goals of philosophy.²⁹

For Aristotle, θεωρία was the most elevated form of thought. In the *Nicomachean Ethics* he ranked the theoretical life, or a life dedicated to contemplation, higher than the practical or political life.³⁰ Aristotle said that "happiness [is] a kind of reflection" and that a life dedicated to theory, if one has enough food and a roof over one's head, would be the happiest kind of life.³¹ The concept of θεωρία entered postclassical Greek and Latin wherever ascetic Christianity flourished. The term now referred to the

---

22 Plato, *Phaedrus*, in *The Dialogues of Plato*, 252. See Nightingale, *Spectacles of Truth*, 161–62.

23 See Pierre-Maxime Schuhl, "Remarques sur Platon et la technologie," *Revue des études grecques* 66 (1953): 465–72.

24 Nightingale, *Spectacles of Truth*, 51–52.

25 See Vernant and Vidal-Naquet, *Myth and Tragedy*, 113–17.

26 Vernant and Vidal-Naquet, *Myth and Tragedy*, 114.

27 Dawson, in Gadamer, *Praise of Theory*, xxvii.

28 Hans-Georg Gadamer, *Truth and Method*, trans. Joel Weinsheimer and Donald G. Marshall (New York: Continuum, 1998), 124 [I.2.1.C].

29 Hadot emphasizes the significance of presence as a category: our presence before the real and, equally, the presence of the real to us. See Pierre Hadot, *Plotinus, or the Simplicity of Vision*, trans. Michael Chase (Chicago: University of Chicago Press, 1993), 3–4, 13, 46.

30 Aristotle, *Nicomachean Ethics*, VI.2 (1139a19–1139a30), trans. Christopher Rowe (Oxford: Oxford University Press, 2002), 177–78.

31 Aristotle, *Nicomachean Ethics*, X.7 (1177a12–1178a8), trans. Rowe, 250–52.

loftiest contemplation of divine truth, or vision. In this sense the term was taken up by the Alexandrian theologians, including Clement and Origen.[32] Origen compared contemplation to a journey through the desert of abandonment, a path taken by a weary traveler who moves quickly and sleeps in a desert tent, because he knows that "here we have no abiding city."[33] Once again there is the image of a traveler, who, like Solon in Herodotus's account, journeys to a distant region as if on a restless pilgrimage. But Origen's standpoint implies that the search for presence is directed toward the divine alone, no longer toward the earthly world that surrounds us: neither seashores, forests, nor fields.

When John Cassian coined the Latin word *theoria*, he gave the term immediate currency in Western lands. It signified the Christian desert ideal to search for celestial realities in place of things of the world. Cassian practiced the monastic life in Bethlehem, Scetis, Kellia, and Nitria in Egypt, observing and writing about the wisdom of the monks he met in those places. Contemplation was now the most important dimension of monastic life, as indicated by terms like *theoria caelestis* and *theoria divina*.[34] To practice *theoria* meant that one's life could be a foretaste of heaven, "feeding on the beauty and knowledge of God alone," as Cassian wrote.[35] Highly influential, too, was Cassian's distinction between the active and contemplative life, which he symbolized in the contrast between Martha and Mary, an image repeated throughout the Middle Ages.[36] The distinction was hierarchical: theory ranked above practice, contemplation above work. In the ancient and early medieval context, work was thought of as something servile, in contrast to the aristocratic life of leisure that was suitable for contemplation, the *otium cum dignitate* of the aristocracy.[37]

---

[32] See Gerhart B. Ladner, *The Idea of Reform: Its Impact on Christian Thought and Action in the Age of the Fathers* (Cambridge, MA: Harvard University Press, 1959), 333.

[33] Jean Daniélou, *Origen*, trans. Walter Mitchell (New York: Sheed & Ward, 1955), 302–4.

[34] Louis Gougaud, "La *theoria* dans la spiritualité médiévale," *Revue ascétique et de mystique* 3 (1922): 381.

[35] Quoted in Columba Stewart, *Cassian the Monk* (New York: Oxford University Press, 1998), 48.

[36] See Stewart, *Cassian*, 47–54; and Gougaud, "La *theoria*," 385–86.

[37] See Jacques Le Goff, "Labor, Techniques, and Craftsmen in the Value Systems of the Early Middle Ages (Fifth to Tenth Centuries)," in *Time, Work, and Culture in the Middle Ages*, trans. Arthur Goldhammer (Chicago: University of Chicago Press, 1980), 71–86.

Theoria was also translated as the Latin *contemplatio*—contemplation, understood to mean contemplation of the deity, as found in the writings of Ambrose, Augustine, Rufinus, and Jerome.[38] An air of sacredness lingered around this ancient Roman term.[39] In *De vita contemplativa*, a work frequently copied and read throughout the Middle Ages, Julian Pomerius (d. 499/505) distinguished two forms of life: the *vita activa* and the *vita contemplativa*. Pomerius was the last word on this topic for most ascetics.[40] For Gregory the Great, who had read Pomerius, the conflict between the active and the contemplative life was existential.[41] *Theoria* even appears in the *Collectio canonum hibernensis* to describe the lives of Irish monks who gave themselves entirely to contemplation (*in contemplatione theorica viventes perseverant*).[42] *Theoria* became a loan-word in Old Irish (*teoir, teuir*).[43] The Benedictine scholar Jean Leclercq has explored the continued relevance of *theoria* in the spiritual practice of medieval monasteries.[44]

The *Consolation of Philosophy*, composed by Boethius during his imprisonment in about 524, encapsulates the long history of theory. In an unforgettable image, Boethius distinguished between theory and practice in the dress worn by Lady Philosophy. A letter Pi was embroidered at the bottom hem of her dress, and a Theta at the top: Pi (Π) for πρᾶξις, and Theta (Θ) for θεωρία. A series of steps showed that one could mount from practice to theory. Theory did not offer Boethius any escape from his imprisonment and fear, but called on him to orient his life toward the

---

38 Alexander Souter, *A Glossary of Later Latin to 600 A.D.* (Oxford: Clarendon Press, 1949), 419.

39 Rausch, *Theoria*, 73.

40 Julianus Pomerius, *De vita contemplativa*, PL 59:415–520. Hannah Arendt would revive this ancient contrast in her own work. See, e.g., Hannah Arendt, *The Human Condition*, 2nd ed. (Chicago: University of Chicago, 1998), 14–15.

41 See R. A. Markus, *Gregory the Great and His World* (Cambridge: Cambridge University Press, 1997), 19; and George E. Demacopoulos, *Gregory the Great: Ascetic, Pastor, and First Man of Rome* (Notre Dame, IN: University of Notre Dame Press, 2015), 21.

42 Hermann Wasserschleben, ed., *Die irische Kanonensammlung*, 2nd ed. (Aalen: Scientia Verlag, 1966), 148 [XXXIX.3].

43 See R. E. Latham, *Revised Medieval Latin Word-List from British and Irish Sources* (London: The British Academy & Oxford University Press, 1994), 483; and Rudolf Thurneysen, *A Grammar of Old Irish*, rev. ed. (Dublin: School of Celtic Studies, 1975), 568.

44 Jean Leclercq, *The Love of Learning and the Desire for God: A Study of Monastic Culture*, trans. Catherine Misrahi (New York: Fordham University Press, 1977), 126–27.

presence of the real.⁴⁵ Prayerful contemplation as the essence of the contemplative life, a life dedicated to love of God, was widely discussed by patristic writers such as Gregory of Nyssa, Pseudo-Dionysius, Augustine, Cassian, and Benedict of Nursia, up into medieval traditions including Hugh of St. Victor, Richard of St. Victor, and Albert the Great.

Thomas Aquinas adapted Aristotle's ideas to the framework of his own philosophy, as Josef Pieper has noted in his book *Happiness and Contemplation*.⁴⁶ Thomas states in his *Commentary on Aristotle's Nicomachean Ethics* that "happiness is the highest activity ... but the highest of human activities is contemplation of truth."⁴⁷ To contemplate the truth is the best way of life and constitutes the highest happiness, according to Thomas, especially if it is done in a community of like-minded companions, presumably a monastery, cathedral chapter, or classroom. Aquinas equated contemplation with the life of the blessed in heaven: "Therefore the last and perfect happiness, which we await in the life to come, consists entirely in contemplation."⁴⁸

In his philosophical treatise *Convivio* (3.14), Dante Alighieri (1265–1321) described contemplation as a state of philosophical rest or leisure.⁴⁹ More profoundly, Jan van Ruusbroec (1293–1381) described the heights of contemplation as an idle state in which the mind stops "working" and becomes a space in which only God is active: the idle mind is "suspended" in God.⁵⁰ As we approach the time of Cusanus, one can point to the "Doctor

---

45 "Harum in extremo margine Π Graecum, in supremo uero Θ legebatur intextum atque in utrasque litteras in scalarum modum gradus quidam insigniti uidebantur, quibus ab inferiore ad superius elementum esset ascensus." Boethius, *Consolatio philosophiae*, I.4, in *Anicii Manlii Severini Boethii Philosophiae consolatio*, ed. Ludwig Bieler, CCSL 94 (Turnhout: Brepols, 1957), 2.

46 See Josef Pieper, *Happiness and Contemplation*, trans. Richard Winston and Clara Winston (South Bend, IN: St. Augustine's Press, 1998).

47 Thomas Aquinas, *Commentary on Aristotle's Nicomachean Ethics*, X.2087, trans. C. I. Litzinger (Notre Dame, IN: Dumb Ox Books, 1993), 624.

48 "Et ideo ultima, et perfecta beatitudo, quae expectatur in futura vita, tota principaliter consistit in contemplatio." Thomas Aquinas, *Summa Theologiae*, I-II, q. 3, a. 5, in *Divi Thomae Aquinatis ordinis Praedicatorum Doctoris Angelici a Leone XIII P.M. ... Summa theologica* (Rome: Ex Typographia Forzani et S., 1894), vol. 2, 45–46; trans. Fathers of the English Dominican Province (New York: Benziger Brothers, 1947), vol. 1, 599–600.

49 Dante Alighieri, *The Convivio*, trans. Philip Henry Wickstool (London: J. M. Dent, 1903), 210. See also Angela G. Meekins, "Contemplative Life," in *The Dante Encyclopedia*, ed. Richard Lansing (London: Routledge, 2010), 216–18.

50 Paul Mommaers, *Jan van Ruusbroec: Mystical Union with God* (Leuven: Peeters, 2009), 155.

Ecstaticus," Denys the Carthusian (1402–1472), especially his 1452 work, *De lumine christianae theoriae*, which identifies metaphysical contemplation as the highest form of thought.[51]

Theoria in Cusanus

Up to this point I have discussed in a rarified way the emergence of *theoria* in terms of its *Wirkungsgeschichte*, tracing a long history extending from the pre-Socratics to Plato and Aristotle, Greek tragic drama, the desert Fathers, medieval monasteries and the schools. But as Claude Lévi-Strauss reminds us, in his work *Tristes Tropiques*: "we live in several worlds.... Some are known to us through action, some are lived through in thought."[52] Ideas must be explored in their multi-dimensionality. We find a personal dimension, and a glimpse into the life-world of the fifteenth century, in Nicholas of Cusa's final book, a discussion of theory.[53] *De apice theoriae* considers theoretical contemplation as the highest form of thought.

There is a distinct self-reflective element in this work, which is quite moving given that Cusanus wrote the treatise at the age of sixty-three, a few months before his death in 1464. The last years of his life were a period of grappling with opposition to his reform efforts, sharp disagreements with the pope, and being assigned new duties, although he longed to retire in seclusion. In spite of all this, he composed a remarkable series of works, which serve as the capstone of his philosophical career.[54] *De apice theoriae* is a slender book having certain parallels with other works of his late period, but I will focus on its distinctive features. The protagonists of the dialogue are "The Cardinal" and "Peter." The latter is meant to be Nicholas's secretary, Peter von Erkelenz, Canon of Aix (ca. 1430–1494). Nearly thirty

---

51 See Denys the Carthusian, *Doctoris ecstatici D. Dionysii Cartusiani Opera omnia in unum corpus digesta ad fidem editionum Coloniensium, cura et labore monachorum sacri ordinis Cartusiensis favente Pont. Max. Leone XIII* (Monstrolii: Typis Cartusiae S. M. de Pratis, 1896–1935), vol. 33, 233–513.
52 Claude Lévi-Strauss, *Tristes tropiques*, trans. John Weightman and Doreen Weightman (New York: Athenaeum, 1975), 412.
53 See Kurt Flasch, *Das philosophische Denken im Mittelalter vom Augustin zu Machavelli* (Stuttgart: Reclam, 2001), 599–606.
54 Donald F. Duclow, "Life and Works," in *Introducing Nicholas of Cusa: A Guide to a Renaissance Man*, ed. Christopher M. Bellitto, Thomas M. Izbicki, and Gerald Christianson (New York: Paulist Press, 2004), 25–56; see esp. 44–47.

years younger than the Cardinal, Peter appears as a devoted student and ideal reader.

As the work opens, we find the Cardinal, Cusanus, seated at his writing desk in his study in discussion with his secretary. Peter has ventured to disturb the Cardinal, remarking that he has been tip-toeing past him for some days, realizing that he was lost in *profunda meditatio*.[55] But the Cardinal's serious expression had suddenly given way to the light of joy. With his discretion and sensitivity, Peter is a perfect companion for the old philosopher. He delicately wonders whether Nicholas may have already said everything he had to say in his previous writings, thus introducing a retrospective mood, for while this dialogue is about aspiring to the pinnacle of theory, it is also about the significance of Cusanus's entire *oeuvre*. Rather than responding to this question directly, Nicholas compares his lifelong quest for understanding to the rapture of Paul to the third heaven described so vividly in 2 Corinthians (2 Cor 12).[56] Nicholas has always hoped to reach this highest degree of understanding, but God escaped him, for he is beyond all comprehension: *qui maior est omni comprehensioni*.[57] So here are the initial, troubling questions of the dialogue: what have your writings amounted to? And what have you been seeking all this time? The answer to the latter question is stated at once: quiddity.

At first Cusanus expresses his insight in a humorous way, a bit like the vaudeville routine "Who's on first?" To paraphrase, Peter asks: "What are you seeking?" Nicholas answers: "What." "That's what I asked you, what are you seeking?" "I am seeking what! [*quid*]." On the basis of his profound meditation Nicholas has reached a summit of thought, discovering one fundamental basis of all being, one quiddity, a single hypostasis of all things, *omnium hypostasis*.[58] This *hypostasis* is possibility. The possibility of all things, the possibility of being, is at the heart of all being—the very possibility itself (*posse ipsum*). It is touching that at the end of his life the old

---

[55] Nicholas of Cusa, *De apice theoriae*, 1, in *Nicolai de Cusa Opera Omnia*, vol. XII, ed. Raymond Klibansky and Hans Gerhard Senger (Hamburg: Felix Meiner Verlag, 1982), 117.

[56] On this passage, see Adolf Deissmann, *St. Paul: A Study in Social and Religious History*, trans. Lionel R. M. Strachan (New York: Hodder & Stoughton, 1912), 82.

[57] Nicholas of Cusa, *De apice theoriae*, 2, ed. Klibansky and Senger, 117; trans. Jasper Hopkins, *Nicholas of Cusa: Metaphysical Speculations* (Minneapolis: Arthur J. Banning Press, 1998), 1423.

[58] Nicholas of Cusa, *De apice theoriae*, 4, ed. Klibansky and Senger, 119; trans. Hopkins, 1424. In this term we hear an echo of the Neoplatonic tradition of *hypostasis* as spiritual substance, as found in Plotinus: see Pauliina Remes, *Neoplatonism* (Berkeley: University of California Press, 2008), 48.

philosopher should meditate on possibility, the most youthful of all values. Equally telling is that he illustrates his point by referring to the lives of little boys, who understand everything about possibility as they engage in their lively activities. The young have an innate sense of possibility as they run, climb trees, or play ball.

Nicholas states that *posse ipsum*, the very possibility of things, is a name for God. Peter, the faithful secretary, is quick to point out that Nicholas already discussed *posse ipsum* in his work *De possest* (1460).[59] Again, there is a questioning tone of retrospection, as the dialogue moves toward ever loftier themes. Possibility is the quiddity of all things. Lying behind the entire world of possibility is Absolute Possibility: absolute, uncontracted, and omnipotent possibility. Absolute Possibility can also be called light, for just as light, which is invisible, gives rise to all colors and all seeing, so possibility is known in all things.[60] Here we can recognize the metaphysical principle that inspired the great cathedral windows of the Gothic age, in which copper or cobalt gives rise to richly colored light that can be seen: an incarnation of the invisible. Similarly, although Possibility itself cannot be grasped, nevertheless the intellect can look beyond itself to see and recognize it, in the presence of light and color.[61]

Here we arrive at the *apex* of theory: the intellectual power reaches beyond its limits, seeing beyond what it can comprehend. *Theoria* here conveys the ancient sense of a wordless beholding, beholding what is beyond comprehension. This is the immeasurable, the greatest of all, the most perfect, the ultimate—and beholding it is the highest power of the mind: this is the *posse supremum mentis*. The mind looks ahead to it "just as a pilgrim foresees the goal of his journey." We must hasten down this road, for possibility is the quiddity that we have been seeking, "the mind's desire" (*mentis desiderium*).[62] The Cardinal is still concerned about his legacy: can his discoveries be conveyed through writing, and will they be understood?

Theoria is finally explained at the end of the dialogue. "The summit of theory is possibility itself" (*apex theoriae est posse ipsum*).[63] Writing as if in breathless haste, Cusanus praises Possibility as "the strength of all strength,

---

59 Nicholas of Cusa, *De apice theoriae*, 5, ed. Klibansky and Senger, 120; trans. Hopkins, 1425.
60 Nicholas of Cusa, *De apice theoriae*, 8, ed. Klibansky and Senger, 122; trans. Hopkins, 1426.
61 Nicholas of Cusa, *De apice theoriae*, 10, ed. Klibansky and Senger, 124; trans. Hopkins, 1427.
62 Nicholas of Cusa, *De apice theoriae*, 11, ed. Klibansky and Senger, 125; trans. Hopkins, 1428.
63 Nicholas of Cusa, *De apice theoriae*, 17, ed. Klibansky and Senger, 130; trans. Hopkins, 1431.

and the might of all might," which is manifest in Christ. Christ leads us to clear-sighted contemplation (*clara contemplatio*) by word and example. This is a happiness that satisfies the mind's ultimate desire.[64] In his old age the Cardinal experiences the contemplation of being as a source of joy, like the happiness of little boys at play.

Theoria in Gadamer

The writings of Cusanus were studied extensively in the twentieth century, as the Cardinal was sometimes seen as a breakthrough figure of the Renaissance.[65] His philosophy was examined and debated by Ernst Cassirer, Hans Blumenberg, and others as a possible harbinger of modernity.[66] Hans-Georg Gadamer was particularly fascinated by Cusanus, seeing in him an exponent of modernity and a key figure in the development of modern language theory and hermeneutics.[67] And as I will demonstrate, Gadamer shared with Cusanus the perception that the wellspring of being is a kind of youthfulness and that a special kind of happiness can be found at the summit of contemplation.

As mentioned above, Gadamer delivered a speech in Salzburg in 1980, titled "Praise of Theory" (*Lob der Theorie*), a topic that appears in other writings of his as well.[68] By then an eighty-year-old man who had lived through both World Wars, Gadamer was facing considerable criticism from students and younger philosophers, because of the quiet professorial life he led during the Second World War. So here again we discover an elderly philosopher taking up the problem of the highest form of thought. Like Nicholas, Gadamer begins by reference to youth and education. Gadamer had trained in classical philology under the Plato scholar Paul Friedländer, and in general his frame of reference relies on a detailed knowledge of

---

[64] Nicholas of Cusa, *De apice theoriae*, 28, ed. Klibansky and Senger, 136; trans. Hopkins, 1434.

[65] See Michael Edward Moore, "Epilogue: Ernst Cassirer and Renaissance Cultural Studies: The Figure of Nicholas of Cusa," in *Nicholas of Cusa and the Making of the Early Modern World*, ed. Simon J. G. Burton, Joshua Hollman, and Eric M. Parker (Leiden: Brill, 2019), 485–506.

[66] See Michael Edward Moore, *Nicholas of Cusa and the Kairos of Modernity: Cassirer, Gadamer, Blumenberg* (Brooklyn, NY: Punctum Books, 2013), 8–13.

[67] On Gadamer's interest in Cusan language theory, see Peter Casarella, *Word as Bread: Language and Theology in Nicholas of Cusa* (Münster: Aschendorff Verlag, 2017), 19–88; and Hans-Georg Gadamer, "Nicolaus Cusanus and the Present," *Epoché* 7 (2002): 71–79.

[68] Gadamer, "Praise of Theory," 16–36.

ancient life and thought, and of the Weimar Classical Period, with its "civilization grounded in cultivation," in Bruford's phrase.[69] Frequent quotations from Goethe, Herder, and Hölderlin mark Gadamer's learned German humanism, which joined classical *paideia* to the tradition of *Bildung*. Gadamer's hermeneutical philosophy frequently returns to the *Leitbegriffe* of humanism.[70] It is legitimate to examine and reexamine the tradition, he often repeated, because questions continually arise out of the past: "the tradition poses questions and points the way to answers."[71]

In ancient times, Gadamer comments, *paideia* was directed toward children and included play. This is one of the ancient sources of θεωρία, and it retains this connection to play and youthfulness. Instead of engaging the active and mature life of a free citizen, θεωρία seems to take up useless matters devoid of profit and to turn its back on practice and politics.[72] Yet theory possesses a tremendous dignity, because it means "sharing in the total order itself."[73] As Gadamer explains, Plato initiated a kind of revolution against the norms of civic life when he founded the Academy as a place dedicated to "the world of enduring thoughts."[74] The Academy was a place of retreat from the life of the polis.[75] This "theory-based education" of the Academy was inherited by the West in its bourgeois education and the ideal of *Bildung*.[76] It would seem at first that the topics taken up in such education should be free from all practical concern. When Aristotle, in his turn, tried to balance the theoretical life with "the ideal of the practical and political life," he still recognized theory as the utmost value.[77] Gadamer readily agrees with Aristotle in his belief that "Man's greatest joy is in 'pure

---

[69] See W. H. Bruford, *Culture and Society in Classical Weimar, 1775–1806* (Cambridge: Cambridge University Press, 1962), 9.

[70] Matthias Baum, *Die Hermeneutik Hans-Georg Gadamers als philosophia christiana: Eine Interpretation von "Wahrheit und Methode" in christlich-theologischer Perspektive* (Tübingen: Mohr Siebeck, 2002), 23.

[71] Hans-Georg Gadamer et al., *Gadamer in Conversation: Reflections and Commentary*, ed. and trans. Richard E. Palmer (New Haven, CT: Yale University Press, 2001), 51.

[72] Gadamer, "Praise of Theory," 17.

[73] Gadamer, *Truth and Method*, 454.

[74] Gadamer, "Praise of Theory," 18.

[75] See the summary in Lucien Jerphagnon, *Á l'école des Anciens: Portraits et préférences* (Paris: Perrin, 2014), 40.

[76] Gadamer, "Praise of Theory," 18.

[77] Gadamer, "Praise of Theory," 19.

theory.'"[78] As Gadamer writes, "He is the creature who has the logos: he has language, he has distance from the things that immediately press upon him, he is free to choose what is good and to know what is true—and he can even laugh. He is a 'theoretical creature to the core.'"[79] In his portrait of the theoretical life, Gadamer moves from the education of the young, to play, to laughter, and onward to θεωρία as a kind of beholding, or observing "the great world-order."[80]

Gadamer suggests that there was a turning-point in late antiquity: along with the Latin translation of *theoria* to *contemplatio* came the sharp distinction between the *vita contemplativa* and the *vita activa*. Christians concluded that the things of this world should not be explored to their very depths, but the soul should instead reflect only on God.[81] The desire for knowledge was demoted, and theory, reduced to contemplation of the divine, retreated into the monasteries. Then with the rise of early modern science, "knowledge became research." In an essay of 1963, Gadamer already suggested that at the "dawning of modernity" the concept of rational theory had become something entirely (merely) practical. It was in order to escape from this kind of reason that Nicholas of Cusa put his loftiest doctrines on the lips of the *Idiota*, rather than the learned *Orator* or *Philosophus*.[82]

For Galileo and Newton, the ideal of theoretical knowledge displayed a supremely confident use of reason understood to be self-certifying. German Idealism later gave priority to practical reason and tried to support both theory and practice upon it: the rehabilitation of τέχνη. Idealism tried to give science a basis in philosophy. Hegel's philosophy attempted to synthesize all the products of human spirit, but the relentless impetus of modern science pushed the dream of Hegel into the background.[83] But by the early twentieth century, Gadamer's narrative continues, science was transformed into pragmatics and technology. Pure research had to hide behind the

---

[78] Gadamer, "Praise of Theory," 20.

[79] Gadamer, "Praise of Theory," 20.

[80] On the connection between human freedom and having a world, see Hans-Georg Gadamer, *Truth and Method*, 444–45.

[81] Gadamer, "Praise of Theory," 22.

[82] Hans-Georg Gadamer, "On the Possibility of a Philosophical Ethics (1963)," in *Hermeneutics, Religion, and Ethics*, trans. Joel Weinsheimer (New Haven, CT: Yale University Press, 1999), 19.

[83] Gadamer, "Praise of Theory," 25.

conceit that it could contribute to technology. Once τέχνη had taken the reins, theory became the servant of practice.

Bourgeois cultural idealism did not survive the First World War, the developing alienation from labor, and the appearance of technological mastery now revealed in "technological slaughter" in the trenches along the Marne and the Somme. Gadamer's train of thought here is marked by certain tragic features of our world: industrialization, poverty, and inequality.[84] It reminds one of the dark, mysterious warning in the forward to *Truth and Method*, that "science expands into a total technocracy and thus brings on the 'cosmic night' of the forgetfulness of being."[85] This statement, with its Nietzschean and Heideggerian overtones, betrays tremendous anxiety about the direction of historical events and the course of intellectual activity. Clearly Gadamer hoped that *theoria* could be salvaged and could restore some form of blessedness for modern humanity in contemplative happiness.

Whereas the body is almost invisible to Cusanus, for Gadamer it is the very gateway to our having a world. Our body calls on us to recognize others and to be recognized by them. Our immersion in social life teaches us to recognize reality and to "acknowledge the reality of far-off times and foreign peoples."[86] The philologist will be alert to Gadamer's message here, with its echo of Herodotean travels in search of knowledge. Hence it is necessary to set aside our prejudices "in order to see what is." In this way, Gadamer returns to the original Greek sense of theory as an observant state of being and a direct approach to reality. It means "being present" and thus recalls the theme of presence.[87] Theory is not exhausted by its servitude to practice.

Finally, as if to conclude the journey we have taken, Gadamer unexpectedly turns our gaze toward the earliest period of human existence, the so-called youth of humankind. As Gadamer notes, archaeology has discovered that prehistoric peoples were not entirely preoccupied with technologies of survival. They also engaged in the apparent superfluity of funeral rites, offering decorative and ritual acts going beyond the demands

---

84 Gadamer, "Praise of Theory," 26–27.
85 Gadamer, *Truth and Method*, xxxvii.
86 Gadamer, "Praise of Theory," 30–31.
87 Gadamer, "Praise of Theory," 31.

of practical necessity.[88] Gadamer does not further specify these "burial rites" or "consecrations."[89] As is known, the bodies in prehistoric gravesites were often sprinkled with red ochre, or decorated with hollyhock flowers.[90] Gadamer's argument about the ornamentation of prehistoric burials leads, in the end, to the question of happiness—ancient tombs were recognized as a meaningful space beyond the mundane boundaries of τέχνη and practice. Funerary rites involved, he notes, "a constantly surprising wealth of superfluous decorations, and not a confinement to what is necessary."[91]

The theoretical encounter with presence, Gadamer concludes, is "almost" a divine consciousness, which turns us toward reality and toward others.[92] In this sense Gadamer's praise of theory is very similar to that of Nicholas of Cusa. By reaching the level of *theoria*, we can find a life to which we can say, "yes"![93]

---

88 Gadamer, "Praise of Theory," 33–34.

89 Gadamer, "Praise of Theory," 34.

90 See e.g. Ernst E. Wreschner et al., "Red Ochre and Human Evolution: A Case for Discussion," *Current Anthropology* 21 (1980): 631–44; and Ralph S. Solecki, "Shanidar IV, a Neanderthal Flower Burial in Northern Iraq," *Science* (N.S.) 190, no. 4217 (1975): 880–81.

91 Gadamer, "Praise of Theory," 34.

92 Gadamer, "Praise of Theory," 35.

93 Gadamer, "Praise of Theory," 36.

4

Blumenberg Reading Cusanus

The Epochal Threshold as a Liminal Space between the "No Longer" and the "Not Yet"

ELIZABETH BRIENT

Hans Blumenberg's interest in Nicholas of Cusa dates back to the beginning of his scholarly career. In 1957, he collected and introduced a selection of Cusanus's writings which he entitled *Die Kunst der Vermutung* (*The Art of Conjecture*).[1] The edition begins with a sophisticated and perspicaciously nuanced reading of Cusanus as a central figure in the epochal transition from the medieval to the modern age. Toward the beginning of this sixty-two-page introductory essay, Blumenberg dryly observes that "a century of Cusanus research can't decide whether Cusanus *still* belongs to the Middle Ages or *already* belongs to the modern age, whether he did more to further the Middle Ages or to prepare for the modern age."[2] Rather than arguing for one reading or the other,

---

1 Hans Blumenberg, ed., *Nikolaus von Cues: Die Kunst der Vermutung; Auswahl aus den Schriften* (Bremen: Carl Schünemann Verlag, 1957). All translations from Blumenberg's introductory essay in *Die Kunst der Vermutung* are my own.
2 Blumenberg, *Die Kunst der Vermutung*, 10.

Blumenberg's introductory essay aims to show why these are the wrong sorts of questions to be asking in the first place, "sterile" lines of inquiry that both mistake the character of Cusan thought and misunderstand the nature of epochal transition generally. Theorists who try to situate a transitional thinker like Cusanus by presupposing rigid epochal divisions and then reading Cusanus's work listening single-mindedly "for the echoes of the past or the anticipatory ring of the future" will certainly "bag a lot of prey," Blumenberg grants, but in the process, the real substance of the threshold itself will escape them.[3] Transitional figures of the caliber of Cusanus, Blumenberg writes, "do not, as it were, come *between* the fixed continental blocks of the epochs, rather *in* these thinkers and *through* them the separations [*Scheidungen*] in the flow of history are first of all accomplished: both the distinctions [*Unterscheidungen*] and the decisions [*Entscheidungen*]."[4] In this essay I consider Blumenberg's reading of Nicholas of Cusa as just such a transitional figure and aim toward teasing out and further developing his understanding of the nature of the epochal threshold as a liminal space that is first of all made (and made visible) by such distinctions and decisions in thinkers like Cusanus.

I will return to Blumenberg's insights in this early introductory essay in what follows, but I begin with a detour through his much better-known reading of Cusanus in part 4 of the *Legitimacy of the Modern Age*, entitled "Aspects of the Epochal Threshold: The Cusan and the Nolan."[5] Here Blumenberg develops a novel conception of the "epochal threshold" in the context of his fundamental rethinking of the dynamics of historical transition in general.[6] Theoretical accounts of the process of historical transition have tended to rely on models that derive their chief explanatory power by focusing either on threads (or elements) of continuity in the transition on the one hand, or on rupture and emergent novelty on the other. The first approach is characteristic of reception history. It focuses on the "reception" of earlier historical content as it is taken up into a new form

---

3 Blumenberg, *Die Kunst der Vermutung*, 11–13.

4 Blumenberg, *Die Kunst der Vermutung*, 11.

5 Hans Blumenberg, *The Legitimacy of the Modern Age*, trans. Robert M. Wallace (Cambridge, MA: MIT Press, 1983). Unless otherwise noted, this and all subsequent references to *Legitimacy* are from Wallace's translation of the revised German edition, *Die Legitimität der Neuzeit (erweiterte und überarbeitete Neuausgabe)* (Frankfurt: Suhrkamp Verlag, 1973, 1974, 1976).

6 See Elizabeth Brient, "Epochenschwelle," in *Blumenberg lesen: Ein Glossar*, ed. Robert Buch and Daniel Weidner (Berlin: Suhrkamp Verlag, 2014), 72–86.

or context. Here the theorist hunts for and seeks to identify the relevant "influences," "precursors," and "forerunners" of the new historical forms. In the second model, historical transformation is understood in terms of a rupture or break with the past and the inauguration of something new. The theorist then hunts for and seeks to identify the "epoch-making" events or agents, the heroes of innovation and discovery, the founders of the new.

Both models tacitly assume that one can chronologically date the epochal turning. It is here that the theorist identifies the "reception" of the old in its new form or context, or points to the "rupture" that inaugurates the new. Both models further assume that one should be able to identify the "cause" or "agent" of historical transition: either the influences or the innovations, either the precursors or the founders, that is, the "makers of history." And both models also tend to assume that we can neatly correlate the history of causes and intents with a history of effects.[7] Blumenberg challenges all of these assumptions in *The Legitimacy of the Modern Age* by critiquing both models and by fundamentally rethinking the dynamics of historical transition and hence the nature of the epochal threshold.

Blumenberg points out that these three assumptions—that there must be some "cause" or "agent" of a given epochal change, that we can chronologically date the particular juncture in time when the epochal transition occurs, and that we can correlate the history of causes and intents neatly with a history of effects—are all actually rooted in the history of the development of the "epoch" *concept* itself. The original Greek term, ἐποχή, simply referred to a halt in motion, or the point at which a halt is made or in which a reversal of direction takes place.[8] The term was not applied to history until the modern age, but even then it was originally used to denote, not periods of time, but rather significant events at points in time. So for example, someone might describe a significant event as a major "epoch" in their life, as a turning point. At the end of the eighteenth and the beginning of the nineteenth century, however, the term began to be used to mean the length of time between significant events and the present moment. The term "epoch" then gradually came to mean the *unity of character* of the time periods inaugurated by significant events and their consequences. Epochs were then not only conceived of as chronologically divided from each other by the events that gave rise to them, but also as characteristically distinct

---

7 See Blumenberg, *Legitimacy*, 476–77; *Legitimität*, 554–55.
8 Blumenberg, *Legitimacy*, 459; *Legitimität*, 533.

from each other and so comparable across the discontinuity of the epochal turning.⁹

This conception of history as divided into characteristically distinct "epochs" is both a product of the modern age and a crucial part of modernity's own self-understanding, as the "new age" that decisively breaks with the past and defines the "Middle Ages" as what comes between it and the ancient world.¹⁰ But is there a reality corresponding to this (characteristically) modern pretension? Blumenberg points out that the debate concerning the real or merely nominal validity of epochal concepts has been dominated by the assumption (on both sides) that *if* historical epochs are real phenomena, then we should then be able to chronologically date the particular juncture in time when the epochal transition occurs. We should be able to identify the agents of change (the precursors or the innovators), their motives and actions, and the epoch-making outcome of their transformations. But just these assumptions have proved untenable. "Those who espouse realism with regard to the epochal concepts," Blumenberg notes, "have always failed as a result of their willingness to accept this demand."¹¹ Indeed, in its drive to demonstrate "the reality of epochs as authentic formations of the historical process," historicism actually worked against itself by bringing to light characteristically medieval qualities in the great "founders" of the modern age (Copernicus, Bacon, and Descartes) from the one side, and then unearthing an ever growing number of "precursors" of supposedly characteristically modern accomplishments on the other.¹²

It is in the context of this search for precursors and founding figures, in the attempt to identify witnesses to the epochal turning, that the debate concerning Nicholas of Cusa's "position" in history has been conducted. Does he still belong to the Middle Ages, or is he a forerunner of modernity? In *Legitimacy*, Blumenberg refuses to "locate" Cusanus in this manner. Indeed, Blumenberg rejects the idea that we must be able to locate the juncture in time that separates one epoch from the next. Blumenberg argues, on the contrary, that "the Middle Ages and the modern age existed for a good bit of history intermeshed or side by side, or at any rate without

---

9 Blumenberg, *Legitimacy*, 459–60; *Legitimität*, 534.
10 Blumenberg, *Legitimacy*, 463; *Legitimität*, 538.
11 Blumenberg, *Legitimacy*, 461; *Legitimität*, 536.
12 Blumenberg, *Legitimacy*, 462; *Legitimität*, 537. See also Blumenberg, *Legitimacy*, 470–71; *Legitimität*, 546–47.

phenotypical distinction."[13] He argues that the epochal threshold lies "below the surface of chronology" and datable events, that a given thinker's relation to the epochal threshold is not (necessarily) chronological,[14] and that it is a mistake to think of these transitional figures as epoch-*making* thinkers or actors.[15] While there is something correct in the modern dictum that man makes history—"Who else should make it for him?" Blumenberg asks—it is a mistake to understand this as though we could unambiguously line up historical actions and the outcomes they bring about. He rejects the idea that there is an unambiguous correlation between intentions and effects, motives and transformations. Man does make history, we might say, but not as an intentional object: what is made is often not at all what is intended.[16] Again, this sort of misunderstanding can be traced back to an earlier conception of history and historical change.

When "history" was still understood as something to "be found in annals and chronicles, in treaties and proclamations," Blumenberg points out, then it made sense to think that "legal instruments and public papers document how history was 'made'" and to identify the great events and actors who "make" history.[17] Here there *is* a clear coordination of historical agents' intentions with historical effects, of motives with historical transformations. Within the rubric of this sort of model of "history-making" agents, later historians are inclined to say that "with the *Revolutiones* Copernicus brought about the changed view of the world that was important to him; that Descartes produced from the motive of absolute doubt the effect of absolute certainty; and that the Cusan, too, by drawing up the program of 'imprecision,' became the overcomer of the Middle Ages that he should have understood himself to be."[18]

Blumenberg, however, rejects this concept of the epoch-making thinker or actor. "The principle that man makes history," he insists, "certainly does not mean that what is made depends solely on the intentions and the precepts as a result of and according to which it was produced."[19] In relation

---

13 Blumenberg, *Legitimacy*, 470; *Legitimität*, 546.
14 Blumenberg, *Legitimacy*, 470; *Legitimität*, 545.
15 Blumenberg, *Legitimacy*, 477; *Legitimität*, 553–54.
16 Blumenberg, *Legitimacy*, 477–78; *Legitimität*, 553–55.
17 Blumenberg, *Legitimacy*, 477–78; *Legitimität*, 554.
18 Blumenberg, *Legitimacy*, 478; *Legitimität*, 554.
19 Blumenberg, *Legitimacy*, 477; *Legitimität*, 554.

to actions that might be said to "make" history, Blumenberg insists, the element of interference always supervenes. Historical action always takes place within the horizon of the historically possible, and the effects of the action occur "in a context of the reciprocal interaction of synchronicity and nonsynchronicity, of integrative and destructive interdependence." An epoch, then, "is the sum total of all the interferences between actions and what they 'make.' In this sense—that actions and outcomes are not capable of unambiguous coordination—we have to recognize that history 'makes itself.' What we grasp in the patterns of history is more the outcomes than the agents."[20]

How then should one think in a more adequate way about the nature of historical change, about transitional figures, and the problem of epochal transition? This problem, Blumenberg suggests, needs to be approached from a transcendental perspective: by considering the question of *the conditions for the possibility of experiencing them at all*. Blumenberg argues that the experience of historical transition, like the experience of any change at all—all succession from old to new—is accessible to us only insofar as it can be related to a constant frame of reference.[21] Here Blumenberg invokes Kant's first analogy of experience, which postulates the principle of the permanence of substance as a condition of the possibility of our experience of variation over time. But rather than assume a permanent historical "substance" as the constant frame of reference, Blumenberg points to a continuity of existentially orienting questions—questions about "self and world"—and the "carry-over" expectation that those questions can and should have answers. These "carry-over" questions and expectations constitute a relatively stable framework of positions within the system of self- and world-understanding, positions that come to be "reoccupied" by new answers in a period of epochal transition.[22] "That what is new in history cannot be arbitrary in each case, but rather is subject to a rigor of expectations and needs, is the condition of our being able to have such a

---

20 Blumenberg, *Legitimacy*, 478; *Legitimität*, 554–55.
21 Blumenberg, *Legitimacy*, 466; *Legitimität*, 541.
22 Blumenberg emphasizes that we ought not to assume that these reference frame conditions are permanent or eternal, only that they "have greater inertia for consciousness than do the contents associated with them, that is, that the questions are relatively constant in comparison to the answers." Blumenberg, *Legitimacy*, 466; *Legitimität*, 542. See also Blumenberg, *Legitimacy*, 469; *Legitimität*, 545.

thing as 'cognition' [*Erkenntnis*] of history at all."²³ Blumenberg's concept of "reoccupation" designates, then, "the minimum of identity that it must be possible to discover, or at least to presuppose and to search for" in even the least stable and most turbulent periods of historical change (*die bewegtesten Bewegung der Geschichte*), namely in periods of epochal transition.²⁴

If, then, we can speak of changes of epoch as something real, and not merely convenient nominalistic devices for the historian, what would one expect to see, or be able to demonstrate, asks Blumenberg, when the question is posed of a real change of epoch? We should be able to identify stable question-positions on both sides of the epochal transition and the carry-over *need* that compels a search for new answers when the old answers no longer serve their function. Equally important, there must be something definitive and irreversible about this change:

> Since all history is composed of changes, the "epoch-making" movements must be assumed to be both copious and rapid but also to move in a single, unambiguous direction and to be structurally interconnected, mutually dependent. He who speaks of the reality of a change of epoch takes on the burden of demonstrating that something is definitely decided. It must be possible to show that something is present that cannot be disposed of again, that an irreversible change has been produced.²⁵

So we can say, for example, that we are clearly no longer living in the medieval world, and that there is no going back. But what is the sense of this "no longer"? Blumenberg's preference for the metaphor of the "epochal *threshold*" (*Epochen*schwelle)—rather than epochal break, or epochal turning—is significant here. In German, one crosses over a threshold to go into a building (another space), but one can also speak of the threshold to adulthood or the threshold of death, and this sense of threshold (*Schwelle*) is crucial here. The epochal threshold, like the threshold to adulthood, or the threshold of death, is uni-directional and irreversible. Once one has crossed this boundary, there is no going back; a definitive transformation has taken place. And like those other thresholds, the epochal threshold is

---

23 Blumenberg, *Legitimacy*, 466; *Legitimität*, 541.
24 Blumenberg, *Legitimacy*, 466; *Legitimität*, 541.
25 Blumenberg, *Legitimacy*, 468; *Legitimität*, 543–44.

not a clear-cut borderline, but rather a liminal area of transition. Consider the threshold between childhood and adulthood. For a long time, we recognize that a young girl is "*still* just a child," until at some point, and without being able to say when it happened, we understand that she has *already* grown into a young woman. She is clearly *no longer* a child. The epochal threshold is just such a liminal space of transition, definitive, irreversible, and occurring over an indefinite period of time. "The epochal turning is an imperceptible frontier, bound to no crucial date or event. But viewed differentially, a threshold marks itself off, which can be ascertained as something either not yet arrived at or already crossed."[26]

Again, we can "recognize" (*erkennen*) that this crossing has occurred only if we have a reference to something relatively stable across the threshold. That means that we will miss it entirely if we are single-mindedly hunting for the supposed epochal agents of change and the "epoch-making" outcome of their reception or innovation. There are no witnesses to "epochal ruptures" (*Epochenumbrüchen*) in this sense, Blumenberg insists. But a "threshold marks itself off" if we take two cross-sections of history on either side of the threshold and compare them differentially, "demonstrating, *through dissection*, an identical fundamental system of elementary assertion needs, notions of the world and the self, on both sides of the threshold."[27] Hence, rather than looking for the agents or events that cause the change of epoch, we need to examine "at least two witnesses," whose relation to the epochal threshold—something *not yet* crossed over, or *already* moved beyond—make it visible and evident. Such witnesses would share the same basic system of elementary assertion needs, of existentially orienting questions, the same sense of what needs to be explained about us and our world, on both sides of the threshold, but would provide decisively different answers to these fundamentally orienting questions. This continuity and this difference make it possible to register that a decisive shift has occurred.

For the threshold leading to the modern age, Blumenberg chooses two such witnesses: Nicholas of Cusa on the medieval side of the threshold and Giordano Bruno on the modern. Here, Blumenberg claims, the fundamental

---

26 Blumenberg, *Legitimacy*, 469; *Legitimität*, 545.

27 Blumenberg, *Legitimacy*, 469; *Legitimität*, 545 (emphasis added). This is an echo of a metaphor Blumenberg used in his introduction to *Die Kunst der Vermutung*, that of examining "epochal" dissections under a microscope in order to see them more clearly. We shall return to this early metaphor in what follows.

assertions of the two thinkers can be recognized as different answers to the same questions, and the epochal transition may then be understood as the reoccupation of formally congruent systematic positions of self- and world-understanding. The epochal "turning" is thus not a turning point at some particular juncture in history, but rather a shift that becomes evident *over* a threshold across which something definitive has been decided. We can observe a period of epochal change differentially in terms of what has *not yet* or *already* been definitively decided. Thus, neither Cusanus nor Bruno may be regarded as a founding figure; neither is the "maker" of an epoch. They are, rather, each "distinguished by their *relation* to the epochal threshold. That threshold is comprehended not with them or in them but by *interpolation* between them."[28]

I have argued in detail elsewhere against Blumenberg's contention that the systems of Cusanus and Bruno represent homologous "position frames" and share the same fundamental "assertion needs" in all crucial respects.[29] In particular, I have argued that Cusanus is aware of, and speaks to, a characteristically new modern problem: the need for an epistemological measure for human knowing in the face of a newly infinite universe. How can our finite, discursive concepts even begin to do justice to the universe as an intensively and extensively infinite object of knowledge? In response to this new problem, Cusanus already sees the need for something like the modern notion of a regulative ideal as a limit-concept of unending conjectural approach toward an ever-elusive but guiding *telos*. In doing so, I argue, Cusanus has added a new "position frame" into the system of self- and world-explanation and offered a new answer to a modern problem that becomes increasingly obvious and unavoidable to early modern thinkers from Descartes to Kant. This is a problem that Bruno has *not yet* recognized, and in this important respect, I would argue, Cusanus and Bruno are related to the epochal threshold in the reverse order.

Blumenberg himself—at least tacitly—assumes a given thinker may relate to the epochal threshold in one direction in a particular regard, and the reverse direction in another regard, as demonstrated by his treatment

---

28 Blumenberg, *Legitimacy*, 478–79; *Legitimität*, 555.

29 See Elizabeth Brient, *The Immanence of the Infinite: Hans Blumenberg and the Threshold to Modernity* (Washington, DC: The Catholic University of America Press, 2002); and Elizabeth Brient, "Blumenberg Reading Cusanus: Metaphor and Modernity," in *Erinnerung an das Humane: Beiträge zur phänomenologischen Anthropologie Hans Blumenbergs*, ed. Michael Moxter (Tübingen: Mohr Siebeck, 2011), 122–44.

of Leibniz. While Blumenberg views Cusanus as moving in the direction of the modern valuation of the individual when he conceived of each created entity as a "finite infinity," it was Leibniz, Blumenberg holds, who first made the decisive modern connection between infinity and individuality.[30] On the other hand, in his conception of a personal God who chooses the best of all possible worlds, Blumenberg argues, Leibniz falls back to a position "behind" that of Giordano Bruno.[31] "Chronological sequence," Blumenberg reminds us in the case of Leibniz, "does not provide an adequate criterion of the direction of relation to the epochal threshold."[32] This implies that Blumenberg's conception of the epochal threshold is more nuanced than is at first obvious. Identifying the epochal threshold isn't a matter of finding the right interval on a timeline by separating those thinkers who are "still medieval" from those who are "already modern." We shouldn't conceive of the threshold as a chronologically definable point or segment in time. The *Epochenwende*, as Blumenberg understands it, is not a turning *point* at a particular juncture in history, but rather a shift in orientation, evident *over* a threshold, *across* which something (definitive) has been decided. We must therefore consider a given thinker's stance (or stances) toward the particularly vexed problems that arise in periods of rapid and dense historical change, and the way in which those positions correspond to what is *still* or becomes *no longer* possible by way of fundamental self- and world-orientation in the changed reality, what is *not yet* or is *already* recognized as decisive. This means that any given thinker might well relate to the epochal threshold in opposite directions *in relationship* to different epochal problems.

The strength of Blumenberg's differential analysis, which looks at two transitional thinkers in terms of their *relationship* to the threshold, is that it allows the complexity of the epochal threshold itself to become visible. Indeed, I want to argue that this differential conception of the epochal threshold invites the consideration of multiple differential parings and crossings. In my earlier work on Blumenberg's reading of Cusanus in *Legitimacy*,[33] for example, I considered the pair Eckhart-Cusanus, in place of Blumenberg's pair Cusanus-Bruno, not, of course, in order to shift the

---

30 Blumenberg, *Legitimacy*, 518 and 523; *Legitimität*, 600 and 607.
31 Blumenberg, *Legitimacy*, 587; *Legitimität*, 689–90.
32 Blumenberg, *Legitimacy*, 587; *Legitimität*, 690.
33 Brient, *The Immanence of the Infinite*, 145–251.

threshold chronologically further back in time, but in order to highlight aspects of the threshold in relation to questions concerning the *intensive* infinitization of the universe. This in turn threw into relief the emergence of an entire nexus of interpretive expectations and orienting questions tied to the pressing problem of finding a measure for human knowing and action in the newly infinite world.

While I believe that this more layered and multivalent conception of the epochal threshold is tacitly suggested by Blumenberg's differential analysis here, it should be recognized that this is a direction Blumenberg himself does not pursue. Indeed, there is a tension in Blumenberg's use of the "threshold" metaphor in *Legitimacy*, which indicates that he would resist moving too far in this direction. I have emphasized those passages in which Blumenberg draws on the sense of a "threshold" (*Schwelle*) as a liminal space of transition that is irreversible but not precisely datable. But a "threshold" can also be used to indicate an entryway into some distinct space, for example, the threshold into a building. To the extent that we understand the "epochal threshold" as an entryway in this sense, we might be tempted to read it as rigidly chronologically fixed, or even as produced by the rhythm of moving toward or across a point or segment in homogeneous, linear time. Nicholas of Cusa would then be read as a figure standing "before" (the chronologically fixed) threshold, not yet having crossed over, and Giordano Bruno as "already" having definitively stepped across it "into" modernity. Then it becomes all too easy to perceive Cusanus and Bruno as in fact "making" the threshold by, on the one hand, walking up to and standing, as it were, just before a turning point in history and, on the other, striding forward past this point and so decisively "making" the change. This sounds like the division in time is "made" by the decision to cross over, and indeed Blumenberg at times evokes just this image. He writes, for example, of "the Cusan, who still stands before this threshold, and the Nolan, who has already left it behind; the cardinal, who relates to the threshold through his concern for the endangered continuance of his system, and the heretic, who is certain, in his triumphant backward glance, of having crossed it."[34]

At the same time, it is clear that Blumenberg was aware of this tension in his use of the threshold metaphor. He addressed it explicitly in the first edition of *Legitimacy*:

---

34 Blumenberg, *Legitimacy*, 469; *Legitimität*, 545.

This notion of the epochal threshold assumes, unchecked, that historical time has a homogeneous linear structure, and that somewhere there is a markable rupture at that time. But historical time can also be imagined on the model of a strand of many individual veins bundled together, a plurality of contexts, traditions, factual-histories and school-histories, receptions and reactions. The epochal threshold would then be nothing other than the pressed together occurrence or appearance of such mutations between two perhaps relatively distant points of the time strand. Assuming, then, that the "epoch" category does not have a purely nominalistic ordering function, the methodological consequence of this approach is that the "event" of epochal change becomes comprehensible only in the manner of interpolation. From two points sufficiently distant in time, it can be said that the turn of the epoch, as seen from the earlier point in time, is still to come, from which later on it has already occurred. This not-yet and this already indicate what lies in between. The choice of the two aspects must (from the point of view of the factually constituting elements) yield approximately the same cross-section through the time-strand. To lend concreteness to this method, I attempt a confrontation spanning a century and a half between Nicholas of Cusa and Giordano Bruno....[35]

I like this supplementary metaphor of the time strand made up of many individual veins bundled together, "a plurality of contexts, traditions, factual-histories and school-histories, receptions and reactions," because it evokes the idea we saw earlier of an epoch as the "sum total of all the interferences" occurring "in a context of the reciprocal interaction of synchronicity and nonsynchronicity, of integrative and destructive interdependence."[36] It allows for the idea that there are multiple aspects to the epochal threshold, that the threshold itself is "an imperceptible frontier,"[37] a "cryptic border,"[38] a liminal space of transition. And it clarifies that the threshold

---

[35] Hans Blumenberg, *Die Legitimität der Neuzeit* (Frankfurt am Main: Suhrkamp Verlag, 1966), 440–41. My translation.
[36] Blumenberg, *Legitimacy*, 478; *Legitimität*, 554–55.
[37] Blumenberg, *Legitimacy*, 469; *Legitimität*, 545.
[38] Blumenberg, *Legitimacy*, 470; *Legitimität*, 546.

is not "made" by the action of crossing, but rather is made *visible* by the comparison of two sufficiently distant and sufficiently similar cross-sections of the time strand, so that it becomes clear that one cannot reverse their actual order in the time strand. As seen from the earlier point in time, the epochal turning is experienced as still to come, and from the later point as something that has already definitely occurred.[39]

Perhaps Blumenberg chose not to include this supplementary metaphor in his revised edition of the *Legitimacy* precisely because it draws too much attention to the multiplicity of veins running through the period in question and so deflects attention from the single narrative strand that he is so keen to highlight: the conditions that led to the decisive turn to self-assertion in the crossing of the epochal threshold. I want to argue, however, that we would do well to follow out multiple strands, and "mark off" multiple pairs of cross-sections in order to examine the character of the epochal threshold from multiple aspects. The particular features of the epochal threshold that become visible would then depend on the pair we chose in relation to the cross-section examined. This is precisely because the "time strand" is *not* homogeneous and because for a good part of history the medieval and the modern coexisted. This means that while we can recognize the directional sequence of "not yet" and "already," of "still" and "no longer," in a differential analysis of two well-chosen figures who make a particular feature of the epochal threshold visible, nevertheless, the liminal space of the epochal threshold itself does not admit of a definitive directionality. Again, Blumenberg makes this explicit in the first edition of *Legitimacy*, where he writes:

> The epochal threshold seems to be below the surface of chronology. *"Standing-before" and "already-having-been" are inextricably superimposed on each other*. The Middle Ages and the modern age are simultaneous for a good bit of history.[40]

---

[39] In this regard the threshold is more like the threshold from childhood to adulthood than the threshold from outside to inside a house. Of course, this metaphor of the threshold to adulthood is problematic in its own right, insofar as it might encourage us to imagine historical transition on the model of the organic growth of a self-identical individual substance, which Blumenberg clearly rejects.

[40] "Die Epochenschwelle scheint gleichsam unter der Oberfläche der Chronologie zu liegen. Bevor-stehen und Schon-geschehen-sein schieben sich unabgrenzbar übereinander. Mittelalter und Neuzeit sind für ein gutes Stück der Geschichte gleichzeitig." Blumenberg, *Die*

In this sense, Cusanus, Bruno, and Leibniz may be seen to stand in *multidirectional* relationships to the epochal transition. That is, medieval and modern coexist, or are intermeshed or superimposed, not only in the same historical period, but also *in the same thinker*. Indeed, I would argue that we can look at these transitional figures not only as comparative reference points, marking the "not yet" or the "already" in various linear differential analyses of the threshold that lies between them, but also as figures involved in a complex web of decisions, differences, and interferences, out of which the liminal space of the threshold itself first of all arises.

This latter approach is much closer to that taken by Blumenberg in his early reading of Cusanus in his 1957 edition of Nicholas of Cusa's selected writings, *Die Kunst der Vermutung*, as is nicely captured in a series of metaphors Blumenberg uses at the beginning of that edition. The first follows immediately after the passage with which I began this essay: "A century of Cusanus research can't decide whether Cusanus *still* belongs to the Middle Ages or *already* belongs to the modern age, whether he did more to further the one epoch or to prepare for the next epoch. These are sterile ways of formulating the questions," Blumenberg insists, "that leave out of account the fact that 'epochs' are dissections [*Präparate*] whose coloring for the purpose of sharper objectification brings to the fore the historical reflection of the particular contemporary self-awareness [*Selbstbewußtsein*]."[41] The metaphor here is of the historian looking at a dissection of history under a microscope. The dissection (the "epoch") has been prepared with coloring that enables us to see what we want to see more clearly, namely the "self-awareness" of the period in question.

This is an interesting metaphor, because "epochs" are identified with the *Präparate*, the dissection. This implies *both* that the "epoch" refers to something man-made, in the sense that we prepare the slide for study by dissecting and coloring the historical period, but also that there *is* a reality that we are trying to make visible with the aid of coloration for sharper objectification.[42] Blumenberg uses the metaphor to draw our attention

---

Legitimität der Neuzeit (1966), 436. The second sentence, which I have italicized in my translation above, does not appear in the revised edition.

41 Blumenberg, *Die Kunst der Vermutung*, 10–11.

42 The *Objektiv* is the name for the part of the microscope's lens closest to the object. Also note the parallel between coloring the specimen so we can see what we are looking for more clearly, and the idea that we have to choose which strand to examine and where to make the cross-sections for comparison.

to the way in which epochal transition becomes visible: first to the historian looking back at the period in question (i.e., visible for the historian who has prepared the cross-section for examination) and second in the self-awareness of the period in question (i.e., *what* is being examined in the cross-section). Once again, Blumenberg is theoretically oriented by the question of what makes the *experience* of epochal change possible. What we are after (again in the language of the metaphor) is not an over-sharpening of the opposition between medieval and modern, but rather the bringing to the fore, the making visible, of the self-consciousness of the period in question. "More important, then, than the direct use of the epochal concepts 'Middle Ages' and 'modern age,'" Blumenberg remarks, "is seeing in what circumstances these concepts begin [to be used] and from whence they derive their legitimacy."43

So it is no accident, Blumenberg underscores, that the term "Middle Ages" appears for the first time—as far as he is aware—in connection with the figure of Nicholas of Cusa, in a eulogy that Giovanni Andrea Bussi gave for the cardinal in 1469, five years after his death. There was something about the cardinal's thought itself that *made visible* an emergent new stage in history and its distinction from one that came before it. Thinkers of the caliber of Cusanus, we recall Blumenberg insisting, "do not, as it were, come *between* the fixed continental blocks of the epochs, but rather *in* these thinkers and *through* them the separations [*Scheidungen*] in the flow of history are first of all accomplished: both the distinctions [*Unterscheidungen*] and the decisions [*Entscheidungen*]."44 It is a misunderstanding of the nature of epochal transition to conceive of such key figures as either "forward looking" proto-moderns or "backward looking" receivers of tradition. Indeed, this distinction is first of all *made possible* by the perspective afforded by the height to which figures like Cusanus take their thought. "Here lies a boundary [*Scheide*] of the incline from whose height the gaze *can* in fact be turned in two opposite directions. To speak of reception or anticipation, to put the accent on one or the other, those are perspectival possibilities

---

43 Blumenberg, *Die Kunst der Vermutung*, 11.

44 "Geister dieses Kalibers geraten nicht gleichsam *zwischen* die starren Kontinentalschollen der Epochen, sondern *an* ihnen und *durch* sie vollziehen sich erst im Fluß der Geschichte der Scheidungen: Unterscheidungen und Entscheidungen." Blumenberg, *Die Kunst der Vermutung*, 11.

that first of all yield themselves up through the marked standpoint of the singular thinking power."[45]

Blumenberg's reading of Cusanus in his introduction to *Die Kunst der Vermutung* is precisely aimed at showing how Cusan thought manifests those perspectival possibilities. To read Cusanus with Blumenberg is to climb the height of the cardinal's thought and to experience how this powerful standpoint makes visible the "not yet" and the "already" that will come to define the liminal field of the threshold itself. Ultimately, I think, Blumenberg's reading of Cusanus in this early introduction is richer, more supple, and truer to the spirit of the great thinker than the one he will subsequently offer in *Legitimacy*. That later interpretation attends all too single-mindedly to one particular vein in the multilayered time-strand that leads from medieval to modern. There Blumenberg's central focus is on making a case for the legitimacy of the modern turn to self-assertion, and so he reads Cusanus rather myopically from the perspective of his readiness for this decisive turn in comparison to Bruno.[46] But in *Die Kunst der Vermutung*, on the other hand, Blumenberg gives a richer and broader reading of the ways in which Cusanus is *still* medieval in his overarching motive, yet also *already* aware of and responding to the growing inadequacies of the medieval relational triad of God-human-world by championing a new vision of the infinity of each, a vision that appears to the historian—who already knows what's coming—as one leading to bold anticipations of fundamental forms of modern self- and world-understanding.

---

[45] Blumenberg, *Die Kunst der Vermutung*, 11–12.
[46] See Brient, *The Immanence of the Infinite*, 243–51.

5

Identifying Difference

Beierwaltes on Cusanus and Hegel

VALENTINA ZAFFINO

Omnis enim contractio est in absoluto,
quia absoluta visio est contractio contractionum;
contractio enim est incontrahibilis.[1]

In what follows I aim to reconstruct Werner Beierwaltes's reading of Nicholas of Cusa and Hegel. This endeavor does not involve simply comparing the last two philosophers, which has already been undertaken by scholars of Cusanus and German Idealism. Rather, I focus on Beierwaltes's role as mediator between Cusanus and Hegel, pointing out how Beierwaltes himself understood some common themes and crucial concepts proposed by these authors. Although Beierwaltes's deep interest in these two German philosophers is clearly attested, a direct influence of Cusanus on Hegel cannot be demonstrated; Hegel seems not to have read Nicholas's

---

[1] Nicholas of Cusa, *De visione Dei*, II (7), in *Nicolai de Cusa Opera Omnia*, vol. VI, ed. Heide Dorothea Riemann (Hamburg: Felix Meiner Verlag, 2000), 11. I would like to thank the Medieval Institute of the University of Notre Dame, and especially the director, Prof. Thomas E. Burman, for hosting me during the research for this essay.

works. Despite this non-negligible detail, the fundamental position occupied by Nicholas of Cusa in the whole of the modern Neoplatonic tradition is evident, for he fixed some pivotal categories that were to be the basis of future Neoplatonic (and other) systems, particularly Idealism.

Like Beierwaltes, we can analyze the relationship between Hegel and Cusanus not by following a direct line of continuity but rather by considering them within their unique philosophical and theological contexts. Since Cusanus and Hegel proposed similar approaches to reality, their relationship can be considered from a theoretical point of view as well as from a historical one. Beierwaltes's reading of Hegel and Cusanus has not yet been deeply investigated.[2] His writings have more often been examined as studies of Platonism and Neoplatonic tradition than as primary sources for research.[3] Beierwaltes's book *Identität und Differenz* contains specific chapters on Cusanus and Hegel.[4] We can also consult his famous volume *Denken des Einen* to understand Beierwaltes's own speculation on the Neoplatonic concepts "One" and "Whole."[5]

This chapter will be divided into three parts, each focusing on some of the most important developments of the Neoplatonic tradition from Nicholas of Cusa to German Idealism as proposed by Beierwaltes. The first part will be devoted to the binary concepts "identity" and "difference" and to the Cusan theme of *non aliud*. The second part will deal with Hegel's concept of God thinking himself, in continuity with Cusanus's notion of *visio absoluta*. The last part of the essay will analyze Beierwaltes's interpretation of the historical and theoretical process from Cusanus to Hegel, revisited in a Neoplatonic manner. As I retrace the work of Beierwaltes, I will highlight three fundamental subjects, each connected to the other: the role of the

---

[2] See, for instance, the critique of Beierwaltes expressed by Marco Maurizi, "La dialettica dell'altro: Cusano e Hegel a confronto," *Rivista di filosofia neo-scolastica* 98, no. 1 (2006): 99–120.

[3] On Beierwaltes as a philosopher of "the One," see Sandro Mancini, *Congetture su Dio: Singolarità, finalismo, potenza nella teologia razionale di Nicola Cusano* (Milan: Mimesis, 2014), 167–99.

[4] See Werner Beierwaltes, *Identität und Differenz* (Frankfurt am Main: Vittorio Klostermann, 1980), 105–75, 241–68. The content of the chapter "Identität und Differenz als Prinzip cusanischen Denkens" was already proposed in *Identität und Differenz: Zum Prinzip cusanischen Denkens. 219. Sitzung am 16. Februar 1977 in Düsseldorf* (Opladen: Westdeutscher Verlag, 1977).

[5] See Werner Beierwaltes, *Denken des Einen: Studien zur neuplatonischen Philosophie* (Frankfurt am Main: Vittorio Klostermann, 1985).

negative in the philosophical and theological discourse on God and being; the role of the notions of self-reflexivity and self-consciousness; and the role of the world as *explicatio Dei*.⁶

Non Aliud and *Epistrophé*: Principle and Dialectic in Cusan Ontology

In *Identität und Differenz*, while discussing the relationship between Cusanus and Hegel, Beierwaltes attests that the latter was not fully familiar with the former, and we can add that Hegel's *Vorlesungen über die Geschichte der Philosophie* makes no mention of Cusanus. Nonetheless, as stated above, reconstructing an indirect comparison between the two authors is not only possible but also useful and important for a better understanding of the historical development of German philosophy. In fact, as Beierwaltes asserts: "In Nicholas of Cusa's thought, the question about identity and difference reaches its apex and, at the same time, leads to a new conception, for which a comparison with Hegel's dialectics is absolutely important, as it discloses and determines the very content of the question."⁷

First of all, we should consider that, according to Beierwaltes, the identity-difference dialectic reaches its climax with Nicholas of Cusa, both in a theoretical and historical sense. *Identität und Differenz* mentions only the "subjective," or methodical aspect of the principle—that is, the activity of thought—which aims at comprehending the possibility of knowing, the structure of being, and the link between the subject and its principle. In Beierwaltes's analysis of the principle, this epistemological perspective is completed by an ontological survey. In this sense, the structural binary identity-difference is understood as already founded in the principle, then included in the absolute itself. Therefore, on the one hand, the term "identity" not only has a logical value, but above all has an ontological meaning, since it expresses the dignity of the being and its foundation. On the other hand, the term "difference" encompasses some other possible meanings,

---

6 On the identity of *Deus* and *esse*, see Werner Beierwaltes, *Platonismus und Idealismus* (Frankfurt am Main: Vittorio Klostermann, 1972), 5ff.

7 "Im Denken des *Nicolaus Cusanus* erreicht die Frage nach Identitat und Differenz die Spitze ihrer Intention, zugleich aber bricht sie in einen neuen Gedanken auf, der eine Konfrontation mit Hegels Dialektik als durchaus sinnvoll, weil die Sache selbst erschließend und fortbestimmend erscheinen läßt." Beierwaltes, *Identität und Differenz*, 105. All translations from Beierwaltes are my own.

which Beierwaltes lists as *distinctio, alteritas, alietas, diversitas, differentia, oppositio,* and *contraria*. None of these notions alone defines "difference" in Cusanus, which is the result of the mutual interpenetration of all these classical concepts.[8]

According to Cusanus, the nexus between identity and difference is related to the nexus between the infinite and the finite, which refers to the correlation between unity and otherness. Thus, both from a logical and ontological point of view, Nicholas's thought is related to the theme of the *coincidentia oppositorum*. In particular, Beierwaltes observes, the finite is identical to itself, and is at the same time different from another finite, which in turn is identical to itself. Identity is therefore also difference, being identity with respect to itself, and difference with respect to the other by itself. Thus, the two terms coincide in the same *contractio*, and consequently in the dialectic of the coincidence of opposites. Therefore, the finiteness produces the difference, because it distinguishes the entity (finite by nature) from another finite entity. In other words, difference is always regulated by a relationship of proportionality.[9] Although both opposites are resolved in their coincidence, this does not mean that one opposite becomes equal to the other, since two differences never become an identity; rather, differences coexist in a unit that includes all *alteritates*, even if it is not any of them (Cusanus calls this *unitas in alteritate*).[10]

Moreover Beierwaltes identifies in Cusanus's thought a relevant reference to the Neoplatonic concept of *epistrophé* (ἐπιστροφή), which describes the return to the unity of identity completed with and coincident with difference. The unity that the process of return comes to in itself is central in every finite entity and is part of the universal dynamism tending toward the fundamental unity—the origin and principle of the whole—which, from a Neoplatonic point of view, corresponds with the One.[11] In this primary unity, the finitude of single entities is poured into the infinity of the absolute. The notion of *epistrophé* is peculiar to the Neoplatonic tradition and

---

[8] See Beierwaltes, *Identität und Differenz*, 105.

[9] See Beierwaltes, *Identität und Differenz*, 109–10.

[10] Nicholas of Cusa, *De coniecturis*, I.10 (46), in *Nicolai de Cusa Opera Omnia*, vol. III, ed. Karl Bormann and Hans Gerhard Senger (Hamburg: Felix Meiner Verlag, 1972), 50. See Beierwaltes, *Identität und Differenz*, 106–7.

[11] For Beierwaltes on the Neoplatonic notion of the unfolding of the One, see in particular *Denken des Einen*, 155ff. On Nicholas of Cusa and the notion of *epistrophé*, see Beierwaltes, *Denken des Einen*, 156.

will also be paramount to Idealism, because it is related to the third moment of Hegel's dialectic.¹²

Just as for the ancient philosophers, for Cusanus *epistrophé* implies that a being is determined not only by Being itself, but also by not being, since every entity is still missing something. Here Beierwaltes introduces a reflection on the *non aliud*, which in Cusan thought is crucial from a metaphysical and theological perspective, as well as from a logical one. In *De non aliud*, the theme of the negative is broached by Cusanus as follows: "for everything which is another must be other than another, since only Not-Other is not other than any other."¹³ Indeed, the *non aliud* defines the identity of each entity with respect to another entity, since it logically and ontologically defines the identity itself. In this sense, the *non aliud* characterizes both the being and at the same time every otherness that is not being (that is, not being that identity). Beierwaltes concludes that being and not being therefore coincide in the *non aliud*, which is both *esse* and *non esse*. In this context, the Aristotelian concept of *posse* cannot be applied, because according to Cusanus every identity is *posse* only of itself, and not also of the identity of its difference. This is true even if, as Peter Casarella notes, "Beierwaltes claims that *possest* indicates that the divine principle is the identity of possibility and actuality prior to the coincidence of opposites, a unity which makes opposition itself possible, including the difference between possibility and actuality."¹⁴

Once again in continuity with late antique Neoplatonic tradition, Nicholas investigates the question of God's names and the possibility that human language can name God. Thus the problem of the *non aliud* occurs also with reference to the names of God, or in the divine principle itself. First of all, the *non aliud* does not define the divine principle, because *non aliud* is a human expression; as such it is limited and not fully applicable to infinity, the absolute, or God. Rather, the *non aliud* should be understood as an image of the divine principle, a *coniectura* or an *aenigma*. The

---

12 See Beierwaltes, *Identität und Differenz*, 107–8.
13 "Oportet enim omne aliud ab alio esse aliud, cum solum non aliud sit non aliud ab omni alio." Nicholas of Cusa, *De non aliud*, Propositiones, 123, in *Nicolai de Cusa Opera Omnia*, vol. XIII, ed. Ludwig Baur and Paul Wilpert (Leipzig: Felix Meiner Verlag, 1944), 64; trans. Jasper Hopkins, *Nicholas of Cusa on God as Not-Other*, 3rd ed. (Minneapolis: Arthur J. Banning Press, 1987), 1165. See also Beierwaltes, *Identität und Differenz*, 115.
14 Peter Casarella, "Nicholas of Cusa and the Power of the Possible," *American Catholic Philosophical Quarterly* 64, no. 1 (1990): 8.

aenigma, in fact, refers to something unnameable and characterizes it negatively, because only the negative can be grasped by the human mind.[15] For instance, in *Sermo CCXXXI*, Nicholas discusses the original beauty that is (in) God. He attests that beauty is present in a visible object, where it is not in itself but in something else, not in truth but in verisimilitude and image, or in an enigma. Such beauty admits a greater and lesser, since when it is in a material entity, it is not substantial Beauty.[16]

The crucial issue of Nicholas's thought on the *non aliud* can be summarized in the question: How is it possible that the absolute is related to the *nihil*? In fact, the *non aliud* has in itself the nature of *nihil*, because its identity is precisely the negative. Cusanus believes that because of the coincidence of opposites and following apophatic theology, the whole and the nothing reciprocally coincide in God. Moreover, the nothing is necessary for human beings to grasp the essence of God, who is incommensurable in relation to the limited nature of humanity and therefore can only be grasped as not having limits or determinations. Therefore, the human being knows God in a privative manner, knowing what he is not.

Beierwaltes states that the *non aliud* is and remains itself, though it manifests itself in each *ens* in a different way: "the not other is not other than the not other" (*non aliud est non aliud quam non aliud*).[17] It is all in all, but it is fully itself only when it is separated from the entities, namely when it is *nihil*. It is the principle, because nothing exists without otherness with respect to the other—that is to say, without otherness with respect to the *non aliud*. Consequently, the negative is the whole because it is the *nihil* that distinguishes each entity. Cusanus draws this paradox from Meister Eckhart, who like him describes it as *indistincta distinctio*.[18] Indeed, in

---

15 José González Ríos has explored the relation between the concept of *aenigma* and that of *non aliud* in "Los nombres enigmáticos como manuductiones en el pensamiento cusano de senectud," in *Manuductiones*, ed. Klaus Reinhardt and Cecilia Rusconi (Münster: Aschendorff Verlag, 2014), 169–90; and idem, "Die zeichentheoretische Bedeutung des 'non aliud,'" in *Nikolaus von Kues: De non aliud / Nichts anderes*, ed. Klaus Reinhardt, Jorge M. Machetta, and Harald Schwaetzer (Münster: Aschendorff Verlag, 2011), 211–24.

16 "Id quod pascit oculum, est pulchritudo, ut inest rei visibili, ubi non reperitur in se, sed in alio, non in veritate, sed in verisimilitudine et imagine aut aenigmate; ideo recipit magis et minus illa pulchritudo, quia non est substantialis." Nicholas of Cusa, *Sermo CCXXXI* 2, in *Nicolai de Cusa Opera Omnia*, vol. XIX/2, *Sermones IV (1455–1463), Fasc. 2*, ed. Marc-Aeilko Aris, Silvia Donati, et al. (Hamburg: Felix Meiner Verlag, 2001), 173–74.

17 Nicholas of Cusa, *De non aliud*, I.4, ed. Baur and Wilpert, 4.

18 Nicholas of Cusa, *Apologia doctae ignorantiae*, 12, in *Nicolai de Cusa Opera Omnia*, vol. II, ed. Raymond Klibansky (Leipzig: Felix Meiner Verlag, 1932), 10. See also Beierwaltes, *Identität*

this indistinction arises the distinction that determines the world, which has its foundation in the alterity of the *non aliud*, that is, the overcoming of the constitutive limit of matter. Matter is the absence of determination, according to Aristotle, but for Nicholas, matter that constitutes the world is open to the otherness of the negative—an infinite otherness not only in potency but in act.

Hegel and "God Thinking Himself"

If we consider the theme of the *non aliud* from a post-Cusan point of view, and specifically from that of Hegel, it cannot be related only to the second moment of the Idealistic dialectic, just as the concept of identity cannot refer only to the first moment of the triad.[19] In fact, the notions of identity and difference have to be integrated into each other according to the coincidence of opposites.[20] Thus identity and difference are reconciled in their dynamic synthesis, reaching a moment of self-reflection or self-consciousness.[21] Therefore, the relationship between Hegel and Cusanus has to be explored within the context of the integration of the notions of identity, difference, and self-reflexivity. This integration is merely outlined by Nicholas of Cusa, but will be expounded upon by Hegel, whose relation to Cusan thought is mediated by Renaissance and early modern sources.

Beierwaltes maintains that Hegel's approach to Neoplatonism was mediated by Aristotelian metaphysics as it was adopted and adapted in late antiquity and Renaissance humanism.[22] Delving into the interesting

---

und Differenz, 116. Regarding Eckhart, see "Unterschied durch Ununterschiedenheit (Meister Eckhart)," in *Identität und Differenz*, 97–104. See further Werner Beierwaltes, *Platonismus im Christentum* (Frankfurt am Main: Vittorio Klostermann, 1998), 100ff.

19 On the theme of the *non aliud* in both Cusanus and Hegel, see Diogo Ferrer, "A dupla negação em Nicolau de Cusa e Hegel," in *Coincidência dos opostos e concórdia: Caminhos do pensamento em Nicolau de Cusa*, ed. João Maria André and Mariano Álvarez Gómez (Coimbra: Faculdade de Letras, 2001), 187–200.

20 "Anknüpfungspunkt in der Sache und in der Denkform waren und sind im Kontext eines sachauslegenden Methodenbegriffs zum Beispiel die Begriffe konkrete Totalität, Triplitität, Einheit der Gegensätze, absolute Reflexion." Beierwaltes, *Identität und Differenz*, 241.

21 Dialectically, this movement also comprises the reflection and the negation of the reflection. See Stephan Grotz, *Negationen des Absoluten: Meister Eckhart, Cusanus, Hegel* (Hamburg: Felix Meiner Verlag, 2009), 282ff.

22 See Beierwaltes, *Identität und Differenz*, 144ff, 170ff. See also Jens Halfwassen, *Auf den Spuren des Einen: Studien zur Metaphysik und ihrer Geschichte* (Tübingen: Mohr Siebeck, 2015), 315ff.

debate concerning the relationship between Platonism and Aristotelianism in Cusanus is beyond the scope of this paper.[23] However, we must observe that Beierwaltes believes Aristotelian philosophy (sometimes reinterpreted from a Neoplatonic viewpoint) to be a fundamental mediation between Cusan and Hegelian thought. Moreover, Beierwaltes states that the main point of contact between the two authors lies in Nicholas's notion of *visio absoluta* and Hegel's central idea of God thinking himself, which are closely connected with the Idealistic notion of "absolute reflection" and which derive from Aristotle's philosophy.

Both Aristotle and Hegel aimed to understand the divine absolute as the being that thinks itself, a topic reminiscent of Cusanus's investigation into the relationship between identity and difference. Beierwaltes asserts that the Idealistic theme of absolute self-reflexivity brings Hegel close to late-medieval Aristotelianism and Neoplatonism, and most of all to Cusanus. In this regard, Beierwaltes uses Hegel's categories to interpret Hegel's own thought, as well as his relationship with the philosophies that came before him. Thus Hegel's thought could be the synthesis between Aristotelianism (the thesis) and Neoplatonism (the antithesis).[24] Furthermore, Beierwaltes notes that Hegel himself draws on the peak of Aristotelian philosophy: at the end of his *Encyclopaedia*, in fact, he cites Book XII of Aristotle's *Metaphysics*, where the Greek philosopher speaks about God thinking himself.[25] Hegel sustains the thesis according to which the substance of thought is thinking, and in this sense, the act of thinking and the subject of thought are one. For this reason, Hegel maintains that Aristotelian philosophy was founded not on the notion of identity, but rather on that of unity. As we can see, Hegel rereads Aristotle in a Neoplatonist light, stating that the activity of Aristotle's First Unmoved Mover is paradoxically a movement that strives for the unity (and thus not only the identity) of its own substance.

There is, however, an important aspect that distinguishes Hegel from Aristotle: the historical *explicatio* of thinking.[26] In this sense, Hegel is the

---

[23] For the theme of Aristotelianism in Cusan thought, see K. Meredith Ziebart, *Nicolaus Cusanus on Faith and the Intellect: A Case Study in 15th-Century Fides-Ratio Controversy* (Leiden: Brill, 2014); and Emmanuele Vimercati and Valentina Zaffino, eds., *Nicholas of Cusa and the Aristotelian Tradition: A Philosophical and Theological Survey* (Berlin: de Gruyter, 2020).

[24] See Beierwaltes, *Identität und Differenz*, 171.

[25] See Aristotle, *Metaphysics*, XII.7 (1072b18–30); see also Beierwaltes, *Identität und Differenz*, 171.

[26] See Beierwaltes, *Identität und Differenz*, 172 ff.

logical conclusion of Aristotle, and not just a revival of the latter. According to Hegel, the activity of thought is life, because God implies the unity of being and thinking, which in turn presents itself as life; consequently, the notion of life is not necessarily linked to the physical dimension of the subject. In fact, according to Hegel, the thinking being's self-reflexivity is fully explained by the Neoplatonic concept of spirit. Hence in both a metaphysical and non-metaphysical sense, the Christian (and most of all Cusan) notion of the absolute emerges. Nicholas of Cusa's idea of *visio absoluta* as perfection itself beyond every mode of seeing is more than the medieval *explicatio* of Greek metaphysics.[27] Rather, it is a concept, deeply rooted in history, that evolves into the modern conception of absolute subjectivity. For Nicholas, in fact, it has a double meaning: it refers both to God seeing himself, and God being seen by those whom he sees.[28]

Nonetheless, we have to note that in *De visione Dei*, the thought of *visio absoluta* and the absolute itself are often correlated, although the first can exist only thanks to the latter. The absolute, in fact, is the foundation of the absolute vision, whose being absolute is only an attribute dependent upon the absolute itself:

> For in Absolute Sight every contracted mode of seeing is present uncontractedly. For all contraction [of sight] is present in Absolute [Sight], because Absolute Sight is the Contraction of contractions. For it is Uncontractible Contraction. Therefore, most simple Contraction coincides with Absolute [Sight]. Now, without contraction nothing is contracted. Thus, Absolute Sight is present in all seeing, since all contracted sight exists through Absolute Sight and cannot at all exist without it.[29]

---

27 Nicholas of Cusa, *De visione Dei*, XII (48), ed. Riemann, 42. See also Werner Beierwaltes, "*Deus oppositio oppositorum*: Nicolaus Cusanus, *De visione Dei* XIII," *Salzburger Jahrbuch für Philosophie* 8, no. 1 (1964): 175–85.

28 See Werner Beierwaltes, "*Visio Absoluta*": *Reflexion als Grundzug des göttlichen Prinzips bei Nicolaus Cusanus* (Heidelberg: Sitzungsberichte der Heidelberger Akademie der Wissenschaften, Philosophisch-historische Klasse 1, 1989).

29 "Sunt enim in absoluto visu omnes contractionum modi videndi incontracte. Omnis enim contractio est in absoluto, quia absoluta visio est contractio contractionum; contractio enim est incontrahibilis. Coincidit igitur simplicissima contractio cum absoluto. Sine autem contractione nihil contrahitur. Sic absoluta visio in omni visu est, quia per ipsam est omnis contracta visio et sine ea penitus esse nequit." Nicholas of Cusa, *De visione Dei*, II (7), ed. Riemann, 11–12; trans. Jasper Hopkins, *Nicholas of Cusa's Dialectical Mysticism: Text, Translation,*

Thus, in the investigation of the notion of *visio absoluta*, the focus must be on the concept of unity, since every identity is comprised in the fundamental unity, which is intrinsically changeable because of the identities reflected in it. Therefore, as Hegel affirms, identity is an active form of unity, and the relationship between the One and the world is characterized as a dynamic relationship that resolves into a unity.[30] Similarly, *visio* is subjected to the category of "becoming," because it is linked to the identity that it represents and that represents it. However, the *visio* is absolute when, so to speak, it reaches the unity of all the individual *visiones*.

Beierwaltes emphasizes that the identity referred to by Hegel is not an empty identity, but that it is active, dynamic, and alive: it is properly an identity to be overcome, according to the dialectical structure of reality. Therefore, he describes a concrete identity, which in itself is dialectical ("konkrete oder in sich dialektische Identität"[31]) and characterized by difference, negation, and contradiction.[32] The *visio absoluta* is structured in the same way, since it is the perfect vision of the differences existing between individual *visiones*. In other words, in God's vision the perfect unity is achieved, because all partial perspectives, integrated into the divine perspective, are dialectically overcome. In light of this, Beierwaltes declares that his interpretation aims to investigate the metaphysical structure of Hegel's logic and philosophy of religion.[33] In particular, he claims that the most relevant aspect of the relationship identity-difference is the metaphysical one, which, according to Aristotle, is also theological. This assumption was already important in Nicholas of Cusa's thought, and the metaphysical approach of the Idealistic logic of the triad was used as the basis for Hegel's crucial notion of *visio absoluta*.[34]

---

and *Interpretive Study of "De Visione Dei"*, 2nd ed. (Minneapolis: Arthur J. Banning Press, 1988), 683. On *contracta visio*, see Werner Beierwaltes, "*Visio Facialis*—Sehen ins Angesicht. Zur Coinzidenz des endlichen und unendlichen Blicks bei Cusanus," in *Das Sehen Gottes nach Nikolaus von Kues. Akten des Symposions in Trier vom 25. bis 27. September 1986*, MFCG 18, ed. Rudolf Haubst (Trier: Paulinus Verlag, 1989), 91–124.

30 See Georg Wilhelm Friedrich Hegel, *Wissenschaft der Logik*, ed. Georg Lasson (Hamburg: Felix Meiner Verlag, 1951), 2:27.

31 Beierwaltes, *Identität und Differenz*, 242. He refers to Hegel, *Wissenschaft der Logik*, 2:239–40, 327–28, 410ff, 485.

32 See Beierwaltes, *Identität und Differenz*, 241–42.

33 See Beierwaltes, *Identität und Differenz*, 243–44.

34 Beierwaltes cites Hegel's *Wissenschaft der Logik*, 1:46: "Die objektive Logik tritt ... an die Stelle der vormaligen Metaphysik, als welche das wissenschaftliche Gebäude über die Welt war, das nur durch Gedanken aufgeführt sein sollte." See *Identität und Differenz*, 244.

Beierwaltes as Neoplatonic and Idealistic Interpreter

Comparing Cusanus and Hegel, Beierwaltes wonders "whether and to what extent an affinity of Cusanus with Hegel's dialectic can be thought— even if, or indeed because, Cusanus further determines the Neoplatonic notions of absolute principle and reflection."[35] First of all, as described above, there exists an undeniable connection and some affinities in the two men's theories.[36] Yet Beierwaltes also identifies aspects of dissimilarity between them, affirming that neither the premises nor the aims of the two philosophers are the same, though their conceptual settings are often remarkably similar. Beierwaltes, therefore, seems to believe that Cusanus and Hegel were moved by different theoretical instances and that they sought different speculative objectives; the differences between these elements are probably due to the historical gap between the two authors, which causes a relationship of imperfect compatibility. However, these differences make the theoretical closeness existing between Cusanus and Hegel, in their pursuit of theological and philosophical truth, all the more interesting and valuable: though their starting and ending points are diverse, they trace speculative lines that somehow overlap. Beierwaltes's investigations focus on this specific theme.

In this context, the common assumption of the indistinction of philosophy and theology is not intended in the same way by Cusanus and by Hegel. In fact, the latter maintains that philosophy is the overcoming of theological

---

35 "Ob und in welchem Maße eine Affinität des Cusanus zu *Hegels Dialektik* gedacht werden könne—obgleich oder gar weil Cusanus die neuplatonische Konzeption von Prinzip und absoluter Reflexion fortbestimmt." Beierwaltes, *Identität und Differenz*, 128.

36 Beierwaltes also investigated the theme of the triad in the dialectical movement with a particular focus on the Christian Trinity, fundamental in Nicholas of Cusa's work. This is not the subject of our research, which deals with the relationship between Cusanus and Hegel on the basis of the binary identity-difference. On the theme of the Trinity in the two authors, see Davide Monaco, "Pensare l'Uno con Cusano: L'interpretazione di Werner Beierwaltes," *Il Pensiero* 48, nos. 1–2 (2009): 115–27; and idem, *Nicholas of Cusa: Trinity, Freedom and Dialogue* (Münster: Aschendorff Verlag, 2016), in particular 118–29. For Beierwaltes on the theme of the Trinity, see his *Platonismus im Christentum*, 25ff, 85ff. Regarding the notion of absolute in Hegel's *Logic*, Beierwaltes attests that "Die Selbstdefinition Gottes ist als eine derartige Reflexions-Bewegung seines Seins als die trinitarische Einheit von Anfang-Mitte-Ende (als des selben Anfangs) zugleich ein »Schluß« in und mit sich selbst." Werner Beierwaltes, *"Catena Aurea": Plotin, Augustinus, Eriugena, Thomas, Cusanus* (Frankfurt am Main: Vittorio Klostermann, 2017), 340.

thought, which reaches its realization in philosophy itself. Cusanus, on the other hand, views philosophy as mostly serving an instrumental function with regard to the unfolding of theology, which he believes can be successful only when permeated by philosophy.[37] Therefore, Beierwaltes argues that according to Hegel, philosophy comprises and surpasses theology, representing its highest conclusion, whereas according to Cusanus, theology is based on philosophy. The two perspectives are very similar to each other but are not precisely the same, and we can say that Hegel represents the historical—and theoretical—consummation of the dialectical process already explored by Nicholas, whereby philosophy and theology aim at the same unitary and organic knowledge.

Focusing on the points of contact and distance between the two German philosophers, Werner Beierwaltes examines the dialectic of the *coincidentia oppositorum*, central to both Cusanus and Hegel. However, once again in this regard, a crucial difference emerges between them. Nicholas considers the coincidence of opposites possible only in God, who is beyond all contradiction. Cusanus thus affirms the primacy of the One, which in itself is the wholeness of being, from which (according to Neoplatonic tradition) the opposites derive. Consequently, opposites are but explications of the One in time and space, while the One is the substance of being. For Hegel, however, the primacy of the One is the result of the dialectic of being, that is, of the reflexive movement immanent to Being itself ("die Bewegung der dem Sein immanenten Reflexion").[38] The result of the dialectical movement is the unfolding of what was abstractly in itself from the beginning. In this sense, opposites interpenetrate one another, giving rise to unity as the self-penetration of the various moments of the dialectic of spirit. In Nicholas of Cusa we find a descending movement, characteristic of Neoplatonism, which goes from one to multiple. In Hegel, however, an

---

37 See Werner Beierwaltes, "Das Verhältnis von Philosophie und Theologie bei Nicolaus Cusanus," in *Nikolaus von Kues: 1401–2001. Akten des Symposiums in Bernkastel-Kues vom 23.-26. Mai 2001*, MFCG 28, ed. Klaus Kremer and Klaus Reinhardt (Trier: Paulinus Verlag, 2003), 76, where Beierwaltes cites two representative texts by Nicholas. "Unum est, quod omnes theologizantes aut philosophantes in varietate modorum exprimere conantur." Nicholas of Cusa, *De filiatione Dei*, V (83), in *Nicolai de Cusa Opera Omnia, vol. IV*, ed. Paul Wilpert (Hamburg: Felix Meiner Verlag, 1959), 59. "Quomodo sacrae litterae et philosophi idem varie nominarunt." Nicholas of Cusa, *De venatione sapientiae*, IX (23), in *Nicolai de Cusa Opera Omnia*, vol. XII, edited by Raymond Klibansky and Hans Gerhard Senger (Hamburg: Felix Meiner Verlag, 1982), 24.

38 Beierwaltes, *Identität und Differenz*, 128.

ascending movement prevails, which proceeds from the diversity of the *non aliud* to the identity of the One, the result of the identities composing it as well as their differences or negations.

While dealing with the theme of the coincidence of opposites, Beierwaltes examines the notion of negation. For Nicholas, it is otherness that, in the context of finiteness, delimits each identity or each opposite. Otherwise, it can be absolute negativity (*nihil omnium*), preceding and overcoming every negation. But Hegel sees negativity as the second moment of the dialectical movement, characterized as the impulse that moves this process and the explication of the process itself, never allowing a certain phase of being to become permanent without looking toward the next phase. The negative is, therefore, the vital impetus ("Triebfeder oder Unruhe") of the dialectic of being, since it is a reflection that overcomes the contradiction and moves to preserve the identity of the previous moment.[39]

In his interpretation of Hegel and Cusanus, Beierwaltes considers Nicholas's thought to be the apex reached by philosophical theology based on Neoplatonic metaphysics. For his part, Hegel is closely linked to Neoplatonism, which is one of his most relevant sources. In fact, despite the two authors' different premises and aims, both try to answer the question concerning the identity of being and thinking. Thus the Platonic dialectic, which Beierwaltes traces back to Plato's *Parmenides*, achieves the overcoming of multiplicity and the opposite in an absolute and self-reflexive unity, which, through the compenetration of *non aliud*, *idem*, and *possest*, arrives at the reality of the One—that is, the fullness of being.[40]

Conclusions

As Beierwaltes writes, the Cusan *visio Dei* displays a twofold aspect expressed by the title of the *De visione Dei* treatise: God himself sees and is seen by those whom he sees. The inseparable link between the two aspects is shown in the fact that God's "being seen" by another still presupposes God's seeing of himself. In this twofold, ever-changing "being seen," God's seeing is the foundation and origin, namely the *principium*. That divine principle is

---

39 Beierwaltes, *Identität und Differenz*, 129.
40 See Beierwaltes, *Identität und Differenz*, 131. On the *Parmenides*'s notion of the One in the Renaissance, see *Denken des Einen*, 216–22; on the *Parmenides* as interpreted by Hegel in the *Logic*, see *Denken des Einen*, 222–25.

in itself dynamic and continuously active, and, for both Cusanus and Hegel, it reflects itself in its own self-reflection. In fact, identity and difference constitute the highest synthesis, which is not only logically necessary, but also metaphysically and theologically necessary, since the coincidence of opposites—in this case the ontologically original opposites—is the foundation of the world, its becoming, and Being itself.

Even at a historical level, Beierwaltes emphasizes, "seeing" takes on various connotations; in Cusanus it mainly indicates opening to being, that is, the operating of the principle. Therefore, seeing is the reflection and self-reflexivity of the divine principle. This is the aspect of Cusan metaphysics that is closest to German Idealism, above all to Hegel and his notion of God thinking himself. According to Beierwaltes, for both Cusanus and Hegel, God sees and thinks himself throughout a constant and productive activity. With help from Aristotelian metaphysics, and not only from formal logic, we have considered how the central topics of the medieval Neoplatonist tradition became the foundation of modern thought in Hegel and German Idealism. In this context, Nicholas of Cusa's philosophical theology—or theological philosophy—plays a fundamental role.

6

The Infinite Sphere from Cusanus to Peter Sloterdijk's Spherology

JOSÉ GONZÁLEZ RÍOS

In his essay, "Pascal's Sphere" (1951), Jorge Luis Borges affirms: "Perhaps universal history is the history of a few metaphors. To outline a chapter of that history is the purpose of this note."[1] Let us take Borges's words as an invitation to further reflection. Like Borges, many others have studied the image of the sphere in the Western philosophical tradition, but Dietrich Manhke's investigation, *Unendliche Sphäre und Allmittelpunkt* (1937), is perhaps the most prominent.[2] Mahnke studies the role of the sphere image

---

1 Jorge L. Borges, "Pascal's Sphere," in *Other Inquisitions (1937–1952)*, trans. Ruth L. C. Simms (Austin: University of Texas Press, 1964), 6.

2 Dietrich Mahnke, *Unendliche Sphäre und Allmittelpunkt: Beiträge zur Genealogie der mathematischen Mystik* (Halle: Max Niemeyer Verlag, 1937). See also Maurice de Gandillac, "Sur la sphere infinie de Pascal," *Revue d'histoire de la philosophie et d'histoire générale de la civilisation* 33 (1943): 32–44; George Poulet, "Le symbole du cercle infini dans la literature et la philosophie," *Revue de métaphysique et de morale* 64, no. 3 (1959): 257–75; Alexandre Koyré, *From the Closed World to the Infinite Universe* (Baltimore: Johns Hopkins University Press, 1968); George Poulet, *Les métamorphoses du cercle* (Paris: Flammarion, 1975); Karsten Harries, "The Infinite Sphere: Comments on the History of a Metaphor," *Journal of the History of Philosophy* 13 (1975): 5–15; Michael Keefer, "The World Turned Inside Out: Revolutions of

in the development of German philosophy, comprising Meister Eckhart, Nicholas of Cusa, Leibniz, Fichte, Novalis, and Schelling, among others. His enquiry incorporates the reception of both pagan and Christian sources, among which the anonymous *Liber XXIV philosophorum* plays an important role. Mahnke sought to show that in its historicity, the image of the sphere shifted first from the theological to the cosmological realm, expressing an infinite universe, but then shifted from the cosmological to the anthropological field, to symbolize an absolute subject during the periods of Romanticism and German Idealism.

More recently, the project of Peter Sloterdijk is even more ambitious. He strives to understand the entirety of Western culture in light of a theory of spheres or *spherology*, presented in the three volumes of *Sphären*: a *Mikrosphärologie* in *Blasen (Bubbles)* (1998); a *Makrosphärologie* in *Globen (Globes)* (1999), and a *plurale Sphärologie* in *Schäume (Foam)* (2004).[3] For Sloterdijk, the sphere means, above all, life. There isn't any life outside spheres; all things live and exist as spheres; all things are spheres.[4]

In the second volume, *Globen*, Sloterdijk proposes a history of Western metaphysics through the image of the sphere, or more precisely, a metaphysics of the sphere or macrospherology. He studies the diverse ways of understanding the "monosphere" (the integral globe, or unity of the whole) from the ancient doctrines of Being as a spherical form up to the contemporary globalization process. In chapter 5 of *Globen*, "*Deus sive sphaera*, or: The Exploding Universal One," Sloterdijk considers the theological stage of the sphere.[5] In this analysis he focuses on the image of the infinite sphere in the *Liber XXIV philosophorum* to suggest that with Definitions II and XVIII we find ourselves at the threshold of the modern world.[6] And in that same chapter, Sloterdijk also refers to Cusanus.[7] He argues that he, the most

---

the Infinite Sphere from Hermes to Pascal," *Renaissance and Reformation* 12 (1988): 303–13; and Pina Totaro and Luisa Valente, eds., *Sphaera: Forma, immagine e metafora tra Medioevo e età moderna* (Florence: Leo Olschki Editore, 2012).

3 References and quotes from Sloterdijk's works are taken from the following English translations: Peter Sloterdijk, *Spheres*, vol. 1, *Bubbles: Microspherology*, trans. Wieland Hoban (Los Angeles: Semiotext(e), 2011); Peter Sloterdijk, *Spheres*, vol. 2, *Globes: Macrospherology*, trans. Wieland Hoban (Los Angeles: Semiotext(e), 2014); and Peter Sloterdijk, *Spheres*, vol. 3, *Foams: Plural Spherology*, trans. Wieland Hoban (Los Angeles: Semiotext(e), 2016).

4 Sloterdijk, *Spheres I: Bubbles*, 10–11, 45–46.

5 See Sloterdijk, *Spheres II: Globes*, 441–552.

6 See Sloterdijk, *Spheres II: Globes*, 511–33.

7 See Sloterdijk, *Spheres II: Globes*, 533–52.

important thinker of his time, failed to get on the shoulders of that giant, the *Liber*. He provocatively affirms: "Cusa's *oeuvre* thus ends in monumental ambiguity: conservative centrism keeps the revolutionary infinitism [of the *Liber*] in check, as if an explosion had frozen at the moment of ignition."[8]

In what follows, I will first address Definitions II and XVIII of the *Liber* and their place in the macrospherology proposed by Sloterdijk. Second, I examine the reception of the *Liber* in the doctrine of learned ignorance (*maxima doctrina ignorantiae*) of Nicholas of Cusa. Finally, I will respond to Sloterdijk's objections to Cusanus's conception of the sphere.

The *Liber XXIV philosophorum* in Sloterdijk's Macrospherology

In his macrospherology, Sloterdijk does not address the historiographical debate about the origin of *Liber*, which has been ongoing since the late nineteenth century, but instead directly confronts its definitions. We can briefly summarize this historiographical discussion. It is well known that the *Liber* appears toward the second part of the twelfth century in the Latin West, but its origins are not well established. Nor has it been settled whether this text is properly a book or a *florilegium* of definitions collected from diverse sources that tradition made into a single work. Despite the fact that in many manuscripts the *Liber* is attributed to Hermes Trismegistus, and in this way transformed into the bearer of a *prisca sapientia*, the author remains unknown, as does the original title.[9] From Meister Eckhart onward, it has been known as *Liber viginti quattuor philosophorum*.[10]

There are two main lines of interpretation in relation to the origins of the *Liber*: the line that inscribes the *Liber* in the development of a Neoplatonic theology in the twelfth century, and the one supported by Françoise Hudry, who was in charge of a critical edition of the *Liber* in 1997. In Hudry's evolving view, the origin of the text certainly goes back

---

8 Sloterdijk, *Spheres II: Globes*, 548–49.

9 Regarding the manuscript's history and the problems of the origin of the *Liber*, including author, title, and structure, see Françoise Hudry, ed., *Liber viginti quattuor philosophorum*, Corpus Christianorum Continuatio Mediaevalis [CCCM]143A (Hermes Latinus, III, Pars I) (Turnhout: Brepols, 1997), v–cxiv.

10 See Meister Eckhart, *Expositio libri Genesis*, c. 2, 2, n. 155 (LW 1.2, 191); and *Expositio libri Exodi secundum recensionem Codicis Cusani 21 et Codicis Treverensis 72/1056*, c. 16, 18, n. 91 (LW 2, 95).

to Late Antiquity, but it could be the reworking of an Aristotelian text (1989),[11] an Aristotelian theology and cosmology handbook from the Harran School (1997),[12] or, according to her later view, a text by Marius Victorinus (2009).[13] In any case, the actual presence of theological and philosophical terms and doctrines belonging to the atmosphere of the Latin twelfth century has been sufficiently documented by many scholars of the *Liber*, even if we find subtle differences among them.[14]

Regarding Definition II and Definition XVIII, the focus of Sloterdijk's reading, let us remember that Definition II (*Deus est sphaera infinita cuius centrum est ubique, circumferentia nusquam*)[15] expresses the impossibility of conceiving of God in rational terms. Projected to infinity, the image of the *sphaera* compels a reconsideration of the terms "center" and "circumference." Indeed, when the center of the sphere is everywhere (*ubique*), it is not in any determined place. On the other hand, the circumference is nowhere (*nusquam*). In this sense the infinite sphere affirms the absence of any limit or determination; the sphere suspends every limit. A center that is everywhere suggests the idea of immanence, yet the fact of being everywhere expresses, at the same time, its transcendence. In this way the image dissolves the antagonism between the immanence and transcendence of God. The short commentary on this definition corroborates this by affirming that the definition leads to imagining the life (*vita*) of the first

---

11 See Françoise Hudry, *Le livre des XXIV philosophes* (Grenoble: Millon, 1989), 20.

12 See Hudry, *Liber viginti quattuor philosophorum*, xviii–xix.

13 See Françoise Hudry, *Le livre des XXIV philosophes: Résurgence d'un texte du IVe siècle*, 2nd ed. (Paris: J. Vrin, 2015), 13–22.

14 See, among many others, Marie-Thérèse D'Alverny, ed., *Alain de Lille: Textes inédits* (Paris: J. Vrin, 1965), 164; Werner Beierwaltes, "*Liber XXIV philosophorum*," in *Die deutsche Literatur des Mittelalters: Verfasserlexikon*, ed. Kurt Ruh et al. (Berlin: De Gruyter, 1985), 767–70; Paolo Lucentini, *Il libro dei ventiquattro filosofi* (Milan: Adelphi, 1999), 13–14; Zénon Kaluza, "Besprechung: 'Liber viginti quattuor philosophorum', ed. Françoise Hudry (Corpus Christianorum, Continuatio Mediaevalis 143/A, Hermes Latinus III.1), Turnhout 1997," *Mittellateinisches Jahrbuch* 35 (2000): 161–66; Zénon Kaluza, "Comme une branche d'amandier en fleurs: Dieu dans le *Liber viginti quattor philosophorum*," in *Hermetism from Late Antiquity to Humanism*, ed. Paolo Lucentini, Ilaria Parri, and Vittoria Perrone Compagni (Turnhout: Brepols, 2003), 109n23, 121–22; Paolo Lucentini, "Il *Liber viginti quattuor philosophorum* nella *Commedia* dantesca e nei suoi primi commentatori," in *Platonismo, ermetismo, eresia nel Medioevo*, ed. Paolo Lucentini, Textes et Études du Moyen Âge 41 (Louvain: Fédération internationale des instituts d'études médiévales, 2007), 238; and Kurt Flasch, *Was ist Gott? Das Buch der 24 Philosophen* (Munich: Beck, 2011), 107–9.

15 Hudry, *Liber viginti quattuor philosophorum*, 7. ("God is an infinite sphere whose center is everywhere and circumference nowhere.")

cause (*prima causa*) as a *continuum*. The definition conceives of God in his immanence and in his transcendence in a non-oppositional way: the infinite sphere expresses a *continuum* of life.[16]

Definition XVIII (*Deus est sphaera cuius tot sunt circumferentiae quot puncta*) clearly evokes Definition II, as mentioned in the *Liber* (*ista sequitur ex secunda*).[17] In this way, it is the *Liber* itself that relates Definition II to Definition XVIII.[18] Nevertheless, it is not a simple replication. Definition II presents one sphere and one center that is everywhere. Definition XVIII, on the other hand, presents a multiplicity of spheres and centers. Here there is not just one center, even though it is everywhere: every point is the center of its own sphere. With this variation, Definition XVIII permits us to give up on the idea of God as the singular center of all things. As Flasch observes in his interpretation of this definition: "God is the infinite unity of the infinite centers."[19]

When Sloterdijk interprets the sense of these definitions, he concentrates on three points. First, regarding the notion of "infinite" referred to the sphere, Sloterdijk argues that the *Liber* breaks open a closed world, making space not only for the infinite universe but also for the "death of the sphere," that is, "the death of God" explicitly announced by Nietzsche.[20] That is, the infinite sphere image starts an infinitist theology that will eventually put an end to theology itself. In Sloterdijk's words, "the infinite sphere forfeited its harboring function. Those contained in it lost their immunity and their harboring."[21] Second, the image of the sphere in Definition XVIII replaces theocentrism. Every point becomes the center of a sphere; everything that receives being becomes in turn a center of irradiation. Every point of the sphere is also the irradiation center of infinite spheres. For this reason, Definition XVIII expresses a principle of immanent plenitude.

---

16 Flasch, *Was ist Gott? Das Buch der 24 Philosophen*, 14–17.

17 Hudry, *Liber viginti quattuor philosophorum*, 25. ("God is a sphere which has as many circumferences as points.")

18 Despite the fact that the text does not establish the correlation, the image of the sphere also appears in the commentary to Definition XIV: "Haec definitio imaginam facit deum esse *sphaeram* in cuius centro nihil incarceratur et est continue agens *sphaera divina* opus divinum quo detinet nihil in suo esse aeternaliter, a quo per exuberantiam suae bonitatis vocavit in esse rem quae est quasi circa centrum. quaesi ad esse actum attrahit, stabit *sphaera*, si ad esse possibile, redibit ad nihilum." Hudry, *Liber viginti quattuor philosophorum*, 21; my emphasis.

19 Flasch, *Was ist Gott? Das Buch der 24 Philosophen*, 64.

20 Sloterdijk, *Spheres II: Globes*, 126–27.

21 Sloterdijk, *Spheres II: Globes*, 528.

There are no regions alienated from being; there are no "weak points."[22] New circumferences are generated in every point, yielding infinite circumferences, as Definition XVIII affirms: as many circumferences as points (*tot circumferentiae quot puncta*).[23] Third, Sloterdijk underscores that the *Liber* makes no attempt to conciliate both systems of spheres—that is, the infinite sphere from Definition II (theocentric system) and the infinity of spheres from Definition XVIII (theoperipheral system)—even though the *Liber* itself indicates a relationship between the two definitions. Sloterdijk argues that in this way the *Liber* announces an irreconcilable tension between two systems of spheres.

Nicholas of Cusa in Sloterdijk's Macrospherology

As noted previously, Sloterdijk thinks Cusanus did not take up the challenges posed by the *Liber*'s definitions. In his opinion, Nicholas of Cusa could not tolerate the cosmological consequences of conceiving the sphere as infinite (Def. II). Neither could he put up with the making of a sphere from each thing (Def. XVIII). Nor could he solve the relationship between both systems of spheres except through his Christology. So, in Sloterdijk's view, Cusanus merely retreats to Christological orthodoxy once confronted with the revolutionary character of the *Liber*.[24] In this section I will reply to Sloterdijk's objections by reviewing the presence of the *Liber* in the Cusan *maxima doctrina ignorantiae*.[25]

The *Liber* and the *Maxima doctrina ignorantiae*

The *Liber XXIV philosophorum* had a plural reception in the Middle Ages and the early modern era. Theologians and philosophers belonging to diverse traditions used the book as a pagan authority to elaborate their thought systems, a tradition of reception that includes Nicholas of Cusa.

---

22 Sloterdijk, *Spheres II: Globes*, 514: "This eighteenth definition of God, as we can see, has an immanent principle of abundance which ensures that there can be no loss of substance in God, no matter how far His emanations might extend away from the mysterious 'first' center. One could equally say that there are no weak points in God, and that, most strictly speaking, regions distant from him are an impossibility."
23 Sloterdijk, *Spheres II: Globes*, 516.
24 Sloterdijk, *Spheres II: Globes*, 539–42.
25 For reasons of space, I will have to forgo an analysis of Cusan Christology in the context of Sloterdijk's spherology.

Sturlese has shown the presence of Hermetic texts, and of the *Liber* in particular, in Albert the Great's works. Sannino has studied the *Liber*'s presence in Berthold of Moosburg, and Beccarisi has analyzed its circulation in Meister Eckhart, in both his Latin and German works.[26] All of these are explicit sources for Nicholas of Cusa. This makes clear that Cusanus had both direct and mediated contact with the *Liber*, and with the metaphor of the sphere in particular, through these sources during the development of his doctrine of learned ignorance. We cannot say which of the *Liber* manuscripts Nicholas of Cusa read, but based on the mentions he makes we can surmise that he was acquainted with the *versio communis*, the one that circulated the most during the Middle Ages and early modernity.[27]

There certainly is a similarity between the *Liber* and Cusan *docta ignorantia*. One of the lost manuscripts of the *Liber* refers to the definitions as "*enigmaticae*."[28] In this way the book was also understood as a collection of enigmas that answer just one question: *quid est Deus?* The definitions of the *Liber* detonate the limits of rational understanding and lead to an intellectual comprehension in which mere rationality (*ratio*) is overcome, guiding the intellect (*intellectus*) toward the most complex and paradoxical

---

26 See Loris Sturlese, "Saints et magiciens: Albert le Grand en face d'Hermès Trismégiste," *Archives de Philosophie* 43 (1980): 615–34; Lori Sturlese, "Proclo e Ermete in Germania da Alberto Magno a Bertoldo di Moosburg," in *Von Meister Dietrich zu Meister Eckhart*, ed. Kurt Flasch (Hamburg: Felix Meiner Verlag, 1984), 22–33; Antonella Sannino, "The Hermetical Sources in Berthold von Moosburg," *Journal of the Warburg and Courtauld Institutes* 63 (2000): 243–58; Antonella Sannino, "Il *Liber viginti quattuor philosophorum* nella metafisica di Bertoldo di Moosburg," in *Per perscrutationem philosophicam: Neue Perspektiven der mittelalterlichen Forschung*, ed. Alessandra Beccarisi, Ruedi Imbach, and Pasquale Porro (Hamburg: Felix Meiner Verlag, 2008), 252–72; Alessandra Beccarisi, "Deus est sphaera intellectualis infinita: Eckhart interprete del *Liber XXIV philosophorum*," in Totaro and Valente, *Sphaera*, 167–92; and Alessandra Beccarisi, "'nich sint ez allez heidenischer meister wort, die niht enbekanten dan in einem natiurlîchen liehte': Eckhart e il *Liber vigintiquattuor philosophorum*," in *Studi sulle fonti di Meister Eckhart* II, ed. Loris Sturlese (Fribourg: Academic Press Fribourg, 2012), 73–96.

27 This *versio communis* contains a preface and the twenty-four definitions, each accompanied by a brief commentary. Federici Vescovini conjectures that Cusanus had contact with the *versio communis*, based on his mention of the commentary on Definition XIV, which he quotes in *De docta ignorantia* II.2 (100). See Graziella Federici Vescovini, "Les Métamorphoses de quelques propositions hermétiques après le *De docta ignorantia* (1440)," in *Identité et différence dans l'oeuvre de Nicolas de Cues*, ed. Hervé Pasqua (Louvain: Éditions Peeters, 2011), 3–4.

28 See MS Erfurt, Kartause Salvatorberg, C. 27: "Libellus de diffinitionibus Dei philosophorum et theologorum et ponuntur ibidem 23 deffinitiones enigmatice Dei." Quoted in Hudry, *Liber viginti quattuor philosophorum*, lxxxi.

comprehension of which it is capable. In this way the *Liber* can be conceived as a singular way for the intellect to comprehend the incomprehensible, as Sloterdijk notes, and to express linguistically the most excessive understanding of God.[29] Likewise, the Cusan *symbolice investigare* also pushes language to the limit of intellectual comprehension, as it takes images to the intellectual extreme where opposites coincide (*coincidentia oppositorum*), a paradoxical situation in which such images make the discourse explode.

From a doctrinal point of view, we can indicate several conceptual affinities between the *Liber* and the *maxima doctrina ignorantiae*: the apprehension of the unitrinity of the principle through the monad concept (Definition I); the principle's immanence and transcendence (Definition II); the definition of *maximitas* as that than which no greater thing can be, which the *Liber* expresses in terms of thought, not being (Definition V); the abundance of the principle, which is above everything that is (Definition XI); the intellectual principle that lives in the intellection of itself (Definition XX); the *via negationis*, among others, in Definition XVI, which affirms that God is the only being that neither words can denote with precision nor minds can understand; and finally, the very heart of the Cusan doctrine—how to know is to not know (*quomodo scire est ignorare*) (to recall the title of the first chapter of *De docta ignorantia*)—resounds in the *Liber*'s Definition XXIII: *Deus est qui sola ignorantia mente cognoscitur*. In any case, beyond this clear "family resemblance" between the *Liber* and some postulates in Nicholas of Cusa's *maxima doctrina ignorantiae*, the *Liber* is one of his sources that he explicitly quotes or otherwise references by means of other sources.

Definition II in the *Maxima doctrina ignorantiae*

Sloterdijk has suggested that Nicholas of Cusa did not tolerate the cosmological consequences of conceiving the sphere as infinite. Nevertheless, we can see that Cusanus assimilates Definition II of the *Liber* both from a theological and a cosmological point of view, first in *De docta ignorantia* (1440) and years later in Book II of *Dialogus de ludo globi* (1463).

Nicholas of Cusa uses the *sphaera infinita* image to refer to the absolute maximum in the context of the proportionality (*transsumptiva proportione*)

---

29 Sloterdijk, *Spheres II: Globes*, 521.

he practices in *De docta ignorantia* I.11–23.³⁰ Without any mention of the *Liber* or any direct quotation of its definitions, Cusanus transposes the image of the *sphaera infinita* onto the actual infinite of God. If he symbolizes absolute straightness with the image of the infinite line, the absolute Trinity with the infinite triangle, and absolute unity with the infinite circle, the infinite sphere refers to the actual existence of all things in the absolute maximum (*actualissima Dei existentia*).³¹

As referred to God, the image of the *sphaera infinita* expresses the *apex* of the geometrical figures that are referred to the absolute (line, triangle, circle). In this sense, it is the greatest thinkable figure, as the actuality of the line, the triangle, and the circle.³² The line reaches the sphere through the triangle and the circle; the triangle reaches the sphere through the circle; and the circle directly accesses the sphere, which is the most perfect of all figures.³³ So the infinite sphere becomes a *manuductio* that allows one to comprehend intellectually that God is the actuality of the whole and, in this sense, the form of being (*forma essendi*) or the maximally actual being (*maxima actualis entitas*). It is the most adequate measure of the universe and of all things. It is the actual perfection of everything and, for that reason, the absolute life of all things, since all vivification (*vivificatio*) is given from, in, and through the absolute infinite sphere.³⁴

Definition II of the *Liber* appears again, complete and in a striking way, in *De docta ignorantia*, Book II. Here Cusanus approaches the maximum from a second perspective: as the contracted universe, that is, as the maximum unity of diversity.³⁵ When one considers the image of the infinite sphere, it is important to remember the distinction that Nicholas of Cusa

---

30 In this respect, Nicholas of Cusa follows a definite theological tradition. See, for example, Alan of Lille, *Regulae*, 7, ed. Nikolaus M. Häring, "Magister Alanus de Insulis Regulae Caelestis Iuris," *Archives d'histoire doctrinale et littéraire du Moyen Âge* 48 (1981): 97–226, esp. 131–32; Alan of Lille, "Sermon sur le thème: Deus est sphaera intelligibilis," in *Textes inédits*, ed. D'Alverny, 297–306; Meister Eckhart, *Lectio I super Ecclesiastici*, c. 24, 23, nn. 17–20 (LW 2, 246–48); and Meister Eckhart, *Expositio libri Exodi*, c. 16, 18, n. 91 (LW 2, 94–95) *et passim*.

31 Nicholas of Cusa, *De docta ignorantia*, I.19 (56), in *Nikolaus von Kues: Philosophisch-Theologische Werke*, vol. 1, ed. Paul Wilpert and Hans Gerhard Senger, rev. ed. (Hamburg: Felix Meiner Verlag, 2002), 74–75.

32 Nicholas of Cusa, *De docta ignorantia*, I.23 (70), ed. Wilpert and Senger, 92–93.

33 Nicholas of Cusa, *De docta ignorantia*, I.23 (73), ed. Wilpert and Senger, 94–97.

34 Nicholas of Cusa, *De docta ignorantia*, I.23 (72), ed. Wilpert and Senger, 94–95.

35 Nicholas of Cusa, *De docta ignorantia*, II.4 (113), ed. Wilpert and Senger, 30–33.

makes between the negative infinity (*negative infinitum*) of the infinite sphere that is God or *maximum absolutum*, and the privative infinity (*privative infinitum*) of the infinite sphere that is the universe or *maximum contractum*.[36] This allows us to specify that God, as center and circumference of the universal sphere, is in actuality every being that is possible, while the universe is actual only contractedly, although nothing else actually limits it. This is the reason why its *infinitum* condition is unlimited only in a privative sense.

Now in *De docta ignorantia*, II.11, Cusanus affirms, based on this conception of contraction (*contractio*), that it is not possible to have any absolute physical center in the universe. Given this impossibility, a universal circumference is not feasible either. For this reason, it is impossible for the world (*mundus*) or universe to have a fixed and unmoving center. If it had a center, and consequently a circumference, it would have a limit, beyond which there would necessarily be something else.[37] Just as the earth is not the center of the cosmos, the sphere of the fixed stars is not its circumference.[38]

Yet Nicholas observes that many pretend, according to their measurements, that they are at the center. Nevertheless, when enfolding (*complicatio*) the different imaginations related to the position of the center, one can notice in an intellectual way (*intellectualiter*) that the world and its movements cannot be accurately apprehended.[39] In this way, and guided by the ignorance doctrine, the intellect perceives that the world, its movement, and its shape can be understood only in an incomprehensible way. Here, quoting Definition II from the *Liber*, Cusanus remarks: "Hence, the world-machine (*machina mundi*) will have its center everywhere and its circumference nowhere, so to speak; for God, who is everywhere and nowhere, is its circumference and center."[40] Therefore God is the center of the world, the earth, and the fixed stars, indeed of every being in the world. At the

---

36 Nicholas of Cusa, *De docta ignorantia*, II.1 (97), ed. Wilpert and Senger, 12–13.
37 Nicholas of Cusa, *De docta ignorantia*, II.11 (156), ed. Wilpert and Senger, 84–87.
38 Nicholas of Cusa, *De docta ignorantia*, II.11 (157), ed. Wilpert and Senger, 86–89.
39 Nicholas of Cusa, *De docta ignorantia*, II.11 (161), ed. Wilpert and Senger, 92–93.
40 "Unde erit machina mundi quasi habens undique centrum et nullibi circumferentiam, quoniam eius circumferentia et centrum est Deus, qui est undique et nullibi." Nicholas of Cusa, *De docta ignorantia*, II.12 (162), ed. Wilpert and Senger, 92–95; trans. Jasper Hopkins, *Complete Theological and Philosophical Treatises of Nicholas of Cusa*, vol. 1 (Minneapolis: Arthur J. Banning Press, 2001), 93.

same time, God is the infinite circumference of all things that is nowhere. The infinite sphere that is the universe has its center and its circumference everywhere, that is to say, in each contraction, even if, from a metaphysical standpoint, it has its center and its circumference in God.

The image of the infinite sphere reappears in *Dialogus de ludo globi*, Book II. In this text Cusanus refers to the image of the sphere in these words: "After you take note of the saying of the wise man who said that God is a circle whose center is everywhere ... so God is present in all things."[41] We must note, above all, that Cusanus uses the two-dimensional concept of circle and not the three-dimensional of sphere, perhaps because he is explaining the two-dimensional game board. In Book II, Albert asks for the explanation of the mystical sense (*mystica sententia*) of the bowling-game.[42] The Cardinal answers that using his *oculus mentis* we can see that nothing is greater or lesser (*maius aut minus*) than that which is in all things.[43] This is the *maximum* and *minimum* exemplar of all things. There is only one exemplar that exists in every exemplification; he is in all things and all things are in him.[44] The same applies to numbers: each number is one number because the unit (*unitas*) is in it, and it is in the unit.

Cusanus identifies this exemplar with the notion of life (*vita*),[45] a concept that appears in the commentary on Definition II within the *Liber*.[46] According to the anonymous commentator, it is necessary that there be life in all things and that all things be in life. Life is thus the center that is in all places, never communicated or participated in a diminished way. This shows that even when Cusanus establishes degrees of contraction, there are no marginal or residual regions of life. Life is in all things and all things are in life, which is the principle, middle, and end of all things. This allows

---

[41] "Et postquam advertis dictum sapientis, qui aiebat deum circulum, cuius centrum est undique ... ita deus in omnibus." Nicholas of Cusa, *Dialogus de ludo globi*, II (84), in *Nicolai de Cusa Opera Omnia*, vol. IX, ed. Hans Gerhard Senger (Hamburg: Felix Meiner Verlag, 1998), 103–4; trans. Jasper Hopkins, *Nicholas of Cusa: Metaphysical Speculations* (Minneapolis: Arthur J. Banning Press, 1998), 1226.

[42] Nicholas of Cusa, *Dialogus de ludo globi*, II (61–62), ed. Senger, 73–75.

[43] Nicholas of Cusa, *Dialogus de ludo globi*, II (62), ed. Senger, 74–75.

[44] Nicholas of Cusa, *Dialogus de ludo globi*, II (63), ed. Senger, 75–76.

[45] Nicholas of Cusa, *Dialogus de ludo globi*, II (69–70), ed. Senger, 81–84.

[46] "Haec definitio data est per modum imaginandi ut continuum ipsam primam causam in vita sua." Hudry, *Liber viginti quattuor philosophorum*, 7.

us to address Sloterdijk's second objection regarding the dissolution of the meaning of Definition XVIII of the *Liber* in the work of Cusanus.

Definition XVIII in the *Maxima doctrina ignorantiae*

According to Sloterdijk, Nicholas of Cusa did not consider things in the world to be immanent to God. He affirms: "Through its bleak marginality, the world becomes impenetrable for the central God himself."[47] For this reason, according to Sloterdijk, all created things lose the immunity of the divine sphere's center in Cusan thought. It is true that Cusanus does not explicitly quote Definition XVIII from the *Liber*, the one that offers the image of the sphere projected all the way to the ambit of what is created, making a sphere of each thing in the universe.[48] Nevertheless, in *Sermones et lectiones super Ecclesiastici*, Meister Eckhart quotes not only Definition II but also Definition XVIII, establishing the relationship between the two systems of spheres. It is noteworthy that Nicholas of Cusa underlines this passage in Codex Cusanus 21.[49] I will briefly show the affinity between this Definition XVIII and Nicholas of Cusa's conception of the singular thing, which makes each being into a *deus occasionatus* or *sphaera occasionata*. In this way, as we shall see, Nicholas intensifies the strength of created things, confronting the former tradition.[50]

---

[47] Sloterdijk, *Spheres II: Globes*, 547.

[48] See Lucentini, *Il libro dei ventiquattro filosofi*, 131–32.

[49] "Rursus tertio in divinis 'quolibet est in quolibet' et maximum in minimo et sic fructus in flore. Ratio, quia 'deus' ut ait sapiens, 'est sphaera' intellectualis 'infinita, cuius centrum est ubique cum circumferentia,' et 'cuius tot sunt circumferentiae, quot puncta,' ut in eodem libro scribitur." Eckhart, *Lectio I super Ecclesiastici*, c. 24, 23, n. 20 (LW 2, 246–48). As can be noted, Eckhart refers to the sphere in Definition II not only as "infinite" but also as "intellectual" (*intellectualis*), no doubt because of the priority of the intellectual principle in Eckhart and, later, in Cusanus. And Eckhart also quotes Definition XVIII side by side with Definition II, in connection with cosmological formulations dear to Cusanus in his conception of the singular being: "quolibet est in quolibet" and "maximum in minimo." Finally, as already mentioned, Nicholas of Cusa marks this passage in his manuscript of the text (cf. MS Cod. Cus. 21, fol. 80r). On these points, see further: Mahnke, *Unendliche Sphäre und Allmittelpunkt*, 144, 172; Herbert Wackerzapp, *Der Einfluss Meister Eckharts auf die ersten philosophischen Schriften des Nikolaus von Kues (1440-1450)* (Münster: Aschendorff, 1962), 141–42; Donald F. Duclow, "Nicholas of Cusa in the Margins of Meister Eckhart: *Codex Cusanus 21*," in *Nicholas of Cusa in Search of God and Wisdom*, ed. Gerald Christianson and Thomas M. Izbicki (Leiden: Brill, 1991), 57–69; and Elizabeth Brient, "Transitions to a Modern Cosmology: Meister Eckhart and Nicholas of Cusa on the Intensive Infinite," *Journal of the History of Philosophy* 37, no. 4 (1999): 575–600.

[50] Brient draws a contrast between Eckhart and Nicholas of Cusa regarding singularity. See Brient, "Transitions to a Modern Cosmology," 593–97.

The *complicatio-explicatio* doctrine, which Nicholas of Cusa presents explicitly for the first time in Book II of *De docta ignorantia*, offers his way of understanding the relationship between the One and the Many. The *maximum* as *absolutum* is the absolute complication (*complicatio absoluta*) of all things, as all things are complicated in the absolute without alterity. From this perspective, all things have in God their *terminus*, *perfectio*, and *totalitas*, the three concepts that Cusanus uses to define his notion of *complicatio*.[51] However, each singular thing has not only an absolute quiddity, or absolute complication, but also a contracted quiddity, which expresses its identity in alterity. In this way, there is a quiddity that makes it one and a quiddity that makes it other in relation to other things.[52] Recall that for Cusanus the universe's unity is not transcendent but immanent in multiplicity, and it does not survive separated from all things, but is rather a contracted unity in multiplicity. What is explicated in the diversity of things is therefore the whole universe, as stated in the title of *De docta ignorantia*, II.5, *Quodlibet in quolibet*.

The difference between singular things, for Nicholas of Cusa, is not only quantitative but also qualitative. Every single thing is unique in its way of being, because what gets actualized in it are determinate potentialities of the universe—drawn from infinite possibilities—that are not actualized in any other. Socrates, for example, is not perfect as man, but is perfect as Socrates: he is the best possible Socrates. For this reason, each individual is perfect in its way of being.[53] This leads Cusanus to conceive the created being as a kind of finite infinity or "created god," in which there shines out, as in a mirror, the first mirror or perfect image that is the divine Word. From this perspective, each created being is a contracted image of the universe, which in its determination manifests or unfolds it (*explicatio*). Every single thing is unique in its expression of the universe, hence it is a *sphaera occasionata*.

Finally, let us consider the viewpoint of concentric circles in the way proposed by the game in *Dialogus de ludo globi*. The infinite sphere as *maximus mundus* or *negative infinitum* is thus the center and circumference of all things, because it is everywhere and nowhere. However, we can assert, based on Cusan cosmology, that the infinite sphere as *magnus mundus* or *privative infinitum*, in its condition as image, has its center everywhere,

---

51 Nicholas of Cusa, *De docta ignorantia*, II.3 (105), ed. Wilpert and Senger, 22–23.
52 Nicholas of Cusa, *De docta ignorantia*, II.4 (115), ed. Wilpert and Senger, 34–35.
53 Nicholas of Cusa, *De docta ignorantia*, II.2 (104), ed. Wilpert and Senger, 20–23.

and that center is every singular being. In this way each single thing in the universe is, at the same time, a center in a contracted sense. That is why Nicholas of Cusa affirms that the whole universe is modalized in every singular thing or *minus mundus*. And every singular being projects, as much as it is able to, its own circumference. Therefore, each thing is in its own way a sphere.[54]

In any case, it is clear that all of the circles deployed from the center of the game board have one and the same center: life or being. Each circle in its singularity expresses roundness in its own way. Roundness is identified with the circulation or movement of life. Therefore, roundness is in everything that is round, as its principle, in the same way that life is in all things alive.[55] But circles do not lose the singularity of their circumferences, which gives them their contracted identities.

Final Considerations

Peter Sloterdijk proposed a theory of spheres or spherology that enriches our understanding not only of our times but also of the history of Western metaphysics. However, we have briefly tried to show that Nicholas of Cusa, far from offering a *summa* of scholastic spherology, as Sloterdijk suggests,[56] in fact productively addressed the challenges brought about by the *Liber*'s definitions of the absolute sphere (Definition II) and contracted spheres (Definition XVIII) in his *maxima doctrina ignorantiae*. In this way, Cusanus offers a spherology that by recovering a plural tradition represents a prelude to the horizon of modern thought. I have shown how Cusanus transfers the infinite sphere image from the theological to the cosmological realm. Even if the cosmological use of the image is still theological and finds its basis in the consideration of the *maximum* as absolute, nonetheless from this notion Cusanus supports a cosmology with conjectures that might seem unusual to some, as he puts it.[57] Contra Sloterdijk, this Cusan

---

54 Nicholas of Cusa, *Dialogus de ludo globi*, II (82), ed. Senger, 100–102.
55 Nicholas of Cusa, *Dialogus de ludo globi*, II (69), ed. Senger, 81–83.
56 Sloterdijk, *Spheres II: Globes*, 533.
57 Nicholas of Cusa, *De docta ignorantia*, III. Ep. (264), ed. Wilpert and Senger, 100–101.

cosmology culminates in the modern conception of an infinite universe, as several scholars have shown.[58]

I have also shown how Cusanus transfers the image of the sphere not only from the maximum absolute to the maximum contracted, but also to every created being, making each one in effect a *sphaera occasionata* in itself. Hence, again contrary to Sloterdijk's interpretation, Nicholas of Cusa does relate the two systems of spheres to each other, in a way that the *Liber XXIV philosophorum* itself only juxtaposed. Cusanus repeatedly warns that the ultimate elucidation about the relationship between the One (*complicatio*) and the Many (*explicatio*) remains incomprehensible to a finite understanding,[59] "for [the world] will appear as a wheel in a wheel and a sphere in a sphere, having its center and circumference nowhere, as was stated."[60] Yet Nicholas of Cusa, guided by *docta ignorantia*, proposes a system of spheres that evidences a *continuum* of life: from the maximum absolute sphere to the maximum contracted sphere, and from this one to the innumerable contracted spheres that are, in their own way, in their singularity, each the center of the universe that is all in all.

---

58 See further: Manhke, *Unendliche Sphäre und Allmittelpunkt*, 76–100; Koyré, *From the Closed World to the Infinite Universe*, 6–8; Harries, "The Infinite Sphere," 5–15; Brient, "Transitions to a Modern Cosmology," 589–97; and Pietro Secchi, "Declinazioni della sfera in Niccolò Cusano," in Totaro and Valente, *Sphaera*, 245–59.

59 "Excedunt autem mentem nostram modus complicationis et explicationis." Nicholas of Cusa, *De docta ignorantia*, II.3 (109), ed. Wilpert and Senger, 26–27.

60 "quoniam apparebit quasi rota in rota et sphaera in sphaera nullibi habens centrum vel circumferentiam, ut praefertur." Nicholas of Cusa, *De docta ignorantia*, II.11 (161), ed. Wilpert and Senger, 92–93; trans. Hopkins, 92.

PART II
New Dialogues

7

Nicholas of Cusa's Contribution to the Final Phase of Kitaro Nishida's Philosophy

KAZUHIKO YAMAKI

The first Japanese scholar to mention Nicholas of Cusa's name was Hajime Onishi 大西祝 (1864–1900), who referred to the German philosopher in his book, *The Origin of Conscience* 良心起源論 (1896). In particular, Onishi referenced the Cusan distinction between reason (*ratio*) and the intellect (*intellectus*). It would be fifteen years later, in 1911, that Kitaro Nishida 西田幾多郎 (1870–1945) published *An Inquiry into the Good* 善の研究, his first book, in which he sought to elaborate his own thoughts of "pure experience." From this first work onward, Nishida maintained a great interest in Nicholas of Cusa, writing a number of articles in which he either mentioned Cusanus or utilized his writings to broaden his own thoughts (see Fig. 7-1).

By 1939, in his late philosophy, Nishida introduced a concept difficult to understand, "the absolutely contradictory self-identity" (*zettai mujunteki jiko douitu* 絶対矛盾的自己同一), in his treatise of the same name. This concept clearly shares elements in common with Nicholas of Cusa's *coincidentia oppositorum*, even though the name "Cusanus" does not appear in the treatise.[1] According to Nishida, the present world is seen as "the absolutely contradictory self-identity," so far as it exists. With this newly designed concept he tries to explain the fundamental structure both of the world and of our existence.

Nishida became further engaged in studying Cusanus from the end of 1942 onward. On March 2, 1944, he finished a new treatise, "Toward a Philosophy of Religion by Way of the Concept of Pre-established Harmony" (*Yotei-chowa wo Tebiki tosite Shukyo-Tetsugaku he* 予定調和を手引きとして宗教哲学へ). This late work can be outlined as follows. This world, which is grasped within the categories of time and space, is an aspect of "the self-determination of the absolute present" as God. Therefore, the world is structured in the manner of pre-established harmony. However, the concept of Nishida's "pre-established harmony" is not a hypothetical one, as in Leibniz, but a real one, in which every being (in the past, present, and future) is even now mirrored in absolute space or contained in the absolute present. From the standpoint of the "self-determination of the absolute present," the relation between God and man is the "absolutely contradictory self-identity." Therefore, there is no clear way for humanity to approach God. Such a way can be opened only by a deepened self-conscious act, in which the self becomes none other than the "absolutely contradictory self-identity." This situation is the fundamental standpoint of religion and is also the standpoint where a study of philosophy comes into existence.

In the process of finishing this treatise, Nishida achieved many remarkable developments in his thinking. In order to explain the ontological nature of "the absolutely contradictory self-identity" (*zettai mujunteki jiko douitu* 絶対矛盾的自己同一), he discovered a decisive conception of "self-determination of the absolute present" (*zettai genzai no jiko-gentei* 絶対現在の自己限定). This new concept of "self-determination of the absolute present" is a change in wording from "self-determination of eternal now" (*eien no ima no jiko-gentei* 永遠の今の自己限定) in the aforementioned treatise on "the

---

[1] According to Prof. Klaus Riesenhuber (Lecture, July 20, 2015, Sophia University, Tokyo), Prof. Torataro Shimomura—one of Nishida's former students who maintained a close connection with him until his death—claimed that Nishida found a hint for this concept in Nicholas of Cusa's notion of *coincidentia oppositorum*. On Nishida's relation to the Cusan concept, see also Michiko Yusa, "Nishida Kitarō and 'Coincidentia oppositorum': An Introduction," in *Cusanus-Rezeption in der Philosophie des 20. Jahrhunderts*, ed. Klaus Reinhardt and Harald Schwaetzer (Regensburg: S. Roderer-Verlag, 2005), 211–26.

Nicholas of Cusa's Contribution to Nishida's Philosophy

Figure 7-1. Kitaro Nishida in his study.

absolutely contradictory self-identity." Remarkably, Nishida made a pencil notation in the margin of his German translation of *De docta ignorantia*, I.21, as follows: "self-determination of the absolute present, March 1944" (*zettai genzai no jiko-gentei, Showa 19 nen 3 gatsu* 絶対現在の自己限定、昭和十九年三月).[2] In that chapter, Cusanus discusses the character of the center, the circumference, and the diameter of an infinite circle. That Nishida noted this with the date makes us think that he recognized this new concept in March 1944.

Nishida developed three meanings of the concept "self-determination of the absolute present." (1) The absolute present is none other than God. (2) The "present" (*genzai* 現在) of the absolute present means not only "to be happening now" in time, but also "to be in a particular place" in space,

---

2 See Nicholas of Cusa, *De docta ignorantia* I.21 (63–66), in *Nikolaus von Kues: Philosophisch-Theologische Werke*, vol. 1, ed. Paul Wilpert and Hans Gerhard Senger, rev. ed. (Hamburg: Felix Meiner Verlag, 2002), 84–89. Nishida possessed only those works of Cusanus that were included, in German translation, in this volume: Franz Anton von Scharpff, *Des Cardinals und Bischofs Nicolaus von Cusa wichtigste Schriften in deutscher Übersetzung* (Freiburg in Breisgau: Herder, 1862).

just as in English. While usually *genzai* is a Japanese word for the present moment with no intimation of space, it is also possible to construe *genzai* as "to be in a particular place." Nishida's idea seems to be inspired by the concept of the *allgegenwärtig* in Dietrich Mahnke's important book, *Unendliche Sphäre und Allmittelpunkt* (1937).[3] (3) Furthermore, it becomes possible for Nishida to conceive the "absolutely contradictory self-identity" of time and space. This conception appeared in his treatise for the first time.[4]

As witnessed by the paragraphs that Nishida discovered in Cusanus and Mahnke, the Japanese philosopher had a great interest in the concept of an infinite globe. He wrote in the margin of *De docta ignorantia*, I.23 (page 25, in his German translation), the Latin word "*Sphera infinita*" (correctly, *sphaera infinita*) with the same pencil and in handwriting similar to his marginal comment noted above ("self-determination of the absolute present, March 1944"). That chapter in *De docta ignorantia* is entitled: "The likening of an infinite sphere to the actual existence of God" (*Transumptio sphaerae infinitae ad actualem exsistentiam Dei*).[5]

---

[3] See Dietrich Mahnke, *Unendliche Sphäre und Allmittelpunkt: Beiträge zur Genealogie der mathematischen Mystik* (Halle: Max Niemeyer Verlag, 1937). Nishida excerpted the following passage from Mahnke in his notebook, with a reference to *De docta ignorantia*: "'jener "unendliche Grenzpunkt", der als solcher dem transfiniten Jenseits zugehört, sei doch zugleich der allgegenwärtige "Mittelpunkt aller Kreise" des indefiniten Diesseits mit ihren ins Unendliche wachsenden Umfängen' (*Docta ignorantia* III 4/5, 7/8) Mahnke op. cit. S. 105).'' Quoted in Nishida Kitaro, *Nishida Kitaro Zenshu* 西田幾多郎全集 [The complete works of Nishida Kitaro] (Tokyo: Iwanami Shoten, 2002–2009), 16:306.

[4] Nishida, *Nishida Kitaro Zenshu*, 10:92. Nicholas of Cusa's *coincidentia oppositorum* does not contain the meaning of the "absolutely contradictory self-identity" of time and space.

[5] See Nicholas of Cusa, *De docta ignorantia* I.23 (70–73), ed. Wilpert and Senger, 92–97. As Mahnke's study shows, the image of the infinite sphere has a long history in European thought. See, e.g., Plotinus, *Enneads* IV.3.17: "All souls then illuminate the heaven and give it the greatest and first part of themselves, but illuminate the rest of the world with their secondary parts; those which come down further throw their light lower, but it is not to their advantage to have gone on so far. For there is a kind of center, and around this a circle shining out from it, and beyond these another, light from light: but outside these there is no longer another circle of light but this next circle through lack of its own light needs illumination from another source. Let this be a wheel, or rather a sphere of a kind which from the third—for it borders upon it—obtains all the illumination which that third receives." Plotinus, *Ennead IV*, trans. A. H. Armstrong, Loeb Classical Library 443 (Cambridge, MA: Harvard University Press, 1984), 89. According to Wackerzapp, Cusanus borrows this image from Meister Eckhart, though he also alludes to *Liber XXIV philosophorum*, Definition II. See Herbert Wackerzapp, *Der Einfluss Meister Eckharts auf die ersten philosophischen Schriften des Nikolaus von Kues (1440–1450)* (Münster: Aschendorff Verlag, 1962), 143.

This attention to the infinite sphere also played a decisive role in Nishida's last treatise. By then he had become dissatisfied with Leibniz's monad,[6] although in August 1941 he had written to his pupil, Torataro Shimomura: "I think that my thought probably has many points in common with Leibniz's thought."[7] Nishida was dissatisfied with Leibniz's concept of monad because it lacks the viewpoint of the embracing space or "place," which embraces monads in itself and has a mutual relation with monads.[8] Because of his critique of Leibniz's monad, Nishida had to develop a new symbolic method to explain his ontology, which has the structure of "the absolutely contradictory self-identity" as the "self-determination of the absolute present." Nishida's final and quite long treatise, entitled "The Logic of Place and the Religious Worldview" (*Bashoteki Ronri to Shukyoteki Sekaikan* 場所的論理と宗教的世界観), was finished on May 10, 1945, about one month before his death.[9]

First, I will try to explain the meaning of "the logic of place." According to Nishida, true comprehension does not occur in a construction in which a subject cognizes an object, as in the cognitive theory of Immanuel Kant. Rather, it is a process by which a subject grasps an object in its own inside, or a subject reflects the object within its own inside. Nishida regards the subject, as it embraces or reflects the object within its own inside during comprehension, as a kind of place where the object is mirrored. In relation to this image of the process of cognition, Leibniz's theory of the monad had seemed very convenient for Nishida until just before he finished "Toward a Philosophy of Religion by Way of the Concept of Pre-established Harmony" in 1944.

At the same time, the concept of place was also important for Nishida to adequately explain the character of reflection as cognition. His characteristic expression "the logic of place" (場所的論理) means the structure in which every being comes into existence from place, which is a kind of

---

[6] On March 3, 1944, when he was writing the treatise, he wrote to another pupil, Goichi Miyake, as follows: "Now I am writing a little treatise, which a little takes up Leibniz's thought 'Pre-established Harmony.' I think Leibniz did not deeply consider space." Nishida, *Nishida Kitaro Zenshu*, 23:194, no. 4038.

[7] Nishida, *Nishida Kitaro Zenshu*, 22:431, no. 3483.

[8] Nishida, "Toward a Philosophy of Religion By Way of the Concept of Pre-established Harmony," in *Nishida Kitaro Zenshu*, 10:103.

[9] See Nishida's diary: Nishida, *Nishida Kitaro Zenshu*, 18:421.

matrix of every being.[10] Because this place is the matrix of every being, it must be so infinitely great that it embraces every being within itself and reflects every being in itself. But according to his thinking-principle of "the absolutely contradictory self-identity," Nishida at the same time regards the matrix as "the place of absolute nothingness," because he did not wish to substantialize place. Instead, he considers it to be the most fundamental reality and thinks that it is grounded in absolutely deep existential self, by virtue of the principle of "the absolutely contradictory self-identity."[11]

To show how Nishida applies Nicholas of Cusa's viewpoints in his thought, let us consider at length a typical paragraph of Nishida's thinking from his final treatise:

> Our "self" [*jiko* 自己] is nothing other than one focus of the world, where the world reflects itself in itself. Our self-consciousness does not take place in a merely closed-up self. It takes place only when the self transcends itself and faces others. Therefore, when we are self-conscious, we are already self-transcending. Man, who substantializes the self through some dogmatism based on objective logic, cannot accept this evident truth.... In the world of "absolutely contradictory identity," every one of many single beings is a focus and has in its manner a character of the world in itself. The situation is similar to one in the monadology [of Leibniz], where every single monad represents the world in itself and becomes a place where the world represents itself.... The world as "a self-determination of the absolute present" has foci in itself in a manner of "the absolutely contradictory self-identity." In the dynamic foci as centers [of the infinitely large sphere as the world] the world forms itself and has its own order. Conversely, individuals in this world are particular foci, and so represent the world in ourselves. On the other hand, we have our own orientation toward the foci of the world to be in accordance with the orientation of foci

---

[10] Nishida writes as follows in the final sentences of his last article, entitled "Concerning My Logic" 私の論理について (1945): "Logic is the discursive form of our thinking. And we will only be able to clarify what logic is by reflecting on the form of our own thinking." Nishida Kitaro, *Last Writings: Nothingness and the Religious Worldview*, trans. David A. Dilworth (Honolulu: University of Hawaii Press, 1987), 126.

[11] See Kunitsugu Kosaka, *Nishida-tetsugaku no Kisoh* 西田哲学の基層 [The basic layers of Nishida's philosophy] (Tokyo: Iwanami Shoten, 2011), 111–12.

of the self-forming world.¹² This situation gives a moral order to the world. That we as individual foci of the world determine ourselves to represent ourselves in the world does not mean that we regard ourselves as necessary beings in the sense of objective logic. Rather it means that we become the individual centers that enfold the eternal past and the eternal future within ourselves. Therefore, I call our individual selves "the self-determination of the absolute present." So our individual selves are self-contradictory. They individually reflect the world in themselves, and at the same time hold themselves in absolutely other being.... Consequently, the world of the absolute present, as an infinite sphere, has no circumference, and every point within it acts as a center [reflecting other points and the sphere itself, which embraces all points].... The world [of absolute present] is no subjective world.... The world, which is regarded as a physical world, must rather be regarded as an aspect of the human historical world, which is none other than "the absolutely contradictory self-identity."¹³

One should observe several points in this lengthy quotation. Not only every individual being but also the world as a whole is a self-determination of "the absolute present" as God. As "the self-determination of the absolute present," each being, on the one hand, has its own character; on the other hand, it is a form of the self-expression of the world. In this sense, our self-consciousness takes place not in a closed-up self, but only when the self transcends itself and faces others by opening itself to others.

To explain the recurring structure of "the self-determination of the absolute present" in the world, Nishida applies Leibniz's *Monadology*, which says that each simple substance is a perpetual living mirror of the universe, but he also, in symbolic manner, applies a modern theory of the concave mirror, a kind of spherical mirror. According to the theory, a concave mirror reflects light inward until it converges on its one focal point (see Fig. 7-2). With the metaphor of reflection, Nishida further deepens his contemplation of the fundamental structure of the universe as "the self-determination of the absolute present." If a concave mirror as a perfect sphere were infinitely large, then it would have an infinite number of focal points in itself. Then

---

12 This notion invokes Nishida's concept of "pre-established harmony."
13 Nishida, *Nishida Kitaro Zenshu*, 10:299–301 (translation is my own).

every point inside the mirror would be a focal point, and in an infinitely large sphere the light coming from the sphere as it embraced itself would converge at every such focus. Nishida thinks that the whole structure of this contemplation on the infinitely large sphere and on the foci should be capable of being symbolically applied to his ontology of "the self-determination of the absolute present."

Nishida's conception of an infinitely large concave mirror may also be

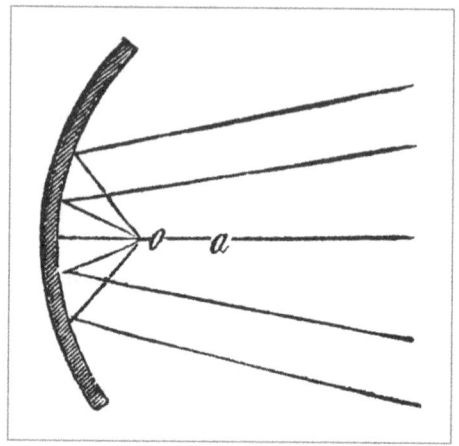

Figure 7-2. A concave mirror reflecting light toward its focal point.

influenced by the Buddhist notion of *adarsa-jnana* (in Japanese, *daien-kyo-chi* 大円鏡智), which means the great perfect mirror wisdom, or wisdom clearly elucidating all things. Nicholas of Cusa also compares God to a mirror on several occasions. In *De dato patris luminum*, Nicholas states: "There is only one Mirror without flaw, viz., God Himself, in whom [what is received] is received as it is. For it is not the case that this Mirror is other than any existing thing; rather, in every existing thing, it is that which is, for it is the Universal Form of being."[14] Later in *De visione Dei*, he writes:

> Since Your sight *is* an eye, i.e., a living mirror, it sees within itself all things. Indeed, because it is the Cause of all visible things, it embraces

---

[14] Nicholas of Cusa, *De dato patris luminum*, II (99), in *Nicolai de Cusa Opera Omnia*, vol. IV, ed. Paul Wilpert (Hamburg: Felix Meiner, 1959), 74; trans. Jasper Hopkins, *Nicholas of Cusa's Metaphysic of Contraction* (Minneapolis: Arthur J. Banning Press, 1983), 376–77.

> and sees all things in the Cause and Rational Principle of all things, viz., in itself. Your eye, O Lord, proceeds to all things without turning. The reason our eye turns toward an object is that our sight sees from an angle of a certain magnitude. But the angle of Your eye, O God, is not of a certain magnitude but is infinite. Moreover, the angle of Your eye is a circle—or better, an infinite sphere—because Your sight is an eye of sphericity and of infinite perfection. Therefore, Your sight sees—roundabout and above and below—all things at once.[15]

Note how this description of God as a living, infinite, and spherical mirror unites both aspects in itself, the infinite sphere and the mirror.

It is clear that this symbolic conception of the "infinitely large sphere" (*sphaera infinita*) played a decisive role in inspiring Nishida's notion of the universe as "the self-determination of the absolute present." As I proposed above, we can trace both concepts back to Nishida's marginal notes in *De docta ignorantia*. Nishida himself makes this connection to Cusanus: "A man, who likened God to an infinite sphere in medieval philosophy, said that in the infinite sphere each point is the center. This is precisely my own concept of 'the self-determination of the absolute present.'"[16] We can be certain that this "man" means Nicholas of Cusa, given how highly Nishida esteemed the German philosopher. Nishida continues: "he [Nicholas] uses a metaphor of a so-called infinite sphere to express God.... The philosophy of '*coincidentia oppositorum*' of Cusanus is able to be best described by my 'logic of place' [場所的論理]."[17]

Yet we must not overlook Nishida's own inventive thinking about the ubiquitous centers of the infinitely large sphere. Cusanus imagines the center of the infinite sphere simply as the center, and Mahnke discusses in detail the medieval symbolism of both the infinite circle and the infinite sphere. Yet neither Cusanus nor Mahnke uses the term "focus" or "focal point." On account of his knowledge of the modern theory of concave mirrors, Nishida was able to introduce the concept "focal point" into his

---

15 Nicholas of Cusa, *De visione Dei*, VIII (30), in *Nicolai de Cusa Opera Omnia*, vol. VI, ed. Heide Dorothea Riemann (Hamburg: Felix Meiner Verlag, 2000), 30–31; trans. Jasper Hopkins, *Nicholas of Cusa's Dialectical Mysticism: Text, Translation, and Interpretive Study of "De Visione Dei"*, 2nd ed. (Minneapolis: Arthur J. Banning Press, 1988), 694–95.

16 See Nishida, "Toward a Philosophy of Religion By Way of the Concept of Pre-established Harmony," in *Nishida Kitaro Zenshu*, 10:335.

17 Ibid.

explanation of "the self-determination of the absolute present." From this viewpoint he could better explain not only the dynamic relation between each being as a focus and the world as an infinitely large concave mirror, but also the dynamism of the individual being as a particular focus, which at the same time has an individual capacity to represent itself.

Nishida sought to elaborate the whole structure of the universe with his symbolic illustration of reflection. The infinitely large sphere has its own light and it converges on its infinite number of foci within the sphere, so that its infinitely many foci appear; quite similarly, the absolute present determines itself to produce infinitely many individual beings. And each focus, on which the whole light of the infinitely large sphere converges, conversely reflects—or rather radiates—that same light, not only to all of the other foci in the sphere, but also to the sphere itself. Yet each being represents its own character not only to each other, but also to that absolute present that is the place or matrix embracing all beings.

We should not overlook another important point on God as "the infinitely large sphere." According to Nishida's concept of "the absolutely contradictory identity," the absolute present as infinitely large sphere must at the same time be regarded as absolute nothingness. For, according to Nishida, God as the absolute present stands as its own absolute self-negation, or as possessing absolute self-negation.[18] Note how "the absolutely contradictory identity" appears symbolically here: on the one hand, the absolute present seems to be substantial, as a kind of place or matrix, from whence every being comes into existence; on the other hand, it is not substantial, because it functions only as a kind of mirror to reflect the radiation of each being as focus.

Here Nishida's philosophy of religion reaches its culmination. He writes:

> It is because of the divine coincidence of absolute nothingness and absolute being that we can say that God can do and know everything, and can speak of the divine omniscience and omnipotence. Therefore, I say that because there is Buddha, there are sentient beings,

---

[18] Nishida, *Nishida Kitaro Zenshu*, 10:316. Nishida's mode of describing God reminds us of Nicholas of Cusa's way of discussing the existence of God in *De coniecturis* I.5 (21), in *Nicolai de Cusa Opera Omnia*, vol. III, ed. Karl Bormann and Hans Gerhard Senger (Hamburg: Felix Meiner Verlag, 1972), 27–28: "Non poterit enim infinitius responderi 'an deus sit' quam quod ipse nec est nec non est, atque quod ipse nec est et non est."

and because there are sentient beings, there is Buddha. Or, [in Christian terms] because there is God as the creator, there is the world of creatures, because there is the world of creatures, there is God as the creator.[19]

Throughout his life, Kitaro Nishida continued to contemplate the deep and wide domain of beings and attempted to grasp it and explain it with words. It seems to me that he accomplished his purpose with help from Leibniz and Nicholas of Cusa. In particular, he fully absorbed Cusanus's conception of the infinitely large sphere, and constructed an elaborate metaphor from it that ended up playing a decisive role in the unfolding of his own concept, "the self-determination of the absolute present."

---

[19] Nishida, *Nishida Kitaro Zenshu*, 10:316; in idem, *Last Writings*, trans. Dilworth, 69 (modified).

8

Maurice de Gandillac's Reading of Nicholas of Cusa and Its Transmission to Gilles Deleuze

ALEXIA SCHMITT

Maurice de Gandillac (1906–2006) was initiated into the study of medieval philosophy by his professor, Étienne Gilson, and through him came to know the writings of Nicholas of Cusa.[1] In 1931, Alexandre Koyré introduced Gandillac to Raymond Klibansky, who together with Ernst Hoffmann had undertaken the publication of the complete works of Cusanus under the patronage of Heidelberg University. By November 1934, Gandillac had traveled to Bernkastel-Kues and visited the St. Nikolaus-Hospital, a visit he recalled many years later with great emotion in his memoirs, *Le siècle traversé*.[2] After six months in Berlin, he returned to Paris and presented his first study: "Nicholas of Cusa, Precursor of the Cartesian Method?", a contribution to

---

1 See Jean Jolivet, "Situation de l'histoire de la philosophie médiévale en France," *Cahiers de civilisation médiévale* 39, nos. 153–54 (1996): 90.
2 See Maurice de Gandillac, *Le siècle traversé: Souvenirs de neuf décennies* (Paris: Albin Michel, 1998), especially chapter 5.

the Descartes Congress of 1937, which he presented while just starting his thesis.³ At that Congress, Gandillac not only highlighted three aspects of Cusan thought that he found similar to the Cartesian method but also warned of the differences between them: for Cusanus, unlike Descartes, the precision of truth exceeds all human effort.⁴

Gandillac Encounters Cusanus: A Historical Survey

In a late essay published in 1999, Gandillac referred again to this first work dedicated to Cusanus. There he repeated his claim that there are three characteristics of Cusan thought that resemble the Cartesian method. He writes: "Preparing then a thesis on this German of the fifteenth century, often misunderstood or marginalized, and following Cassirer, . . . I highlighted three features of his doctrine, where it seemed more legitimate to see some kinship with the Cartesian method." The first feature is "the Layman who does not need secret initiation." The second is "the privilege of mathematics." The third is the Layman placed "in a privileged position, because he is capable . . . of creating all arts."⁵ Gandillac's words allow us to reconstruct his intellectual path toward Cusanus:

> About this elusive Descartes, my professor Étienne Gilson showed me all he owed to Scholasticism . . . as taught to him by the fathers of La Flèche. . . . It was while reading Bruno, and not only Cassirer, that I had discovered his "*divino Cusanus*," this "Cusa" that Descartes quotes, I believe, just one time, but to rightly recall, this German cardinal dared to profess the infinity of the world in the fifteenth century, without 'being accepted by the Church.'"⁶

---

3 See Maurice de Gandillac, "Nicolas de Cues, précurseur de la Méthode cartésienne," in *Travaux du IXe Congrès international de philosophie, Congrès Descartes*, vol. 5, ed. Raymond Bayer (Paris: Hermann et cie, 1937), 127–33.

4 See Maurice de Gandillac, *Oeuvres choisies de Nicolas de Cues* (Paris: Aubier-Montaigne, 1942), 27.

5 Maurice de Gandillac, "Du Cusain à Descartes," *Enrahonar: An International Journal of Theoretical and Practical Reason* [Special issue] (1999): 359–60.

6 Gandillac, "Du Cusain à Descartes," 362: "Ce Descartes insaisissable, mon maître Étienne Gilson a bien montré tout ce qu'il devait à la scolastique . . . que lui enseignèrent les pères de La Flèche. . . . C'est en lisant Bruno, et non pas seulement Cassirer, que j'avais découvert son 'divino Cusano,' ce 'Cusa' que Descartes ne cite, je crois, qu'une fois, mais pour rappeler à

In 1939, Gandillac wrote the first chapters of his thesis, which was directed by Emile Bréhier, and in January 1942 he defended it. To highlight only one of its main ideas, Cusanus is presented as a precursor of Hegelian dialectic.[7] After its publication, Gandillac's interest in Cusanus never decreased, but on the contrary accompanied him throughout his life.[8]

The year after finishing his thesis, he published a selection of works by Cusanus, a volume that became decisive for the diffusion of Cusan thought into Gilles Deleuze's philosophy, as we shall see. Gandillac's anthology includes the three complete *Idiota* dialogues and extracts from the majority of his works, including fragments of some sermons and letters.[9] In this way Gandillac sought to offer a pathway through the works of Cusanus that was as complete as possible and highlighted the diversity of the cardinal's interests. One can appreciate the importance of this work for the dissemination of Cusan thought, especially when we recall that the Heidelberg critical edition was still in preparation.

In order to present Nicholas of Cusa's philosophy, Gandillac wrote an introduction to the anthology that provides an overview of the main currents that nourished the cardinal's thinking, including Pythagoreanism, Platonism, Aristotelianism, and Neoplatonism, highlighting the influence not only of Pseudo-Dionysius, but also of Augustine of Hippo, John Scottus Eriugena, and Meister Eckhart, among others.[10] After this general outline of his sources, Gandillac introduces Cusanus's philosophy itself, warning that the cardinal's intention, more than teaching the truth from the outside, is to "help the spirit to rediscover the truth in himself."[11] "In order to receive this message, which is offered to the simple man rather than to the

---

bon droit que ce cardinal allemand, sans 'être repris par l'Église,' osa professer, au XVe siècle l'infinité du monde."

7 See Gandillac, *Oeuvres choisies de Nicolas de Cues*, 31. See also Jean-Marie Nicolle, "Hommage à Maurice de Gandillac," in *Die Sermones des Nikolaus von Kues. Merkmale und ihre Stellung innerhalb der mittelalterlichen Predigtkultur*, MFCG 30, ed. Klaus Kremer and Klaus Reinhardt (Trier: Paulinus Verlag, 2005), xxix–xxxiii.

8 See Maurice de Gandillac, *La philosophie de Nicolas de Cues* (Paris: Aubier, 1941).

9 These include: *De concordantia catholica, De docta ignorantia, De coniecturis, De filiatione Dei, De quaerendo Deum, Apologia doctae ignorantiae, Coniectura de ultimis diebus, De visione Dei, De pace fidei, De theologicis complementis, De beryllo, Dialogus de ludo globi, Compendium, De venatione sapientiae,* and *Cribatio Alkorani.*

10 See Gandillac, *Oeuvres choisies de Nicolas de Cues*, 18–25.

11 Gandillac, *Oeuvres choisies de Nicolas de Cues*, 26: "aider l'esprit à redécouvrir la vérité en soi."

learned," writes Gandillac, "it is enough to reflect on the very nature of the knowing mind.... The sign of truth is not for [Cusanus] a 'given' perfection at the summit of a scale of diminishing imperfections, but rather the subtle presence in the finite itself of an invisible fire that by means of *ever truer* conjectures and *less inadequate* images feeds on new sources."[12]

Between 1942 and 1943, Gandillac began to delve into two important sources for Cusan thought: Meister Eckhart and Pseudo-Dionysius. During these years he wrote two major articles in *Dictionary of Spirituality*, not only on Nicholas of Cusa,[13] but also on Pseudo-Dionysius, in which he traced the Areopagite's influence upon the cardinal.[14] In a lecture in Bernkastel-Kues on August 11, 1964, Gandillac emphasized Cusanus's intention to achieve peace, not only from the theoretical foundations of his thought, but also in his political-ecclesiological tasks.[15] A few years later, in a brief but interesting essay from 1967, the Sorbonne professor points out some affinities between the interpretation of Aristotle in *De venatione sapientiae* and the new interpretation offered by his friend and student, Pierre Aubenque, in the latter's book, *The Problem of Being in Aristotle*.[16]

In 1973, Gandillac published the volume dedicated to the Renaissance in the Pléiade encyclopedia for the history of philosophy and began it with a chapter on Nicholas of Cusa. As in his earlier work, Gandillac highlights the presence of the infinite in human being through our vocation as microcosm.[17] In this work he returns to another topic frequently addressed ever

---

12 Gandillac, *Oeuvres choisies de Nicolas de Cues*, 25, 28: "Pour recevoir ce message qui est offert aux simples, plus encore qu'aux doctes, il suffit de réfléchir à la nature même de l'esprit connaissant.... Le signe de la vérité, ce n'est point pour lui une perfection 'donnée' au sommet d'une échelle d'imperfections décroissantes, mais bien la présence subtile dans le fini lui-même, à travers les conjectures *toujours plus vraies* et les images *moins inadéquates*, d'un feu invisible qui se nourrit des foyers nouveaux."

13 See Maurice de Gandillac, "Nicolas de Cues," in *Dictionnaire de spiritualité: Ascétique et mystique, doctrine et histoire* (Paris: Beauchesne, 1942), 11:262–69.

14 See Maurice de Gandillac, "Denys l'Aréopagite," in *Dictionnaire de spiritualité*, 3:375–78.

15 See Maurice de Gandillac, "El problema de la comprensión entre los pueblos según los principios teóricos y las sugerencias de orden práctico del Cardenal Nicolás de Cusa," *Folia humanistica* 2, no. 23 (November 1964): 939–52.

16 See Maurice de Gandillac, "Die aristotelische erste Philosophie nach *De venatione sapientiae*," in MFCG 6, ed. Rudolf Haubst (Mainz: Matthias-Grünewald-Verlag, 1968), 30–34; and Pierre Aubenque, *Le problème de l'être chez Aristote* (Paris: Presses Universitaires de France, 1962).

17 See Maurice de Gandillac, "Nicolás de Cusa," in idem, *Historia de la filosofía*, vol. 5, *La filosofía del Renacimiento* (Mexico City: Siglo XXI Editores, 2006), 37.

since his first article on Cusanus: the aspects of Cusan thought that modern thinkers such as Cassirer found to be close to their own philosophical conceptions.[18] Gandillac ends by highlighting a central theme of Nicholas of Cusa's philosophy, which he calls "the harmonic and progressive globality, where singularity and difference retain their own value."[19]

Nor should we neglect the Cusan dialectic, he adds, for in different ways it presaged that of Hegel.[20] Later that same year, Gandillac raised similar questions at his opening remarks at the Cusanus Symposium in Trier. To what extent did Cusanus and Hegel share one and the same Platonic tradition? Is Cusanus a precursor of the Hegelian dialectic? Regarding the first question, Gandillac answers that Cusanus knew the *Timaeus* translation by Calcidius quite well, but that he considers works to belong to the Platonic tradition that even in a broad sense could be taken as such—for example, the *Corpus Areopagiticum*, the *Commentary on Parmenides* by Proclus, or the *Elements* in the translation of William of Moerbeke, among others.[21] On the second point, while Hegel seeks to understand a progressive development of consciousness through a series of dialectical opposites, according to Nicholas no finite mind can capture or pronounce the absolute truth without the mediation of images, whether more or less adequate.[22]

The following year, Gandillac gave a paper at a colloquium of the Centre d'études supérieures de la Renaissance, an essay that would be republished with others under the title *Genesis of Modernity*. Attending to the conference theme, "Plato and Aristotle in the Renaissance," he explored the meaning of Platonism and Aristotelianism in Cusanus. Plato discerns that God governs the whole universe; but Aristotle makes a fair criticism regarding the separate forms, describing the intellect as a producer of

---

18 Here the *Idiota* dialogues particularly stand out. See Gandillac, "Nicolás de Cusa," in *Historia de la filosofía*, 5:39.

19 Gandillac, "Nicolás de Cusa," in *Historia de la filosofía*, 5:44: "El tema que nos parece central es el de la globalidad armónica y progresiva, en donde la singularidad y la diferencia conservan su propio valor."

20 Gandillac, "Nicolás de Cusa," in *Historia de la filosofía*, 5:44.

21 Cf. Maurice de Gandillac, "Nikolaus von Kues zwischen Platon und Hegel," in *Nikolaus von Kues in der Geschichte des Erkenntnisproblems. Akten des Symposions in Trier vom 18. bis 20. Oktober 1973*, MFCG 11, ed. Rudolf Haubst (Mainz: Matthias-Grünewald-Verlag, 1975), 25–26.

22 Gandillac, "Nikolaus von Kues zwischen Platon und Hegel," 26–27. See also Werner Beierwaltes, "Identidad y diferencia como principio del pensamiento Cusano," in *Cusanus: Reflexión metafísica y espiritualidad*, trans. Joaquín Alberto Ciria Cosculluela (Pamplona: Ediciones Universidad de Navarra, S.A., 2005), 168–69.

concepts and implicitly recognizing the existence of a higher principle.[23] Gandillac concludes that when we take into account the prominence of Pseudo-Dionysius, we discover in Cusanus ultimately the primacy of Plato, reaching toward the speculative philosophy attached to theological wisdom, but remembering that signs remain intrinsically conjectural.[24]

The works of Gandillac that we have reviewed evince not only a solid knowledge of Cusanus's multifaceted writings, but also a movement in two directions. On the one hand, Gandillac attempts to identify and then deepen the cardinal's ancient and medieval sources, enabling a better understanding of them; on the other hand, by locating Cusan doctrines in relation to Renaissance and early modern thought, Gandillac considers the extent to which Cusanus can be viewed as their predecesor.

Two Perspectives on Gandillac's Interpretation

In his influential study, *The Method of Cusanus's Philosophy* (1969), Klaus Jacobi dedicates a section to a comparison of Koch's and Gandillac's readings of Cusanus, entitled "Cusanus and Neoplatonism."[25] Koch traces the Cusan metaphysics of unity historically from Proclus and Pseudo-Dionysius: "the metaphysics of unity is not metaphysics from below, as the metaphysics of being, but it is metaphysics from above: ... it starts from the absolute unity as the first given and descends from there to understand the world."[26] Likewise, Gandillac views Proclus as the main source of Cusanus's philosophy. Both Koch and Gandillac emphasize the fundamental difference between Cusan philosophy and the Scholastic theory of analogy.[27] However, according to Jacobi, Gandillac focuses on a particular aspect of this issue: "According to Koch, Cusanus must reject the theory of analogy, because this is a manifestation of the metaphysics of being. ... Gandillac shows how closely the Cusan metaphysical project is linked to Cusanus's

---

23 See Maurice de Gandillac, *Gêneses da modernidade* (São Paulo: Editora 34, 1995), 199.

24 Gandillac, *Gêneses da modernidade*, 199.

25 See Klaus Jacobi, *Die Methode der cusanischen Philosophie* (Freiburg: Karl Alber Verlag, 1969), 66.

26 Jacobi, *Die Methode der cusanischen Philosophie*, 66: "... die Einheitsmetaphysik ist nicht, wie die Seinsmetaphysik, Metaphysik von unten, sondern Metaphysik von oben: ... sie geht von der absoluten Einheit als dem Erstgegebenen aus und steigt von da zum Verständnis der Welt herab."

27 See Jacobi, *Die Methode der cusanischen Philosophie*, 68.

critical reflection on the human itself and the condition of the possibility of his knowledge of truth. This critical reflection sharpens the claim to methodological rigor, a claim for which the method of analogical knowledge no longer suffices. In its place he [Cusanus] substitutes a method of the Trinitarian dialectic of thesis, antithesis, and synthesis."[28]

More recently, Hubert Benz has commented in *Individuality and Subjectivity* (1999) on Gandillac's interpretation of Cusanus.[29] Benz quotes the following text from the German edition of Gandillac's thesis, which discusses how the Cusan philosophy leads to the threshold of Cartesianism: "The essence of Cusanus's revolution is limited to the critical analysis of human thought, . . . [and] to the consciousness of man's sovereignty."[30] However, Gandillac also notes that "at the inner core of the knowledge process you will find . . . the primordial darkness of the coincidence of opposites."[31] Therefore, according to Benz, Cusanus does not propose a closed construction of knowledge, but all the elements of his philosophizing should be understood only "as moments of a universal method."[32] Both Jacobi and Benz underscore the same aspect of Gandillac's reading of Cusanus: that Nicholas establishes a structural link between the difference in the cosmos and the Creator's unity on the grounds of a method more rigorous than the *analogia entis*. On this view, the cardinal is proposing that, instead of a system of transcendent substance, "the immanence of the

---

28 Jacobi, *Die Methode der cusanischen Philosophie*, 68: "Nach Koch muss Cusanus die Analogielehre ablehnen, weil diese eine Ausprägung der Seinsmetaphysik. . . . Gandillac zeigt, wie eng der cusanische metaphysische Entwurf mit der von Cusanus durchgeführten kritischen Reflexion des Menschen auf sich selbst und die Bedingung der Möglichkeit seiner Wahrheitserkenntnis verknüpft ist. Diese kritische Reflexion schärft den Anspruch auf methodische Strenge, einen Anspruch, dem die Methode der analogischen Erkenntnis nicht mehr genüge. An deren Stelle trete eine Methode der dreiheitlichen Dialektik von Thesis, Antithesis und Synthesis."
29 See Hubert Benz, *Individualität und Subjektivität: Interpretationstendenzen in der Cusanus-Forschung und das Selbstverständnis des Nikolaus von Kues* (Münster: Aschendorff Verlag, 1999), 57–60.
30 Benz, *Individualität und Subjektivität*, 57: "Das Wesentliche der cusanischen Revolution beschränkt sich auf die kritische Analyse des menschlichen Denkens, . . . auf die Bewusstwerdung der Souveränität des Menschen . . . ."
31 Benz, *Individualität und Subjektivität*, 58: ". . . im innersten Kern des Erkenntnisvorganges wird man . . . die Urdunkelheit des Zusammenfalls der Gegensätze . . . finden."
32 Benz, *Individualität und Subjektivität*, 58.

infinite is revealed in the synthetic act of the mind."[33] Indeed, the hypothetical infinity of the *ars oppositorum* is only a methodological artifice: it is not a type of substance, according to Benz, but a truly infinite synthetic capacity for the realization of consciousness.[34]

Gandillac and the Diffusion of Cusan Thought to Deleuze

Jean-Michel Counet has observed that, despite few explicit allusions to Nicholas of Cusa in Gilles Deleuze's works, there are surprising convergences between both thinkers on at least four themes.[35] Counet concludes that Deleuze finds in Cusanus's works a deep source of inspiration, adding that such convergences "are obviously not a product of chance. Deleuze knows this author probably through Maurice de Gandillac."[36] Without pretending to exhaust an issue so complex as the assimilation of one thinker by another—especially one as rich as Cusanus and idiosyncratic as Deleuze—I will examine three aspects of Deleuze's conception of philosophy that coincide with Nicholas of Cusa's ideas. Moreover, I suggest that each aspect was highlighted in Gandillac's own interpretation of Cusanus, making all the more plausible the hypothesis that Deleuze absorbed the thought of Nicholas of Cusa through his thesis director, Maurice de Gandillac.

Philosophy as Creation of Concepts

For Deleuze, philosophy is an activity that creates concepts.[37] José González Ríos recalls the fragment of *Dialogues* (1977) in which Deleuze narrates his initiation to philosophy.[38] Deleuze says he was first captured

---

33 Benz, *Individualität und Subjektivität*, 59: "... die Immanenz des Unendlichen im synthetischen Akt des Verstandes offenbart."

34 See Benz, *Individualität und Subjektivität*, 59–60.

35 Cf. Jean-Michel Counet, "Philosopher, c'est faire l'idiot: Le Cusain en filigrane dans l'oeuvre de Gilles Deleuze," *Noesis* 26/27 (2015–2016): 247–63. Counet discusses the concept of *idiota* (247–55), the fold (256–57), the moving image (257–59), and the question of world (259–62). See also the essay by David Albertson, "Inside the Fold: Gilles Deleuze and the Christian Neoplatonist Tradition," in *Mystical Theology and Platonism in the Time of Cusanus: Essays in Honor of Donald F. Duclow*, ed. Jason Aleksander, Sean Hannan, Joshua Hollmann, and Michael Edward Moore (Leiden: Brill, 2023), 347–83.

36 Counet, "Philosopher, c'est faire l'idiot," 247.

37 See Counet, "Philosopher, c'est faire l'idiot," 251.

38 See Gilles Deleuze, "Una entrevista, ¿qué es?, ¿para qué sirve?" in *Confesiones filosóficas*, ed. José González Ríos (Buenos Aires: Editorial quadrata, 2006), 165–69.

by the history of philosophy—this would represent his early monographic works—and then sought his own "liberation" in a second stage, when Deleuze aimed to describe the exercise of thought in opposition to the traditional image that philosophy has projected. Nicholas is distinguished in the history of philosophy for having been a master creator of concepts, such as the enigmatic names *possest* or *non aliud*. In *De mente*, he highlights the "creative" aspect of human knowledge. However, for Cusanus, human beings are creators of concepts because they are the image of God, who is the true and only Creator, for two reasons. Divine creation is ontological (God creates beings), such that divine creation grants the precise measure of each entity; but human knowledge is only conjectural.

According to Counet, Deleuze understands that "a concept has several components, compared to which it has an outstanding position, being fully present in each of them at every moment, by a kind of infinite circulation of a point, [and] this invariably makes Nicholas's reader think about his conception of Trinity."[39] The notion of "concept" in Deleuze as something present in and at the same time different from each of its components, could be illustrated by the Cusan example of the point, line, and surface, which Gandillac included in his anthology of Nicholas of Cusa's writings.[40]

The Indefinite Universe and the Plane of Immanence

The Cusan concept of an indefinite universe should be considered a milestone on the pathway toward the discovery of what Deleuze came to call the immanent plane. As Counet writes, "this universe knows no spatial or temporal limits; . . . and it can also be considered as the place of infinite movements."[41] Counet sees here a dynamic version of the world as an infinite sphere, whose center is everywhere and whose circumference is nowhere; in the same way, the concepts are like multiple waves, which rise up and go down, but the immanent plane is a single sea, which enfolds and

---

[39] Counet, "Philosopher, c'est faire l'idiot," 253: ". . . un concept possède diverses composantes, par rapport auxquelles il garde une position de surplomb, tout en étant pleinement présent en chacune d'elle à chaque instant, par une sorte de circulation infinie d'un point, cela fait immanquablement penser le lecteur de Nicolas à la conception cusaine de la Trinité."

[40] See Gandillac, *Oeuvres choisies de Nicolas de Cues*, 295. Cf. Nicholas of Cusa, *Idiota de mente*, IX (118), in *Nicolai de Cusa Opera Omnia*, vol. V, ed. Renate Steiger (Hamburg: Felix Meiner, 1983), 173–74.

[41] Counet, "Philosopher, c'est faire l'idiot," 254: ". . . cet univers ne connaît aucune limite spatiale ni temporelle; . . . et il peut également être considéré comme le lieu de mouvements infinis."

unfolds (or more literally, wraps and unwraps) them. This folding refers us to Cusanus's concepts of *complicatio* and *explicatio*. Counet notes that Gandillac systematically translates *complicatio* and *explicatio* by the same terms *enveloppement* and *développement*.[42]

The *idiota*, Precursor of the *cogito*

In a course that he taught on Spinoza's *Ethics*, Deleuze makes the following statement about Nicholas of Cusa:

> The cardinal of Kues sets out the theme of the *idiota*. And in what sense? In a very simple one. It is the idea that the philosopher is one who has no knowledge and has only one faculty, natural reason. The *idiota* is the man of natural reason. He has nothing more than a kind of natural reason or natural light—seen in opposition to the light of knowledge and in opposition to revealed light. The *idiota* is the man of natural light. So begins Nicholas of Cusa. Descartes will write a short text, otherwise little known but in his *Complete Works*, which has *idiota* in the title and is an exposition of the *cogito*.[43] And indeed, when Descartes sets out his great formula, "I think, therefore I am," is it not the formula of the *idiota*? It is presented by Descartes as the formula of the *idiota*, because man is reduced to natural reason.[44]

But is the *idiota* of Cusanus the "man of natural light," as Deleuze states here? Throughout all his works, Nicholas strives to lead us to a way of

---

[42] See Counet, "Philosopher, c'est faire l'idiot," 254–55.

[43] Counet speculates that this short text could be *La recherche de la vérité par la lumière naturelle*, although, contrary to what Deleuze claims, it does not include the word *idiota* in the title.

[44] Gilles Deleuze, Spinoza Course, December 2, 1980: "Le Cardinal de Cuses lance le thème de l'idiot. Et ça a quel sens? Ça a un sens très simple. C'est l'idée que le philosophe c'est celui qui ne dispose d'aucun savoir et qui n'a qu'une faculté, la raison naturelle. L'idiot c'est l'homme de la raison naturelle. Il n'a rien qu'une espèce de raison naturelle, de lumière naturelle. Voyez par opposition à la lumière du savoir et aussi par opposition à la lumière révélée. L'idiot c'est l'homme de la lumière naturelle. Ça commence donc à être Nicolas de Cuses. Descartes écrira un petit texte qui est d'ailleurs peu connu mais qui est dans les oeuvres complètes où il y a l'idiot dans le titre et qui est un exposé du cogito. Et en effet, lorsque Descartes lance sa grande formule 'je pense donc je suis,' en quoi c'est la formule de l'idiot? Elle est présentée par Descartes comme la formule de l'idiot parce que c'est l'homme réduit à la raison naturelle." See "La Voix de Gilles Deleuze," accessible at: http://www2.univ-paris8.fr/deleuze/article.php3?id_article=131. Cf. Gilles Deleuze, *Qu'est-ce que la philosophie?* (Paris: Éditions de Minuit, 1991), 60–61.

knowing that overcomes rational knowledge.[45] Therefore, in the Cusan figure of the *idiota* there is an implicit critique not only of academic knowledge, but of rational ways of knowing. Theology and philosophy constitute an indissoluble unity for Cusanus, which absorbs the negative theology of Neoplatonism and finds there a way to overcome the limits of rational knowledge.[46]

However, Deleuze links the *idiota* topic with the notion of paradox. As Counet puts it, paradox is "when the thought can only verify the existence of a fact but finds itself unable to think it.... This paradoxical capture of existence is what Nicholas of Cusa calls comprehending the incomprehensible incomprehensibly: something is comprehended which transcends our capacity for comprehension, which is thus understood as incomprehensible, that is, at the same time despite its incomprehensibility and because of this same incomprehensibility."[47] Considered from this perspective, the Deleuzean theme of the "idiot" seems close to the Cusan sense of "learned ignorance" as represented in the figure of the *idiota*.

We have seen that Gandillac was attracted to the cardinal's works precisely because he finds there an antecedent of the Cartesian method, referring among other reasons to the figure of the *idiota*. This emphasis in his reading of Cusanus's works remains present through Gandillac's final publications.[48] Deleuze himself chooses the *idiota* as an example to illustrate the conceptual character of Cusanus, and in this context he refers in a footnote to Gandillac and his anthology of selected writings of Nicholas of Cusa.[49] Despite identifying Cusan thought as a precursor of the *cogito*, Gandillac knows that the cardinal's times remain at some distance; for Nicholas, the precise truth abides beyond human capacities for knowledge.[50]

---

45 See Nicholas of Cusa, *De coniecturis*, I.6 (24), in *Nicolai de Cusa Opera Omnia*, vol. III, ed. Karl Bormann and Hans Gerhard Senger (Hamburg: Felix Meiner Verlag, 1972), 30–32; and Nicholas of Cusa, *Idiota de mente*, VII (105–6), in *Nicolai de Cusa Opera Omnia*, vol. V, ed. Renate Steiger (Hamburg: Felix Meiner, 1983), 157–60.

46 See Claudia D'Amico, "Introducción general," in *Todo y nada de todo*, ed. Claudia D'Amico (Buenos Aires: Ediciones Winograd, 2008), 27–28.

47 Counet, "Philosopher, c'est faire l'idiot," 262.

48 See Gandillac, "Du Cusain à Descartes," 359–62; and Maurice de Gandillac, *Nicolas de Cues* (Paris: Ellipses, 2001), 12–13.

49 See Deleuze, *Qu'est-ce que la philosophie?*, 60–61.

50 See Gandillac, *Oeuvres choisies de Nicolas de Cues*, 26.

Conclusion

Maurice de Gandillac contributed significantly to the dissemination of Cusan thought not only through Deleuze's works, but throughout other French thinkers of the twentieth century, including Jacques Derrida.[51] The works of the Sorbonne professor offer us a double perspective on Nicholas of Cusa, combining a historical view that studies Cusan sources with a gaze toward modern philosophy, in which, for Gandillac, the thought of the German cardinal critically reflects on the nature of being and knowing.

These three aspects of Deleuze's conception of philosophy—philosophy as concept creation, the immanent plane, and the figure of the *idiota*—resemble that of Cusanus, although differences remain. It would certainly be interesting to investigate whether Deleuze's positions resembled the cardinal's in other ways. Which works of Cusanus does Deleuze know, and when and how does he know them? Regarding both questions, we can provide an initial and partial answer: Deleuze at least knows the excerpts from the works of Nicholas of Cusa that Maurice de Gandillac included in his extensive anthology of selected works, and in all likelihood he knew them well from his student days onward.

But from these three aspects, can we surmise that Cusanus and Deleuze share the same conception of the philosophical enterprise? Counet doubts this is the case, given that the general point of view of each thinker is opposed: "Nicholas remains a deeply traditional thinker, where the one is first in relation to the multiple, which is nothing more than a shadow, an effect, a decline. In Deleuze ... it is the other way around: it is the multiple, the different, that comes first, and unity is nothing more than an effect of the forces that animate and amass the multiple."[52] Nevertheless, as Gandillac has noted, singularity and difference gain in importance as Nicholas's thought develops, a fact that Beierwaltes sums up with the Cusan formula: *unitas in alteritate*.[53]

---

51 See Hans Gerhard Senger, *Nikolaus von Kues: Leben—Lehre—Wirkungsgeschichte* (Heidelberg: Universitätsverlag Carl Winter, 2017), 277–78.

52 Counet, "Philosopher, c'est faire l'idiot," 263: "Nicolas reste un penseur profondément traditionnel où l'un est premier par rapport au multiple, qui n'en est qu'une ombre, un effet, une déchéance. Chez Deleuze ... c'est l'inverse: c'est le multiple, le différent qui est premier et l'unité n'est qu'une effet des forces animant et pétrissant le multiple."

53 Beierwaltes, "Identidad y diferencia como principio del pensamiento Cusano," in *Cusanus: Reflexión metafísica y espiritualidad*, 147. See Gandillac, "Nicolás de Cusa," in *Historia de la filosofía*, 5:44; and Rodrigo Núñez Poblete, *Metafísica de la singularidad* (Buenos Aires: Biblos, 2015).

9

Jacques Lacan and Learned Ignorance

JEAN-MARIE NICOLLE

It can be said that psychoanalysis is a meeting between two ignorances: that of the patient and that of the analyst. The patient does not know why he is sick; he comes to psychoanalysis to know his truth, and thereby admits he is ignorant of himself. He does not understand what's happening to him. He addresses the psychoanalyst by highlighting his symptoms, and the psychoanalyst must show him that it's something else—the symptoms are not the most important thing. The patient believes that his psychoanalyst will know how to decipher the hidden meaning of his illness. It's an illusion for the patient and a trap for the psychoanalyst. Faced with the patient, the psychoanalyst doesn't know exactly why he is sick, because the psychoanalyst still doesn't know everything about his life and knows nothing about his unconscious. Like the patient, he too must recognize his own ignorance. Under these conditions, what should be the attitude of the psychoanalyst?

Jacques Lacan (1901–1981) was a psychiatrist and psychoanalyst and, with Freud, one of the greatest theoreticians in the field of psychoanalysis. Throughout his life his principal preoccupation was the training of psychoanalysts.¹ To this end, for thirty years he taught a weekly seminar in Paris that was open to all. His lectures were attended by many intellectuals, including Louis Althusser and Paul Ricoeur, as well as Michel de Certeau, who was an active member of the school of psychoanalysis created by Lacan. Lacan was not a philosopher, but he had a great knowledge of philosophy. He referenced the concepts of Plato, Pascal, Kant, Hegel, and others, reworking them according to what he wanted to demonstrate, and, of course, he also created his own concepts. He did not want to construct a philosophical theory; his work was aimed at psychoanalysts. But since there can be no good technique without sound concepts, he borrowed from philosophers whatever served him best. Imagine my surprise when my wife drew my attention to the concept of learned ignorance in Lacan, and this in his very first seminar.² Still we mustn't forget that what Lacan says about learned ignorance, he says in the field of psychoanalysis, in relation to the psychoanalytic cure, and not as a central concept in his theory.

In 1954, Lacan declared: "The analyst's attitude must be that of an *ignorantia docta*, meaning formal rather than scholarly, which can be formative for the subject." Lacan warns his students: "There is a great temptation ... to transform *ignorantia docta* into *ignorantia docens*. If the psychoanalyst thinks he knows something, in psychology for example, then he is already bound to fail."³ *Ignorantia docens* is the pedantic ignorance of one who thinks that as a scholar he knows everything, and who thus misses the truth of his patient. *Ignorantia docta* is the wise and informed ignorance of one who is aware of the difficulty of psychoanalytic work. The psychoanalyst is in the background, suspended. He is the one who doesn't use the power of suggestion, advice, or influence. More fundamentally, he must give up the idea that he already knows—or thinks he knows—what his patient has to say.

---

1 See Jacques Lacan, "Note italienne," *Ornicar? Bulletin periodique du champ Freudien* 25 (1982): 7–10, reprinted in Jacques Lacan, *Autres écrits* (Paris: Seuil, 2001), 307–11.

2 Lacan, who knew Maurice de Gandillac personally, explicitly attributes "learned ignorance" to cardinal Nicholas of Cusa. See Jacques Lacan, "Lesson, November 4, 1971" (available online: http://staferla.free.fr/S19b/S19b%20Le%20savoir%20du%20psychanalyste.pdf).

3 "La position de l'analyste doit être celle d'une *ignorantia docta*, ce qui ne veut pas dire savante, mais formelle, et qui peut être, pour le sujet formante.... La tentation est grande ... de transformer l'*ignorantia docta* en ... une *ignorantia docens*. Que le psychanalyste croie savoir quelque chose, en psychologie, par exemple, et c'est déjà le commencement de sa perte." Jacques Lacan, *Séminaire*, vol. 1, *Les écrits techniques de Freud (1953–1954)* (Paris: Seuil, 1975), 306–7. Nicholas of Cusa first uses the term extensively in 1440. See *De docta ignorantia* I.1 (2–4), in *Nikolaus von Kues: Philosophisch-Theologische Werke*, vol. 1, ed. Paul Wilpert and Hans Gerhard Senger, rev. ed. (Hamburg: Felix Meiner Verlag, 2002), 6–9.

Throughout his teaching, Lacan warned his students against the temptation to understand too quickly, or rather, to believe to have understood, what the patient means. He criticizes the premature aspect of interpretation and stresses that in every understanding there is a danger of illusion. Instead, the psychoanalyst must question what he understands to try to reach what he does not understand. On this point, Lacan is very close to what the Layman says in Nicholas of Cusa's dialogue *Idiota de sapientia*: "Perhaps the difference between you and me is the following: you think that you are a scholar, although you are not; hence, you are haughty. By contrast, I know that I am a layman; hence, I am quite humble. In this respect, perhaps, I am more learned."[4] From the beginning of *De docta ignorantia*, Cusanus frequently refers to Plato and Aristotle. He relates that Socrates believed himself to know nothing except that he did not know. This is the same Socrates whom we encounter in the seminar that Lacan devotes to transference, that is to say, to the relationship between love and knowledge. He explains the lived experience of transference in the psychoanalytic cure by drawing an analogy with the lived experience of Alcibiades's love for Socrates.

At the end of the *Symposium*, Alcibiades praises Socrates. He compares him to the statuettes of Silenus, whose exteriors are grotesque, but which contain extraordinary marvels inside: figurines of the gods in gold, the ἀγάλματα: "I say, that he is exactly like the busts of Silenus, which are set up in the statuaries' shops, holding pipes and flutes in their mouths; and they are made to open in the middle, and have images of gods inside them [ἀγάλματα θεῶν]."[5] Socrates, who was said to be very ugly, possesses a beauty not physical but infinitely superior, an inner beauty. He charms those who hear him, and that is why Alcibiades finds such treasure in Socrates, this precious object that has unleashed his desire, the ἄγαλμα. Then, he tells of his attempts to seduce Socrates, in order to obtain from him everything he knows. We might say that knowledge, so to speak, has an "agalmatic" value to a subject, and so Alcibiades expects an exchange of knowledge for beauty.

---

4 "Haec est fortassis inter te et me differentia: Tu te scientem putas, cum non sis, hinc superbis. Ego vero idiotam me esse cognosco, hinc humilior. In hoc forte doctior exsisto." Nicholas of Cusa, *Idiota de sapientia* I (4), in *Nicolai de Cusa Opera Omnia*, vol. V, ed. Ludwig Baur and Renata Steiger (Hamburg: Felix Meiner Verlag, 1983), 6; trans. Jasper Hopkins, *Nicholas of Cusa on Wisdom and Knowledge* (Minneapolis: Arthur J. Banning Press, 1996), 498.

5 Plato, *Symposium*, 215ab; trans. Benjamin Jowett, *The Dialogues of Plato* (New York: Random House, 1937), 1:338.

Lacan's thesis is that love is a metaphor, that is to say, a substitution. He distinguishes two functions: the lover and the beloved. The lover, the ἐραστής, is the subject of the desire. What characterizes the ἐραστής is what he is missing, but he does not know what he is missing. The beloved, the ἐρώμενος, is the one who is desired, but he does not know why. He doesn't know what's hidden in him and what makes him attractive. But when the function of ἐραστής, the lover, comes to substitute for the function of ἐρώμενος, the beloved object, then love is produced. In other words, for love to be produced, the beloved, the one who is loved, must become the lover, the one who loves.

Now, how does this relate to knowledge and ignorance in the psychoanalytical cure? On the side of the patient, he is first an ἐρώμενος, because, in the context of an analysis, he is the one who is worthy of love and interest. The psychoanalyst is there for him. Furthermore, the subject who comes into analysis assumes his ignorance and knows that he doesn't know—why he is anxious, or why he is suffering from his symptoms—and on top of that, he is asking himself: who am I? This position of non-knowing correlates to the attribution of knowledge to the analyst himself, who thus becomes "the subject supposed to know," and the relationship between love and knowledge is such that the supposition of knowledge corresponds to love: "I love him who knows." This is the love of transference, a tool that is indispensable to the process of psychoanalysis. At this moment, the patient embodies the lover (ἐραστής). On the side of the patient, there is therefore the metaphor of love, a substitution of the lover for the beloved.

But how does Socrates react to Alcibiades's discourse, which identifies Socrates as one who contains the precious object of Alcibiades's desire? He avoids the position of ἐρώμενος by declaring himself unworthy of Alcibiades's love. Socrates answers Alcibiades: "Truly you must see in me some rare beauty of a kind infinitely higher than any which I see in you. And therefore, if you mean to share with me and to exchange beauty for beauty, you will have greatly the advantage of me; you will gain true beauty in return for appearance—like Diomede, gold in exchange for brass." Then Socrates adds: "But look again, sweet friend, and see whether you are not deceived in me," for one day Socrates's beauty will also fail. [6] Socrates refuses to show to Alcibiades the metaphor of love. He refuses to be part of the metaphor, to have been ἐρώμενος, the desirable, who is worthy of being loved.

---

6 Plato, *Symposium*, 218d–219a; trans. Jowett, I:341.

According to Lacan, the analyst has to follow the example of Socrates by refusing to enter into the metaphor of love or to provide the sign of his own desire. Such an avowal could stop the analytic process, and constitute the fall of the subject who is supposed to know, upon whom analysis is based. That is why the analyst must limit himself to producing only the signifier of the lack implied by desire. This is the meaning of Socrates's response to Alcibiades: do not be fooled, for you are mistaken; you thought that you saw something interesting in me, but I am nothing. Socrates means by this that his essence is emptiness, the hollow; in other words, he represents desire as a lack, the "pure desire."

What kind of knowledge does such ignorance have to learn? Of the three passions of being named in Buddhism—love, hatred, and ignorance—Lacan considers ignorance the only passion worthy of the analyst. It's the most positive of the three, because as learned ignorance it emphasizes the limits of what one is able to know. According to Lacan, the psychoanalyst must not be satisfied with not knowing and give up working on it; on the contrary, his ignorance must be "cultivated" in the double sense of maintained with passion—as learned ignorance—and supported by theoretical reflection. Ignorance must not be understood as an absence of knowledge, but as a passion for being: a way in which being is formed. The revelation of ignorance is non-knowledge, which is not a negation of knowledge, but its most elaborate form.[7]

In 1967, Lacan returns to the ethical precept of learned ignorance: "In no way does this authorize the psychoanalyst to be content with knowing that he knows nothing, because the question is what he needs to know."[8] There is no question of settling in the comfort of stupidity. The psychoanalyst must be ignorant but not uneducated. Throughout his teaching, Lacan constantly reminds us that psychoanalysts must learn from the texts of great authors (Sophocles, Shakespeare, Claudel) and should study linguistics, mathematics, history, and philosophy, as well.

---

7 "L'ignorance en effet ne doit pas être entendue ici comme une absence de savoir, mais, à l'égal de l'amour et de la haine, comme une passion de l'être; car elle peut être, à leur instar, une voie où l'être se forme.... Le fruit positif de la révélation de l'ignorance est le non-savoir, qui n'est pas une négation du savoir, mais sa forme la plus élaborée." Jacques Lacan, "Variantes de la cure-type," in *Écrits* (Paris: Seuil, 1966), 358.

8 "... ceci n'autorise nullement le psychanalyste à se suffire de savoir qu'il ne sait rien, car ce dont il s'agit, c'est de ce qu'il a à savoir." Jacques Lacan, "Proposition du 9 octobre 1967 sur le psychanalyste de l'école," *Scilicet* 1 (1968): 20.

For the psychoanalyst, learned ignorance is a straining for knowledge. To clarify this search for knowledge, Lacan invites us to distinguish two meanings of zero: the void and nothingness. Nothingness is marked as the first degree of a measure; to be ignorant in the sense of knowing nothing is to be incompetent. The void is a virtuality; ignorance in the sense of an absence of knowledge doesn't mean stupidity, but a desire to know. Just as a blank page calls for writing, learned ignorance calls out for knowledge. Hence learned ignorance can be defined as a position in relation to others. The psychoanalyst must forget all that he knows and respond to the ignorance of his patient by his own ignorance, if he is to avoid enclosing the patient immediately in alienating knowledge. That is, the learned ignorance of the psychoanalyst is a necessary condition of the freedom of his patient. It's not a renunciation of understanding, but, on the contrary, a drive to seek truth.

Cusanus scholars may wonder quite legitimately: Hasn't Lacan completely transformed Nicholas of Cusa's concept? Indeed, the differences between the Cusan theory and Lacan's objectives are important. We can discern at least three. First, for Cusanus, the incomprehensible is God, and knowledge must be wholly focused toward God. For Lacan, the unknown is the unconscious: "What psychoanalysis reveals is knowledge that is unaware of itself."[9] Unlike the traditional affirmation that "knowledge is knowing that we know," psychoanalysis shows that the unconscious is knowledge that is not known, and that a psychoanalytic effort is necessary in order to discover a part of it. When it comes to talking and language, one is always saying things one doesn't know one is saying.

Second, for Cusanus, who in part follows Aristotle, all people are animated by a desire for knowledge (*sciendi desiderium*), and this desire is fulfilled by experiencing the limits of knowledge as we approach the absolute truth. Nicholas of Cusa, taking up the words of the Apostle Paul ("For now we see in a mirror, dimly, but then we will see face to face. Now I know only in part; then I will know fully, even as I have been fully known" [1 Cor 13:12]), promises the knowledge of oneself and God in the afterlife. For Lacan, on the contrary, the desire not to know drives individuals; here he differs from Freud, who defended the existence of an epistemic drive. Of course, the patient would like to know what is wrong with him, but he wants to know only up to a point, and this point, in the analysis, appears when a resistance stops him. There is a rejection of knowledge that can go

---

[9] "Ce que la psychanalyse révèle, c'est un savoir insu à lui-même." See Lacan, "Lesson, November 4, 1971."

so far as to become a hatred of knowledge. From the psychoanalytic point of view, Lacan considers that there is no desire to know, no impulse to know, no search for knowledge. And while he always thought learned ignorance positive, he also stressed the negative aspect of ignorance, which he calls "wanting to know nothing about it." Thus, throughout the course of the cure, the analyst must support the desire to know.

Finally, the learned ignorance of Nicholas of Cusa is neither a philosophical wisdom in the style of the Skeptics, nor even an instruction for a Christian life. Above all, it is a weapon against the medieval Aristotelians in the battle for faith, because only faith can triumph over ignorance. Learned ignorance is a strategy for establishing certainties and overcoming problems.[10] For Cusanus, access to truth is possible only through faith in Jesus Christ, where love and knowledge coincide. But for Lacan, access to the truth passes through the subject's word, and one must acknowledge that the truth can only be "half-said."

Our two authors have in common a consistently positive vision of learned ignorance, which they define as the knowledge that surrounds what we cannot know. It is the pinnacle of possible knowledge. However, Nicholas of Cusa did not forge his concept of learned ignorance in order for his readers to find their own inner truth. He was a preacher, a teacher of theology, and his concept of learned ignorance was meant to give weight to his discourse—that of a master teaching religious truth. The analytic discourse announces that there is no absolute knowledge or total knowledge of the unconscious. The unconscious is a knowledge that does not know itself. Therefore, Lacan argues that psychoanalytic knowledge could not be written as textual knowledge, since the truth is never fully said. Michel Foucault grasped that Lacan the theoretician wanted to liberate psychoanalysis from medicine in order to restore the complexity of the subject. This is why his texts are complicated and very difficult to read. As Foucault writes, "Lacan wanted the obscurity of his *Écrits* to become the very complexity of the subject, and the work necessary to understand it to become a work performed on oneself."[11]

---

[10] "... docta ignorantia omnia scibilia venatur in fine indagationis." Nicholas of Cusa, *De caesarea circuli quadratura*, 18, in Jean-Marie Nicolle, *Nicolas de Cues: Écrits mathématiques* (Paris: Honoré Champion, 2007), 424.

[11] "Lacan voulait que l'obscurité de ses *Écrits* fût la complexité même du sujet, et que le travail nécessaire pour le comprendre fût un travail à réaliser sur soi-même." Michel Foucault, "Lacan, le libérateur de la psychanalyse," in *Dits et écrits, tome II: 1976-1988*, ed. Daniel Defert and François Ewald (Paris: Gallimard, 2001), 1024.

10

The Wild Science

Michel de Certeau and Cusan Topology

DAVID ALBERTSON

Most scholars of Nicholas of Cusa are now familiar with Michel de Certeau (1925–1986) and his famous essay on *De visione Dei*, but few know its genesis. As befits the ingenious French Jesuit who traced the ruptures and absences in the history of Christian mysticism, Certeau's study of the Cusan treatise was delivered in fragments over three decades. A first short version appeared in the French review *Traverses* in 1984, published by the Centre Georges Pompidou under the title: "Nicolas de Cues: Le secret d'un regard."[1] In 1987, a similar version, now containing a few more notations, was translated into English by Catherine Porter for the American journal *Diacritics*.[2] Not until 2013 was that long version published in French with a revised apparatus, based this time upon a typed manuscript corrected by Certeau himself. This complete essay, "Le regard: Nicolas de Cues," appeared in the

---

[1] Michel de Certeau, "Nicolas de Cues: Le secret d'un regard," *Traverses* 30–31 (1984): 70–85.
[2] Michel de Certeau, "The Gaze: Nicholas of Cusa," *Diacritics* 17 (1987): 2–38.

second volume of *La Fable mystique*, published several years after Certeau's death by his editor Luce Giard. That final version is nearly twice as long as the original one, supplemented as it is with a new section on the geometry of mystical language: "Le discours circulaire."³

Given that three versions emerged over several years, Certeau apparently returned again and again to Nicholas of Cusa. For Certeau, the German cardinal was not one subject among others, but a guide who came to shape his thinking. Certeau had overseen the publication of the first volume of *La Fable mystique* in May 1982, but by the middle of 1985 he realized his worsening illness might prevent him from finishing the second. After his death in January 1986, Giard began to organize and publish scores of the prodigious historian's unfinished manuscripts: four volumes of new essays, seven older works newly re-edited, and four conference volumes.⁴ Only then could she return to the task of compiling the second volume of *La Fable mystique*, which she published in 2013. Certeau left detailed notes for its structure. The first volume focused on Teresa of Ávila and John of the Cross and addressed the formation of a new "science" of mysticism, which Certeau called *la mystique*, or "mystics" (like "physics" or "aesthetics"). The unfinished second volume was to discuss "the content itself of that science, from Nicholas of Cusa ... to Fénelon and Pascal."⁵ His famous Cusanus essay is the first and longest chapter in that second book. By investigating the mystical gaze of the icon in *De visione Dei*, Certeau formulates the first principles of *la mystique*.⁶

Certeau approached *De visione Dei* as an opportunity to probe the meaning of Christian mysticism per se and draw conclusions well beyond the parameters of the fifteenth-century treatise. Yet even as a work of

---

3 Michel de Certeau, "Le regard: Nicolas de Cues," in *La Fable mystique. XVIe-XVIIe Siècle, tome II*, ed. Luce Giard (Paris: Éditions Gallimard, 2013), 51–121; trans. Michael B. Smith, "The Look: Nicholas of Cusa," in *The Mystic Fable*, vol. 2, *The Sixteenth and Seventeenth Centuries* (Chicago: University of Chicago Press, 2015), 23–70.

4 More details can be found in Luce Giard, "Presentation," in *Mystic Fable*, 2:ix–xi. Most recently, see Luce Giard, ed., *Michel de Certeau: Le voyage de l'oeuvre* (Paris: Éditions Facultés Jésuites de Paris, 2017).

5 Quoted in Giard, "Presentation," in *Mystic Fable*, 2:xii.

6 Jocelyne Sfez points out that Cusanus is not a "mystic" in Certeau's distinctively historicized early modern sense, even if the cardinal contributed significantly to "mystical" discourse in the tradition of Dionysian commentaries: see Sfez, "Michel de Certeau, lecteur de Nicolas de Cues: Nicolas de Cues était-il un mystique?," *Archives de sciences sociales des religions* 172 (October/December 2015): 71–73.

historical scholarship, Certeau's essay testifies to his impressive knowledge of the Cusan oeuvre. He makes specific references to *De concordantia catholica, De docta ignorantia, De quaerendo Deum, Dialogus de Deo abscondito, Apologia doctae ignorantiae*, the *Idiota* dialogues, *De theologicis complementis, De beryllo, Cribratio Alchorani*, and at least two of the mathematical works on quadrature—in several instances, well before the respective volumes of the Hamburg critical edition were finished.[7] Certeau had absorbed the seminal scholarship of Ernst Cassirer, Rudolf Haubst, Edmond Vansteenberghe, Maurice de Gandillac, and Erich Meuthen, as well as then-younger scholars Mariano Alvarez-Gómez, Hans Gerhard Senger, and John Monfasani; and he made his own connections to the work of Erwin Panofsky, Ernst Gombrich, Michael Baxandall, and Gilles Deleuze. At one point, Certeau casually remarks: "There are, incidentally, pages in Jacques Lacan on *le regard* that are very close to Cusa's analysis."[8]

In sum, Michel de Certeau did not write in passing on a single work of Nicholas of Cusa, nor as an outsider peering in the windows of *Cusanus-Forschung*. His grasp of the cardinal's oeuvre was detailed and substantial, and we often find traces of it elsewhere in his thought. For example, in a chapter on Pierre Bourdieu's *habitus*, Certeau describes how practices speak louder than words, and calls the phenomenon "*docta ignorantia*" without further explanation.[9] The contrast of landscape and architecture in Manhattan, described as "a texturology in which extremes coincide," he names "*coincidatio* [sic] *oppositorum*."[10] His anthropological account of "belief" seems based on the dialogical model of *De visione Dei*, here termed the "anteriority of the other": only as others believe with me can I trust them, credit them as faithful, and so come to believe along with them—just as Cusanus counseled the quarreling Benedictines at Tegernsee.[11] And in Certeau's remarkable prose fragment "White Ecstasy," the protagonist

---

7 Like his contemporary, Gilles Deleuze, Certeau probably made use of the compilation of Cusan works published by Maurice de Gandillac in 1941, which he mentions in each version of his essay. On Gandillac's pivotal role, see Alexia Schmitt's essay in chapter 8 of this volume.

8 Certeau, *Mystic Fable*, 2:243n104. On this question, see the essay by Jean-Marie Nicolle in chapter 9.

9 Michel de Certeau, *The Practice of Everyday Life*, trans. Steven Rendall (Berkeley: University of California Press, 1984), 50–56.

10 Certeau, *Practice of Everyday Life*, 91.

11 Michel de Certeau, "What We Do When We Believe," in *On Signs*, ed. Marshall Blonsky (Baltimore: Johns Hopkins University Press, 1985), 201.

reports that in a distant land, the strange foreigners can perceive the world only through subject and object, whereas his own culture natively experiences seeing God and being seen by God as identical. "They separate what appears to us to be one and the same," he relates, pitying their unfortunate ways. In effect, Certeau takes the world of *De visione Dei* as his homeland and renders the modern world a foreign country.[12]

Jocelyne Sfez calls Certeau "a pioneer in the rediscovery in France of Nicholas of Cusa," noting that "when the first volume of *The Mystic Fable* appeared, Nicholas of Cusa was not studied in France."[13] A Jesuit until his death, Certeau had a superb training in the Christian theological tradition; his achievements as a historian and cultural theorist should not overshadow his status as a modern Christian thinker of great distinction.[14] He was educated in the *nouvelle théologie* by Henri de Lubac,[15] and his intellectual projects were deeply marked by his Jesuit identity.[16] The more we appreciate the nature of Certeau's particular Cusan adventure, the more central it appears to be to his thinking in general about what mysticism is and what it might signify today, as it wanders about in exile among the more properly "scientific" disciplines.

A Hermeneutics of Space

Certeau's long essay on Cusanus effectively opened up a new dialogue, one still unfolding today, between the cardinal's dialectical iconology and the theological turn in French phenomenology. In *De visione Dei*, the Christ

---

12 Michel de Certeau, "White Ecstasy," in *The Postmodern God: A Theological Reader*, ed. Graham Ward (London: Wiley Blackwell, 1997), 155–58.

13 Sfez, "Michel de Certeau, lecteur de Nicolas de Cues," 68–69.

14 On Certeau as theologian, see Frederick Christian Bauerschmidt, "The Abrahamic Voyage: Michel de Certeau and Theology," *Modern Theology* 12, no. 1 (1996): 1–26. Certeau's theological writings about Christianity are few. In English translation, see especially Michel de Certeau, "The Weakness of Believing: From the Body to Writing, A Christian Transit," trans. Saskia Brown, in *The Certeau Reader*, ed. Graham Ward (Oxford: Blackwell, 2000), 214–43; and Certeau, "How Is Christianity Thinkable Today?," in *The Postmodern God*, 142–55.

15 See Brenna Moore, "How to Awaken the Dead: Michel de Certeau, Henri de Lubac, and the Instabilities between the Past and the Present," *Spiritus: A Journal of Christian Spirituality* 12, no. 2 (2012): 172–79. For a good biographical overview, see Willem Frijhoff, "Michel de Certeau (1925–1986)—A Multifaceted Intellectual," in *Spiritual Spaces: History and Mysticism in Michel de Certeau*, ed. Inigo Bocken (Leuven: Peeters, 2013), 5–23.

16 See Philip Sheldrake, "Michel de Certeau: Spirituality and the Practice of Everyday Life," *Spiritus: A Journal of Christian Spirituality* 12, no. 2 (2012): 207–16.

icon organizes a perspectival play between particular reductions of the visible and the transcendental vision of God. In his essay, Certeau names this iconic manifestation of the gaze of the Other with language reminiscent of the early works of Jean-Luc Marion: "There is no longer any *object seen* for the person *looked at*.... The look of the other excludes the possession of an image. It deprives of sight, it bedazzles, it blinds ... *Being* itself is a *subject looked at*."[17] Truth, continues Certeau, is "all the *more true* the more it *disappears*, the more it escapes vision, the more it approaches the true, so that it is ultimately in a blind bedazzlement of the eyes of the body and of reason."[18] Without making any claims of influence, we should note that Marion's *Dieu sans l'être* appeared in 1982, just as Certeau was writing the original short version of his Cusanus essay published in 1984.[19] In 2014, Emmanuel Falque followed Certeau's example by reading *De visione Dei* through the lens of the phenomenological tradition, hailing Certeau's essay as "pour la première fois ... une véritable lecture 'philosophique'" and adding his own cross-references to Husserl and Merleau-Ponty.[20] By 2016, Jean-Luc Marion also finished an essay on *De visione Dei*.[21] Marion praised Cusanus for anticipating the phenomenology of the icon but disputed Falque's interpretation of *icona*.[22]

More than most readers, Certeau notices the fundamental geometrical matrix that undergirds the project of *De visione Dei*, influenced as it is by *De theologicis complementis*, a treatise on speculative geometry penned by Nicholas a few months earlier in the same year. Certeau calls the implicit geometry of *De visione Dei* "topology."[23] In his peculiar sense, topology is a

---

17 Certeau, "The Look," in *Mystic Fable*, 2:45.

18 Certeau, "The Look," in *Mystic Fable*, 2:52.

19 See Jean-Luc Marion, *God Without Being: Hors-Texte*, trans. Thomas A. Carlson, 2nd ed. (Chicago: University of Chicago Press, 2012), 11–22.

20 Emmanuel Falque, "L'Omnivoyant: Fraternité et vision de Dieu chez Nicolas de Cues," *Revue des sciences philosophiques et théologiques* 98, no. 1 (January/March 2014): 37–73. See the English translation by Kyle H. Kavanaugh and Barnabas Aspray: "The All-Seeing: Fraternity and Vision of God in Nicholas of Cusa," *Modern Theology* 35, no. 4 (September 2019): 1–28.

21 Jean-Luc Marion, "Voir, se voir vu: L'apport de Nicolas de Cues dans le *De visione dei*," *Bulletin de littérature ecclésiastique* 117, no. 2 (April/June 2016): 7–37. See the English translation by Stephen E. Lewis: "Seeing, or Seeing Oneself Seen: Nicholas of Cusa's Contribution in *De visione dei*," *The Journal of Religion* 96, no. 3 (July 2016): 305–31.

22 On this controversy, see the essay by Emmanuel Falque in chapter 14 of this volume.

23 Certeau, "The Look," in *Mystic Fable*, 2:28, 40–41. For context: Guy-Félix Duportail, "Le moment topologique de la phénoménologie française: Merleau-Ponty et Derrida," *Archives de philosophie* 73, no. 1 (2010): 47–65.

practice of measuring space that precedes division into different ontological domains, encompassing not only mathematical topology or physical topography, but also social, psychic, or discursive spaces—a mode of measurement indifferent to the category of quantity, we might say. There are resonances here with Michel Foucault's complex deployment of spatial models across his works, or Henri Lefebvre's reconceptualization of spatial representation. But unlike Foucault and Lefebvre, Certeau is especially interested in a mystical topology, that is, the way that Christian mystical texts invent and explore spaces.[24] He gives us a vocabulary to construe Cusan mystical theology not as one more flavor of spirituality among others, but as a discursive grammar of mysticism in the peculiar idiolect of geometrical measures, that is, a general topology, or a hermeneutics of space.

For Certeau, Nicholas's fascination with geometry is not the arcane pastime of a world-weary cardinal, but the very center of his philosophical and theological practice. Geometry grounds the iconology of *De visione Dei*, Certeau suggests, because geometrical space establishes the original "topology" within which mental insight coincides with optical seeing. "Geometry's first concern," he writes, "is operations relative to seeing, since it unfolds entirely in that element and since it makes the visible the very field of intellectual visions.... [Geometry] consists in a seeing of the invisible in a visible space...."[25] But seeing the invisible in the visible is not only the mission of every geometer; it is the function of the iconic gaze in *De visione Dei*. Certeau's insight is that space unifies the visual and the geometrical, so long as space is construed as a universal, pre-quantitative topology.[26]

Certeau's attention to space in Cusanus is striking in several regards. While Nicholas of Cusa weaves geometrical ideas and images into many, even most, of his theological works, it never appears in *De visione Dei*.

---

[24] On Foucault and Lefebvre, see Carmel Bendon Davis, *Mysticism and Space: Space and Spatiality in the Works of Richard Rolle, "The Cloud of Unknowing" Author, and Julian of Norwich* (Washington, DC: The Catholic University of America Press, 2008). Cf. David Albertson, "Cataphasis, Visualization, and Mystical Space," in *The Oxford Handbook of Mystical Theology*, ed. Edward Howells and Mark A. McIntosh (Oxford: Oxford University Press, 2020), 347–68.

[25] Certeau, "The Look," in *Mystic Fable*, 2:34.

[26] Cusanus discusses the possibility of geometrical space *sine quantitate*. See, e.g., Nicholas of Cusa, *Trialogus de possest*, 46, in *Nicolai de Cusa Opera Omnia*, vol. XI/2, ed. Renata Steiger (Hamburg: Felix Meiner Verlag, 1973), 57; and Nicholas of Cusa, *De theologicis complementis*, 12, in *Nicolai de Cusa Opera Omnia*, vol. X/2a, ed. Heide Dorothea Riemann and Karl Bormann (Hamburg: Felix Meiner Verlag, 1994), 67.

Undaunted, Certeau was determined to reveal the geometry hidden within the folds of the 1453 treatise, however absent on the surface. "Nicholas of Cusa invents, in his own way," writes Certeau, "a geometry of the relations of position that anticipates topology."[27] Certeau describes the monks in procession around the icon as a "mathematical liturgy [that] stages a space distributed in places by a system of differences between singularities constituted by their reciprocal positions."[28] Thus Certeau discovers in the treatise not only an opposition between two kinds of sight, contracted and absolute, or seeing and being-seen. More importantly, he discovers a "torsion" and "an opposition between two kinds of space ... two visual practices of space ... that of the eye and that of the look."[29]

Certeau the Jesuit spiritual director calls the spatial order of *De visione Dei* a "composition of place," much like that commended in Ignatius's *Spiritual Exercises*, as several scholars have noted.[30] The gaze from monk to icon, or monk to monk—the "look" named in the essay's title—establishes its own "geometrical perspective." "The look is a vector," he writes, "a line and an action in space." Each point in that space unfolds in three dimensions: "as a 'figure' in a geometrical space; as a scene in a theatrical space; and as a map in a geographical or cosmological space." What matters is the "play of spaces" that Cusanus activates in the dialogue.[31] Certeau himself invents a series of Cusanesque diagrams to delineate the spatial logic of the icon, gently supplementing the cardinal's missing geometry.

The French Jesuit was ahead of his time in appreciating the spatial aspect of Cusan thought. Thanks to recent discoveries, we can now supply the historical grounds for Certeau's intuitions about the centrality of

---

27 Certeau, "The Look," in *Mystic Fable*, 2:41.
28 Certeau, "The Look," in *Mystic Fable*, 2:41.
29 Certeau, "The Look," in *Mystic Fable*, 2:45–46.
30 "The diversity of his concepts for phenomena of place and space is directly connected with the multiplicity of places according to the spiritual method of 'composition of place' (*compositio loci*) that Ignatius of Loyola taught in the *Exercises*." Georg Eickhoff, "Geschichte und Mystik bei Michel de Certeau," *Stimmen der Zeit* 126, Bd. 219 (2001): 249. "The Jesuit describes Cusan works as a process of spatialization in an Ignatian style, pursued, however, as a problem posed for historiography." Johannes Hoff, *Kontingenz, Berührung, Überschreitung: Zur philosophischen Propädeutik christlicher Mystik nach Nikolaus von Kues* (Freiburg: Verlag Karl Alber, 2007), 290.
31 Certeau, "The Look," in *Mystic Fable*, 2:42.

geometry for Cusan thought.³² Remarkably, Certeau already understood much of this in the early 1980s:

> The painting's gaze constitutes a *point*. According to Nicholas of Cusa's constant theory as he repeats it in the *Theological Complement* [*De theologicis complementis*], the point itself is a "quasi-nothingness" (*prope nihil*), but it is endowed with an infinite "fecundity".... It is inseparably, being the simplest unit, the epistemological principle of the geometrical definition and, by its fecundity, the genetic principle of spatial construction. There is, therefore, the *generation of a space* thanks to the equal lines drawn from the point.³³

Certeau was able to grasp the point's fecundity as a general epistemological principle and the foundation of a general topology. The cardinal's treatise became a vehicle that allowed him to tap into a deeper stratum of Cusan thought: its inchoate dynamics of a mystical, imaginal, or pre-quantitative space. But it was not simply as a disinterested observer that Certeau mapped Cusan topology. In fact, it informed his own approach to interpreting mysticism in modernity and probing the topographic capabilities of other discourses. That is, the discovery of Cusan topology latent in Certeau's historiography allows us to explore new dimensions of Certeau's thought.

Certeau envisioned a Christian mystical science of the future that challenged secular modernity's epistemic comforts yet remained equally foreign to contemporary Christian institutions. Neither old nor new, neither familiar or strange, Certeau's third way has challenged commentators to explain *la mystique* and in particular the postmodern spatiality it represents. Bauerschmidt sees Certeau as an avant-garde theologian who aims beyond both modern nihilism (there is no Other) and premodern

---

32 Irene Caiazzo recently identified a mathematical manuscript in Stuttgart as Thierry of Chartres's lost commentary on Boethius's *De arithmetica*, which she edited as *Thierry of Chartres: The Commentary on the "De arithmetica" of Boethius* (Toronto: Pontifical Institute of Mediaeval Studies, 2015). Caiazzo shows that Thierry's theology of folding has a geometrical basis in points and lines, and not the other way around; See also Thierry of Chartres, *Super Arithmeticam*, II.iv.4 (lines 230–75), ed. Caiazzo, 163–65. It is highly likely that Cusanus had direct access to this earliest stratum of Thierry's thought: see David Albertson, "*Boethius Noster*: Thierry of Chartres's *Arithmetica* Commentary as a Missing Source of Nicholas of Cusa's *De docta ignorantia*," *Recherches de théologie et philosophie médiévales* 83, no. 1 (2016): 143–99.

33 Certeau, "The Look," in *Mystic Fable*, 2:41; emphasis in the original.

analogy (God as wholly Other). Rather, Certeau's God is best described using a Cusan notion, God as Not-Other (*non aliud*), a heterological theology. "Because Certeau's God haunts the interstices of thought and speech, appearing in the middle ground of believing that lies between self and other," Bauerschmidt observes, "he is not so easy to banish."[34]

Graham Ward finds a similar third way in Certeau, but characterizes the terrain as more topological than theological.[35] For Ward, Certeau clearly opposes two spaces; the riddle is how to relate them. The first is the "rational" space of modernity, or Cartesian extension: transparent, full of objects, visible to the transcendental subject, a secularized world. The second is ordered by "heterological" practices that organize a "transgressive" counter-modernity, "places of ecstasy and desire." Here the subject is a voice from elsewhere, and the landscapes are non-objective, interiorized geographies, whose invisibility eludes reason's gaze. But how should we relate the univocal, homological space of modern rationalism and the equivocal, heterological space of the mystics? Ward suggests that Certeau can be read either way. His vision of space is not necessarily the rational space of modernity. In fact, Certeau's genealogy of an alternative space might be read as deconstructive—an aporetic Nietzschean wandering that leads into an endless eddy of interpretation. "Is Certeau's heterological project, then, finally a species of nihilism?" Ward rightly asks. "Is he simply announcing the politics of knowledge and belief such that all truth is relative and pragmatic?"[36] Ultimately Ward contends that Certeau indicates a third way beyond the opposition of homological and heterological spaces. Ward calls this option liturgical, eucharistic, or doxological space.[37] Ward's analysis is sound, but his conclusions are sometimes vague.[38] I will try to offer a

---

[34] Frederick Christian Bauerschmidt, "The Otherness of God," *South Atlantic Quarterly* 100, no. 2 (Spring 2001): 359.

[35] Graham Ward, "Michel de Certeau's 'Spiritual Spaces,'" *South Atlantic Quarterly* 100, no. 2 (Spring 2001): 501–17.

[36] Ward, "Michel de Certeau's 'Spiritual Spaces,'" 507.

[37] Ward, "Michel de Certeau's 'Spiritual Spaces,'" 510–15.

[38] This lack of precision can invite optical illusions: Ward's final account sounds as if Certeau left Roman Catholicism for progressive Anglicanism. "The Church as place has to collapse, but the Church as that space for communal living characterized by eucharistic practices? This can remain. For this space is doxological, not institutional. Its practices are liturgical.... [H]e was pushing toward a new space, a rewriting of the traditional space that is not the denial but the affirmation of tradition; in order for tradition to be tradition, it must move forward." Ward, "Michel de Certeau's 'Spiritual Spaces,'" 514.

more specific account by looking to Cusan topology as both inspiration and index of Certeau's distinctive approach.

In order to behold Certeau's mystical topology and its foundation in Cusan questions, one has to look outside the well-thumbed pages of his vaunted Cusanus essay and instead to four dense methodological *opuscula* collected in the two volumes of *The Mystic Fable*.[39] In these often-overlooked texts on the emergence and decline of "mystics" (*la mystique*), we find further connections between Certeau's method and Cusan mysticism, as I will show. By stepping outside the Cusanus essay, we see the depth of Certeau's engagement with Cusanus; and by stepping outside of Certeau's works altogether, we see the significance of that engagement as part of a broader effort in modern philosophy to articulate a non-Cartesian ontology. Hence, after exploring Certeau's understanding of mystical space, I compare Heidegger's attempt to define measurement without quantity: a necessary postulate of any general topology.

Mystical Space and the Sciences

As Certeau revisited his Cusanus essay again and again, he formulated a distinctive approach to mysticism. What Certeau found in *De visione Dei* was not only a proto-phenomenology, but a model of topology that confirmed and perhaps informed his evolving account of "mystical science." The final and longest version of that Cusanus essay—the one with a completely new conclusion—ends with these words: "The text [of *De visione Dei*] ... narrates its relation to a center of darkness circumscribed by an inability, a deficit, a madness. This black sun haunts the discourse ... [Cusanus] prides himself on only one thing, ... to 'hear' the word of other witnesses and thus try to open up a trail for that madness in history [*tenter ainsi d'ouvrir à cette folie un chemin dans l'histoire*]."[40] Those who open Nicholas's *De visione Dei* may not easily find the cardinal opening a trail for madness in history, as Certeau says, still less a *noir soleil*. However, these pregnant phrases are an astute characterization of Certeau's own handling of mysticism in the

---

[39] These are his introduction to *The Mystic Fable*, vol. 1, *The Sixteenth and Seventeenth Centuries*, trans. Michael B. Smith (Chicago: University of Chicago Press, 1992), 1–30; "A Topics," in *The Mystic Fable*, 1:75–78; "The New Science," in *The Mystic Fable*, 1:79–112; and "Mystic Historicities," in *The Mystic Fable*, 2:1–22.

[40] Certeau, "The Look," in *Mystic Fable*, 2:70. See also Certeau, "Le regard: Nicolas de Cues," in *La Fable mystique*, vol. 2, *XVIe–XVIIe Siècle*, 120–21.

two volumes of *The Mystic Fable*. The madness of the past erupts within the hermeneutical horizon of Certeau's reader, the present-day scholar, who is bound in responsibility to the past but painfully aware that she remains exiled from it. As Bauerschmidt has noted, Certeau frequently "describ[es] Cusa in terms that make him sound remarkably like Certeau."[41]

Certeau paints a rather bleak portrait of scholars who study the history of Christian mysticism. The modern academic is an expatriate far from the homeland of her premodern subject, surviving on crumbs of nostalgia. The historian's challenging texts conspire against her "like statues erected to mark the boundaries of an 'elsewhere' that is not remote, a place they both produce and guard, . . . a frontier that divides space."[42] For Certeau, historiography plays out in the contested space where the Other (divine or otherwise) is missing; the act of writing becomes a poor but necessary surrogate for the Other's absence.[43] Mystical science is therefore a topological or topographical practice, in which the historian begins from the spatial position of exile. Each mystical text offers a "theater" or "laboratory" in which to invent what Certeau calls different mystical "styles." Yet by "styles" he plainly means spatial models, since his examples of "styles" are Euclidean geometry, Cartesian geometry, and vectorial geometry.[44] Mystics is therefore a science of measuring spaces, analyzing spaces, and inventing spaces.

Mystical texts absolutely prohibit the reification of the divine Other into something denotable, let alone cede the question of God to the theologians. Likewise, they refuse to hand God over to modern conceptions of religion, since religious experience in our age has been "excluded from the scientific field and fetishized as the substitute for what is lacking."[45] Instead of allowing mysticism to be captured by theology or religion, Certeau proposes that mystical science (*la mystique*) should assert its own domain, procedures, and techniques. "At the beginning of my analysis, therefore," he writes, "there is isolation of a 'mystic' unit in the system of differentiation of

---

[41] Bauerschmidt, "Otherness of God," 353.

[42] Certeau, introduction to *The Mystic Fable*, 1:2.

[43] Certeau's historiography—where practices substitute for the lost body of the beloved—is indelibly Christian, something he knew well yet many of his readers forget or elide. See Marian Füssel, "Writing the Otherness: The Historiography of Michel de Certeau SJ," in Bocken, *Spiritual Spaces*, 25–44.

[44] Certeau, "Mystic Historicities," in *The Mystic Fable*, 2:22.

[45] Certeau, introduction to *The Mystic Fable*, 1:15.

the discourses that articulates a new area of knowledge."[46] "Mystics" is thus an autonomous zone where the alien nature of mystical texts is permitted to stand without compromise on its own, relieved of the burden of categorization under the aegis of any contemporary scholarly discipline, whether anthropology, religious studies, gender theory, or neuroscience.

At the same time as he defends its freedom, Certeau does not wish to "exclude" *la mystique* from the field of the sciences altogether, for as he insists, mysticism authentically poses a "new area of knowledge." It adds something to the field of the known, even if something elliptical, opaque, radical, or subversive. He defends this complex contemporary situation of *la mystique* by narrating its initial emergence. According to Certeau, after the professionalization of theology in the twelfth century (and the concomitant resurgence of "heresy," its twin), mysticism began with Hadewijch of Brabant and Meister Eckhart around 1300.[47] The late-medieval adjective "mystical" slowly congealed into the nominative *la mystique*, becoming an "autonomous science" of mystics for the first time. Initially, mystical science "took its place within a modified distribution of scientific fields, . . . a configuration of knowledge that distributed the practices of knowing in a different way."[48] But around 1700, after the French Quietist controversies surrounding François Fénelon and Madame Guyon, the epistemic configuration supporting mystical science collapsed. *La mystique* was partly absorbed by its neighbors, theology and philosophy, and partly redistributed into the new sciences of psychology and medicine.[49]

According to Certeau's narrative, one would expect this decline to be inevitable demise. The impossible divine Object of mystics rendered its scientific field permanently unstable and hence impossible to organize with fixed principles and procedures. In its later stages, mystical science was briefly sustained as an appendage of poetry, whose arts of language provided a center the discipline had lacked. But this too could not hold. And yet, Certeau insists, although mystical science dissolved into other disciplines, it never died; it was only sleeping. "Of that passing and contradictory science there has survived a ghost that continues to haunt Western

---

46 Certeau, introduction to *The Mystic Fable*, 1:16.

47 On the subtle importance of Hadewijch for Certeau's approach to mysticism, especially her elliptical and equivocal temporality, see Amy Hollywood, "Love Speaks Here: Michel de Certeau's *Mystic Fable*," *Spiritus: A Journal of Christian Spirituality* 12, no. 2 (2012): 198–206.

48 Certeau, "A Topics," in *The Mystic Fable*, 1:76.

49 Certeau, introduction to *The Mystic Fable*, 1:16.

epistemology," he avers. "This phantom of a passage, repressed during periods secure in their knowledge, reappears in the gaps within scientific certainty."[50] In other words, the absence of mystical science from our contemporary disciplinary map continues to destabilize those disciplines that have survived. Mystics is not a tame science like the others that arose from the disciplinary formations of the seventeenth or nineteenth centuries; it is a "wild science" (*science sauvage*) that prowls about disturbing their neat measurements.[51]

But why exactly did mystical science decline? Certeau's claim that it collapsed and dissolved in early modernity is crucial to his genealogical narrative, which in turn justifies the anomalous location of *la mystique*—in the world of the sciences, but not of it.[52] Yet the explanation provided by Certeau does not suffice, for it fails to explain the timing. Why did mystical science suddenly dissolve after four centuries of health? If it was doomed from the outset by virtue of its impossible theonymic task, how could it be reawakened again today, as he suggests? What happened in the seventeenth century that suddenly overwhelmed the epistemological capacities of *la mystique*? If mystical science haunts the new certainties of early modern science, as he maintains, what generated that new, rival mode of certainty?

One obvious candidate for the missing causal link in Certeau's genealogy is the emergence and valorization of mathematical models of the universe in Galileo, Descartes, and Newton. The mathematization of physics that began with the Oxford Calculators accelerated and expanded in those centuries into a philosophical program, the Cartesian *mathesis universalis*, a totalizing epistemology in which only numerical order and quantitative extension can guarantee certain knowledge.[53] If this were the silent precip-

---

50 Certeau, "A Topics," in *The Mystic Fable*, 1:77.

51 Certeau, "Mystic Historicities," in *The Mystic Fable*, 2:14. Certeau sometimes broadens this claim in other methodological texts, such that theology poses the most significant challenges to the writing of history: "The treatment of religious ideology by contemporary historiography requires us to recognize the ideologies that are already invested in history itself." Michel de Certeau, "Making History: Problems of Method and Problems of Meaning," in *The Writing of History*, trans. Tom Conley (New York: Columbia University Press, 1988), 21.

52 See Koenraad Geldof, "Ökonomie, Exzess, Grenze: Michel de Certeaus Genealogie der Moderne," in *Michel de Certeau: Geschichte—Kultur—Religion*, ed. Marian Füssel (Konstanz: UVK Verlagsgesellschaft, 2007), 91–151.

53 The locus classicus is René Descartes, *Regulae ad directionem ingenii*, IV, in *Oeuvres de Descartes*, vol. 10, ed. Charles Adam and Paul Tannery (Paris: Léopold Cerf, 1908), 377; trans. in *The Philosophical Writings of Descartes*, ed. John Cottingham, Robert Stoothoff, and Dugald Murdoch (Cambridge: Cambridge University Press, 1985–1991), 1:19.

itating cause of the decline of *la mystique* in Certeau's narrative, we could understand mystical science to have collapsed under the pressure of a novel, competing, mathematical determination of space. Then we might surmise that it was the geometrization of space, and the installation of its universal, homogenizing topology, that put an end to mystical topology and its heterogeneous spaces.

On the other side of that epistemological upheaval, where we late moderns reside, "mystical space" is now constrained to mean something different than it meant before. Today we have only the modest possibility of wielding "topology" as a poetic metaphor.[54] If we say, for instance, that there is a Cusan "topology" in *De visione Dei*, we can only mean by this an analogy to what occurs properly in the discipline of contemporary mathematics or physics. A mystical "space" can be no more than metaphorical, parasitic on the reality of quantitative space, or relegated to the domain of the literary imagination. Yet Certeau insists that this missing mystical topology survives in a ghostly form that continually "haunts" scientific certainty. For this to be true, its continuing critical force—and its enduring disciplinary autonomy—can be sustained only by refusing its exile into the domain of poetic metaphor. The defiance of *la mystique* today threatens the complacency of totalizing mathematical measurement. While he never states it definitively, Certeau's narrative leads us to ask: Does mystical space expose the insufficiency of geometrical space? Does the sheer notion of "mystical topology" already begin to relativize the universality, the precision, the homogeneity, the self-evidence, of the Cartesian *mathesis universalis*? Are mystical spaces somehow an antidote to the technologization of the late modern world?

Such suspicions are confirmed when we notice that Certeau himself invokes Edmund Husserl's *The Crisis of the European Sciences* in the second volume of *The Mystic Fable*.[55] Writing in 1936, Husserl feared that the natural and social sciences had so exhaustively analyzed human being that they left no space for philosophy. This precipitated our modern crisis: we find ourselves rich beyond belief in advanced sciences that produce world-altering technologies, and yet increasingly impoverished in existential meaning.

---

54 Despite its poetic confinement, "space" can offer a new theoretical platform for literary analysis: see, e.g., W. J. T. Mitchell, "Spatial Form in Literature: Toward a General Theory," *Critical Inquiry* 6, no. 3 (Spring 1980): 539–67; or Angus Fletcher, *The Topological Imagination: Spheres, Edges, and Islands* (Cambridge, MA: Harvard University Press, 2016).

55 Edmund Husserl, *The Crisis of the European Sciences and Transcendental Phenomenology*, trans. David Carr (Evanston, IL: Northwestern University Press, 1970), 23–59.

Husserl traces the origin of this crisis to the geometrization of space in Descartes and Galileo, the ugly ditch between the world as measured and the world as lived. He predicts that modern philosophy will languish until the wound is healed, and points to phenomenology as the cure.

Certeau insinuates that "mystical science" might play this role instead—not phenomenology, but *la mystique*. After quoting Husserl's *Crisis*, Certeau remarks: "Thus mystics becomes one of the places in which the appropriation of the religious by the new sciences and the crisis of philosophy interrelate."[56] In other words, the question of the Other (threatened by theological reductions) and the loss of human meaning (threatened by scientific measurements) both find their solution in the same "place": *la mystique*. Mystical science defends the alterity of God from its capture by "religion," to be sure; but it also applies its powers toward recovering the experience of worldhood lost in post-Cartesian philosophy. In this role mysticism would no longer be a matter of interior authenticity, but a means of measuring the exterior differently. Once the sciences have anatomized the world into so many objects, Certeau explains, mystics gains a new "epistemological function."[57] It exposes the scientist to the threat of a "heterogeneous epistemological system."[58] It stands as a "non-place"[59] or "atopic space"[60] outside the disciplinary cartography of modern science. It is like a ghost haunting the ill-gained certainty of the modern science[61]—a "wild science" that frightens the domesticated ones.[62]

Possibilities of Measure

Certeau's genealogy of the rise and fall of *la mystique* implies a clash between two opposed regimes of space: mystical space (non-quantitative topology) and geometrical space (quantitative topology). The former suffered discursive collapse and dissolution when the latter became the ascendant hegemonic episteme after the seventeenth century. Yet for Certeau the

---

56 Certeau, "Mystic Historicities," in *The Mystic Fable*, 2:10.
57 Certeau, "Mystic Historicities," in *The Mystic Fable*, 2:11.
58 Certeau, "Mystic Historicities," in *The Mystic Fable*, 2:9.
59 Certeau, "Mystic Historicities," in *The Mystic Fable*, 2:14.
60 Certeau, "Mystic Historicities," in *The Mystic Fable*, 2:13.
61 Certeau, "Mystic Historicities," in *The Mystic Fable*, 2:12.
62 Certeau, "Mystic Historicities," in *The Mystic Fable*, 2:14.

mathematical measures of physics remain haunted by the wild science of mystics, which sustains the premodern epistemic alternative by asserting a different modality of measurement. Unlike the infinite geometrical grid of *mathesis universalis*, however, the mystical spaces traversed in *la mystique* are permitted today to appear only as fantasy—poetic, metaphorical, or imaginary. This is the contemporary disjunction between precise measurement and existential meaning that troubled Husserl: increasing technological sophistication in the face of philosophical stagnation and deflation; a divorce between the visible and the sayable; and ultimately, a chasm between the exterior world and the interior self.

After Husserl, many continental philosophers have addressed the very same problem, including Maurice Merleau-Ponty, Henri Lefebvre, Michel Foucault, and most recently the Americans Yi Fu Tuan and Edward Casey.[63] Yet their continued investments in ever more nuanced spatial theories testify to the durability of that stubborn separation between geometrical and poetic measure. In his classic work from 1957, *The Poetics of Space*, Gaston Bachelard rejected what he called the Cartesian "cancerization" of space by geometry. For Bachelard, space is always first experienced through poetic images of enclosure that protect the thinker, the "topography of intimate being" of eggs, nests, corners, huts. Once properly sheltered, the human mind can unfold vast regions of abstract mathematical space. But that topography of scientific precision is secondary, for "inhabited space transcends geometrical space."[64] In 1988, Alain Badiou distinguished two orientations to nature that broke apart after the "Galilean rupture" of the seventeenth century: the *matheme*, or presence as subtraction from being, and the *poeme*, presence as manifestation of being.[65] Peter Sloterdijk's trilogy on "spheres" (1998–2004) outlines a contemporary anthropology by means

---

[63] See Maurice Merleau-Ponty, *Phenomenology of Perception*, trans. Donald A. Landes (New York: Routledge, 2012), especially part 2, chapter 2; Henri Lefebvre, *The Production of Space*, trans. Donald Nicholson-Smith (Oxford: Blackwell, 1991); Yi-Fu Tuan, *Space and Place: The Perspective of Experience* (Minneapolis: University of Minnesota Press, 1977); and Edward S. Casey, *The Fate of Place: A Philosophical History* (Berkeley: University of California Press, 1997).

[64] Gaston Bachelard, *The Poetics of Space*, trans. Maria Jolas (Boston: Beacon Press, 1994), 47. See further Mary Tiles, "Technology, Science, and Inexact Knowledge: Bachelard's Non-Cartesian Epistemology," in *Continental Philosophy of Science*, ed. Gary Gutting (London: Wiley Blackwell, 2005), 157–75.

[65] See Alain Badiou, *Being and Event*, §11, trans. Oliver Feltham (New York: Continuum, 2005), 123–29.

of a hierarchy of non-quantitative spaces: bubbles, globes, and foam.[66] For Sloterdijk, to become human is to enter "immunological" spheres that form complex systems of intimacy and interiority. "Living in spheres," he writes, "means creating the dimension in which humans can be contained. Spheres are immune-systemically effective space creations for ecstatic beings that are operated upon by the outside."[67]

Behind all of these stand the late writings of Martin Heidegger. Building on Husserl's analysis of the post-Cartesian plight of modernity, Heidegger opposed ontotheological metaphysics to true thinking, and the "calculability" of technological objects to the poetry that allows Being to appear. Heidegger takes up the problem most directly in two essays from 1951, where he squarely confronts the problem of equivocal measure and defends a principled account of poetic space that exceeds, and in fact precedes, numerical measures.[68]

In "Building Dwelling Thinking" (August 1951), Heidegger argues that one understands architecture only by thinking the essence of "dwelling" (*wohnen*).[69] To dwell, "to remain, to stay in a place" (*das Bleiben, das Sich-Aufhalten*), is how humans abide in being, tethered to the earth by virtue of our mortality, but miraculously able to open a clearing in which beings are spared to be themselves (*in sein Wesen schonen*) by remaining at peace (*in Frieden bleiben*).[70] The contrary of alienation, such dwelling is a kind of keeping-with things that cultivates them within a human-scale world, just as a bridge constructed over a river gathers earth, water, and sky into

---

66 On Sloterdijk's "mathematical turn," see Scott Lash, "Deforming the Figure: Topology and the Social Imaginary," *Theory, Culture & Society* 29, nos. 4–5 (2012): 261–87.

67 Peter Sloterdijk, *Spheres*, vol. 1, *Bubbles: Microspherology*, trans. Wieland Hoban (Los Angeles: Semiotext(e), 2011), 28. On the connections between sphericity and Cusanus in Sloterdijk's trilogy, see the essay by José González Ríos in chapter 6 of this volume.

68 In addition to the essays considered here, see also Martin Heidegger, "The Age of the World Picture (1938)," in Heidegger, *Off the Beaten Track*, ed. and trans. Julian Young and Kenneth Haynes (Cambridge: Cambridge University Press, 2002), 57–85; and Heidegger, "Art and Space," trans. Charles H. Seibert, in *Man and World*, vol. 6, no. 1 (The Hague: Nijhoff, 1973), 3–8.

69 Martin Heidegger, "Bauen Wohnen Denken," in *Vorträge und Aufsätze*, in *Gesamtausgabe* [*GA*], vol. 7, ed. Friedrich-Wilhelm von Herrmann (Frankfurt am Main: Vittorio Klostermann, 2000), 145–64. The original English translation is by Albert Hofstadter, "Building Dwelling Thinking," in Martin Heidegger, *Poetry, Language, Thought* (New York: Harper & Row, 1971), 145–61. Hofstadter's translation is adapted with some changes in Martin Heidegger, *Basic Writings*, ed. David Farrell Krell (New York: HarperCollins, 1993), 347–63; page numbers cited refer to this latter version.

70 Heidegger, "Building Dwelling Thinking," in *Basic Writings*, 350–51 (GA 7, 150–51).

one locale.[71] Heidegger contends that such human settlements exist prior to the abstract spaces whose dimensions we can measure with number. The bridge makes the place, and not the place the bridge, for "spaces [*Räume*] receive their essential being from locales [*Orten*] and not from 'space' ['*dem*' *Raum*]."[72] Spaces are places where a thing is sustained in a realm of unencumbered dwelling. Its preservation is guaranteed by a boundary (πέρας) or a horizon (ὅρος), but these derive from the existential posture of dwelling, not from practices of measurement.[73]

Dwellings, then, are folds of proximity: the bridge brings earth, river, and sky into nearness within its horizon, and keeps the mountain or forest further away. But once near and far are subjected to measure, the distance (*Abstand*) between definite positions becomes calculated as an interval (*Zwischenraum*) (στάδιον, *spatium*).[74] Positions can be occupied by things, but also by verbal signifiers or graphic marks, such that distance (*Entfernung*) can be measured abstractly as height, breadth, and depth, rather than sky, earth, and river. According to Heidegger, this converts the meaning of space into sheer *extensio*: "the possibility of the purely mathematical construction of manifolds with an arbitrary number of dimensions."[75] Space as mathematical extension is univocal and homogenized, and in fact "contains no spaces and no places." In lieu of the dwelling that opens up human worlds, we find only bare dimensions indifferent to human presence, abstracted from the thinking that cultivates nearness:

> *Spatium* and *extensio* afford at any time the possibility of measuring things and what they make room for, according to distances, spans, and directions [*nach Abständen, nach Strekken, nach Richtungen*], and of computing these magnitudes. But the fact that they are *universally* applicable to everything that has extension can in no case make numerical magnitudes the *ground* of the essence of spaces and locales that are measurable with the aid of mathematics.[76]

---

[71] Heidegger, "Building Dwelling Thinking," in *Basic Writings*, 354–55.
[72] Heidegger, "Building Dwelling Thinking," in *Basic Writings*, 356 (GA 7, 156).
[73] Heidegger, "Building Dwelling Thinking," in *Basic Writings*, 356.
[74] Heidegger, "Building Dwelling Thinking," in *Basic Writings*, 357 (GA 7, 157).
[75] Heidegger, "Building Dwelling Thinking," in *Basic Writings*, 357.
[76] Heidegger, "Building Dwelling Thinking," in *Basic Writings*, 357–58 (GA 7, 158).

Humanity and space are mediated by dwelling, not calculation.[77] Architectures (or mystical texts?) that open a space for dwelling remain "closer to the essence of spaces ... than any geometry" could hope to be and assume for themselves the tasks of "traversing and measuring."[78] Here, says Heidegger, prior to mathematical measurement, humanity awaits the arrival of divinity.[79]

Heidegger develops this philosophy of measure in a second lecture, "... Poetically Man Dwells..." (October 1951), centered around a poem by Friedrich Hölderlin.[80] Once again, the quantitative "space" of extensive magnitudes is not the authentic "space" of earthly dwelling. Now we might be tempted to say that the latter is no more than a poetic expression, relegated to the realm of metaphor—particularly given Heidegger's conspicuously mythical images of "sky" and "mortals." But, as Heidegger points out, poetry is itself nothing less than a "letting dwell" (*Wohnenlassen*), namely, the most human mode of "building," in the original Greek sense of the poem as a "making" (ποίημα > ποίησις).[81] Poetry responds to the call of language, which can be heard only in a deep listening that awaits the "unforeseen" (*das Unvermutete*), a kind of grateful prayer.[82] This is the very opposite of the calculability of number, which decides what to say in advance and repeats its abstractions heedless of occasion or locale. If poems make possible authentic dwelling, they open spaces; and if they make space, they must have a metric function of some kind, Heidegger reasons, a mode of measurement that is prior to numerical magnitudes. Explaining the essence of poetic measurement—quite deliberately in mythopoetic terms—is the task of this second lecture.

"Poetry is a measuring," Heidegger observes. "But what is it to measure? ... In poetry there takes place what all measuring is in the ground of its being. Hence it is necessary to pay heed to the basic act of measuring."[83] To begin with, Heidegger asserts that true measuring is not yet a science or a

---

77 Heidegger, "Building Dwelling Thinking," in *Basic Writings*, 359.
78 Heidegger, "Building Dwelling Thinking," in *Basic Writings*, 360.
79 Heidegger, "Building Dwelling Thinking," in *Basic Writings*, 360.
80 Martin Heidegger, "... dichterisch wohnet der Mensch ...," in *Vorträge und Aufsätze*, 189–208. English translation by Albert Hofstadter, "... Poetically Man Dwells ...," in *Poetry, Language, Thought*, 213–29.
81 Heidegger, "... Poetically Man Dwells ...," in *Poetry, Language, Thought*, 215 (GA 7, 193).
82 Heidegger, "... Poetically Man Dwells ...," in *Poetry, Language, Thought*, 216 (GA 7, 194).
83 Heidegger, "... Poetically Man Dwells ...," in *Poetry, Language, Thought*, 221.

matter of instrumental precision, or even numeration at all. True measure precedes our modern reduction of measure to calculation:

> By the use of something known—measuring rods and their number [*Maßstäben und Maßzahlen*]—something unknown is stepped off and thus made known, and so is confined within a quantity and order [*Anzahl und Ordnung*] which can always be determined at a glance. Such measuring can vary with the type of apparatus employed. But who will guarantee that this customary kind of measuring, merely because it is common, touches the nature of measuring? When we hear of measure, we immediately think of number and imagine the two, measure and number [*Maß und Zahl*], as quantitative. But the *nature* of measure is no more a quantum than is the *nature* of number.[84]

Geometrical measures of quantity are strictly confined to earth (as the μέτρον of γῆ, geo-metry), namely to an immanence of objects that lack human depth. Truly human measures, Heidegger proposes, span from the earth up to the sky, from mortality to divinity, from the given to the possible. To remain human, to secure a human dwelling, begins with a primordial "dimension" that "spans the between" (*durchmißt das Zwischen*), bridging humanity and divinity. As Heidegger writes, "taking the measure of the dimension is the element within which human dwelling ... securely endures [*währt*]."[85] That vector running from earth to sky opens the possibility of dwelling in being and time, and thus of making space.

Poetry is just that action of "spanning" (*Durchmessung*) earth and sky and thus exercising an autonomous capacity for a "distinctive kind of measuring" (*ein ausgezeichnetes Messen*).[86] Poetry takes the measure of the co-givenness of earth and sky that enables human being to remain itself. This is a trans-quantitative, but therefore more authentic, way of measuring space. This suggests that a "poetic" use of space is by no means merely a metaphoric transfer from a real mathematical instance to a fictive one marked with ironic punctuation. Rather, the visibility of "earth" that invites

---

84 Heidegger, "... Poetically Man Dwells ...," in *Poetry, Language, Thought*, 224 (GA 7, 203). See Heidegger's analysis of Descartes in "The Question Concerning Technology," in *Basic Writings*, esp. 277–78.
85 Heidegger, "... Poetically Man Dwells ...," in *Poetry, Language, Thought*, 221 (GA 7, 198–99).
86 Heidegger, "... Poetically Man Dwells ...," in *Poetry, Language, Thought*, 221, 224 (GA 7, 202).

quantitative measure through the repetitions of number exhibits its length and breadth thanks only to the invisible presence of its antipode, the "sky" reflecting it from above. The spanning of earth and sky endows earth with an image-character that conceals a hidden depth which always delivers more to sense. That is, what we call "image" is "the appearance of sky that manifests the invisible invisibly in the visible." Or in Heidegger's deliberately poetic image: "The radiance of its height is itself the darkness of its all-sheltering breadth."[87]

Poetic images are not merely metaphors; they are the initial manifestation of dwellings not yet flattened and dulled by the mechanical repetitions of quantitative measurement.[88] They are "not mere fantasies and illusions but imaginings [*Ein-Bildungen*] that are visible inclusions of the alien [*Fremden*] in the sight of the familiar."[89] Hence the importance of the sky or the "alien"—the dimension of God—within the measures that poetry effects. For Heidegger, God is not the measure of all human measuring, for God remains entirely unknown, and in this complete withdrawal makes possible human dwelling. "The unknown god appears as the unknown by way of the sky's manifestness," he writes. "This appearance is the measure against which man measures himself."[90] Human being measures quantities, while poetry measures the human itself; but in a sense, the measure of poetry itself is the absent God. Precisely through that absence, the crucial alien invisibility is guaranteed: "that to which the invisible imparts itself in order to remain what it is—unknown."[91]

Poetry "spans the between" of earth and sky, meting out a space in which God appears as a trace of absence. The space of poetry could well be called mystical: a mystical topology, which folds together a play of presence and absence, all within a space that secures the remaining-together of the sayable and unsayable, the familiar and the alien. Heidegger's reference to brightness and darkness remind one of the cataphatic and apophatic mystical traditions that captivated Cusanus and Certeau: "The poetic saying of images gathers the brightness and sound of heavenly appearances into

---

[87] Heidegger, "... Poetically Man Dwells ...," in *Poetry, Language, Thought*, 226.

[88] Heidegger, "... Poetically Man Dwells ...," in *Poetry, Language, Thought*, 228. By the same token, our contemporary boredom with poetry is a symptom of a totalizing mania for quantitative space, "a curious excess of frantic measuring and calculating."

[89] Heidegger, "... Poetically Man Dwells ...," in *Poetry, Language, Thought*, 226 (GA 7, 205).

[90] Heidegger, "... Poetically Man Dwells ...," in *Poetry, Language, Thought*, 223.

[91] Heidegger, "... Poetically Man Dwells ...," in *Poetry, Language, Thought*, 225.

one with the darkness and silence of what is alien. By such sights the god surprises us. In this strangeness he proclaims his unfaltering nearness [*unablässige Nähe*]."[92] Beyond the familiarity of objective presence, beyond the silence of total absence, perdures an alien but indelible "nearness," the intimate curvature of space pressing upon us, the sky brushing our face.

Mystical Topology in Four Dimensions

Heidegger's first essay describes a non-quantitative spatial architecture that is more original, more human, and more transparent to divinity than physical structures measured geometrically. His second essay argues that poetic apprehensions of space are more authentic moments of measurement than calculations made with numbers. What Heidegger describes seems eminently close to Certeau's notion of the alternative topology practiced by *la mystique*, which haunts our complacent distinction of quantitative space from non-quantitative space. Certeau detected a fundamental "topology" in Cusanus, one present in Cusan mysticism more than others and perceptible even within the pages of *De visione Dei*, that rare work where Nicholas managed to avoid mentioning geometry altogether. Did Certeau simply reflect his own spatial interests back upon Cusanus, or in this case, did Nicholas of Cusa actually help Certeau define, in his own words, "the content itself" of the wild science of mystics?

For Certeau, mystics is the discipline in which Christian thinking makes its best response to the crisis of modern philosophy. Certeau's opposition to mathematized space—much like the anti-Cartesian alternative explicated by Heidegger—is aided considerably by Cusan thought. Indeed, Certeau's confidence in a mystical "topology" at the heart of *la mystique* seems largely inspired by the German cardinal, as if Cusan mystical theology were the exemplar that encouraged Certeau to dream of a post-Cartesian spatial hermeneutics. But if this is the case, it stands to reason *a fortiori* that Cusan topology is intrinsically opposed to that totalizing quantitative extension that Heidegger critiques under the name *mathesis universalis*.[93] Cusan space is profoundly geometrical—hence its appeal to Certeau—but its geometry boasts analogical theonymic functions that counteract the universal claims of merely quantitative measure. Cusanus, in effect, geometrizes the rocky,

---

[92] Heidegger, "... Poetically Man Dwells ...," in *Poetry, Language, Thought*, 226 (GA 7, 205).
[93] On Cusanus and Heidegger, see the essay by Stephen Gersh in chapter 15 of this volume.

moss-addled terrain of the myriad mystical spaces unfolded in ancient and medieval Christian traditions, thereby establishing the conditions for a more fundamental resistance to the totalizing modern episteme. Hence not only is Nicholas of Cusa's mysticism a propaedeutic, a warrant, and a resource for Certeau's historiographical project in general; the particular contours of the Cusan "style" of mystical topology, its signature features, shed light on a possible future for *la mystique* beyond the strictures of *mathesis universalis*. Let us name four such features by way of conclusion.

Circularity

Mathesis universalis is universal: its numerical measure is always pre-calculated, endlessly repeated, and enforced heedless of context. By contrast, mystical topology emerges only through networks of relations, continually and systematically displaced and displacing, circulating without attaining its object in an infinitely asymptotic approach toward discursive unity.

Certeau envisions a mystical science—incomplete, eccentric, and parasitical—that haunts the conscience of scientific certainty: "*Mystics* does not have its own content: it is an exercise of *the other* in relation to a given *site*; it is characterized by a set of specific 'operations' in a field that is not its own."[94] It secretly "traces" and "inscribes" the divine into conventional "networks of knowledge."[95] If mystical science were to re-emerge, Certeau contends, it would have to appear within a fourfold disciplinary "frame." The four "lines" forming this square frame, he says, are four extant discourses that Certeau adopts but deliberately deforms.[96] They are: (1) the discourse of eroticism (the body prior to the text); (2) the discourse of psychoanalysis (speech-acts deciphering the body); (3) the discourse of historiography (mourning the absent body); and (4) the discourse of fable (orality prior to textuality). Certeau names this fourfold disciplinary nexus—and with it, his fundamental project in *The Mystic Fable*—"squaring the circle."[97]

The phrase "squaring the circle" is not a rhetorical commonplace, but denotes a specific geometrical problem from ancient to Renaissance mathematics, the quadrature of the circle. In the fifteenth century, no one had yet discovered a rational proportion between the square and the circle. That

---

[94] Certeau, "Mystic Historicities," in *The Mystic Fable*, 2:22.
[95] Certeau, "Mystic Historicities," in *The Mystic Fable*, 2:22.
[96] Certeau, introduction to *The Mystic Fable*, 1:4–14.
[97] Certeau, introduction to *The Mystic Fable*, 1:3.

mystery drove Nicholas of Cusa to compose one geometrical treatise after the other, as he sought the solution in twelve works between 1445 and 1458, roughly one a year. He never succeeded, and professional mathematicians like Paolo Toscanelli gently asked the good cardinal to cease.[98] But despite his amateur mistakes, the very attempt remains philosophically valuable.[99] In *De docta ignorantia*, Nicholas compares the human mind to a polygon or square that infinitely approaches the perfect circularity of God.[100] If he could actually formulate the ratio of square to circle, Nicholas was convinced it would be a theological breakthrough. If God appears at the coincidence of opposites, the squared circle would be a kind of theophany.

What does Certeau mean when he calls a reinvigorated mystical science "squaring the circle"? The four proximate disciplines form a square (erotics, psychoanalysis, historiography, fables), leaving "mystics" to be the ineffable circle. The square approaches circularity, but the ratio between them eludes us. Certeau's Cusan image suggests that his exemplary mystical science cannot and should not emerge as one integral discipline. Its only procedure is to maximize its fourfold base, pushing those four disciplines beyond themselves, ever reinscribing their interior topography, yet never tracing a separate figure. Certeau's mystical science, which promises to restore the lost epistemological unity that troubled Husserl, can only be infinitely approximated, much like Nicholas's serial proofs, as an unsystematic

---

[98] On Cusanus's geometrical works, see Jean-Marie Nicolle, *Mathématiques et métaphysique dans l'oeuvre de Nicolas de Cues* (Villeneuve d'Ascq: Presses Universitaires du Septentrion, 2001); and Marco Böhlandt, *Verborgene Zahl—Verborgener Gott: Mathematik und Naturwissen im Denken des Nicolaus Cusanus (1401–1464)* (Stuttgart: Franz Steiner Verlag, 2009). On the quadrature of the circle in Cusanus, see Tom Müller, *Perspektivität und Unendlichkeit: Mathematik und ihre Anwendung in der Frührenaissance am Beispiel von Alberti und Cusanus* (Regensburg: S. Roderer-Verlag, 2010), 47–74.

[99] This is not an uncontroversial point; see Jean-Marie Nicolle, *Le laboratoire mathématique de Nicolas de Cues* (Paris: Éditions Beauchesne, 2020), esp. 13–14, 206–7. Nicolle's conclusions might appear differently in light of Certeau's *la mystique*. If there is nothing more to think or experience than quantitative space measured technologically, then we should indeed take Cusan mysticism as an ill-advised chimera that fails both as mathematics and as theology; like a child, the cardinal only distracts the laboratory of working mathematicians as he plays with geometrical "symbols." But if there is the possibility of a pre-quantitative apprehension of space—as Heidegger and Bachelard *inter alia* maintain—then experiments with mathematical models inside of mystical theology signal a powerful philosophical critique.

[100] See Nicholas of Cusa, *De docta ignorantia*, I.3 (10), in *Nikolaus von Kues: Philosophisch-Theologische Werke*, vol. 1, ed. Paul Wilpert and Hans Gerhard Senger, rev. ed. (Hamburg: Felix Meiner Verlag, 2002), 14.

collection of insights—a *mathesis* that is definitively not universal, because it maps a space that is non-quantitative, subject to another measure.

Itinerancy

Mathesis universalis projects a static grid of positions separated by intervals of distance, erasing difference through the eternal sameness of calculative measure. Mystical topology is always in movement, carving out irregular, unpredictable pathways and rippling folds, unconstrained, organic, alive, and free.

At the end of the first volume of *The Mystic Fable*, Certeau famously praises the figure of the Wanderer: "He or she is mystic who cannot stop walking and, with the certainty of what is lacking, knows of every place and object that it is *not that*; one cannot stay *there* nor be content with *that*.... Places are exceeded, passed, lost behind it. It makes one go further, elsewhere. It lives nowhere."[101] To wander through locales without arresting one's movement is to be a mystic, but only because that spatial practice induces the topological experience that is properly mystical: nomadic itinerancy.

Certeau's image of wandering echoes his famous chapter, "Walking in the City," in *The Practice of Everyday Life* (1980). Manhattanites are *Wandersmänner*, perpetual walkers who pass through the masses like bodies inscribing poems. Viewed abstractly, the titanic metropolis seems a "'geometrical' or 'geographical' space," but the circumambulations of the walkers, bustling and chaotic, yet spontaneously harmonized, construct "'another spatiality' (an 'anthropological,' poetic and mythic experience of space)," writes Certeau, citing Merleau-Ponty.[102] Their "pedestrian enunciation" is a legible speech-act, and their footsteps are an "appropriation of the topographical system," that links here to there.[103] The "long poem of walking" has its own rhetoric and grammar: "Walking affirms, suspects, tries out, transgresses, ... the trajectories it 'speaks.'"[104] At the same time, metaphors and narrative are equally "spatial trajectories" that "traverse and

---

[101] Certeau, *The Mystic Fable*, 1:299.

[102] Certeau, *Practice of Everyday Life*, 93; 117. On Certeau's debts to Merleau-Ponty, see Ian Buchanan, "Heterophenomenology, or de Certeau's Theory of Space," *Social Semiotics* 6, no. 1 (1996): 111–32.

[103] Certeau, *Practice of Everyday Life*, 97–99.

[104] Certeau, *Practice of Everyday Life*, 100–101, 99.

organize places." They "regulate" our shift through imaginal space, but they also "organize walks," achieving the journey before our feet.[105] A "metaphor" is fundamentally a transportation system.[106]

Certeau's account of walking as a practice of spatial construction is highly reminiscent of the dramatic setting of *De visione Dei*, when the monks perambulate around the icon.[107] Their footsteps tread out a geometrical space attuned to the optics of the omnivoyant face of Christ, and their walking creates the possibility of shared language and mutual belief. That projective geometrical space can be measured and diagrammed (as Certeau does, adding his diagrams where Cusanus had none), but its topology is not founded on number. Its measure is sustained by the embodied dwelling of the community together, cloistered and yet wandering before the icon with nomadic freedom, ever within the gaze of divine Vision—"the invisible invisibly in the visible," in Heidegger's words.[108]

---

[105] Certeau, *Practice of Everyday Life*, 115–16. Inigo Bocken calls Certeau's consistent attention to lived space—whether the nomadism of the mystics or the flânerie of the urbanite—a "rhetoric of dwelling" that responds to contemporary "placelessness" (*Ortlosigkeit*). "The silence of God, in Certeau's analysis, opens up space for the technocratic, calculative mastery of the modern world. There is no longer any privileged place for human being to orient itself and where God's voice can be heard.... In the emptiness of a silent God we have no alternative but to establish new discourses and build new mental dwellings.... In this sense it is understandable that, toward the end of his life, Michel de Certeau paid great attention to Nicholas of Cusa. For Cusanus was quite aware of this problem...." See Inigo Bocken, "Nirgendwo zu Hause? Die Rhetorik des Wohnens nach Michel de Certeau," in *Wohnen*. vol. 3 of Felderkundungen Laienspiritualität, ed. Ulrich Dickmann and Wolfgang Christian Schneider (Schwerte: Katholische Akademie, 2011), 38–39.

[106] "In modern Athens, the vehicles of mass transportation are called *metaphorai*. To go to work or to go home, one takes a 'metaphor'—a bus or a train. Stories could also take this noble name; every day, they traverse and organize places; they select and link them together; they make sentences and itineraries out of them.... Every story is a travel story—a spatial practice." Certeau, *Practice of Everyday Life*, 115.

[107] I thank Victoria Pérez Rivera for this insight. See Nicholas of Cusa, *De visione Dei*, Praef. (3–4), in *Nicolai de Cusa Opera Omnia*, vol. VI, ed. Heide Dorothea Riemann (Hamburg: Felix Meiner Verlag, 2000), 5–7.

[108] On wandering and its connections to Cusanus, see Inigo Bocken, "Nomad and Layman: Spiritual Spaces in Modernity—Mysticism and Everyday Life in Michel de Certeau," in Bocken, *Spiritual Spaces*, 111–23. For Bocken, Certeau demonstrated that cultural theory must be a "topographical practice" that maps spaces and cuts pathways through them. If Certeau is too theological for the theorists, and too theoretical for the theologians, "this is exactly his intended position ... the very expression of the modern condition itself—the position of the nomad" (123).

Depth

Mathesis universalis is devoid of matter, quality, and phenomenal presence, a pure possibility that drains locales of particularity thanks to the imperative to measure through quantity alone. Mystical topology, by contrast, is also a variety of negation, but one that leaves intact, indeed outlines in bas-relief, the cut and texture of particular beings in their singularity. In its failures of precise measurement, mystical space bears witness to a divine depth of which it cannot speak. If *mathesis universalis* negates the phenomenal world to gain certain knowledge of order and quantity, mystical topology negates itself instead to preserve the richness of the world.

Certeau recognizes that topology can operate as a meta-science only if it can bridge two modes of measuring: numbers and language. In the new section added to the final version of his Cusanus essay, Certeau identifies three discursive moments in Cusan mysticism.[109] The first is figural: the geometry of point and line in space, what Certeau calls a "scenic construction." The second is constative: positive statements intended as true, or "rational discourse." If the first is mathematical, the second is linguistic. The third moment is the relation of first and second, coordinating the visible and the sayable.[110] Certeau proposes that this third moment is "alogical" and "cannot be thought." All theory begins from folly and madness, as one credits the Other's word without reason and "an irrational initiates the rational."[111] It escapes both the seen and the said, yet silently joins them. Figure and statement, or what Badiou calls *matheme* and *poeme*, can only be placed into endlessly "mutual referral," tending toward a point of coincidence infinitely deferred. Mystical science has little to do with the predicative speech of scripture or doctrine, but is rather the ceaseless disjunctions of non-closure and non-encounter. For this reason, Certeau calls Cusan wisdom a "theory of failure."[112]

---

109 Certeau, "The Look," in *Mystic Fable*, 2:53.
110 Certeau, "The Look," in *Mystic Fable*, 2:54.
111 Certeau, "The Look," in *Mystic Fable*, 2:53.
112 Certeau, "The Look," in *Mystic Fable*, 2:68. Hoff compares Certeau's interest in Cusanus to Derrida's encounter with negative theology, but Derrida knew the cardinal fairly well, thanks to his teacher, Maurice de Gandillac. See Johannes Hoff, "Philosophie als performative Praktik: Spuren cusanischen Denkens bei Jacques Derrida und Michel de Certeau," in *Cusanus-Rezeption in der Philosophie des 20. Jahrhunderts*, ed. Klaus Reinhardt and Harald Schwaetzer (Regensburg: S. Roderer-Verlag, 2005), 93–119.

Here Certeau clearly has in mind Nicholas of Cusa's theory of measure in *De docta ignorantia*. The mind measures through number and, in its struggle to apprehend the physical world, projects mathematical quantities. The instruments of arithmetic, geometry, harmonics, and astronomy allow us to make precise measurements, and yet, Cusanus observes, the experience of precision is fundamentally negative. Exact measurement never reaches its terminus, but stretches out into ever greater degrees of precision. Precision is that which is most impossible for the human geometer, the limit that can be approached only infinitely and asymptotically.[113] Instead, Cusanus reserves perfect precision for God alone, making God the sole successful geometer—and for Nicholas, the point is that this not a metaphor. At the same time, Cusanus discovered that at the heart of the new scientific rendering of mathematical space was hidden an experience of apophatic mysticism. Measure is negation, as the world recedes infinitely beyond the grasp of the measurer, leaving him bereft of knowledge. But as the greatest Renaissance commentator on Pseudo-Dionysius, Nicholas knew that the most profound mystical experience was unknowing: one names God best by withdrawing from names and entering into silence. Once precise measurement is grasped as negative theophany, even the geometrical experience of space leads one back to a prior mystical experience of space, the priority of the non-quantitative. Cusan topology is replete with interior absences. Crevasses of the infinite loom behind every definite edge, as a mesh of perforations unravels space from within, quietly ruptured by the divine depths (τὰ βάθη τοῦ θεοῦ) (1 Cor 2:10).

Proximology

Mathesis universalis stretches out into infinite cosmic reaches. The calculable extensive distances, endlessly repeated, are the warp and weft that project the vast mathetic field. These are the infinite distances whose silence terrified Pascal.[114] But mystical topology, while also a measured spatial field, is ordered not by unimaginable distances, but by a luminous nearness, an unthinkable proximity that projects itself like the gaze of an icon into the space of the measuring subject, preserving her singular locale.

---

113 See Nicholas of Cusa, *De docta ignorantia*, I.3 (9–10), ed. Wilpert and Senger, 12–14.

114 "The eternal silence of these infinite spaces frightens me." Blaise Pascal, *Pensées*, 206; in *Pascal's Pensées*, trans. W. F. Trotter (New York: E. P. Dutton & Co., 1958), 61.

According to Certeau, Nicholas of Cusa does not think of geometry as an ontology of forms, as in ancient Platonism. Rather, geometry furnishes an overarching "scientificity" that is "capable of formulating and regulating the productions of the mind in all the disciplines."[115] Certeau christens this alternative Cusan mode of universal geometry a "proximology."[116] Proximology is the science of radical nearness, he says, operating within a distinctive "space of coincidence."[117] As a master "hermeneutic of figures," proximological geometry is the principle (necessarily pre-quantitative) that grounds scientificity as such by coordinating diverse practices of measure. Certeau even claims, controversially, that Cusanus abandons the medieval *analogia entis* and adopts proximology in place of analogy to think God. Proximology is a conjectural logic of infinite approach without identity, a spatialization of theonymy that Cusanus beautifully calls "brilliant nearness" (*fulgida propinquitas*)—a figure Certeau hastens to adopt.[118] Or in Heidegger's words: "By such sights the god surprises us. In this strangeness he proclaims his unfaltering nearness."

---

[115] Certeau, "The Look," in *Mystic Fable*, 2:33–34.
[116] Certeau, "The Look," in *Mystic Fable*, 2:51.
[117] Certeau, "The Look," in *Mystic Fable*, 2:33.
[118] Certeau, "The Look," in *Mystic Fable*, 2:51. See also "The Look," 40, where Certeau foregrounds *De theologicis complementis*.

11

The Gift in Cusanus

The Neo-Augustinian Humanism of Louis Dupré

PETER CASARELLA

In memoriam Louis Dupré (1925–2022)

Louis Dupré introduced me to the phenomenology and philosophy of religion when I was a freshman in Yale College. I had the great fortune to be able to converse with him about many topics that flowed from this initial encounter. The relevance of Cusanus to my studies, however, did not arise until four years later, during my first semester of graduate school. Soon after that I was a teaching assistant in a popular lecture course that Dupré taught with Cyrus Hamlin of the German department on "The Shape of Modernity." It was in these years that I first began to speak to him about writing a dissertation on Nicholas of Cusa, and by 1988, I had left to study for two years with Prof. Rudolf Haubst at the Institut für Cusanus-Forschung in Trier. Dupré's work on Cusanus began to appear in the years that followed. At the time, I had only a vague idea of what Dupré would outline in the years to follow: how Cusanus might be placed into the matrix of the passage to modernity and the revival of an Augustinian theology of the self that was marked by the humanism of the Italian quattrocentro. Dupré took an approach that was different from that of Ernst Cassirer, Hans-Georg Gadamer, Hans Blumenberg, and even his Yale colleague and fellow Cusanus devotee, Karsten Harries, and he led me to ask different questions than had been asked by these eminent scholars of Cusanus. Dupré connected the cardinal from Kues to the origins of modernity in a way that was more theological and more humanistic than any of the scholars just mentioned. How this theological and humanistic matrix came together as a hermeneutical lens for the study of Nicholas of Cusa is the subject of this essay.

The Passage to Cusanus

Dupré wrote four substantial essays on Nicholas of Cusa: "Nature and Grace in Nicholas of Cusa's Mystical Theology" (1991), "The Mystical Theology of Nicholas of Cusa's *De visione Dei*" (1992), "The Question of Pantheism from Eckhart to Cusanus" (2006), and "Justifying the Mystical Experience" (2019).[1] There are striking similarities between these treatments that are confirmed by the excursus on Cusanus in his groundbreaking work, *The Passage to Modernity* (1993), as well as in other places. Cusanus's main legacy in the history of Western thought, according to Dupré, was to rethink the unification of nature and grace in the wake of their "fateful separation."[2] By "separation," Dupré is referring to the twin problems of a nominalist absolute potency in God that empties nature of any intrinsic meaning or worth and a humanist naturalism that subsumes the positive content of revelation into a preordained and rationally conceived whole. By "fateful," he is referring to the ripple effect that these two opposed and, ultimately,

---

[1] Louis Dupré, "Nature and Grace in Nicholas of Cusa's Mystical Philosophy," *American Catholic Philosophical Quarterly* 64, no. 1 (1990): 153–70; idem, "The Mystical Theology of Nicholas of Cusa's *De visione Dei*," in *Nicholas of Cusa on Christ and the Church: Essays in Memory of Chandler McCuskey Brooks for the American Cusanus Society*, ed. Gerald Christianson and Thomas M. Izbicki (Leiden: Brill, 1996), 205–20; idem, "The Question of Pantheism from Eckhart to Cusanus," in *Cusanus: The Legacy of Learned Ignorance*, ed. Peter J. Casarella (Washington, DC: The Catholic University of America Press, 2006), 74–88; and idem, "Justifying the Mystical Experience," in *Thinking the Unknowable* (Notre Dame, IN: University of Notre Dame Press, forthcoming). The citations from this last work are given below based on Dupré's original typescript.

[2] Louis Dupré, *The Passage to Modernity: An Essay in the Hermeneutics of Nature and Culture* (New Haven, CT: Yale University Press, 1993), 167.

irreconcilable currents will have on modern and contemporary spiritual life.

This ill-fated separation has an outcome similar to what Charles Taylor in *A Secular Age* calls a "ratchet effect."[3] Once separated, there is no return to the symbolic world that held together what is now experienced as shattered fragments. We need to pause and grasp the immensity of the task for thought presented by what appears to be an unbridgeable chasm. In much the same vein, David Tracy composed a stimulating essay on Dupré's thought on modernity entitled: "Fragments of a Synthesis? The Hopeful Paradox of Dupré's Modernity."[4] Tracy writes with genuine and rightful admiration of Dupré's work: "Dupré leaves one amazed again at the newness of modernity and thinking again about our culture's original passage to modernity. . . . Dupré also helps one to think through anew the most central issues of philosophy (form, nature, culture, the self, transcendence) by rethinking our culture's history. No small accomplishment that."[5]

The placement of Cusanus in this narrative is thus critical to grasping the full scope of Dupré's interest in the fifteenth century. No other figure occupies this same role, even though other figures are tasked by Dupré with the same impossibly Herculean act of reunification. Cusanus does not just happen to be at the place of the separation, as a "forerunner" or rare beacon of light at the cusp of the truly modern age. Cusanus's attempted synthesis in a certain sense brings into view *for the very first time* what has already begun to fall apart in and through Scholasticism and what can *never*, in spite of Cusanus's mightily creative labors, be brought together again. As with the Dionysian "secret" that Cusanus references in *De non aliud*, the cardinal from Kues discloses a hidden truth about reality through a radical process of negation.[6] What Cusanus *cannot* reconstruct is the modern predicament in microcosm: the flame of faith burns from within seeking

---

[3] Charles Taylor, "Comparison, History, Truth," in *Myth and Philosophy*, ed. Frank Reynolds and David Tracy (Albany: State University of New York Press, 1990), 52.

[4] David Tracy, "Fragments of a Synthesis? The Hopeful Paradox of Dupré's Modernity," in *Christian Spirituality and the Culture of Modernity: The Thought of Louis Dupré*, ed. Peter J. Casarella and George P. Schner, SJ (Grand Rapids, MI: Eerdmans, 1998), 9–24.

[5] David Tracy, "Fragments of a Synthesis?," 24.

[6] See Peter Casarella, "Cusanus on Dionysius: The Turn to Speculative Theology," in *Re-Thinking Dionysius the Areopagite*, ed. Sarah Coakley and Charles M. Stang (Malden, MA: Wiley-Blackwell, 2009), 141; and Jacques Derrida, "On How Not to Speak: Denials," in *Languages of the Unsayable: The Play of Negativity in Literature and Literary Theory*, ed. Sanford Budick and Wolfgang Iser (New York: Columbia University Press, 1989), 3–70.

to find God in all things, even while unsure that any path is available to be traversed that might lead from subjective intimacy to cosmic fullness.[7]

The nature of this particular unconcealment comes even more prominently into view if one compares the image of Cusanus in Dupré's narrative with other bridge figures that he configures in a similar manner: Jan van Ruusbroec, Ignatius of Loyola, and Hegel. Ruusbroec died in Groenendaal just twenty years before Nicholas's birth in nearby Kues.[8] The Flemish mystic had integrated a neo-Augustinian concept of the Trinitarian image of God with the flowing rhythms of a social commitment to everyday life. In the common foreword to *Light from Light*, his anthology of Christian mysticism co-edited with James Wiseman, Dupré writes: "The human person is called to partake in the *outgoing* movement of the Trinity itself and, while sharing the common Life of the Triune God, to move outward into creation."[9] Ruusbroec inherits from Augustine the notion that the Trinitarian image of the soul relates first to the divine origin of the soul and then to the way outward. This particular rhythm is even more explicit in Dupré's treatment of the bridge figure of Ignatius, as Paul Levesque has observed:

> [For Ignatius] action is itself perceived as participating in the "outgoing" movement of the trinitarian life of God. Humans are called to fulfillment not by resting in the divine but by descending with the Son into creation in order to sanctify it.[10]

---

[7] See Peter Casarella, "'Modern Forms Filled with Traditional Spiritual Content': On Louis Dupré's Contribution to Christian Theology," in *Christian Spirituality and the Culture of Modernity*, ed. Casarella and Schner, 275–310.

[8] I estimate the distance between the two places to be about 160 miles. There is no evidence, to my knowledge, that Cusanus knew the works or even the person of Ruusbroec, but there is a common font of Rhineland mysticism shared between them. That this very terrain is the terrain of Louis Dupré, who even visited me once from Belgium when I lived in Trier, is the more salient point. Dupré maintains without evidence that Cusanus probably knew, "directly or indirectly," the *Spiritual Espousals* of Ruusbroec. See Dupré, "The Question of Pantheism from Eckhart to Cusanus," 85.

[9] Louis Dupré and James A. Wiseman, OSB, introduction to *Light from Light: An Anthology of Christian Mysticism*, ed. Louis Dupré and James A. Wiseman, OSB, 2nd ed. (Mahwah, NJ: Paulist Press, 2001), 9–10. Italics in the original.

[10] Paul Levesque, "Symbol as the Primary Religious Category in the Thought of Louis Dupré: Foundations for Contemporary Sacramentology" (PhD diss., Katholieke Universitaeit Leuven, 1995), 300. Levesque is commenting on Louis Dupré, "Ignatian Humanism and Its Mystical Origins," *Communio: International Catholic Review* 18, no. 2 (1991): 164–82.

From late fourteenth-century Flanders to sixteenth-century Spain, Dupré finds bridge figures on either side of the divide of the fateful separation. The more robust Trinitarian spirituality of both Ruusbroec and Ignatius (in Dupré's view) effectively negotiated a way forward that could have avoided the fateful separation. All three figures—Ruusbroec, Cusanus, and Ignatius—willy-nilly reverse a pattern that Hans Blumenberg attributed to the beginnings of modernity. Blumenberg maintained in *The Legitimacy of the Modern Age* that because of modern self-assertion traditional religious forms would become imbued with a wholly new content (an epochal shift Blumenberg ties most explicitly to Giordano Bruno). Dupré's bridge-makers fill a free and modern *imago Dei* with traditional religious content.[11]

This development in the transition to the modern age brings Dupré close to both Hegel and Transcendental Thomism.[12] Dupré was an avid reader of Hegel from the beginning of his career. Hegel, he says, achieves the movement from the inner to the outer by hyperbolizing the uniqueness of the Trinitarian revelation in a rational manner and transmuting the facticity of the absolute potency of God into the strenuous toil of the philosophical notion. The early modern opposition between residual nominalism and pre-Enlightenment naturalism is overcome through a synthesis that is even less religiously satisfying than the former dichotomy. Yet Dupré still persists in distilling a panentheistic truth from Hegel that suffuses his reading of Cusanus and will reappear in other contexts as well. Dupré maintains "that Hegel wanted to preserve the Christian idea of God."[13] Hegel as a modern Gnostic failed to teach believers how to interpret Christian doctrine philosophically; for this task, Cusan mysticism is far more adequate. But Hegel's *felix culpa* was not without its progeny, for Hegel liberated the modern idea of God from religious representation as such but paradoxically maintained the necessity of a revealed Word.

Dupré repudiates Hegel's philosophy of the Absolute as hermeneutically untenable, but Dupré's own hermeneutics of how mysticism enables the modern believer to encounter the idea of God intelligibly has a visibly Hegelian watermark. Through Hegel, he negates the capacity of modern thought to incorporate the richness of the fourfold sense of divine causality

---

11 Dupré, "Ignatian Humanism and Its Mystical Origins," 181; See also Levesque, "Symbol as the Primary Religious Category," 300n251.
12 Part of this paragraph borrows from my preface to *Thinking the Unknowable*.
13 Dupré, *Thinking the Unknowable*, Essay 5, 49.

that Plato and Aristotle bequeathed to the Christian tradition.[14] Dupré contends in many contexts that the Aristotelian-Thomistic response, whereby there is no *real* relation between God and the world, only conceptual relations, is thoroughly inadequate. Dupré's positive solution is thoroughly Cusan, that is, that in God's "pure actuality" God also has "the potential to 're-act' to events and circumstances in a manner that requires the acting subject to move out toward the other in order to return to itself in a new manner."[15] This form of divine agency does not apply to God in God's very own being but to the simultaneous emergence in the act of creation of an active and a passive God. In sum, the Hegelian swerve to process metaphysics, away from what Dupré perceives to be a nascent dualism in the ancient Aristotelian order of being, applies retroactively.[16]

Dupré's debt to Henri de Lubac and Karl Rahner is clearly evident throughout his work but comes to the fore only in *Thinking the Unknowable*, the still-unpublished manuscript that he completed in 2018. Dupré finds in these two authors parallel approaches to the problem of the separation of nature and grace as it relates to the secular age. In the wake of de Lubac and Rahner, Dupré transforms the Scholastic question of the natural desire to see God according to God's essence into an investigation of the possibility in a secular age of acknowledging a transcendent horizon to all finite knowing and loving. Thomas Aquinas, he says, inherited from Aristotle the idea that the mind must desire the cause of its being by virtue of some connaturality that joins the seeking intellect to its origin. For Dupré, the condemnation of 1270 marks the turning point at which the resolution of the philosophical problem is relegated to faith and the dynamics of the seeking intellect become supplanted by the vicissitudes of a nominalist God. Even the contested reconstruction of Thomas's original view by Henri de Lubac, with minimal recourse to the thesis of a historical pure nature, remains unable to respond adequately to radical empiricists and phenomenologists

---

14 Dupré, *Thinking the Unknowable*, Essay 6, 54.

15 Dupré, *Thinking the Unknowable*, Essay 6, 68.

16 Dupré considers Friedrich Schleiermacher, interestingly, to have repristinated the Cusan coincidence of opposites in a panentheistic manner. See Louis Dupré, *Religion and the Rise of Modern Culture* (Notre Dame, IN: Notre Dame University Press, 2008), 100n3. There is a panentheistic commonality that, in spite of their famous historical differences, binds Hegel and Schleiermacher as dialecticians of a transcendently immanent God, a commonality that cannot be found in any other continental critics of traditional theism in the nineteenth century. See Louis Dupré, "Schleiermacher's Religion as Feeling," in idem, *A Dubious Heritage: Studies in the Philosophy of Religion after Kant* (New York: Paulist Press, 1977), 16–24.

alike who question the notion of knowledge presupposed in the intellect apart from the givens of actual experience.[17] This critique leaves open a path to Transcendental Thomism, one that Dupré in *Thinking the Unknowable* traces through Maurice Blondel, Karl Jaspers, Martin Heidegger, Max Scheler, and finally Karl Rahner.

Rahner skirts the problem of apriorism that arises for other modern phenomenologists by claiming that the pre-apprehension of being that leads us to God is not *a priori* knowledge, but rather the actual existing horizon against which judgments are made. Dupré interestingly notes the reprise in Rahner's thinking of Descartes's proof for God's existence on the basis of divine infinity in Descartes's *Third Meditation*. Dupré nonetheless concludes that Rahner has proved only the possibility, not the actuality, of God as the end of all desire.[18] Dupré was nursed by the Transcendental Thomism of Joseph Maréchal from his early days at Louvain and therefore never dismisses out of hand its central premises. His approach to Cusanus marks him as a critical and sympathetic reader of both de Lubac's work on the supernatural and Rahner's *Hearer of the Word*.[19] Neither de Lubac nor Rahner spent much time with Cusanus, but their response to secularization is clearly present in the background of Dupré's own narrative of the separation of nature and grace.

Nature and Grace in Cusanus's Mystical Theology

Having laid out the contours of the larger narrative, we turn now to what Dupré actually says about nature and grace in Nicholas of Cusa. In 1976, Louis Dupré gave an address to the Catholic Theological Society of America on "Transcendence and Immanence as Theological Categories," which provoked a robust criticism from Notre Dame theologian and grammatical Thomist, David Burrell, CSC.[20] Both the language and tenor of

---

[17] Louis Dupré, "On the Natural Desire of Seeing God," *Radical Orthodoxy: Theology, Philosophy, Politics* 1, nos. 1–2 (August 2012): 92–93.

[18] Dupré, *Thinking the Unknowable*, Essay 13, 140.

[19] See Henri de Lubac, *The Mystery of the Supernatural*, trans. Rosemary Sheed (New York: Crossroad, 1998); and Karl Rahner, *Hearer of the Word*, trans. Joseph Donceel (New York: Continuum, 1994).

[20] Louis Dupré, "Transcendence and Immanence as Theological Categories," in *Proceedings of the Thirty-First Annual Convention of The Catholic Theological Society of America* (New York: Catholic Theological Society of America, 1976), 1–10. Fr. Burrell's response appears in the same volume (11–14).

Dupré's remarks, which Burrell subjected to a blistering criticism, foreshadowed the shape of the narrative that would unfold across three volumes, starting fifteen years later: *The Passage to Modernity* (Yale University Press, 1991), *The Enlightenment and the Intellectual Foundations of Modern Culture* (Yale University Press, 2004), and *The Quest of the Absolute: The Birth and Decline of European Culture* (University of Notre Dame Press, 2013).

Back in 1976, here is how Dupré began to outline the central problem of his narrative of modernity as it relates to the idea of God:

> Transcendence is the religious category *par excellence*. It refers to that particular quality by which the source and terminus of the religious relation surpasses absolutely the mind's and all other reality. It introduces separation into the most intimate union, negation into the most affirmative assertion. It provides the dynamic tension without which the religious act would grow slack and eventually collapse into its own immanence.... Our problem today is hardly an excessive awareness of transcendence, but much rather its total decline.[21]

Dupré blames the loss of transcendence not in the first instance on modern atheism, which he sees as a symptom of a larger problem. Fairly consistently he cites the failure to understand the relationship between transcendence and immanence as the central problem of modern spiritual life.[22] The argument is as much synchronic as diachronic. Before one loses one's belief in God, one is bedeviled either by a false confidence in naturalism (which becomes the primary problem for and in Enlightenment Christianity) or an undue fear of an omnipotent God's disruption of the causal order of being.

To Burrell's consternation, Dupré goes so far as to blame the Thomistic theory of causal dependency for this situation. To be clear, from this early stage until his trilogy, Dupré is intimately aware of the doctrine of participation in Aquinas, the notion of God as *esse ipsum subsistens* (self-subsistent being), and the mysticism of the Angelic Doctor. But the charge he makes about causality as it relates to the relationship between transcendence and immanence is both devastating and lingering:

---

21 Dupré, "Transcendence and Immanence as Theological Categories," 1.
22 Dupré, "Nature and Grace in Nicholas of Cusa's Mystical Philosophy," 153.

> [W]hen it comes to defining the nature of this divine immanence, Thomas concludes, in the end, that it consists in a relation of causal dependency. Now causality is a typical category of juxtaposition. If God's immanence is restricted to causality, then in the final analysis his presence to the creature is reduced to the impact of one being upon another.... Thus with one stroke Aquinas has lowered both the immanence and the transcendence which he had raised so highly in principle. In addition,... causal determinations are particularly *inappropriate* for describing the intrinsic dependency of a free agent.[23]

One could debate, as Burrell did vehemently, whether Dupré has made the mistake of associating Thomas's doctrine of created being too closely with modern mechanistic causality. What is not debatable is the perdurance of this theme—the overcoming of causal dependency—throughout the later works of Dupré.

In Dupré's view, the road not taken in Nicholas of Cusa's mystical philosophy better affirms religious transcendence, while allowing for even more nuances regarding the distinction between Creator and creature than Dupré himself could provide to Burrell in the exchange of 1976.[24] I will focus on four dimensions of this narrative: possibility and actuality in God, God and otherness, the valency of symbolic disclosure in a multi-perspectival world, and the Incarnation.

Dupré writes that "the nominalist concept of *potentia absoluta* [absolute power]... had severed intelligibility from divine omnipotence."[25] Cusanus sometimes speaks like a nominalist, since his language about God and divine power is always uttered in reference to absolutes, but Nicholas's real goal was to rethink God *ante differentiam actus et potentiae* (before the distinction between act and potency). "Possibility," says Dupré, "emerges from the divine Being simultaneously with actuality."[26] This differentiation allows Cusanus to distinguish an absolute potency from an ordained potency in

---

[23] Dupré, "Transcendence and Immanence," 3. Italics added.
[24] Dupré remarks that the phrase "road not taken" came from the poem of the same name by Robert Frost by way of his former student, Clyde Lee Miller, but this leaves unspoken whether Miller was an oral or written source. See Clyde Lee Miller, "A Road Not Taken: Nicholas of Cusa and Today's Intellectual World," *Proceedings of the American Catholic Philosophical Association* 57 (1983): 68–77.
[25] Dupré, "Nature and Grace in Cusanus's Mystical Philosophy," 155.
[26] Dupré, "Nature and Grace in Cusanus's Mystical Philosophy," 155.

God without separating one from the other. The confidence that God never acts inconsistently goes hand in hand with clear demarcation between the divine reason and its expression in the world that God has created. The actual world does not represent one side of a duality between possibility and actuality. On the contrary, the world constitutes the otherness of God's own being, and God is the non-otherness of created being.[27]

The Proclian-Dionysian figure of the Not-Other plays a prominent role in Dupré's reconstruction of the Cusan doctrine of God, but so too does Cusanus's debt to Eckhart regarding what Dupré refers to as "inverted analogy." The Cusan doctrine of analogy does not proceed from creatures up to the prime analogate in the divine being. The Not-Otherness of God is shared downward by God in the otherness of creation.[28] Cusanus postulates an identity between the non-otherness of created being and God's uncreated being as the Not-Other. Cusanus also clarifies a point that had already been made by Franciscan theologians like Alexander of Hales and Bonaventure. The likeness between creature and Creator extends in principle to the general presence of God in everything; "but only in a spiritual being," notes Dupré, "is that likeness an image of God."[29] Both Eckhart and Ruusbroec understand the *imago Dei* as the mind growing nearer to God. Cusanus leaves his readers with the elements of this position, especially when he develops the Eckhartian dialectic of *intelligere* (thinking) and *esse* (being) through the metaphor of seeing in *De visione Dei*.[30] The creative mind as image of God grows asymptotically toward the divine Not-Other, but, in the end, Dupré is still confident that "Cusanus maintains an insurmountable distinction between God and the created mind, and this places his position beyond any suspicion of pantheism."[31]

One distinctive aspect of Dupré's entire philosophical project is to think about God, nature, and culture in terms of their inner harmony. They are distinct domains but not separate problems for thought. The two authors to whom he dedicated the most focused aspects of his life-long research were Jan Ruusbroec and Karl Marx, and the polarity that separates and unites the contemplative mystic and the praxis-oriented social theorist figures into

---

27 Dupré, "Nature and Grace in Cusanus's Mystical Philosophy," 156.
28 Dupré, "Nature and Grace in Cusanus's Mystical Philosophy," 159.
29 Dupré, "The Question of Pantheism from Eckhart to Cusanus," 85.
30 Dupré, "The Question of Pantheism from Eckhart to Cusanus," 84.
31 Dupré, "The Question of Pantheism from Eckhart to Cusanus," 86.

his work as a whole. Dupré's shortest but arguably most revealing book is entitled *Metaphysics and Culture*, in which he maintains that "the possibility of metaphysics then rests on the presence of a genuine transcendence as an essential factor operative within culture itself."[32]

Cusanus also contributes to the discussion of this triadic relationship in the idiom of the Italian humanism of his milieu and especially through the adoption of the theory of perspective of Ambrogio Lorenzetti and Leon Battista Alberti.[33] Cusanus sees God represented through a symbolic disclosure in a multi-perspectival world.[34] For Dupré, the cardinal meets the modern turn to the subject halfway, for he still holds out the vision of a knowledge of the absolute that is not conditioned by perspective:

> Cusanus assumes that the mind *represents* the real according to its subjective capacity. Yet, Cusanus's metaphor then points in a direction opposite to that taken by modern epistemology. Far from being the sole source of truth, the human mind *receives* its representational truth only by reflecting a perspective of the perspective-less divine mirror.[35]

The Cusan form of understanding is like and unlike its Kantian counterpart. It receives and represents on the basis of the free spirit of its own creativity, but that spiritual freedom is actualized in a manner that is a virtual inversion of Kant's autonomy. The free use of neologisms and symbols (such as being seen in the face of one's Creator) are unfoldings of this new doctrine of freedom. Dupré contrasts Jean-Paul Sartre's notion of the coincidence of knower and known in God with the Cusan *separateness* out of which an original perspectival form of knowing takes its departure.[36] Without separation in the act of knowing, there is no perspective. Without perspective, there is no creativity. The new metaphysics of unity therefore also yields a philosophically necessary confirmation of the difference between divine and human creativity.

A polemic against Thomas still emerges in this discussion. Yet in both *The Passage to Modernity* (1993) and "The Question of Pantheism" (2006),

---

32 Louis Dupré, *Metaphysics and Culture* (Milwaukee: Marquette University Press, 1994), 57.
33 Dupré, "Nature and Grace in Cusanus's Mystical Philosophy," 160.
34 Dupré, "Nature and Grace in Cusanus's Mystical Philosophy," 159–69.
35 Dupré, "Nature and Grace in Cusanus's Mystical Philosophy," 161; emphasis in original.
36 Dupré, "Nature and Grace in Cusanus's Mystical Philosophy," 162.

Dupré leaves room for a Thomism that circumvents his own harsh remarks against Thomas in 1976.[37] In both texts, he cites Aquinas's Neoplatonic notion of divine immanence: "Being is innermost in each thing and most fundamentally present within all things, since it is formal in respect of everything found in a thing.... Hence it must be that God is in all things and innermostly [*intime*]."[38] But he also maintains that this balanced view of God's presence in his creation is still explicated, in the very same article, in terms of Aristotelian causality.[39] Dupré is not arguing against God as the cause of being, but he finds "formal, or at least a quasi-formal, causality" as preferable to a strictly efficient causal presence.[40] Aquinas, he concedes, is clearer than Eckhart by avoiding an exclusive use of Neoplatonic metaphysics to define divine immanence. But he still represents the genesis of ambiguity for later generations in at least two respects. First, the very terms "nature" and "supernatural" differentiate two formally distinct aspects of one reality, which Thomas did not intend to separate, but which later Thomists, not heeding his subtlety, did in fact separate. Second, his analogizing of divine immanence with efficient causality and the physics of motion is problematic, since it renders divine presence into an entity alongside the created order rather than its spiritual interiority.[41]

One clear trajectory in Cusanus research in the past forty years is the seriousness with which scholars now take Nicholas's theology of the incarnate Word.[42] This is a new development that would have surprised interpreters from the first half of the twentieth century, like Ernst Cassirer and Anne Forbes Liddell. It would not have surprised H. Lawrence Bond, who practically inaugurated the theme in Anglophone literature with his Duke

---

37 Dupré, *The Passage to Modernity*, 173; and Dupré, "The Question of Pantheism from Eckhart to Cusanus," 87–88.

38 Thomas Aquinas, *Summa Theologiae*, Ia, a. 8, q. 1, in *Summa Theologiae*, vol. 2, *Existence and Nature of God*, trans. Timothy McDermott, OP (New York: McGraw-Hill, 1964), 112–13; as quoted in Dupré, *The Passage to Modernity*, 276n13.

39 Oddly, Dupré holds in *The Passage to Modernity* that the explanation is in terms of efficient causality, while in "The Question of Pantheism" he suggests that God as "the cause of being of all things" is not defined any further by Aquinas.

40 Dupré, "The Question of Pantheism from Eckhart to Cusanus," 87–88. On Cusanus's critique of Aquinas's existential formalism in the name of a Platonic and Neoplatonic "form essentialism," see also Dupré, "The Mystical Theology of Cusanus's *De visione Dei*," 215–16.

41 Dupré, *The Passage to Modernity*, 17.

42 See, for example, Peter Casarella, *Word as Bread: Language and Theology in Nicholas of Cusa* (Münster: Aschendorff Verlag, 2017), esp. 2–9 and 356–63.

doctoral dissertation.[43] Dupré's interpretation of Cusanus is particularly consonant with this new emphasis.

Dupré returned to the Christology of *De visione Dei* at least three times in his writings on Cusanus.[44] In one text he actually questions the Cusan "idea of a universe that culminates in the nature of the God-man" as an unbiblical, *a priori* construction.[45] Dupré favors the mystical path to Christ that emerges in *De filiatione Dei* and afterward to the more Anselmian and even mathematical Christ found within the idea of an absolute maximum in *De docta ignorantia*. Cusan mysticism, he states, is neither "a pure intellectualism nor an intellectual naturalism."[46] With those caveats, Dupré suggests that the cardinal's recourse to the mystical union of divinity and humanity "through love and faith" is the lynchpin of Cusan thinking:

> In his reconstruction of Trinitarian theology, Christ's humanity realizes the union between God and man. The distance between Christ's humanity and the divine Word remains as great as it is in other human beings. Yet Christ's total openness to the divine nature singles him out for a unique role in the sanctification of human nature.[47]

For Cusanus, Christ's human participation in the life of the Trinity is *the* paradigm for joining a theology of mystical union with a decisively apophatic—and, thus, even more emphatically cosmic—sense of astonishment before the reality of divine immanence. But that participation comes to the believer only as a *gift of faith*, even if the intellect is being uplifted in a unique fashion in the process.

---

[43] This is summarized in H. Lawrence Bond, "Nicholas of Cusa from Constantinople to 'Learned Ignorance': The Historical Matrix for the Formation of the *De docta ignorantia*," in *Nicholas of Cusa on Christ and the Church*, 107–26.

[44] See Dupré, "Nature and Grace in Nicholas of Cusa's Mystical Philosophy," 166–69; Dupré, "The Mystical Theology of Nicholas of Cusa's *De visione Dei*," 217–20; and Dupré, "Justifying the Mystical Experience," in *Thinking the Unknowable*, 161–62.

[45] Dupré, "Nature and Grace in Nicholas of Cusa's Mystical Philosophy," 168.

[46] Dupré, "The Mystical Theology of Nicholas of Cusa's *De visione Dei*," 219.

[47] Dupré, "Justifying the Mystical Experience," in *Thinking the Unknowable*, 161.

The Theology of the Gift in Nicholas of Cusa

As we have seen throughout Dupré's long engagement with Cusanus, he found in the cardinal a "road not taken" in modernity, one that avoided the tendency, which Dupré frequently associated with Thomist traditions, to divide nature from grace. His interest in the theme of nature and grace in Cusanus ran deep, but he himself did not expand on the multifaceted grammar of *donum* ("gift") in Cusanus. Consequently, before concluding I would like to explore further the theme of the gift in Nicholas of Cusa, to which only a few studies have been dedicated. A thesis prepared in Trier in 1993 under the direction of Rudolf Haubst already studied this question in a comprehensive fashion as it relates to three of the speculative works from 1445–46.[48] But the theme returns in the later sermons, and my brief reflection here is based upon Sermon 280, which Cusanus delivered to the clergy of Brixen in the Synod of 1457. The main theme of the sermon is Christ as the Good Shepherd, which is interpreted Neoplatonically. For example, he asks the clergy of Brixen to "consider attentively how Christ is *all in all*, in the shepherd as a shepherd, in the subject as subject and as obedient."[49] The humanity of Christ is basically a pedagogical example that teaches the clergy how to preside as good shepherds and the laity how to be humble and merciful as Christ was in both word and deed.

There Cusanus also relates the theme of the gift of God to the ignorance of the Greeks, which Paul sought to dispel when he arrived at the Areopagus. Cusanus quotes directly from the account in the Acts of the Apostles: "God has overlooked the times of ignorance, but now he demands that all people everywhere repent because he has established a day on which he will 'judge the world with justice' through a man he has appointed, and he has provided confirmation for all by raising him from the dead" (Acts 17:30–31). Christ is the one to whom the Father gave the gift of being greater than all.[50] This gift functions here not just as an exemplum. There is no gift

---

[48] For a summary, see Meinholf von Spee, "'*Donum Dei*' bei Nikolaus von Kues: Zum Verständnis von Natur und Gnade nach den Schriften *De quaerendo Deum, De filiatione Dei* und *De dato patris luminum*," in MFCG 22, ed. Klaus Kremer and Klaus Reinhardt (Trier: Paulinus Verlag, 1995), 69–120. See also Martin Thurner, "Die Philosophie der Gabe bei Meister Eckhart und Nikolaus Cusanus," in *Nicolaus Cusanus zwischen Deutschland und Italien*, Veröffentlichungen des Grabmann-Institutes 48, ed. Martin Thurner (Berlin: De Gruyter, 2002), 153–84.

[49] Nicholas of Cusa, Sermon 280 (38), in *Nicholas of Cusa: Writings on Church and Reform*, trans. Thomas M. Izbicki (Cambridge, MA: Harvard University Press, 2008), 511.

[50] Nicholas of Cusa, Sermon 280 (51), in Izbicki, *Writings on Church and Reform*, 519.

that the believer can expect from God that is greater than the humanity of Christ. Then, referring to the passage from Acts just cited, Cusanus states that *hoc est donum sublationis ignorantiae Dei* ("this is the gift of taking away ignorance of God"). This gift is therefore equally positive and negative. It is an actual gift received freely by the believer, but also a gift that takes away a darkness that comes from ignorance of God. One does not place the gift in the hands of the unbeliever, but transforms the ignorance of unbelief into what Cusanus in *De docta ignorantia* calls sacred ignorance.[51] The act of martyrdom by the good shepherd is such a use of the gift.[52] Teaching with many words is not excluded but will inevitably fail to rise to the maximality of the sharing of the gift that is symbolized by the shepherd who gives himself for his flock even unto death. You will find your life, Cusanus states, by losing your soul or life *propter caritatem* ("on account of charity").[53] This passage confirms that the notion of the gift in Cusanus is thoroughly Christocentric and based upon a kind of language or mode of expression that is more performative than informative.[54]

In sum, Cusanus is offering us here a revision of the symbolically ecclesial mysticism of *De concordantia catholica* (1430), which is itself a humanistic revision of Pseudo-Dionysius the Areopagite's *Ecclesiastical Hierarchy*.[55] The negative gift of *sublatio ignorantiae Dei* is the highest form of learned ignorance, both Pauline and Augustinian. Both Paul and Augustine preached the cross of Christ before tombs to the unknown God in their own Areopagi, but Cusanus in his theology of the gift is able to offer a new synthesis of apophaticism and Christocentrism that surpasses that of the ancients in its ethical and social exhortation.

---

[51] "Docuit nos sacra ignorantia deum ineffabilem; et hoc, quia maior est per infinitum omnibus, quae nominari possunt; et hoc quidem quia verissimum, verius per remotionem et negationem de ipso loquimur, sicuti et maximus Dionysius, qui eum nec veritatem nec intellectum nec lucem nec quidquam eorum, quae dici possunt, esse voluit." Nicholas of Cusa, *De docta ignorantia*, I.26 (87), in *Nikolaus von Kues: Philosophisch-Theologische Werke*, vol. 1, ed. Paul Wilpert and Hans Gerhard Senger, rev. ed. (Hamburg: Felix Meiner Verlag, 2002), 110.
[52] Nicholas of Cusa, Sermon 280 (52), in Izbicki, *Writings on Church and Reform*, 521.
[53] Nicholas of Cusa, Sermon 280 (54), in Izbicki, *Writings on Church and Reform*, 523.
[54] See Benedict XVI, *Jesus of Nazareth*, vol. 1 (New York: Doubleday, 2007), 47.
[55] Jovino Miroy, *Tracing Nicholas of Cusa's Early Development* (Leuven: Peeters, 2009).

Nicholas of Cusa's Mysticism and Contemporary Theology

In 1965, Hans Urs von Balthasar wrote a famous chapter called "Nicholas of Cusa: The Knot." His concept of the knot was somewhat similar to Rudolf Haubst's idea that Cusanus was the doorkeeper of the modern era, whose carriage, full of precious ancient and medieval manuscripts from the library of Kues, was salvaged and transported to the very brink of modernity.[56] For both of these Catholic thinkers (who, incidentally, had some written contact with one another), Cusanus delivered a new synthesis of ancient and medieval thought to the very precipice of a new epoch. Haubst was sure that Cusanus preserved the ancient tradition of analogical thought, a thesis that finds a new and different reverberation in the recent work of Johannes Hoff.[57] Balthasar lauded Cusanus's attempt at a metaphysics of analogy as an important strand in the bundle, but was ambivalent about whether "the knot" in the ecclesial personage and philosophical work of Nicholas of Cusa could actually be held together in the same way that Cusanus intended.[58]

Dupré harbors nostalgia neither for Cusanus's bibliophilia nor for his sometimes strong proclivities in favor of the *via antiqua*. Dupré thus unties "the knot" and places Cusanus's synthesis under a critical and thoroughly modern interpretive lens. He is no less appreciative than either Haubst or Balthasar of the cardinal's reverence for the religious thought of the past. Dupré also has no interest in branding Cusanus with the ill-fated label of "precursor." The act of untying is not a good in itself in Dupré's hermeneutical project. He is not trying to dissect or deconstruct the strands that are so tightly and originally brought together into a new synthesis in order to leave them strewn about in a new play of signifiers. Rather, Dupré likes to use the word "assay" to describe the methodological purposes of his genealogical inquiries. It is a scientific word that indicates a process that yields questions as well as answers. Like Cusanus's *De staticis experimentis* (1450), Dupré is

---

56 Rudolf Haubst, *Nikolaus von Kues—Pförtner der neuen Zeit*. Kleine Schriften der Cusanus-Gesellschaft (Trier: Paulinus Verlag, 1988).

57 Johannes Hoff, *The Analogical Turn: Rethinking Modernity with Nicholas of Cusa* (Grand Rapids, MI: Eerdmans, 2013).

58 On analogy, see Hans Urs von Balthasar, *Herrlichkeit. Eine theologische Ästhetik. Bd. III, 1: Im Raum der Metaphysik. Teil II: Neuzeit*, 3rd ed. (Einsiedeln: Johannes Verlag, 2009), 568–76. According to Balthasar, Cusanus sheds even more light than Aquinas on how biblical revelation and Platonic-Plotinian religious universalism might be reconciled with one another, but he does not think the synthesis is fully worked out in Cusanus. His final word is interesting: "Die Neuzeit wird die Konsequenzen enthüllen" (591–92): modernity would reveal the consequences.

weighing and testing with new tools of interpretation that have been uncovered only in recent times. He gestures toward a strictly phenomenological reading based upon his reading of Husserl and especially Henry Duméry, but never settles on that mode of inquiry as a final position.

In the end, are the fragments of the synthesis going to come together? That critical question is never answered in *any* of Dupré's works. The open-endedness of that question shows his preference for modern hermeneutical reflection over the restoration of ancient metaphysics. He is confident that assaying the synthesis that we have inherited from Nicholas of Cusa will point toward a new future for the study of philosophy, theology, and mysticism. The relationships among those three sciences will be revealed in a new way, one very different from the Scholastic synthesis. What emerges as new in Cusanus is then brought by Dupré into conversation with Hegel and Whitehead, yet not for the sake of a Hegelian or Whiteheadian Cusanus.[59]

Dupré as a reader of Cusanus is finally both a humanistic and a neo-Augustinian interpreter. The former label is plain from his attention to Cusanus's quattrocento synthesis of rational faith, the perspectival knowing of the artist, and a new theology of culture and work. I can demarcate what this second label means in two different ways. First, in the end Dupré is closer to Blondel and de Lubac than to Karl Rahner on the meaning of the supernatural. Rahner maintained in *Hearer of the Word*: "The *Vorgriff* [pre-apprehension of being] is not an *a priori* knowledge of an object, but the manner, given with our very nature and in that sense *a priori*, in which we take up a sense object given *a posteriori*, the *a priori* way of knowing what appears *a posteriori*. It is not a self-subsisting grasp of being as such, but the anticipation [*Vorgriff*] of being, which is possible only in grasping the appearance."[60] According to Dupré, the supernatural as such is grasped only in an anticipatory manner with the expectation of a fulfillment through a concrete revealed symbol of a particular faith. The Rahnerian project of knowing God on the basis of a *Vorgriff auf esse* is not sufficiently steeped in the paradox of the supernatural or the negativity of

---

[59] "Only recently have a few thinkers, foremost among them Maurice Blondel, Karl Jaspers, and Paul Ricoeur, begun to rethink the relation between freedom and transcendence in non-causal terms." Louis Dupré, *The Passage to Modernity*, 163.

[60] Rahner, *Hearer of the Word*, 122. Cf. Dupré, *Thinking the Unknowable*, Essay 13, 140n9.

being outlined by Heidegger.⁶¹ The Cusan *praegustatio* ("foretaste") of God cited by Dupré is a limited phenomenon, in the terminology of Emmanuel Falque.⁶²

Second, there is a close parallel between Dupré's neo-Augustinian philosophy of religion and mystical phenomenology and the neo-Augustinianism of Nicholas of Cusa himself. Augustinian interiority is a theme that cuts through the entire work of Dupré.⁶³ Dupré's main interest in Augustine is the interiority of memory and what he conceives of as an apophatic mysticism of the Trinitarian image in the human person growing asymptotically closer to God.⁶⁴ Is this genuinely Cusan? Do we find such an explicit recourse to the Augustinian theology of the image in *Confessions* and *On the Trinity*? This question is now much easier to answer in the affirmative on the basis of Alexia Schmitt's *Interioridad y trascendencia*.⁶⁵ First, she notes that the Augustinian theme highlighted by Dupré is cited by Cusanus in Sermon 38 and *De aequalitate*. Second, Schmitt comprehensively reviews the presence of Augustinian interiority in the middle works *De filiatione*, *De quaerendo Deum*, and *De visione Dei*.⁶⁶ Third, she records the copious underlinings and marginal notations that appear in Nicholas's own copies of the *Confessions*, which in turn confirm his fascination with Augustinian memory and the Trinitarian *imago Dei*.⁶⁷ Through his reading of Eckhart, Nicholas sometimes radicalizes the inversion implicit in the Augustinian *cor inquietum* ("restless heart"), yet never abandons the basic Augustinian insight into the true ground of being oneself. By becoming oneself in the deepest level of selfhood, one realizes the principle that God is in all things from within and without.⁶⁸ The separation of nature from grace could have

---

61 Dupré, *Thinking the Unknowable*, Essay 13, 140–41.

62 Dupré, *Thinking the Unknowable*, Essay 13, 138. See Emmanuel Falque's essay in chapter 14 of this volume.

63 Casarella, "'Modern Forms Filled with Traditional Spiritual Content,'" 288–93.

64 On memory, see Louis Dupré, *The Deeper Life: An Introduction to Christian Mysticism* (New York: Crossroad, 1981). On the mysticism of the image, see the commentary on selected texts from Augustine in Dupré and Wiseman, *Light from Light*, 57–58.

65 Alexia Schmitt, *Interioridad y trascendencia. Asimilación de la interioridad agustiniana en el pensamiento Cusano: hacia la subjetividad moderna* (Buenos Aires: Editorial Biblos, 2017).

66 Schmitt, *Interioridad y trascendencia*, 103–7, 123–68.

67 Schmitt, *Interioridad y trascendencia*, 225–307.

68 Schmitt concludes by quoting a formula of her colleague and teacher Jorge Machetta: "El camino es ser lo que se es, porque precisamente lo que se es, en su nivel más profundo, es en tanto el principio es presente en todo lo que de él proviene" ('The path is to be that which you

been avoided by following this Augustinian path to the deeper self of the spiritual life. Cusanus did not invent this path, but he gave it a new impetus. The deeper self of Augustine was in fact rediscovered by Nicholas of Cusa in *and through* the passage to modernity.

The final essay in Dupré's final book likewise ends with a comment on how the grace of the Holy Spirit in Cusanus "drives the mind in its quest of God." He then concludes: "To follow him here would have been a giant step into Christian theology, which, of course, was not my task in this book. I realize that with this final section on theology I have already passed beyond the limits of philosophy."[69]

Endings are revealing for what they say about what came before and even more so for what they wager cannot be said. As a philosopher trained in a post-Hegelian tradition of philosophical reflection, Louis Dupré always remained in awe of the diligence with which Cusanus upheld the *cognitive* nature of the mystical quest. At the same time, he concludes with an important nod to the uplifting experience of a gift of self-surpassing love, which no cognitive quest has ever been able to grasp. The Flemish Louis Dupré and the cardinal from the Mosel River Valley inhabited adjoining lands, but their real sense of proximity is anything but territorial. In gesturing to an innate desire to go beyond his own limits as a philosopher of religion, the scholar of Christian mysticism from Flanders reveals his true admiration for the life-long project of the thinker from Kues.

---

are to yourself, because precisely in being oneself, at the deepest level of selfhood, one becomes in that way the principle that is present in all that comes from [God]). Schmitt, *Interioridad y trascendencia*, 167, quoting Jorge M. Machetta, "'Sé tú tuyo y yo seré tuyo': síntesis cusana de antropología y mística," in *Memoria y silencio en la filosofía medieval*, ed. Carlos Ruta (Buenos Aires: Jorge Baudino Ediciones, 2006), 212.

69 Dupré, *Thinking the Unknowable*, Essay 15, 162.

12

A Constant "Re-presenter" of the World's Reality

Karsten Harries on Cusanus, Art, and Architecture

IL KIM

Philosopher Karsten Harries (1937–) has written about art and architecture for more than five decades. His particular interest in architecture stems from Hegel's *Lectures on Aesthetics* (first published in 1835 by one of his students) that discusses architecture as human beings' first attempt to express the realm of the divine:

> Architecture is in fact the first pioneer on the highway toward the adequate realization of the Godhead. In this service it is put to severe labor with objective nature, that it may disengage it by its effort from the confused growth of finitude and the distortion of contingency. By this means it levels a space for the God, informs His external environment, and builds Him his temple....[1]

---

1 G. W. F. Hegel, *Sämtliche Werke*, vol. 12, *Vorlesungen über die Aesthetik*, ed. Hermann Glockner (Stuttgart: Fromann Verlag, 1937), 125; trans. in F. P. B. Osmaston, "Selections from *The Philosophy of Fine Arts*," in *Philosophies of Art and Beauty:*

Martin Heidegger took up Hegel's view, yet there was a fundamental difference between the two of them. Although for Hegel art is a highway to the Godhead, at the same time he states that science and technology are more masterful of the earth than art or architecture.[2] Hegel placed architecture as the opposite of nature, whereas Heidegger saw architecture as embedded in the earth or its surrounding context, stating that "the Work [of architecture] lets the earth be an earth," giving architecture a more positive existence.[3] Harries agrees with many, if not all, of Heidegger's philosophical stances and has inherited his views on architecture.

The Death of Art and Architecture

One of Harries's main arguments regarding architecture derives from Heidegger's focus on its ethical function. Hegel had written that "the highest function of fine art (including architecture) is to share its sphere with religion and/or philosophy, becoming a mode and form through which the Divine"—meaning the Truth, something transcendent, the most profound interests of human beings—is expressed and "brought home" to human consciousness.[4] Heidegger agreed with Hegel on this point, and although Harries is an atheist, he too agrees, even if his definition of the divine being differs, as I will discuss shortly.

What Hegel calls the "highest function," Harries calls "the ethical function" of art and architecture, the importance of which he has emphasized throughout his writings, especially in his book, *The Ethical Function of Architecture*, which deals with both art and architecture. Yet Harries stresses that, like Hegel and Heidegger, he believes this "highest function" has been increasingly denied to art and architecture in the course of the Enlightenment, confining them within, or reducing them to, the realm of inward reflection: "art for art's sake" of purely conceptual art, or purely

---

Selected Readings in Aesthetics from Plato to Heidegger, ed. Albert Hofstadter and Richard Kuhns (Chicago: University of Chicago Press, 1964), 439. Quoted in Karsten Harries, *The Ethical Function of Architecture* (Cambridge, MA: MIT Press, 1998), 352.

2 For Hegel's rather pessimistic notion of art (including architecture), see Karsten Harries, "Hegel on the Future of Art," *The Review of Metaphysics* 27, no. 4 (1974): 677–96.

3 Martin Heidegger, "The Origin of the Work of Art," in *Poetry, Language, Thought*, trans. Albert Hofstadter (New York: Harper and Row, 1971), 46; quoted in Harries, *The Ethical Function of Architecture*, 352.

4 Hegel, *Vorlesungen über die Aesthetik*, 27; trans. Osmaston, 388. Quoted in Harries, *The Ethical Function of Architecture*, 353.

A Constant "Re-presenter" of the World's Reality 191

Figure 12-1. Claude-Nicolas Ledoux, *Maison de gardes agricoles* (1789).

Figure 12-2. Walter Gropius, Gropius House in Lincoln, Massachusetts (1938).

Figure 12-3. Mies van der Rohe, Farnsworth House (1951)

conceptual architecture.[5] According to Harries, these signal the death of art and architecture. For Harries, conceptual art by artists like Carl Andre or Donald Judd would represent the death of art, because they are too cerebral.

Conceptual architecture, such as Peter Eisenmann's "House 6," is no more than an appropriation of Deconstructivism in linguistics, and therefore means the death of architecture as well. On the other hand, Harries would praise the architecture of Claude-Nicolas Ledoux, who pursued simple geometric forms in his spherical house; or that of Walter Gropius, who tried at Bauhaus to revive the spirit of Gothic architecture shared by medieval citizens; or Mies van der Rohe, who eliminated superfluous elements in architecture, as exemplified in his Farnsworth House. All of these challenge us and open up new ways of thinking about and re-presenting truth (see Figs. 12-1–12-3).[6] Similarly, Harries finds great potential even in the "anarchitecture" of Lebbeus Woods, which deliberately has nothing to do with nature (see Fig. 12-4). He states that Wood's drawings of modern ruins stimulate the viewer with a sense of sublime "being."[7]

---

5 Harries, *The Ethical Function of Architecture*, 360.

6 Karsten Harries, "The Dream of the Complete Building," *Perspecta: The Yale Architectural Journal* 17 (1980): 38–39.

7 Karsten Harries, "Journeys into the Wilderness of Artifice," in *Lebbeus Woods: Experimental Architecture*, ed. Tracy Myers, Lebbeus Woods, and Karsten Harries (Pittsburgh: Carnegie Museum of Art, 2004), 38–51, especially 42–45.

Figure 12-4. Lebbeus Woods, Horizon House (2000)

Harries's reading of historical buildings is consistent with his discussion of modern art and architectural movements. For example, in his *The Bavarian Rococo Church: Between Faith and Aestheticism*, Harries applies this manner of thinking when analyzing Bavarian Rococo architecture and its design characteristics, as he demonstrates that the design shifted toward inward thinking and that ornament became independent. Harries calls this phenomenon "ornament for ornament's sake."[8] He stresses that such churches successfully blended requirements of sacred space and those of art for only a short period of time; eventually the synthesis disintegrated as beauty became separated from truth and the sacred, and ornament came to exist solely for ornament's sake. Thus, according to Harries, Bavarian Rococo churches reached a splendid dead end, unlike German Gothic architecture, which later inspired Gropius and other early Bauhaus instructors. Nevertheless, Harries concedes that Rococo's aesthetic impulses were a bridge to modern art.[9]

---

[8] Karsten Harries, *The Bavarian Rococo Church: Between Faith and Aestheticism* (New Haven, CT: Yale University Press, 1983), 243–58.

[9] According to Harries, even the end of great art could inspire a new beginning in the future: see Karsten Harries, "Hegel on the Future of Art." See further Otto Pöggeler, "Heidegger on Art," in *Martin Heidegger: Politics, Art, and Technology*, ed. Karsten Harries and Christoph Jamme (New York: Holmes & Meier, 1994), 106–24, especially 109.

Harries notes that, before Hegel, Kant had also recognized the failure of the human search for pure art, or art for art's sake. Kant insists that art should aim at more than just beauty; it should edify people. For him, art should speak to the human person of his or her essence and vocation. Following Kant, Hegel, and Heidegger in this regard, Harries warns that if art and architecture are liberated from their ethical function and instead form an autonomous province in an aesthetic sphere (where, for example, Rococo ornamentation ended up), this condition fails to illuminate the world of human existence, and therefore we should strive against it.[10]

Dasein and Re-presentations of "Being There"

In *The Origin of the Work of Art* (1935–36), Heidegger cites Hegel's well-known propositions in the *Lectures on Aesthetics* and then comments as follows:

> Art no longer counts for us as the highest manner in which truth obtains existence for itself.... One may well hope that art will continue to advance and perfect itself, but its form has ceased to be the highest need of the spirit.... In all these relationships art is and remains for us, on the side of its highest vocation, something past.[11]

Heidegger does not agree with the pessimistic view presented by Hegel. Heidegger's main concern regarding art and architecture is how they reveal the special traits that belong to nature and life, that is, traits embedded in the earth.[12] According to Heidegger, art and architecture can reveal more of those traits when set within their original location or context, not in the museum, even if they have ceased to re-present beliefs in religion or philosophy about the divine.[13]

Heidegger's philosophy centers on his reflections on dwelling (*Wohnen* or *Aufenthalt*), which essentially addresses the ontological "question of Being" (*Seinsfrage* or *Frage nach dem Sein*). His thinking about being is intimately connected with his fundamental ontology of "being-in-the-world"

---

10 Harries, *The Bavarian Rococo Church*, 255.
11 Heidegger, "The Origin of the Work of Art," in *Poetry, Language, Thought*, 80; quoted in Harries, *The Ethical Function of Architecture*, 354.
12 Pöggeler, "Heidegger on Art," 119.
13 Harries, *The Ethical Function of Architecture*, 354–56.

(*In-der-Welt-sein*), which he expressed by the term Dasein ("being-there," or "being here"), which comprises "the fourfold" (*das Geviert*) of "earth and sky, divinities and mortals" (*Erde und Himmel, die Göttlichen und die Sterblichen*). Human beings as mortals exist within the "fourfold" by way of dwelling, that is, by staying with things in being-in-the-world.[14] This concept of Dasein is important for understanding Heidegger's interpretation of art and architecture.

Following Heidegger, Harries recounts visiting great works of architecture on their original sites, such as the Parthenon, the Pantheon, the cathedral in Amiens, or St. Peter's in Rome. All of these—unlike, say, the ancient Altar of Zeus located today in the Pergamon Museum in Berlin—allow us to connect art and architecture with its highest function in the past, revealing or re-presenting the truth both in past and present about specific lives, which Harries calls "our own place in the world."[15] Buildings like those still hold on to their ethical function of revealing the world or earth even after they have lost their original ties with religion or philosophy. In another example, Harries writes that the world of divinities within which Bamberg Cathedral (see Fig. 12-5) used to stand has perished, but because of this loss, today we appreciate more keenly other aspects re-presented by the cathedral, such as its pure design elements or historical value as a monument. It is not the work it once was, but it still holds its place in our world.[16]

Harries contends that Heidegger's understanding of art and architecture as re-presentations of "being there" in the world remains significant, because unlike Hegel, who thought that our reasoning and reality are commensurable, Heidegger saw the rift or chasm between the human spirit and nature, or between the word and reality. Because of that chasm, nature and reality require re-presentations. Harries says that Descartes was right to hold that we understand reality precisely to the extent that we can model it and reproduce it. However, it is easy to understand that even

---

14 Martin Heidegger, *Basic Writings*, ed. David Farrell Krell, 2nd ed. (New York: Harper Collins, 1993), 352–53. This interpretation of Heidegger owes much to Nader El-Bizri, "Being at Home among Things: Heidegger's Reflections on Dwelling," *Environment, Space, Place* 3, no. 1 (Spring 2011): 45–69. As El-Bizri points out, some architectural historians and theorists misappropriate Heidegger's reflections on dwelling (*Wohnen*) by taking the word literally to indicate the spatial conditions in which a person resides.

15 Harries, *The Ethical Function of Architecture*, 356–57.

16 Harries, *The Ethical Function of Architecture*, 356–57.

Figure 12-5. Bamberg Cathedral, Germany (1012)

when contemplating some concrete natural object, such as rock or a tree, we notice the "inadequacy of all our attempts to describe it," recognizing, as Harries writes, that "reality will finally always transcend and elude our grasp."[17] We use different measures to understand various aspects of the same reality in order to grasp it more clearly and distinctly, but Harries asserts that "something is experienced as real precisely when we know that we cannot finally understand it. Reality transcends our understanding. Art recalls us to this transcendence. Heidegger's 'earth' gestures toward this dimension...."[18] The transcendence that can be recalled by art or architecture is the divine for Harries. Here is where Cusanus finally comes in.

Mind Unfolding Unity in Measure and Number

Harries is interested in several of Nicholas of Cusa's notions that recur throughout his works: that "the mind is an unfolding unity in search of unity," that "the human being himself provides the measures by which he knows," and that although mathematics provides the form or measure for

---

[17] Harries, *The Ethical Function of Architecture*, 361.
[18] Harries, *The Ethical Function of Architecture*, 361.

our best conjectures, even then "our often chaotic perceptions" hinder us from approaching unity.[19] Harries summarizes Cusanus's understanding of the human mind as follows:

> Because we are finite knowers, cast into a seeming chaos, this search for unity has to express itself in unending attempts to subject the manifold of the world to unity, to discover the same in what at first seems different, to reduce what is many to one. If there is thus a sense in which the human mind can be called a living unity that unfolds itself in measure and number, such an unfolding must realize itself in the world if it is not to substitute arbitrary invention for understanding. The Unity we seek, which draws us toward a contemplation of true being, demands that we confront an often labyrinthine world of which we are not the authors, demands that our unfolding of the living unity that we are be at the same time a discovery of unity in that world.[20]

Thus, Harries recognizes in Cusanus the tension between his understanding of the mind as an unfolding unity and his desire that such an unfolding should not "lose touch" with reality.[21]

However, here there is a danger of confusing appearances (that is, constructed re-presentations) and reality—of confusing perceiving and knowing.[22] Plato in his *Theaetetus* accused Protagoras (ca. 490–420 BCE) of this confusion, but this passage was not yet known to Cusanus, since Ficino had not finished his translation of the dialogue. However, Harries contends that Cusanus questioned the same distinction between appearance and reality with his usual higher-order reflections, since according to Cusanus the knower gives to what he claims to know his human measure, "subjecting them to a humanly constructed linguistic or conceptual space." Harries

---

19 See Karsten Harries, *Infinity and Perspective* (Cambridge, MA: MIT Press, 2001), especially his chapter, "Homo Faber: The Rediscovery of Protagoras," 160–99. Harries discusses in particular *De coniecturis* (1442–43), *Idiota de mente* (1450), and *De visione Dei* (1453). He references Maurice de Gandillac's suggestion that in the word *coniectura* Cusanus "hears the German *Mut-massung* it translates, implying a measuring with the mind." Harries, *Infinity and Perspective*, 192–93.
20 Harries, *Infinity and Perspective*, 193.
21 Harries, *Infinity and Perspective*, 194.
22 Harries suggests that the philosophical structure that our reason has built since antiquity is still valuable if we widen the possibilities of different interpretations of reality. See Karsten Harries, *Wahrheit: Die Architektur der Welt* (Munich: Wilhelm Fink Verlag, 2012).

contends that precisely for this reason both Cusanus and Leon Battista Alberti call man a second God. Man is a creator of conceptual forms (or space) in which he mirrors or unfolds himself and by means of which, supported by his various measures, he re-constructs, re-creates, or re-presents in his own lesser image the manifold of the world presented to his senses.[23]

Immediately before mentioning Protagoras, who said "Man is the measure of all things," Alberti writes in *Della pittura* (1435) that all things are known by comparison assisted by measure. However, he also demonstrates that the knowledge gained through measure does not touch the quiddity of things and is often fragile. He notes, for instance, that the ancient hero Aeneas was tall among ordinary mortals, but placed next to Polyphemus he seemed a dwarf; young Spanish girls who appear fair seem dusky and dark when seated next to German maidens.[24] Thus, as Harries rightly stresses, both Cusanus and Alberti clearly know that reality always surpasses the human mind and that there is an incommensurability of the finite and infinite—the incommensurability between reality itself and all of our concepts, re-presentations, or words. Yet, there is hope: as if inspired by Cusanus's untiring metaphysical speculations, Harries writes:

> Whatever we grasp of reality is shadowed by what has escaped the activity of our understanding, shadowed by transcendence. This transcendence announces itself in the failure of our attempts to describe [or re-present] adequately or grasp conceptually what we are given. What remains unmastered reminds us that what we have arrived at is only a conjecture concerning reality and that it is in principle always possible to improve on that conjecture.[25]

Alberti knew well that even his proud invention of perspectival construction contained serious defects. It forces us to use a single-eye perspective (as opposed to our two-eyed vision); it requires a stationary view (as opposed

---

23 Harries, *Infinity and Perspective*, 190.

24 See Leon Battista Alberti, *Della pittura*, I.18, in *On Painting: A New Translation and Critical Edition*, ed. and trans. Rocco Sinisgalli (Cambridge: Cambridge University Press, 2011), 38. Cited in Harries, *Infinity and Perspective*, 185.

25 Karsten Harries, "Problems of the Infinite: Cusanus and Descartes," *American Catholic Philosophical Quarterly* 64, no. 1 (Winter 1990): 104.

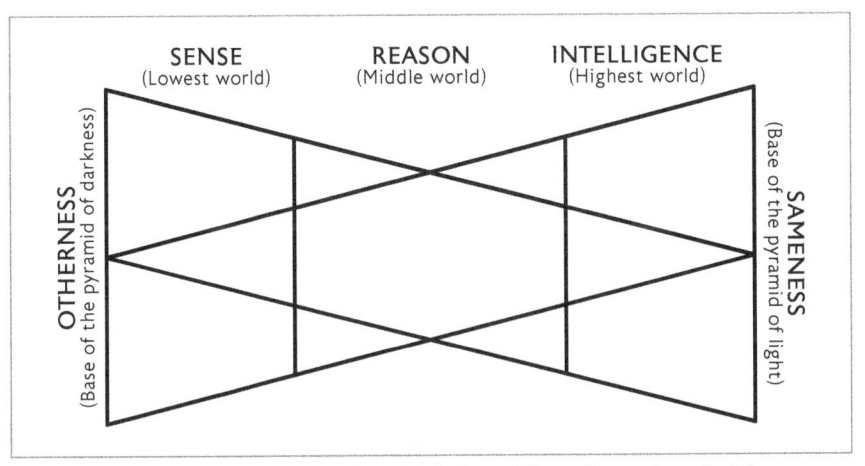

A Constant "Re-presenter" of the World's Reality   199

Figure 12-6. Diagram based on Nicholas of Cusa, *De coniecturis*, I.9. *Unitas* and *alteritas* in *Figura paradigmatica* (Figura P). Jacques Lefèvre d'Étaples added the image to *De coniecturis* in his 1514 Paris edition, vol. I, fol. 46r.

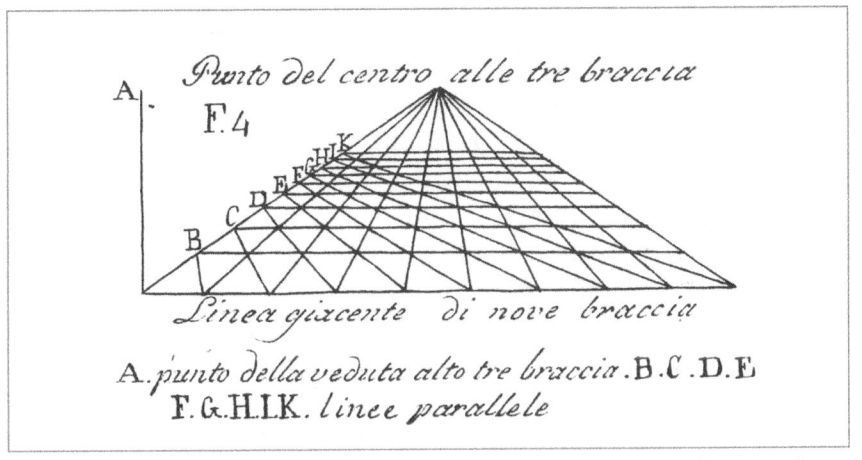

Figure 12-7. Leon Battista Alberti, *Della pittura*, Book I: illustration of perspective. From the 1804 edition of *Della pittura*.

to our constantly moving eye); and it severely distorts forms located more than 45 degrees from our visual line toward the central vanishing point.[26]

Some scholars have noted the similarity between Cusanus's Figure P (*figura paradigmatica*) in *De coniecturis* and Alberti's perspectival

---

[26] On Alberti's self-criticisms regarding single-eye perspective, see Alberti, *Della pittura*, I.6; in *On Painting*, trans. Sinisgalli, 27–28.

construction in Book I of *Della pittura* (1435): in each case, two triangular cones are placed in opposite directions, showing the relationship between the finite and the infinite, or *alteritas* and *unitas* (see Figs. 12-6 and 12-7).[27] While this is true, the two images remain fundamentally different.[28] Cusanus's Figure P does not require the panel placed at the crossing of the two cones, which in Alberti's perspectival construction indicates the plane on which an artist constructs a view where everything converges on the single vanishing point. By contrast, Cusanus does not define the crossing area of Figure P at all. For both men there is an absolute chasm between finite and infinite. While Cusanus's Figure P fails to acknowledge the chasm, Alberti clearly states that the vanishing point in his perspectival construction is located not in infinity, but in "seemingly infinite space" re-presented on the panel, thus emphasizing the chasm, and invoking the realm beyond it.[29] Although Harries does not discuss this point, he would agree that even after the Renaissance, perspectival paintings of religious *historia* cease to have any religious connotation, yet even for an atheist like himself they still recall something transcendent and beyond human reach, fulfilling the proper ethical function of art and architecture.

Karsten Harries's interest in writing about Cusanus was guided by his knowledge of Heidegger and his keen interest in art and architecture. Following Hegel and Heidegger, yet introducing his own concept of "re-presentation," Harries establishes a vision of an optimistic future in art and architecture. Within this context, he turns his eye to Cusanus. Harries sees a parallel structure between "the ethical function of art and architecture" and Cusanus's speculative thought (some aspects of which were shared by Alberti). Like the ethical function of good art and architecture, which edify us and recall something transcendent to us even after they cease to have a connection with religion, Cusanus's conjectural speculation, assisted by various measures, can encourage us to pursue reality or transcendence, which is divine even to the atheist Harries.

---

[27] Nicholas of Cusa, *De coniecturis*, I.9 (37–43), in *Nicolai de Cusa Opera Omnia*, vol. III, ed. Karl Bormann and Hans Gerhard Senger (Hamburg: Felix Meiner Verlag, 1972), 42–47. The image first appears in Jacques Lefèvre d'Étaples's 1514 Paris edition of Nicholas of Cusa's works. See further Charles H. Carman, *Leon Battista Alberti and Nicholas Cusanus: Towards an Epistemology of Vision for Italian Renaissance Art and Culture* (Burlington, VT: Ashgate, 2014), 106–9.

[28] For an explanation of the colors that Cusanus added to the Figure P diagram and their theological implications, see Jeffrey F. Hamburger, *Color in Cusanus* (Stuttgart: Hiersemann Verlag, 2021), 86–91.

[29] Leon Battista Alberti, *Della pittura*, I.19; in *On Painting*, trans. Sinisgalli, 40.

PART III
Thinking with Cusanus

… 13

The Contemporary Relevance of the Philosophical Presuppositions of Interreligious Dialogue in Cusanus

JOÃO MARIA ANDRÉ
TRANSLATED BY ISABEL PEDRO

The merit of great thinkers lies in their ability to project themselves beyond their times, in which they live intensely as a result of the density, depth, and fecundity with which they respond to the conceptual challenges of their age, opening the door to modes of thinking that transcend the limited circumstances of their historical existence.[1] Although this is true of all great philosophers, it applies even more appropriately to those who lived on the border between different worlds, predicting the dawn of future ages from the autumn of a given age. This is exactly the case with Nicholas of Cusa, who has been defined as "a thinker at the border

---

1 This research is financed by national funds through FCT—Fundação Para a Ciência e Tecnologia, I.P., Research project UIDB / FIL / 00010/2020.

of two worlds,"² the medieval world and the modern world, and who has become, in his presuppositions and his intuitions, a contemporary of ours. In order to discuss the contemporary relevance of this fifteenth-century mystic and thinker, I will focus on interreligious dialogue in the framework of what is now called intercultural dialogue.

The issue of interreligious dialogue in Nicholas of Cusa can be approached from two different perspectives. The first consists in analyzing how Cusanus specifically responded to the conflicts of his time, which incidentally were not insignificant. Two of Nicholas of Cusa's works focus on these immediate concerns: *De pace fidei*, written in 1453, and *Cribratio Alchorani*, written in 1461, when Pope Pius II was planning a new military expedition against the Turks. The second possible perspective consists in exploring the general philosophical presuppositions of his thought and their implicit openness to the practice of a constructive inter-relationship with other peoples, other cultures, and other religions. The former approach can lead to the conclusion that, in practice, Nicholas of Cusa held an openly inclusivist view: through dialogue the truth of the Christian religion can be established, measuring other religions's proximity to truth by the way in which they consciously or unconsciously incorporated fundamental principles of the Christian creed. The second approach opens up other dialogical perspectives that have a greater capacity to relativize one's points of view; they invite a greater openness to the wealth of alterity and singularity manifested in the various ways other peoples and other cultures conceive of, name, and worship the divinity. Thus there seems to be a gap between the theoretical principles that can inspire interreligious dialogue and Cusanus's practical application of such principles, especially in his analysis of the Qur'an. I therefore agree with Wilhelm Dupré when he writes that "from this perspective, his thinking offered him more possibilities than he himself understood or could have understood."³

My approach in what follows will be fundamentally the second one, which I believe is much more open and fruitful than the first. The second approach is much more universalizing and forward-looking, and therefore, much more contemporary in its potentialities and in its dynamism. In order

---

2 See Eusebio Colomer, "Nicolau de Cusa (1401–1464): Um pensador na fronteira de dois mundos," *Revista portuguesa de filosofia* 20 (1964): 5–62.

3 Wilhelm Dupré, "Menschsein und Mensch als Wahrheit im Werden," in *Der Friede unter den Religionen nach Nikolaus von Kues. Akten des Symposions in Trier vom 13. bis 15. Oktober 1982*, MFCG 16, ed. Rudolf Haubst (Mainz: Matthias-Grünewald-Verlag, 1984), 323.

to grasp the topical quality of the philosophical presuppositions of interreligious dialogue in Cusanus, I will not just focus on the two works that are typically invoked as references in the discussion of this topic, but instead, taking *De pace fidei* as a landmark, I will trace the presence of these presuppositions in *De docta ignorantia*, the true starting-point of Cusanus's speculative efforts and the basis for his dialogue-focused attitude vis-à-vis God, humanity, and the world in their reciprocal relations. I will also address *De coniecturis*, some opuscula from the 1440s, the *Idiota* dialogues (with a special emphasis on *De sapientia*), and *De visione Dei*, a text contemporary with *De pace fidei*, before focusing on *De venatione sapientiae*, which affords a panoramic, retrospective view of Nicholas of Cusa's entire work.

I

Insofar as it can be seen as an epistemology, a hermeneutic, and an anthropology of finitude, *De docta ignorantia* introduces the first foundations and the most significant presuppositions of interreligious dialogue. By this I mean that the concepts of the finite and of the infinite are the first key to envisioning the potentialities of interreligious dialogue, inasmuch as they establish a perception of human access to truth as a dialogical process, and a perception of human nature itself as an itinerant, dialogical essence. The entire path through the first chapter of the book, titled precisely "How it is that knowing is not-knowing," aims to introduce the concept of ignorance. It rests on the tension between the desire to know (which defines human nature) the infinite (to which knowledge aspires and which defines its horizon), on the one hand, and the condition of finitude, in which such desire is inevitably circumscribed, on the other. Thus, the confrontation between this condition of finitude and the infinite results not in skepticism, but rather in a special form of being human and of knowing called "learned ignorance."[4] In a very fine analysis of this first chapter, Wilhelm Dupré describes the ontic, logical, and ontological dimension of learned ignorance based on this discursive movement.[5] Karl-Heinz Volkmann-Schluck considers "learned ignorance" to be the expression of a movement toward truth

---

4 Nicholas of Cusa, *De docta ignorantia*, I.1 (4), in *Nikolaus von Kues: Philosophisch-Theologische Werke*, vol. 1, ed. Paul Wilpert and Hans Gerhard Senger, rev. ed. (Hamburg: Felix Meiner Verlag, 2002), 8.
5 See Wilhelm Dupré, "Von der dreifachen Bedeutung der 'docta ignorantia' bei Nikolaus von Kues," *Wissenschaft und Weltbild* 15 (1962): 264–76.

that defines the mind exactly as infinite movement—infinite movement being what characterizes the mind in its fundamental constitution.[6] In a previous text, I have discussed learned ignorance as a hermeneutical experience of finitude.[7]

I would thus identify learned ignorance as the first presupposition from which to address interreligious dialogue, for since religions are human forms of relating to God, they are necessarily more than just their specific rituals or forms of worship, and include a cognitive dimension. They are therefore different expressions of human knowledge about, and experience of, the divine. As expressions of knowledge, and more specifically as expressions of knowledge about the divine, religions are no exception to the rule of learned ignorance according to which there is no proportion between finite and infinite. The next chapters of *De docta ignorantia* take significant steps toward approaching this infinite, which Cusanus identifies from the start as Maximality. A few pages later, he adds: "Since the unqualifiedly and absolutely Maximum (than which there cannot be a greater) is greater than we can comprehend (because it is Infinite Truth), we attain unto it in no other way than incomprehensibly."[8] The tone is set not only for the whole of Nicholas of Cusa's first work but also for all of his future works: recognizing our finitude in the face of divine infinitude requires an attitude of humility to which only comprehension in an incomprehensible way—learned ignorance—can correspond. Reaching absolute truth, whether in rational knowledge, intellectual discourse, or theological conceptualization, is thus impossible.

Nicholas of Cusa introduces a metaphor that expresses this infinite movement of incomprehensible comprehension and already implicitly contains the valorization of plural approaches and movements toward the exactness of the truth identified with God, whether philosophical or theological: the metaphor of the polygon inscribed in a circle, which is in itself a profoundly dialogical metaphor.[9] It would seem that each religion, in its

---

[6] Karl-Heinz Volkmann-Schluck, "La filosofía de Nicolás de Cusa: Una forma previa de la metafísica moderna," *Revista de filosofía* 17 (1958): 450.

[7] See João Maria André, "Dimensões antropológicas da douta ignorância," in *Manuductiones. Festschrift zu Ehren von Jorge M. Machetta und Claudia D'Amico*, ed. Cecilia Rusconi and Klaus Reinhardt (Münster: Aschendorff Verlag, 2014), 93–121.

[8] Nicholas of Cusa, *De docta ignorantia*, I.4 (11), ed. Wilpert and Senger, 16; trans. Jasper Hopkins, *Nicholas of Cusa on Learned Ignorance* (Minneapolis: Arthur J. Banning Press, 1985), 8.

[9] Nicholas of Cusa, *De docta ignorantia*, I.3 (10), ed. Wilpert and Senger, 14.

attempt to reach God, is a polygon inscribed within the circle, each of them different from all the others—some with more angles, some with fewer, but none in fact resolved into identity with the circle, none of them identifiable with absolute truth.

The most immediate consequence of learned ignorance for an approach to interreligious dialogue emerges at the end of Book I of *De docta ignorantia*, when the author focuses on God's names, both negative and positive, and begins a hermeneutic of divine names that will continue to his last work, *De apice theoriae*. The reason why all affirmative names bestowed to God are relativized is that "they befit Him only in relation to created things," that is, they are marked by the finitude that characterizes all created beings.[10] To avoid suggesting that this concerns only other religions, let us stress that this relativizing process first applies to the names given by the Christian religion itself: "The aforesaid is so true of all affirmations that even the names of the Trinity and of the persons—viz., 'Father,' 'Son,' and 'Holy Spirit'—are bestowed on God in relation to created things."[11] In the following chapter, when Cusanus discusses the names by which other religions or the pagans denominate God, he relativizes them on the same grounds: they are based on a consideration of creatures, but he also valorizes them for symbolizing particular perfections. He concludes: "All these names are unfoldings of the enfolding of the one ineffable name. And as accords with [this] proper name's being infinite, it enfolds an infinite number of such names of particular perfections. Therefore, the unfolded [names] could be many without being so many and so great that there could not be more of them. Each of them is related to the proper and ineffable name ... as what is finite is related to what is infinite."[12] A dialogue among religions presupposes that, even in their effort to name God, each religion is relative in the way it approaches the naming of creatures, and therefore each religion, and also each name, should be understood as a finite explanation (thus complementary to others) of the infinite and ineffable name of God.

Another presupposition of *De docta ignorantia* that can be highlighted for interreligious dialogue is the *contractio* theory. The basis for

---

10 Nicholas of Cusa, *De docta ignorantia*, I.24 (79), ed. Wilpert and Senger, 100; trans. Hopkins, 41.
11 Nicholas of Cusa, *De docta ignorantia*, I.24 (80), ed. Wilpert and Senger, 102; trans. Hopkins, 42.
12 Nicholas of Cusa, *De docta ignorantia*, I.25 (84), ed. Wilpert and Senger, 106; trans. Hopkins, 43–44.

this theory is developed, in an especially profound way in Book II, from the Anaxagorean idea that "everything [is] in everything."[13] This thought is developed from an ontological and anthropological perspective in this book, but it can also be approached gnoseologically, as suggested in Book II and later discussed in more depth in *De coniecturis*. Fundamentally, Cusanus's *contractio* theory, which is inseparable from the *complicatio-explicatio* theory and which intensifies the dynamism inherent in the very concept of contracting (*contrahere*), means that all things are in everything and that anything is in anything, not in itself but in the way it presents itself in the contracted form of that thing. Ontologically, this means that the whole universe and all concrete beings are in each concrete being in its contracted form and, anthropologically, that the whole of humanity and all human beings are in each specific human being in their contracted forms—all because God, who is the absolute form of all forms, is contracted in each concrete form, and each concrete form is in God's absolute form.

The first gnoseological transposition of this theory is present in the idea that all things are senses in the senses, imagination in the imagination, reason in reason, and intellect in intellect.[14] Applying this idea to the diversity of religions that address the ineffable unity of truth, it might be argued that all religions are in each religion under its specific contracted form, and each religion is in all religions, in the same way that truth is in each statement that contracts it, and that each statement or position abides in all statements or positions. Thus, it is the hidden presence of the infinite in the finite, as highlighted by Mariano Álvarez-Gómez,[15] that grounds interreligious dialogue in articulation with an epistemology of complexity inspired by the hologrammatic principle developed by Edgar Morin in his reflections on ethics and the ecology of ideas, according to which "the whole is in a certain manner included in the part that is included in the whole."[16]

---

13 See Anaxagoras, Fr. 6, in *Die Fragmente der Vorsokratiker*, ed. Hermann Diels (Berlin: Weidmannsche Verlagsbuchhandlung, 1952), II.A. See Nicholas of Cusa, *De docta ignorantia*, II.5 (117–18), ed. Wilpert and Senger, 36–38.

14 Nicholas of Cusa, *De docta ignorantia*, II.5 (119), ed. Wilpert and Senger, 40.

15 See Mariano Álvarez Gómez, *Die verborgene Gegenwart des Unendlichen bei Nikolaus von Kues* (Munich: Anton Pustet, 1968).

16 Edgar Morin, *O método*, vol. 3, *O conhecimento do conhecimento/1*, trans M. G. Bragança (Mem Martins: Publicações Europa-América, 1987), 98.

II

The second step in this search for the philosophical presuppositions of interreligious dialogue is to be found in *De coniecturis*, starting with the very concept of "conjecture." According to Cusanus, a conjecture is "a positive assertion that partakes—with a degree of otherness—of truth as it is [in itself]."[17] The context of this definition is quite interesting: the author discusses the image of the pope's face as produced by his interlocutor when looking at it. Since his eye is contracted to the position from which he looks at the pope, as well as to the contingencies of his gaze, the image will never be complete. Instead, it is a necessarily limited, partial image, which needs other images seen by other eyes and from other places in order to be completed and to afford a fuller perception of the pope's face. Our knowledge is thus not absolute knowledge, but rather a personal reconstruction produced by the human mind.[18]

At this point I should stress the kinship between the concept of "conjecture" and that of "symbol." The former is largely the translation of the Greek *etyma* into a word of Latin origin: *coniectura* derives from *conjicere*, which means to throw together or to assemble, the same as the Greek *symballein*, that is, a conjecture should be interpreted as a symbol that enables us to come closer to grasping a meaning, even though it is not a univocal translation or expression of that meaning.[19] Hence the need to reunite the different conjectures or the different symbols in a movement such as interreligious dialogue, because symbols and myths ultimately enhance dialogue

---

17 "Coniectura igitur est positiva assertio, in alteritate veritatem, uti est, participans." Nicholas of Cusa, *De coniecturis*, I.11 (57), in *Nicolai de Cusa Opera Omnia*, vol. III, ed. Karl Bormann and Hans Gerhard Senger (Hamburg: Felix Meiner Verlag, 1972), 58; trans. Jasper Hopkins, *Nicholas of Cusa: Metaphysical Speculations*, vol. 2 (Minneapolis: Arthur J. Banning Press, 2000), 190.

18 Nicholas of Cusa, *De coniecturis*, I.1 (5), ed. Bormann and Senger, 7–8.

19 On this point, see Stephan Meier-Oeser, "Symbol (Antike, Mittelalter, Neuzeit)," in *Historisches Wörterbuch der Philosophie*, vol. 10, ed. Joachim Ritter and Karlfried Gründer (Basel: Schwabe & Co., 1998), 710, 717. See also Harald Schwaetzer, "Viva similitudo: Zur Genese der cusanischen Anthropologie in den Schriften 'Responsio de intellectu evangelii Iohannis', 'De filiatione Dei' und 'De genesi,'" in *Nicolaus Cusanus: Perspektiven seiner Geistphilosophie. Internationale Tagung junger Cusanus-ForscherInnen von 24.-26. Mai 2002*, ed. Harald Schwaetzer (Regensburg: S. Roderer-Verlag, 2003), 85n25. See also João Maria André, "Conocer es dialogar: Las metáforas del conocimiento y su dimensión dialógica en el pensamiento de Nicolás de Cusa," in *El problema del conocimiento en Nicolás de Cusa*, ed. Jorge Machetta and Claudia D'Amico (Buenos Aires: Editorial Biblos, 2005), 25–26.

more effectively than logical and rational approaches themselves, as Raimon Panikkar argues in his conceptualization of dialogue and tolerance.[20]

Insofar as all human knowledge, even positive knowledge, has a conjectural dimension, it nonetheless can be superseded indefinitely. Yet despite its rich diversity, knowledge can lack awareness of that conjectural nature, a lack that itself corresponds to the introduction of learned ignorance into the positivity of conjecture itself.[21] One might ask if such conjectural dimensions pertain even to the knowledge of religion or religions, but Nicholas of Cusa himself suggests in *De coniecturis* that this specific type of knowledge, culture, and all that is associated with them are governed by conjecture and, with it, by the *figura universorum*, which is ultimately a development of what he calls Figure P, or the paradigmatic figure.[22] In the same chapter, Cusanus relates religion to humankind's diversity and multiplicity and makes a threefold distinction: a specific religion is characterized by a higher participation, above reason or the senses; another religion is more marked by contraction as concerns reason; and a third one by contraction as concerns the senses.[23] This determines the mutability of different parts of each religion, for "preciseness of truth can be pursued by us only by way of surmise [*in coniectura*]."[24]

If we apply Nicholas's "paradigmatic figure" to religions, one could argue that no religion is absolutely or entirely situated in the region of the most simple light, nor is it absolutely and entirely situated in the utter dark of the region of darkness; rather, all religions lie in the intermediate space where light and darkness meet and combine. Incompleteness is therefore their distinctive mark. This brings us to one of the conditions for intercultural dialogue identified by Boaventura de Sousa Santos, who posits the incompleteness of all cultures as both the basic assumption and the starting point for a diatopical hermeneutics.[25] This procedure, inherited from Panikkar,

---

20 See Raimon Panikkar, *Mito, fe y hermenéutica* (Barcelona: Herder, 2007), 55–58.
21 See Helmut Meinhardt, "Konjekturale Erkenntnis und religiöse Toleranz," in *Der Friede unter den Religionen nach Nikolaus von Kues*, 329.
22 See Nicholas of Cusa, *De coniecturis*, II.15 (147), ed. Bormann and Senger, 147.
23 See Nicholas of Cusa, *De coniecturis*, II.15 (147), ed. Bormann and Senger, 148.
24 Nicholas of Cusa, *De coniecturis*, II.15 (148), ed. Bormann and Senger, 148; trans. Hopkins, 239.
25 Boaventura de Sousa Santos, "Toward a Multicultural Conception of Human Rights," in *International Human Rights Law in a Global Context*, ed. Felipe Gómez Isa and Koen de Feyter (Bilbao: University of Deusto, 2009), 107.

"consists in the work of interpretation between two or more cultures aiming to identify common isomorphic concerns and the different responses that they supply to those concerns."[26] According to Santos, its starting point is "the idea that the topoi of an individual culture, no matter how strong they may be, are as incomplete as the culture itself," and therefore, the proposed objective is "to raise the consciousness of reciprocal incompleteness to its possible maximum by engaging in the dialogue, as it were, with one foot in one culture and the other in another."[27]

III

Among the shorter texts written after *De coniecturis*, the dialogue *De Deo abscondito* is the first to draw the consequences that follow from the conjectural dimension of knowledge regarding the nature of religions, and also the first to coordinate religion with the concept of learned ignorance, although this expression is not mentioned in the text. A dialogue between a pagan and a Christian, *De Deo abscondito* might be expected to consist in an exaltation of the superiority of the Christian religion. However, the words spoken by the Christian and the conclusions suggested in the dialogue are the conclusions of a believer who could equally be a Christian, a Jew, or a Muslim. Since God is identified with truth, and truth is associated with unity and unity's ineffable nature, God and the truth will forever remain hidden. In the exact center of the dialogue, Nicholas relativizes the conceptual content of religions and thus stresses the need to overcome their respective limitations: "I know that whatever-I-know is not God and that whatever-I-conceive is not like God but that God excels [all this]."[28] As the dialogue progresses, the radical nature of this statement eventually leads the author to deny that any of God's names, including the word "God," is adequate to God's ineffable truth.[29]

---

[26] Boaventura de Sousa Santos, *A gramática do tempo: Para uma nova cultura política* (Porto: Afrontamento, 2006), 115.

[27] Santos, "Toward a Multicultural Conception of Human Rights," 108.

[28] Nicholas of Cusa, *Dialogus de Deo abscondito*, 8, in *Nicolai de Cusa Opera Omnia*, vol. IV, ed. Paul Wilpert (Hamburg: Felix Meiner Verlag, 1959), 6–7; trans. Jasper Hopkins, *A Miscellany on Nicholas of Cusa* (Minneapolis: Arthur J. Banning Press, 1994), 302.

[29] Nicholas of Cusa, *Dialogus de Deo abscondito*, 13, ed. Wilpert, 9. Mariano Álvarez-Gómez connects this short dialogue to *De pace fidei* in two interesting ways. On the one hand, he explains that knowledge in its finitude finds its condition of possibility in its presupposed truth and works as an occultation of truth through the finite veil with which it covers its

In *De filiatione Dei*, Cusanus introduces the metaphor of a mirror, which he develops and expands later in the text and which provides some valuable assumptions for a fruitful interreligious dialogue. After describing the metaphor's vehicle, a perfectly flat mirror surrounded by several curved mirrors, the author offers the following considerations:

> One [and the same] reflected-brightness appears variously in all mirror-reflections. But in the first, most straight Reflected-brightness all the other mirrors appear as they are. (This occurrence can be observed in the case of material mirrors turned toward one another in a facing circle.) But in each of the other mirrors, which are contracted and curved, all the other mirrors appear not as they themselves are but in accordance with the condition of the receiving mirror, i.e., with some diminishment because of the receiving mirror's deviation from straightness.[30]

This mirror metaphor can be interpreted as focusing on the singularity of creatures, although it can also suggest the interpretation of the nature of religions, since the whole chapter discusses the realization of both filiation and *theosis*. However, the consummation of this sonship can only be eschatologically realized, and therefore, in our temporality and finitude, we are condemned to live among more or less curved mirrors with the possibility of becoming living mirrors ourselves in a movement of approximation toward unity. When applied to religions, this mirror metaphor is particularly meaningful insofar as it again translates the hologrammatic relationship between religions based on the concept of contraction. By delving deeper into it we can surmise that each individual religion is not only a contraction of the ineffable truth and the perfectly straight mirror that is the divine Word, but it is also the contraction of all other religions within itself, which establishes an inclusive relation among all religions in the context of each specific singularity. Naturally, this is a useful presupposition

---

infinitude. On the other hand, he shows how the metaphor of the light-color relationship aptly translates this knowledge dialectics. See Mariano Álvarez-Gómez, "Hacia los fundamentos de la paz perpetua en la religión según Nicolás de Cusa," *La Ciudad de Dios* 212, no. 2 (1999): 334–36.

30 Nicholas of Cusa, *De filiatione Dei*, III (66), in *Nicolai de Cusa Opera Omnia*, vol. IV, ed. Paul Wilpert (Hamburg: Felix Meiner Verlag, 1959), 49; trans. Jasper Hopkins, *A Miscellany on Nicholas of Cusa* (Minneapolis: Arthur J. Banning Press, 1994), 347.

for interreligious dialogues that seek to find the isomorphisms and the trans-religious nature common to all religions.

Written in 1447, Cusanus's short dialogue *De genesi* is particularly significant as concerns the philosophical presuppositions of interreligious dialogue. Although the major aim of this text is to examine more closely a new concept in Nicholas of Cusa's itinerary through divine names—the concept of *idem* (the Same)—the hermeneutic considerations made in *De genesi* go far beyond fifteenth-century hermeneutics and speak to the differences among religions. The starting point for this dialogue is the naming of God in Psalm 101: all things change, "but you are the same" (*tu autem idem ipse es*) (Ps 101:26–28). I now want to transpose this idea into discourse about God, converting a metaphysical principle into a hermeneutic principle. Cusanus writes: "Those who have spoken about the genesis [of all things] have spoken of the same thing in different ways.... Why, then, are you amazed that the Same [*idem*] is the Cause of [all] the different things?"[31] These words set the tone for the whole speech: the link between a metaphysical principle (from itself Oneness generates multiplicity) and a hermeneutical principle (the same motif can be the object of different interpretive expressions). Thus, both a metaphysical and a hermeneutical meaning should be ascribed simultaneously to the claim that "Infinity—which coincides with the absolute, unattainable Same—shines forth quite brightly in the countless multitude of particular beings."[32] If infinity shines better in the multiplicity of creatures, then infinite truth also shines brighter in the multiplicity of religions.

This assumption is echoed in the following chapter of *De genesi* in a set of methodological and hermeneutical rules, which immediately affect the reading of the biblical text and indirectly affect the interpretation of the diversity of religions.[33] These rules, all formulated from the capacities of reason, can be summarized as follows. First, the biblical text (and along with it, the sacred texts of any religion) should be expressed in human language and in accordance with the human ability to express and comprehend

---

31 Nicholas of Cusa, *Dialogus de genesi*, I (143), in *Nicolai de Cusa Opera Omnia*, vol. IV, ed. Paul Wilpert (Hamburg: Felix Meiner Verlag, 1959), 104; trans. Jasper Hopkins, *A Miscellany on Nicholas of Cusa* (Minneapolis: Arthur J. Banning Press, 1994), 394.

32 Nicholas of Cusa, *Dialogus de genesi*, II (154), ed. Wilpert, 111; trans. Hopkins, 399.

33 Giovanni Santinello describes those principles in a short article on the subject: "L'Ermeneutica scritturale nel 'De genesi' del Cusano," *Archivio di filosofia* 3 (1963): 81–90.

ideas.³⁴ Second, the multiplicity of expressions of truth invite an assimilative movement leading from the different contractions back to the *idem* (the fact that the word "contraction" is used here again is quite significant), contractions that unfold it, manifesting the relative nature of each.³⁵ Third, the same principle is to be applied to all interpretations, including the interpretations of the wise and of the Church Fathers (or, extrapolating this principle, the interpretations of the "priests" or interpreters of any religion), since they are but "different concepts of [that] inexpressible manner" of apprehending the absolute *idem*, "which each [of those wise] has endeavored to befigure assimilatively."³⁶

IV

I would now like to look at the first books of *Idiota de sapientia*, the Cusan dialogue on wisdom, in order to highlight two elements that will later find an important echo in *De pace fidei*. From these books I will extract three quite productive presuppositions for a discussion of the plurality of religions. Based on the identification of God with wisdom ("Orator: Is Eternal Wisdom anything other than God? Layman: Far be it that it is anything but God!"),³⁷ the first of these presuppositions transposes the infinitude of God into Wisdom, something that no human power whatsoever can ever apprehend.³⁸ This implies that no religion can apprehend divine Wisdom in its ineffable character:

---

34 Nicholas of Cusa, *Dialogus de genesi*, II (159), ed. Wilpert, 114–15.

35 "Ipsi [prudentes atque peritiores] enim absolvunt eum a contractione illa, quantum eis possibile fuerit, ut intueantur tantum idem absolutum identificare." Nicholas of Cusa, *Dialogus de genesi*, II (160), ed. Wilpert, 115–16. This contraction is even assigned a historical dimension, as Cusanus argues at the beginning of the following chapter. See Nicholas of Cusa, *Dialogus de genesi*, III (161), ed. Wilpert, 116.

36 Nicholas of Cusa, *Dialogus de genesi*, II (160), ed. Wilpert, 116; trans. Hopkins, 403.

37 Nicholas of Cusa, *Idiota de sapientia*, I (21), in *Nicolai de Cusa Opera Omnia*, vol. V, ed. Ludwig Baur and Renata Steiger (Hamburg: Felix Meiner Verlag, 1983), 44; trans. Jasper Hopkins, *Nicholas of Cusa on Wisdom and Knowledge* (Minneapolis: Arthur J. Banning Press, 1996), 507.

38 This is also highlighted by María del Carmen Paredes Martín, "Sabiduría y mística en Nicolás de Cusa: El *Idiota de sapientia*," in *Filosofía, arte y mística*, ed. María del Carmen Paredes Martín and Enrique Bonete Perales (Salamanca: Ediciones Universidad Salamanca, 2017), 162–64. For a detailed analysis of the different meanings of the concept of wisdom in these dialogues, see María del Carmen Paredes Martín, "El concepto de 'sabiduría' en *Idiota de sapientia*," *Anuario filosófico* 28, no. 3 (1995): 671–94.

Hence, Wisdom (which all men seek with such great mental longing, since by nature they desire to know) is known in no other way than [through the awareness] that it is higher than all knowledge and is unknowable and is inexpressible by any speech, incomprehensible by any intellect, unmeasurable by any measure, unlimitable by any limit, unboundable by any bounds, disproportional in terms of any proportion, incomparable in terms of any comparison, unbefigurable by any befiguring, unformable by any forming, immovable by any movement, unimaginable by any imagining, unsensible by any sensing, unattractable by any attracting, untasteable by any tasting, inaudible by any hearing, unseeable by any seeing, inapprehensible by any apprehending, unaffirmable by any affirming, undeniable by any negating, undoubtable by any doubting, inopinable by any opining... Wisdom, through which and in which and from which are all things.[39]

The consequence of this for the relativity of all religions as well as for their intrinsic movement toward unity is revealed some pages later: "Unmultipliable Infinity is unfolded in the best way by means of a varied reception," observes Nicholas. In this interpretation, each religion participates in divine Wisdom, some more distantly, some more closely, though none perfectly. As Nicholas concludes: "Wisdom, received in various forms in various ways, brings it about that each form, called to sameness [with Wisdom], partakes of Wisdom in the best way it can."[40]

The second presupposition concerns the configuration of wisdom through multidimensional sensitivity, following the description of wisdom as nourishment for the spirit,[41] which introduces the relationship between knowledge and love. This is the context in which we find the statement: "Eternal Wisdom is tasted in everything tasteable. It is the delightfulness in everything delightful."[42] This means that wisdom, to which all cognoscitive efforts converge and toward which all religions are directed, does not belong solely to the realm of logic and knowledge, for it also includes taste, delight, beauty, and desire. And all knowledge, including knowledge

---

39 Nicholas of Cusa, *Idiota de sapientia*, I (9), ed. Baur and Steiger, 15–16; trans. Hopkins, 501.
40 Nicholas of Cusa, *Idiota de sapientia*, I (25), ed. Baur and Steiger, 52–53; trans. Hopkins, 509.
41 See Nicholas of Cusa, *Idiota de sapientia*, I (12), ed. Baur and Steiger, 22–26.
42 Nicholas of Cusa, *Idiota de sapientia*, I (14), ed. Baur and Steiger, 30; trans. Hopkins, 504.

that can be translated into religious propositions, contains this multidimensionality. This is what underlies both the hermeneutical dynamics of pre-understanding in the quest for wisdom (based on a cognitive *a priori*) and the pathic, sensitive dynamics of love (based on an affective *a priori*). These two *a priori* principles are not independent, nor do they run parallel, even from an ethical point of view.[43] Rather, they are mutually inscribed, as Klaus Kremer aptly shows in his discussion of the implications of the concept of wisdom.[44] I will deal with the connection between knowledge and love later in what follows, but note that it is a key dimension in the discussion of interreligious dialogue as not only a confrontation of ideas but also a convergence of affections.

The third presupposition does not concern the concept of truth or the concept of wisdom so much as it inscribes itself in the very practice or exercise of dialogue. We now proceed from Book I to Book II of *Idiota de sapientia*. While Book I is focused on the concept of wisdom, Book II focuses on the concept of God as the presupposition of all concepts. While discussing the most appropriate type of theology to approach and elaborate on the concept of God, after clarifying both the method and the nature of positive theology and the method and nature of negative theology, Cusanus introduces the concept of *theologia sermocinalis*,[45] which can be translated as locutional theology, the theology of speech, or dialogical theology, to describe the best way in which to discuss God.[46] Therefore, when seeking God or the adequate discourse about God, one has to overcome the dichotomy between positive theology and negative theology in order to benefit from a theology grounded on dialogue and the force of the word. As Cusanus writes: "Now, it is God who is being sought. Hence, this is locutional theology, by which I am endeavoring to lead you unto God—in the easiest and truest way I can—through the meaning of a word [*in vi vocabuli*]."[47]

---

43 This is Klaus Kremer's conclusion in "Das kognitive und affektive Apriori bei der Erfassung des Sittlichen," in Klaus Kremer, *Praegustatio naturalis sapientiae: Gott suchen mit Nikolaus von Kues* (Münster: Aschendorff Verlag, 2004), esp. 144–46.

44 See Klaus Kremer, "Weisheit als Voraussetzung und Erfüllung der Sehnsucht des menschlichen Geistes," in Kremer, *Praegustatio naturalis sapientiae*, 51–91.

45 On *theologia sermocinalis* in Cusanus, see Peter J. Casarella, *Word as Bread: Language and Theology in Nicholas of Cusa* (Münster: Aschendorff Verlag, 2017), 89–164.

46 Nicholas of Cusa, *Idiota de sapientia*, II (33), ed. Baur and Steiger, 66.

47 Nicholas of Cusa, *Idiota de sapientia*, II (33), ed. Baur and Steiger, 66; trans. Hopkins, 514.

This approach offers us a model applicable to interreligious dialogue: a dialogue based on the force of the word (*vis vocabuli*) and the power of unity that it means to express. The force latent within the word causes an impact on the speakers, bringing them closer to the unity of wisdom.[48] Note how in Book I of *Idiota de sapientia*, force (*vis*) denotes the force of the unity of wisdom prior to being the force of the word. It is precisely this unifying power of wisdom that shines forth in all efforts to apprehend it, whether philosophical or religious, and in the words used to convey and describe it. The conception of dialogue postulated here is thus profoundly dynamic.

V

We can also extract important presuppositions for interreligious dialogue from *De visione Dei*, written the same year as *De pace fidei* (1453). These presuppositions emerge from Nicholas of Cusa's development of the vision metaphor. I would highlight two aspects: one concerning the enhancement of singularity, and the other concerning the dynamics of love. The valorization of singularity is present in the organization and expansion of the metaphor itself. The vision of God's icon is omnidirectional, and each observer can perceive this omnidirectional gaze only from the contraction of the place where they are situated,[49] from the penetration of their eyes,[50] and their sensitivity, characteristics, and emotions.[51] The same can be said of the perception of the movement of the painting's gaze on the part of each of the observers who move in opposite directions.[52] This means that all finite, contracted gazes are necessarily limited and incomplete in the perception they have of the gaze that gazes back at them, and that only complementary gazes can provide an approximate access to the absolute gaze in its entirety.

To apply this metaphor to the diversity of religions—themselves contracted forms of looking at the divine gaze—is to recognize the inevitable singularity of each religion and its enhancement as a complementary form

---

48 On the concept of "force of the word" in Nicholas of Cusa, see João Maria André, *Nikolaus von Kues und die Kraft des Wortes* (Trier: Paulinus Verlag, 2006).

49 Nicholas of Cusa, *De visione Dei*, Praef. (3), in *Nicolai de Cusa Opera Omnia*, vol. VI, ed. Heide Dorothea Riemann (Hamburg: Felix Meiner Verlag, 2000), 5–6.

50 See Nicholas of Cusa, *De visione Dei*, I (5), ed. Riemann, 10.

51 See Nicholas of Cusa, *De visione Dei*, II (7), ed. Riemann, 11–12.

52 See Nicholas of Cusa, *De visione Dei*, Praef. (3), ed. Riemann, 5–6.

of approach to the divine. However, this valorization of singularity entails the inscription of the ethical motif of care, which is crucially important in the dialogical relation between the observers's gazes and God's gaze. The words of the German cardinal express exactly that:

> And while he considers that this gaze does not desert anyone, he sees how diligently it is concerned for each one, as if it were concerned for no one else, but only for him who experiences that he is seen by it. This [impression] is so strong that the one who is being looked upon cannot even imagine that [the icon] is concerned for another. [The one who is pondering all this] will also notice that [the image] is most diligently concerned for the least of creatures, just as for the greatest of creatures and for the whole universe.[53]

Transposing the metaphor from the ontological or anthropological sphere to the sphere of the diversity of religions, we may say first that God takes the most diligent care of each religion in its specificity and its singularity. But since "Absolute Sight is present in all seeing, since all contracted sight exists through Absolute Sight,"[54] this care is transfused into each gaze, which makes each religion look upon all the others with the same diligent care. An ethics of care would thus complement a metaphysics of singularity in enhancing the specificity of each religion.

The second aspect emerges at the very end of *De visione Dei*, and it too inscribes the dynamics of love into the dynamics of the gaze. While the dialogical dimension is a necessary component of this text, as I have sought to demonstrate elsewhere,[55] the dialogical nature of the gaze cannot be understood without the affective component, which translates into the love relationship. In chapter 25 in particular, Cusanus discusses the complementarity of all intellectual spirits, which are innumerable; were they not so, God could not be known in the best way, which means that the religions

---

53 Nicholas of Cusa, *De visione Dei*, Praef. (4), ed. Riemann, 6; trans. Jasper Hopkins, *Nicholas of Cusa's Dialectical Mysticism: Text, Translation, and Interpretive Study of "De Visione Dei"*, 2nd ed. (Minneapolis: Arthur J. Banning Press, 1988), 681–82.
54 Nicholas of Cusa, *De visione Dei*, II (7), ed. Riemann, 11; trans. Hopkins, 683 (caveat: Hopkins's chapter numbers differ).
55 See João Maria André, "Sehen ist auch Hören und Sprechen: Dialogische dimensionen in *De visione Dei*," in *Nikolaus von Kues—Denken im Dialog*, ed. Walter Andreas Euler (Münster: LIT Verlag, 2019), 27–42.

within which these intellectual spirits act are themselves a condition for knowing God in the best possible manner. Nicholas combines this motif and the love motif: "For each intellectual spirit sees in You-my-God something [without] which the others—unless it were revealed to them—could not in the best possible manner attain unto You-their-God. Full of love, the spirits reveal to one another their respective secrets; and, as a result, their knowledge of the one who is loved and their desire for Him is increased; and the sweetness of their joy is aflame."[56] This shows how, in tandem with the enhancement of singularity and the ethics of care, the love dynamic is another characteristic of interreligious dialogue.

VI

In line with my reading of the vision metaphor in *De visione Dei*, and regarding the contemporary relevance of the presuppositions of interreligious dialogue, I would stress how Nicholas of Cusa gives singularity special attention in his later works, most notably in *De venatione sapientiae*, where *singularitas* appears as a special meadow in the "field" of equality.[57] In this treatise, the cause of singularity is identified as unity, which in itself is maximally singular and non-multipliable. That is why "each thing rejoices over its singularity."[58] "Since what is singular is made singular by an eternal Cause, it can never be resolved into what is not singular," Nicholas observes, a claim that entails that "a singular good never ceases to be [a singular good], since everything singular is good."[59] Applying these considerations to the singularity of each religion, one can conclude that singularity is positive and ought not to be annulled by artificial unifications. This does not

---

[56] Nicholas of Cusa, *De visione Dei*, XXV (117), ed. Riemann, 88; trans. Hopkins, 735 (caveat).

[57] Without denying its presence in other works, Gerda von Bredow stresses the importance of singularity in Cusanus's later works. See Gerda von Bredow, "Der Gedanke der Singularitas in der Altersphilosophie des Nikolaus von Kues," in Gerda von Bredow, *Im Gespräch mit Nikolaus von Kues: Gesammelte Aufsätze 1948–1993*, ed. Hermann Schnarr (Münster: Aschendorff Verlag, 1995), 31–39. See also Rodrigo Núñez Poblete's research on this concept in *Metafísica de la singularidad* (Buenos Aires: Editorial Biblos, 2015).

[58] Nicholas of Cusa, *De venatione sapientiae*, XXII (65), in *Nicolai de Cusa Opera Omnia*, vol. XII, ed. Raymond Klibansky and Hans Gerhard Senger (Hamburg: Felix Meiner Verlag, 1982), 63; trans. Jasper Hopkins, *Nicholas of Cusa: Metaphysical Speculations* (Minneapolis: Arthur J. Banning Press, 1998), 1319.

[59] Nicholas of Cusa, *De venatione sapientiae*, XXII (66), ed. Klibansky and Senger, 64; trans. Hopkins, 1320.

mean that the movement of approximation (which translates to dialogue, ultimately) should not be encouraged, because it corresponds to the desire that all religions feel for their own cause.[60] Yet this does imply something decisively important for a dialogue of religions: unification does not come to fruition in the form of actualized unity, but is instead realized in an ongoing process of approximation within which singularity permanently remains.

Underlying the field of praise, Cusanus acknowledges the fact that each creature, in its singularity, is a hymn to God. Although the concept of singularity is explicitly mentioned only in connection with sun, it remains implicit in all references to the other divine hymns. This leads Hans Gerhard Senger, as well as Nuñez Poblete, to argue that singularity can be included in the extended sphere of the *laudabiles*, not because it is explicitly mentioned but because of its implicit importance.[61] It would not be too far-fetched a reading of the Cusan text to suggest that among human discourses religious discourse is perhaps the most laudatory, or even that it is realized as a *scientia laudis*. All religions can therefore be considered to be hymns of divine praise, in various degrees and in their own particular specificities.

VII

The last idea to discuss as a Cusan presupposition with consequences for interreligious dialogue concerns the oft-stated coincidence of love and knowledge. Besides its presence in some of the most significant letters exchanged between Nicholas of Cusa and the Tegernsee monks, this coincidence is especially argued for in some of Cusanus's sermons and emerges again later in his letter to Nicholas Albergati, written shortly before the author's death.[62]

By way of illustration, let us focus on Sermon 172. At the beginning of the sermon, Nicholas incisively states: "But there is no love without

---

60 Nicholas of Cusa, *De venatione sapientiae*, XXII (66), ed. Klibansky and Senger, 64.

61 See Hans Gerhard Senger, "Warum es bei Nikolaus von Kues keine Transzendentalien gibt und wie sie kompensiert werden," in *Die Logik des Transzendentalen: Festschrift für Jan A. Aertsen*, ed. Martin Pickavé, Miscellanea Medievalia 30 (Berlin: De Gruyter, 2003), 575. See also Poblete, *Metafísica de la singularidad*, 196–201.

62 See Maria Simone Marinho Nogueira, "Amor, caritas e dilectio—Elementos para uma hermenêutica do amor em Nicolau de Cusa," (PhD diss., University of Coimbra, 2008), esp. 110–48.

knowledge. Thus, it is necessary for that Nature [created by God] to be capable of God through knowledge, so that it may taste the gentleness of the Lord, whom it should love, for nothing can be loved which is unknown."[63] This dialogical relationship between love and knowledge seems to be aimed at knowing God, but the text has a wider scope and becomes more categorical by proclaiming that "there is no love without knowledge" and by maintaining against some mystical traditions that one cannot love something that one does not know. Moreover, in the next paragraph, the author insists: "Consider also how assimilating and being assimilated coincide in the mind, just like understanding [*intelligere*] and loving. Indeed, the mind does not understand in the absence of desire and it does not desire in the absence of the intellect. The mind is therefore the source of the intellect and of affection. The mind is the simple, noblest power, where understanding and loving coincide."[64]

In Cusanus's letter to Albergati, this knowledge-love coincidence is sublimely called *scientia amoris*. According to his reinterpretation in this letter, the complete return to God (*completa reditio*) happens through love: "Just as all things come into being from love, which is God, so all things are preserved and returned to God by love." This is why, he continues, love is a *sine qua non* for the life of the intellect: "The intellect, however, cannot live in ignorance without joy and love. Since it is lacking, the knowledge of love [*scientia amoris*] is in its ignorance. It is necessary that the intellect, if it would live in eternal joy, which cannot lack love, should know love, which it cannot know except by loving."[65]

The intersection of the "science of praise" and the "science of love" allows us to transpose this idea into interreligious dialogue. Dialogue cannot be understood as something that happens merely at a logical-conceptual

---

[63] Nicholas of Cusa, Sermo CLXXII (Suscepimus, Deus, misericordiam tuam in medio templi tui), 2, in *Nicolai de Cusa Opera Omnia*, vol. XVIII, *Sermones III (1452–1455), Fasc. 3*, ed. Silvia Donati, Isabella Mandrella, and Harald Schwaetzer (Hamburg: Felix Meiner Verlag, 2003), 249–50. See also Sermo CLV (Vere filius Dei erat iste), 2, in *Nicolai de Cusa Opera Omnia*, vol. XVIII, *Sermones III (1452–1455), Fasc. 2*, ed. Heinrich Pauli (Hamburg: Felix Meiner Verlag, 2001), 167.

[64] Nicholas of Cusa, Sermo CLXXII, 3, ed. Donati et al., 250–51.

[65] Nicholas of Cusa, "Epistola ad Nicolaum Bononiensem," 12, in *Cusanus-Texte IV. Briefwechsel des Nikolaus von Kues. Dritte Sammlung: Das Vermächtnis des Nikolaus von Kues. Der Brief an Nikolaus Albergati nebst der Predigt in Montoliveto (1463)*, ed. Gerda von Bredow (Heidelberg: Carl Winter Verlag, 1955), 31. I thank Thomas Izbicki for the use of his unpublished translation.

level, since it needs to be brought to fruition at the affective level. What this means is that the approximation of religions requires a reciprocity of affections to be added to mutual knowledge. The words of Raimon Panikkar, a Catalonian of Spanish and Indian descent whose life was an ongoing existential search for interreligiosity and interculturality, are fully in line with such Cusan intuitions, of which they are a most fruitful development. Panikkar describes a sacred marriage, a *hieros gamos*, of knowledge and love: "All loveless approximation to another culture is a violation of this culture. All approximation without knowledge is a more or less immoral approximation." And he adds: "The love-knowledge relationship is not dualistic. One does not go without the other, although they are not one and the same thing. Love is not only the prime condition for knowledge ('*de ignoto nulla cupido*'). Knowledge is not only the previous condition for love ('*nihili volitum quin praecognitum*'). Their relationship is intrinsic and constitutive."[66] The Latin expressions used by Panikkar to underpin his opinion could almost seem to have been transcribed from Nicholas of Cusa.

VIII

Having concluded this survey from *De docta ignorantia* to *De venatione sapientiae*, and having examined some of the philosophical presuppositions in Nicholas of Cusa that might throw light on his views on interreligious dialogue, we must now address *De pace fidei*, the text in which this subject was most directly approached, and check whether such presuppositions were incorporated into the author's dialogical attitude. As we read *De pace fidei*, we are again confronted with two hermeneutic possibilities: on the one hand, specific answers to different issues under discussion, which have a narrower scope than what the theoretical presuppositions might suggest; and on the other, the potential for greater openness found in the text and in the considerations that precede the dialogue on the specific topics under discussion, which point toward broader presuppositions. To validate this second, broader hermeneutic, it is important to bear in mind the structure of the text. In the prologue Cusanus stages a fictive council in which the wisest representatives of the different peoples, cultures, and religions (for instance, the Greek, the Arab, and the Chaldean) engage in dialogue. This

---

[66] Raimon Panikkar, *Pluralisme et interculturalité*, in Raimon Panikkar, *Oeuvres*, 6/1 (Paris: Éditions du Cerf, 2012), 409.

is followed by three dialogue scenes, whose interlocutors are first the Word, then Peter, and finally Paul. Within this structural framework, the most concrete issues, whether theological or sacramental or ecclesiological, are dealt with in the dialogues with Peter and Paul, whereas the dialogue with the Word focuses particularly on philosophical questions or even on the philosophical presuppositions of certain theological themes, such as the Trinity or Creation. The prologue and the dialogue with the Word are precisely where the presuppositions that I have analyzed throughout the work of Nicholas of Cusa shine forth most evidently.

The basis of a metaphysics and a hermeneutic of finitude, exercised as learned ignorance, is the perception of God as infinite. This is decisive for the movement of dialogue. The words uttered by the Word could not be more incisive and fruitful in their dialogical reach: "As Creator, God is trine and one; as Infinite, He is neither trine nor one nor any of those things that can be spoken of. For the names that are ascribed to God are taken from creatures, since in Himself God is ineffable and beyond all that can be named or spoken of."[67] Potentially, these words relativize all theological formulations, including those that concern the very dogma of the Trinity, reducing that divine name to the conditions of human speech, constrained by the limitations of each and every creature. This statement inscribes all discourses about God under the principle of learned ignorance and has repercussions for divine names. Cusanus continues with another affirmation, which, following other medieval authors, reformulates philosophically the Trinitarian conception as habitually formulated in the Christian creed: "Some name Oneness *Father*, Equality *Son*, and Union *Holy Spirit* because these terms, though not proper, nonetheless signify the Trinity suitably.... And if simpler terms could be found, they would be more fitting—as are Oneness, Itness, and Sameness."[68] The religious, theological nomenclature of Father, Son, and Holy Spirit is here subordinated

---

[67] See Nicholas of Cusa, *De pace fidei*, VII (21), in *Nicolai de Cusa Opera Omnia*, vol. VII, ed. Raymond Klibansky and Hildebrand Bascour, 2nd ed. (Hamburg: Felix Meiner Verlag, 1970), 20; trans. Jasper Hopkins, *Nicholas of Cusa's "De pace fidei" and "Cribatio Alkorani": Translation and Analysis*, 2nd ed. (Minneapolis: Arthur J. Banning Press, 1994), 643.

[68] Nicholas of Cusa, *De pace fidei*, VIII (24), ed. Klibansky and Bascour, 25; trans. Hopkins, 645–46. Nicholas of Cusa again repeats the proposition presented in *De docta ignorantia*, I.9 (25), ed. Wilpert and Senger, 34. In his book on the evolution of Cusan thought, Kurt Flasch stresses the distance that is implicit in this expression and emphasizes the "philosophical correction" of the church's traditional Trinitarian theory. See Kurt Flasch, *Nikolaus von Kues: Geschichte einer Entwicklung* (Frankfurt am Main: Vittorio Klostermann, 1998), 356.

to another, clearly philosophical nomenclature that echoes the concepts laid down in *De docta ignorantia*.[69]

Second, in addition to the philosophical reformulation of the theological concepts, based on learned ignorance, I would also emphasize the primacy of the concept of wisdom understood as "infinite force," which gives a dynamic dimension not only to wisdom, but to all interreligious dialogue, based on this force of wisdom and on the force of words. This idea is developed in the first dialogue with the Greek (chapter 4), which we find summarized in the following words: "You all agree, then, that there is one most simple Wisdom, whose power is ineffable. And in the unfolding of Wisdom's power, each [of you] experiences this ineffable and infinite power."[70] This conception of mind and wisdom as power or force continues from the concept of *contractio* into the *Idiota* dialogues and through the whole of *De sapientia*, which *De pace fidei* encapsulates. After alluding to the sensorial multidimensionality of wisdom, Nicholas returns through the light metaphor to his meditations in *De filiatione Dei*, which describe the existential dimension of dialogue as a *conversio spiritus* that leads to *filiatio*.[71] Rewriting the relationship between one infinite wisdom and plural finite (human) wisdoms through the light metaphor, as this paragraph does, allows us to perceive the relationship's contemporary translation into the hologrammatic principle mentioned above. Indeed, all the examples of contraction presented in *De docta ignorantia* are repeated here in the concepts of organism, its members, order, life, harmony, movement, and rational spirit.

Third, I would say that, if each people's wisdom and the wisdom inherent to each religion are explications of the one, infinite, and ineffable wisdom, as we saw above, then their singularity is an indispensable wealth that must be positively evaluated and heuristically enhanced, rather than devalued as something expendable, as I outlined in my reading of *De venatione sapientiae*. Two examples can support this view: (a) Cusanus's statement in the prologue concerning the diversity of rites, which clearly demonstrates that diversity is wealth rather than fragility;[72] and (b) his idea throughout the entire prologue: God holds the diversity of religions in such

---

69 See Nicholas of Cusa, *De docta ignorantia*, I.9 (25), ed. Wilpert and Senger, 34.
70 Nicholas of Cusa, *De pace fidei*, IV (11), ed. Klibansky and Bascour, 12; trans. Hopkins, 638.
71 See Nicholas of Cusa, *De pace fidei*, IV (12), ed. Klibansky and Bascour, 12–13.
72 Nicholas of Cusa, *De pace fidei*, I (6), ed. Klibansky and Bascour, 7.

esteem that each religion has been granted protective guards, significantly presented as "intellectual virtues,"[73] envoys and guardians of the people,[74] or angelic spirits.[75] This aspect is underscored by Josef Stallmach in his study of the text.[76]

Fourth and last, a special mention must be made of the place of love in this discourse, which introduces an affective, rather than a merely cognitive dynamic in the realization of interreligious dialogue. In the dialogue with the Arab (chapter 6), this affective dynamic can first be deduced from the fact that all the wise men and the representatives of the different peoples and religions attending this council are "lovers of wisdom" who desire wisdom because it is the life of the intellect.[77] As a presupposition of the Trinity, love is also explicitly mentioned in the dialogue with the Chaldean (chapter 8), where it is described as connection impregnated with the power of unity.[78] Next, in his dialogue with Peter (chapter 10), the Scythian declares that "love unites" and concludes: "Hence, this spirit, whose power [*vis*] is diffused throughout the universe, can be said to be Love-that-is-God."[79] Note that the word "force" or "power," which had been used to describe wisdom, is used here to describe love, introducing a profoundly dynamic dimension. Finally, and overlooking some other similar references to love, Paul's dialogue with the Tartar (chapter 16) raises the practical question of how people can come to understand one another if each people and each religion has its own commandments. To this, Paul offers a very emphatic and conclusive answer:

> The divine commandments are very terse and very well known to everyone and are common to all nations. Indeed, the light that shows us these [commandments] is created together with the rational soul. For God speaks within us, [commanding us] to love Him from whom

---

[73] "Non enim habitu ut homines sed intellectuales virtutes comparebant." Nicholas of Cusa, *De pace fidei*, I (2), ed. Klibansky and Bascour, 4.

[74] See Nicholas of Cusa, *De pace fidei*, I (6), ed. Klibansky and Bascour, 7.

[75] See Nicholas of Cusa, *De pace fidei*, III (9), ed. Klibansky and Bascour, 10.

[76] See Josef Stallmach, "Einheit der Religion—Friede unter den Religionen. Zum Ziel der Gedankenführung im Dialog 'Der Friede im Glauben,'" in *Der Friede unter den Religionen nach Nikolaus von Kues*, 65–66.

[77] See Nicholas of Cusa, *De pace fidei*, VI (16), ed. Klibansky and Bascour, 15.

[78] See Nicholas of Cusa, *De pace fidei*, VIII (23), ed. Klibansky and Bascour, 23–24.

[79] Nicholas of Cusa, *De pace fidei*, X (27), ed. Klibansky and Bascour, 29; trans. Hopkins, 648.

we receive being and not to do unto another anything except that which we want done unto us. Therefore, love is the fulfilment of God's law, and all [other] laws are reducible to the law of love.[80]

Here again is the love dynamic we identified in *De visione Dei*, which is defined in a number of Cusan sermons as "the form or life of all the virtues" or described as the full realization of God's law and the practical materialization of concord: the ultimate goal of interreligious dialogue.[81] However, in his explicit reference to the commandment of love, Cusanus identifies it with the Golden Rule—"not to do unto another that which we do not want done unto us"—a rule often present in his texts and sometimes referred to as the *regula aequalitatis*.[82]

This reference to love as the foundation for interreligious concord is yet another profoundly topical characteristic of Nicholas of Cusa's presuppositions for interreligious dialogue. In his *Project for a Global Ethic*, while sifting through the "ethical perspectives of world religions," Hans Küng identifies the Golden Rule of love as one of the transversal traits common to nearly all religions, both in its positive formulations (What you wish done to yourself, do to others) and in its negative ones (What you do not wish done to yourself, do not do to others). Küng goes so far as to argue that Kant's categorical imperative corresponds to the modernization and secularization of the Golden Rule.[83] The rational level, where Cusanus believes that interreligious dialogue should take place as a means to reach concord, is the register and the horizon of these presuppositions.[84] This means that Nicholas of Cusa's aim was to seek the grounds for a peaceful coexistence between believers of different religions in the "loftiest domain of reason" (i.e., in philosophy), more than in any other domain, this rational debate being the basis for building "perpetual peace" among men. Perpetual peace,

---

80 Nicholas of Cusa, *De pace fidei*, XVI (59), ed. Klibansky and Bascour, 55; trans. Hopkins, 665.

81 On the constitutive nature of love both ontologically and ethically, see Wilhelm Dupré, "Liebe als Grundbestandteil allen Seins und 'Form oder Leben aller Tugenden,'" in *Sein und Sollen: Die Ethik des Nikolaus von Kues*, MFCG 26, ed. Klaus Kremer and Klaus Reinhardt (Trier: Paulinus Verlag, 2000), 65–91.

82 For some instances of this rule in Cusanus's text and its connection with equality, see Hans Gerhard Senger, "Gerechtigkeit und Gleichheit und ihre Bedeutung für die Tugendlehre des Nikolaus von Kues," in *Sein und Sollen: Die Ethik des Nikolaus von Kues*, 48–49.

83 See Hans Küng, *Projekt Weltethos* (Munich: Pieper, 1990), 84–85.

84 Nicholas of Cusa, *De pace fidei*, XIX (68), ed. Klibansky and Bascour, 62–63.

a concept outlined by Nicholas of Cusa approximately three hundred years before Kant, is also the objective of Hans Küng's global ethic, based on what he calls an "ecumenical theology for peace."[85]

As we have seen, there is great openness in the philosophical presuppositions for interreligious dialogue in Nicholas of Cusa—surely greater than his own limited application of those presuppositions, often guided by a too-reductionist or inclusivist perspective found in specific proposals of *De pace fidei* and in *Cribratio Alkorani*. However, this gap between the openness of his presuppositions and the limitation of their application is possibly no more than a sign that, once again, Cusanus's interpretation and concrete application of interreligious dialogue is itself a contraction—marked by the space, time, and historical and societal contingencies of his life—of what interreligious dialogue could become in the future, as a quest for the one, ineffable force of Wisdom.

---

[85] Küng, *Projekt Weltethos*, 162–66.

14

Image or Icon

Phenomenologies of Nicholas of Cusa

EMMANUEL FALQUE
TRANSLATED BY CHRISTOPHER C. RIOS

Behind a simple question of translation is hidden an even more profound difference of perspective on the world, and therefore of how to read Nicholas of Cusa. I have come to understand that it is on a single point, in a single place, where my opposition to the philosophy of Jean-Luc Marion is direct and explicit—precisely in the interpretation of Cusanus. For where Marion proposes to translate the title of the work, *De visione Dei sive de icona*, literally as "The Icon or the Vision of God," I have translated it as "The Image (or Painting) and the Vision of God." Honor due to the master means one will go no further than this unique difference, which, taken as more than a matter of custom, introduces a disagreement as well. I have always said, and even written, that the "saturated phenomenon" and the "limited phenomenon" are not two antagonistic visions, but rather two complementary ways of seeing the world. To take a simple example, we can read the passage of the disciples on the road to Emmaus in the Gospel of Luke either by emphasizing the end ("Then their eyes were opened, and they recognized him; and he vanished from their sight," Luke 24:31), or by referring to the rereading made by the disciples from the beginning ("Were not our hearts burning within us while he was talking to us on the road, while he was opening the scriptures to us?" Luke 24:32).[1] On the one hand, there is the extraordinary moment of the apparition, following the example of the apophaticism of Mount Horeb (saturated phenomenon, Pseudo-Dionysius), and on the other hand, the everyday, ordinary moment of God condescending into flesh (limited phenomenon, Bonaventure). Every dissimilarity in theological reference on one side produces a divergence in philosophical conception on the other: a Dionysian vision of excess and of distance on the one hand, and a Franciscan pilgrimage of fraternity and proximity on the other.

But there is even more in this difference, which in fact would remain trivial if kept only to this simple disparity of views. For one, this eristic or simple opposition of supposed contraries has never produced good fruit; second, the divergence of ways finds, precisely in Nicholas of Cusa, its possible resolution. Indeed, in the figure of the cardinal and in exemplary fashion, apophaticism (Dionysius) and cataphaticism (Bonaventure) can be joined, and in this synthesis—or rather in this coincidence of opposites—a practically unexpected resolution is discovered. If there is no third term or *Aufhebung* between the saturated phenomenon and the limited phenomenon as between Dionysius and Bonaventure (for one must always be careful with such overcomings), the act of holding the twofold interpretation simultaneously in the coincidence of opposites does not resolve it, but rather makes it visible, and shows how in God everything is paradoxically unified.

The sequence of events, in the order of life as well as of thought, therefore can now commence. Behind the somewhat incredible scenario is hidden a truly philosophical, indeed, Cusan question, one that also involves philosophy as such. To translate the formula *De icona* as "Image" or "Icon" introduces exclusion rather than inclusion, and no doubt the resolution will be found in God. But so long as we remain human, we live according to varied human perspectives far from the coincidence of opposites. We remain committed to supporting the differences of aims or intentions, not to fight or bicker but to understand that in the respective positions there are different ways of doing philosophy.

---

[1] [Trans.: All quotations of scripture follow the NRSV translation.]

A Western or Whodunit

One must recognize—and perhaps I can say this in the United States more than in France, for no prophet is welcome in his own country—that the debate over the image and the icon, at least as it pertains to the interpretation of Nicholas of Cusa, has its own genesis, as well as its own genealogy and chronology.[2] It is a little like a western, a detective novel or whodunit, where re-watching the film is the best way to see what is happening, or to know what it is all about. Moreover, it should be noted, this debate over image and icon is the only place where Jean-Luc Marion is explicitly opposed to one of my interpretations, in a footnote of rare severity, which nevertheless could not sully our real friendship. (It is probably the Cartesian tradition of responses to objections, itself rooted in the medieval *disputatio*, that allows one, at least in France, to differ without getting angry and always remain quite close.)

The genesis first: Everything begins with an article that I published in the *Revue des sciences philosophiques et théologiques* in March of 2014, following a seminar on the *De icona* given at the Catholic University of Paris in the first semester of the year 2013. A warm exchange followed, which resulted in a common agreement on the grandeur of this text, probably the most surprising and persuasive text of the whole medieval and Renaissance periods (at least in my eyes). The coincidence was that Jean-Luc Marion had been invited, some months later and at the request of the Société française Cusanus, to give a lecture on Nicholas of Cusa on December 15, 2014, at the University of Nice in France. This was, then, the occasion if not of a response, then at least of a debate behind the scenes, as it were, between the position of "the painting or the image," sustained in my lengthy article of March 2014, and that of the "icon," largely defended by Marion in the lecture at Nice and published in French two years later in a specialized journal.[3]

---

2 See also two other essays of mine on Nicholas of Cusa: Emmanuel Falque, "Le Pouvoir-Est (*De Possest*) ou le 'Dieu im-possible' (Nicolas de Cues)," *Archivio di filosofia* 78, no. 1 (2010): 131–42; and Emmanuel Falque, "Un Dieu ineffable? La querelle de la docte ignorance chez Nicolas de Cues," in *L'Unique seul importe: Hommage à Pierre Magnard*, ed. Alain Galonnier (Leuven: Peeters, 2019), 103–19.

3 Emmanuel Falque, "L'omnivoyant: Fraternité et vision de Dieu chez Nicolas de Cues," *Revue des sciences philosophiques et théologiques* 98, no. 1 (January/March 2014): 37–73; Jean-Luc Marion, "Voir, se voir vu: L'apport de Nicolas de Cues dans le *De visione Dei*," *Bulletin de littérature ecclésiastique* 117, no. 2 (April/June 2016): 7–37.

But as is often the case, it is on the other side of the Atlantic, that is to say, in the United States, that purely French disputations are triangulated to greatest effect. Numerous papers heard or delivered there (Thomas Carlson, David Albertson, Stephen Lewis *inter alia*) already made mention of this quarrel, without the protagonists having access to it as long as the texts were not published in full. *The Journal of Religion* in Chicago kicked things off in July 2016 (the same year as the French original) by publishing the English version of Jean-Luc Marion's text following his lecture for the American Cusanus Society in 2015, "Seeing, or Seeing Oneself Seen: Nicholas of Cusa's Contribution in *De visione Dei*."[4] The 2015–2016 academic year was also the year in which, for my part, I composed a sort of synthesis or rereading of the body of my own work under the title *Parcours d'embûches*. A final note, added to this text some weeks before sending it to the editor, responded point by point to the sometimes sharp accusations of Jean-Luc Marion regarding my interpretation.[5] The final act or resolution of this film's scenario, before the conclusion that I offer here, was the translation and publication in English, this time in *Modern Theology*, of my initial article on Cusanus, "The All-Seeing: Fraternity and Vision of God in Nicholas of Cusa," where the quarrel started—to which is added an appendix with the translation of the note from *Parcours d'embûches* responding to Marion.[6]

It must be said: all of this certainly has to make us smile, and must indeed be understood in the sense of a *combat amoreux*, rather than as a vague dispute where each one is only as right as the other is wrong. But behind that, not without a certain irony, and never without the honor and exigency to dispute and discuss equally, one finds a veritable "struggle for the sense of the human" (so Husserl in an appendix to *Crisis* in 1936) or a "struggle which is that of the thing itself" (so Heidegger in his *Letter on Humanism* in 1946). For in this noble joust of words, what is at stake is the interpretation of *De visione Dei*, to be sure, and even the disagreement and the difference between the image and the icon. But also at stake are two differentiated views of the relation of the human to God, or at least of the sense and status of phenomenology on the one hand and theology on the other.

---

[4] Jean-Luc Marion, "Seeing, or Seeing Oneself Seen: Nicholas of Cusa's Contribution in *De visione Dei*," trans. Stephen E. Lewis, *The Journal of Religion* 96, no. 3 (July 2016): 305–31.

[5] See Emmanuel Falque, *Parcours d'embûches: S'expliquer* (Paris: Éditions franciscaines, 2016), 186–87n19.

[6] Emmanuel Falque, "The All-Seeing: Fraternity and Vision of God in Nicholas of Cusa," trans. Kyle H. Kavanaugh and Barnabas Aspray, *Modern Theology* 35, no. 4 (September 2019): 1–28.

Plunged into the invisible, or the absolute requirement of distance on the one hand: such is the status of the icon. The recognition of the thickness of the visible, or even of the necessary proximity to God made man: such is the meaning of the image. Mount Horeb on the one hand (Dionysian aim), and the newborn babe in the crèche on the other (Franciscan vision). In the time when the Renaissance surpasses the medieval, and even more in the Byzantine world, chances are that the borderlands shift, and therefore philosophy does so as well. The distance from Dionysius the Areopagite to Nicholas of Cusa continues to grow, like that of a negative or apophatic theology, which, this time, could not do without its just-as-essential positive or cataphatic dimension. Here I must agree with Agnès Minazzoli, French translator of *De icona*, who suggests, in concert with the celebrated works of Erwin Panofsky on the Renaissance, that nothing assures us up front that we must translate *De icona* by "The Icon," since "the term icon could reduce the semantic richness of the painting in orienting the imagination of the reader toward the unique domain of Byzantine iconography which, as Nicholas of Cusa was aware, is here relegated to the rank of a mere evocation."[7]

The Question of the Title

The scene is set. The film, however, is not yet over. We still need to lay out the plot and to let the point be seen where in fact everything is played out, and where the conflict, or at the very least the "loving struggle," takes shape. For one cannot be satisfied with images or the unwinding of events without grasping the framework where the problem is posed and the protagonists exposed.

Let us note at the outset that one way of resolving the difficulty between "image" or "icon" in translating *De icona* is simply to suppress it. As Immanuel Kant says in speaking on the problem of evil and *On the Failure of All Attempted Philosophical Theodicies* (1793), there are two ways to undo the knot: either to untie it or cut it.[8] The first way—the untying

---

[7] Agnès Minazzoli, commentary in Nicholas of Cusa, *De visione Dei*, trans. Minazzoli as *Le tableau ou la vision de Dieu*, (Paris: Les Éditions du Cerf, 1986), 101.

[8] Immanuel Kant, "L'insuccès de toutes les tentatives en matière de théodicée (1793)," in *Oeuvres completes*, vol. 2 (Paris: Gallimard, 1991), 1939. [Trans.: The English translation of this text reads: "By referring in this way to the supreme wisdom, one can cut the knot; one does not untie it, which was what theodicies promised in the first place." Immanuel Kant, "On the

resolution—is the one that I pursue here, which the debate on the French translation of the title of Nicholas of Cusa's treatise requires. The second way—to resolve the problem by suppressing it—is paradoxically the one adopted by other languages or other countries, which shorten the translation of the title or keep only a part of it, as if the issue did not arise. So, with some exceptions, *De visione Dei sive de icona* is translated only as "The Vision of God" (English), "Die Gottes-Schau" (German), or "La visión de Dios" (Spanish). The icon or the image falls away and only the vision of God remains. To be sure, the choice is justified if not philologically, at least historically. For Nicholas of Cusa himself gave different titles to his own work: *De icona*, *De visione Dei* or even *Tractatus de visione*, or *De visione Dei sive de icona* in full.[9] One can therefore resolve the question by a simple choice of the initial formula: in its short formulation without the term icon and with the vision of God alone (the English, German, or Spanish decisions), or in its longer wording with the term icon always combined with the vision of God (the French decision).

What is most surprising in this affair, then, is seeing or noticing that the French have not suppressed the difficulty, but have brought it out, if not emphasized it, at least in the latest translations. That is where the scenario picks up from where it remained unfinished. To get to the point, we know that the current French translation of *De icona* is that of Agnès Minazzoli, published by Éditions du Cerf, who translates it as *Le tableau ou la vision de Dieu* or "The Painting or the Vision of God" (1986). But the debate surrounding the exact translation of the term *icona*—by icon and not image, according to Jean-Luc Marion—then demanded a new translation of the whole work, a new translator, and therefore a new title. So the work of Nicholas of Cusa appears anew, translated now by Hervé Pasqua, this time under the title, *L'icône ou la vision de Dieu*, or "The Icon or the Vision of God," published with Presses Universitaires de France in the collection *Epiméthée* (directed by Jean-Luc Marion) in 2016, the same year as the publication of Jean-Luc Marion's article on Nicholas of Cusa and two years after his first 2014 lecture in French. The choice of translating in full "The Icon or the Vision of God" (2016), of course, as opposed to "The Painting or the

---

Failure of All Attempted Philosophical Theodicies (1791)," trans. Michel Despland, in *Kant on History and Religion: With a Translation of Kant's "On the Failure of All Attempted Philosophical Theodicies"* (Montreal: McGill-Queen's University Press, 1973), 287.]

9 The different titles are noted in Nicholas of Cusa, *L'icône ou la vision de Dieu*, trans. Hervé Pasqua (Paris: Presses Universitaires de France, 2016), 9.

Vision of God" (1986), is all the more surprising since the work itself, within the text, opens exclusively with the title *La vision de Dieu* or "The vision of God," translating the formula *Tractatus de visione Dei* with reference to Augustine's Letter 147.[10] In short, the plot thickens, not by virtue of a simple quarrel among authors or translators, which would have little importance here, but because a veritable battle of wills has taken shape in France with respect to the translation of *De icona* by "Painting" or "Icon"—a polemic cleverly avoided in other languages or other countries, allowing them to believe it never existed.

The Terms of the Debate

It is the body of the text itself, and in particular the preface of Nicholas of Cusa's *De icona*, that makes it the object if not of conflict, at least of disagreement. Let us first cite the formula in Latin, at least to do right by Nicholas of Cusa himself, who was certainly far from imagining that a simple formula spoken in passing could one day in another text nourish such a "dispute" in the medieval sense of the word: *habere potui, caritati vestrae mitto tabellam figuram cuncta videntis tenentem, quam eiconam dei appello.*[11] Translated in French either as: "J'envoie à votre bonté un petit tableau portant cette figure de l'omnivoyant et *que j'appelle le tableau de Dieu*"—which I call the painting of God (as translated by Minazzoli), or as: "j'ai pu me procure un petit tableau que je vous envoie par amour pour vous: il représente l'expression de quelqu'un qui voit tout, *que j'appelle l'icône de Dieu*"—which I call the icon of God (as translated by Pasqua).

The issue is clear. It is a question here, and in the Latin as well, of a "petit tableau," "little painting" (*tabellam*), and therefore of the material basis of the work of art sent in support of the treatise to the brother monks of the Abbey of Tegernsee on the one hand; and on the other hand of the subjective, intentional, and decided appellation of this work as *eicona* by Nicholas of Cusa himself. The material basis would therefore be a painting, and the intention would be an icon if one translates *eicona* literally by icon. Thus, to take the first, literal version of the cardinal's phrase, it would be a matter of sending to the abbot, Caspar Aindorffer, a representation or image

---

10 See Nicholas of Cusa, *L'icône ou la vision de Dieu*, 46–47.
11 Nicholas of Cusa, *De visione Dei*, Praef. (2), in *Nicolai de Cusa Opera Omnia*, vol. VI, ed. Heide Dorothea Riemann (Hamburg: Felix Meiner Verlag, 2000), 5.

accompanying the treatise entitled *De visione Dei sive de icona*, painted on a medium of small size, which would not *be* an icon (since it is a painting or a little painting), but with the intention to *make* it an icon. In short, Nicholas of Cusa would willingly look at the image otherwise in order to convert it into an icon—he would lead the Renaissance world back to the Byzantine world, even return everything profane to the religious. *Tabellam quam eiconam dei appello*: "ce petit tableau que j'appelle icône de Dieu," "this little painting that I call an icon of God," because this is not an icon, and because I wish, or I would wish, that it at least be looked upon or considered as an icon.

But one could simply say the opposite, even formally. *Eiconam dei appello*: "I call an icon of God" this little painting (*tabellam*), not because it is an icon, but because it is only a way of naming it. I call it an "icon" though I know very well that it is a "painting" in every sense of the word. But to name it so will be more appropriate for your community, because it is a matter of seeing or being seen by God, to be sure, but above all because at the start of the Renaissance the term icon can also quite simply mean "image," albeit of God. In other words, you monks of Tegernsee who will receive this painting, it is indeed a matter of a painting or image of an all-seeing visage, just as one finds in recent paintings of human and non-divine figures. But I see in this pictorial method a way of expressing God as well, or of using later cultural and artistic transformations (in particular, the influence of Flemish and Italian art) to make him known in your monastery today. In short, take it for an icon, and I present it to you in this way because that is what you are used to, and because one must speak of God. In fact, however, it is a "painting," or at least an "image," for it is also through human beings, or by referring to men and women in community, that God gives himself.

The first interpretation, the *lectio facilior*, sees the image and makes it function as an icon, where one remains in the purely religious sphere and in a pictorial and theologically Byzantine representation—one in fact little present in the Catholicism of the fifteenth century because of a schism from which it does not recover and which the cardinal will strive to resolve. The second interpretation, the *lectio difficilior*, departs from what one ordinarily calls or knows under the name of icon and makes it function as an image. Here one recognizes the importance of the profane and the possibility of going "to divine things by human means" (*humaniter ad divina vehera*), as the beginning of Cusanus's preface emphasizes.[12] In this second interpretation we give every inch to the novelty of perspective, such that it is not the one who sees who is absorbed in the seen (humanity within God in the invisibility of his depths), but the seen which returns the viewer to himself and his entire community (God within humanity in the visibility of his expressivity). "What I call an icon of God"—*eiconam dei appello*—therefore functions either as a designation of some content (this image is in fact an icon), or as a formal denomination (what I here call an icon is a way of speaking in order to make myself understood to the community, but in fact it is an image or a painting as we understand it today in this new age of rebirth).

In the second perspective, and in it alone (where one makes a representation of God function as an image or a painting in the sense of the contemporary aesthetics of the time, without requiring it to appear as an icon in the religious sense of the term), the treatise *De visione Dei sive de icona* is the place of a true novelty, theological to be sure, but also pictorial and philosophical. For it is a matter here of a painting by the painter Rogier van der Weyden, also named Roger de la Pasture, who mastered this inversion of perspective: the viewer in the Renaissance sees not so much in order to be drawn into the seen (the icon) as to be returned to his own seeing as seen (the image). As Erwin Panofsky emphasizes in *Perspective as Symbolic Form* (1925), regarding painters such as Ambrogio Lorenzetti in Siena (*The Annunciation*, and in particular the tiled paving of the floor), his brother Pietro (*The Nativity of the Virgin*), and especially Paolo Uccello (*The Miracle of the Profaned Host*), the art of the quattrocento consists in "reversing the meaning of perspective" and "including the one looking within the represented space." Set up in this "reversed perspective," according to the celebrated art critic, is "a de-theologized form of the world, where God would be absent, the multiple vanishing points this time being oriented horizontally towards the earth, as well as towards matter."[13]

---

12 Nicholas of Cusa, *De visione Dei*, Praef. (2), ed. Riemann, 5.
13 See Erwin Panofsky, *Perspective as Symbolic Form*, trans. Christopher S. Wood (New York: Zone Books, 1991), 81. According to Panofsky, we find the first example of reversed perspective in the tiled floor in *The Annunciation* painted by Ambrogio Lorenzetti (1344), taken up next in Siena by his brother Pietro in *The Nativity of the Virgin*. One must await the *Miracle of the Profaned Host* of Paolo Uccello (1469) to definitively construct a perspective whose ensemble of vanishing points converge toward the spectator. For my part, I would note that Nicholas of Cusa's *De icona* marks an entirely new attempt to join the novelty of perspective with the presence of God itself through a "painting" (rather than an "icon").

One should understand, then, that the translation of *eicona* in Latin by "icon" in French or any other language, at least in the Byzantine sense of the word, does not go without saying. Such a transcription is so little self-evident that Nicholas of Cusa sets out to name the painting alone, never the icon, in the celebrated letter accompanying the delivery of his treatise and the work of Rogier van der Weyden. The same word, in French (*tableau*) as in Latin (*tabula*), can mean at the same time the support (the frame that suspends a painting) and the image (the painting itself that I see).[14] Even better, the first French translation of the Latin text by the Lord of Golefer (1630), nearly two centuries after the composition of the treatise by Cusanus (1453), will actually use the term "image" and not "icon" to translate *eiconam*: "j'ay recouvert un tableau [*tabellam*] que j'appelle *l'image* de Dieu [*quam eiconam dei appello*]."[15] This illustrates how much, in the time of the Renaissance at least, a work of art moves increasingly away from the religious representation of the icon, and how it tries to see and say something according to its own aesthetic, including the religious—the return to the human (the image) more than the submersion of the human in the divine (the icon).[16]

Revenge of the Image

All the arguments are here. We have set them out in order to express the true meaning of the delivery of this "little painting," which thus represents "a face looking at everyone and each one individually," so that "the infinite

---

[14] As Nicholas writes in the letter: "I have shown [in this chapter] from a *painting* I have which represents a face looking at everyone and each one individually, how sensible experience itself can lead us to mystical theology in showing us intuitively that the infinite vision sees at the same time all together and each one individually.... I know a painter [Rogier van der Weyden] who will work to reproduce a face similar to the one in my *painting*. By following the teaching of the little book which I intend to add as a companion [the treatise *De visione Dei sive de icona*], you will be delighted to seek in an experimental practice [*praxim experimentalem*], so to speak, all that can be known, particularly in the field of mystical theology." Nicholas of Cusa, *Lettre aux moines de Tegernsee* (1453–1454), in *Oeuvres choisies de Nicolas de Cues*, ed. Maurice de Gandillac (Paris: Aubier-Montaigne, 1942), 368; quoted in Falque, "The All-Seeing," 3–4 (emphasis added).

[15] Translation of Lord Golefer (1630), *Traité de la vision de Dieu*, reproduced as an appendix in Maurice de Gandillac, *Nicolas de Cues* (Paris: Ellipses, 2001), 376.

[16] This includes the Christological perspective, as perfectly shown by Pierre Magnard, specialist on Nicholas of Cusa and the Renaissance: "L'invention de l'homme," in *La couleur du matin profonde: Dialogue avec Eric Fiat* (Paris: Les Petits Platons, 2013), 91–116.

vision sees at the same time all together and each one individually."[17] Here it is a matter of an "image" or a "painting" first in the profane sense of the term—which will continue as such (or break new ground) by always functioning as an image and not as an icon. It will suffice simply to recall these arguments, while relying on the *Preface* of the treatise and the *Letter of Dedication* to the monks of Tegernsee, in order to face the facts.

(1) First, the circumstances: It is indeed a matter of sending a painting to illustrate a treatise of theology, which itself follows a work on mathematics. "To *The Mathematical Complements*," Cusanus declares still in the same letter, "I added another opusculum on the *Theological Complements*, where I applied mathematical figures to the theological infinite [*in quo transtuli mathematicas figuras ad theologicam infinitatem*]."[18] That the *eicona* had been sent to the monks does not directly make of it an icon; quite the contrary. It is a matter of passing from mathematics to theology without losing what makes the figures mathematical: this arc of the circle coming from a point where we are all seen together rather than seeing ourselves (the inversion of perspective or reverse perspective).[19]

(2) Second, the examples of paintings: Far from being referred to icons or to the art of the icon, a number of choice models of all-seeing paintings come from profane art or profane figures, not from sacred art or art with religious ends. Thus Nicholas of Cusa mentions "the *Sagittarius* of Nuremberg"; another painting executed by Rogier van der Weyden in Brussels, none other than "The Justice of Trajan," a copy or rather a tapestry of which remains in the museum in Bern, and in which, moreover, one can make out the figure of the painter himself as all-seeing; "the angel holding the arms of the church" in the castle of Brixen, not a religious edifice; and "many others elsewhere."[20] It is enough for us to mention Leonardo da Vinci's celebrated but later Mona Lisa (1503).

(3) Next, the addressees: These are certainly monks, and everything would therefore suggest that the cardinal might invite each of them and

---

[17] Nicholas of Cusa, *Lettre aux moines de Tegernsee*, 368; quoted in Falque, "The All-Seeing," 3.

[18] Nicholas of Cusa, *Lettre aux moines de Tegernsee*, 368; quoted in Falque, "The All-Seeing," 3. See Nicholas of Cusa, *De theologicis complementis*, 1–2, in *Nicolai de Cusa Opera Omnia*, vol. X/2a, ed. Heide Dorothea Riemann and Karl Bormann (Hamburg: Felix Meiner Verlag, 1994), 3–13.

[19] Nicholas of Cusa, *Lettre aux moines de Tegernsee*, 368.

[20] Nicholas of Cusa, *De visione Dei*, Praef. (2), ed. Riemann, 5; trans. H. Lawrence Bond, *Nicholas of Cusa: Selected Spiritual Writings* (New York: Paulist Press, 1997), 235.

the whole community to pray before this image, at least if it functioned as an icon. But he does nothing of the sort. There is not one mention of prayer or praise before the little painting. Quite the contrary, the cardinal invites them to a sort of choreographic dance or street theatre, far from the fixed liturgy of the pulpits or stalls of the abbey church. "Nicholas of Cusa conceives as a mathematician the exercise that the monks have to carry out," Michel de Certeau comments in his celebrated article on the *De icona*, "not with a compass but with their legs, during a ceremony that also prolongs the 'games,' mimicry, and 'juggling acts' that were a long-standing tradition at the abbey of Tegernsee, and that had the odd audacity of replacing the liturgy with a geometric order, and especially the altar and the Bible with a painting."[21]

(4) Hence, finally, the places of exercise: By asking the monks to "fix the image wherever you wish, for example on the north wall [*septentrionali*]," in order to then look at it in a semi-circle, first a leading member of the community and then his brother thereafter, the author of the treatise most likely does not have the abbey church in mind, even if he uses the Latin term *icona* or "icon of God" (*quam eiconam dei appello*).[22] And this for several reasons. First, because one no longer exercises or dances in the church in the Renaissance, in contrast to the concentration of all of life in the churches or cathedrals in the Middle Ages. Second, because the abbey church would be oriented toward the east, that is to say toward the Orient or Jerusalem, but certainly not toward the north.

Thus, the conclusion is obvious. If it is indeed an exercise, even a physical exercise, to which the cardinal invites them in proposing they walk around the painting of the all-seeing, this spiritual physicality would more likely take place in the chapter room or refectory than in the abbey church. But there is still nothing here about an icon, only an image—all the more so because the very idea of "hanging on the wall," and even of "fixing on any place" (*hanc aliquo in loco . . . affigetis*)[23] would in no way pertain to an icon, even an Orthodox one, which in its placement as well as in physical practice would call for prostrations of some sort rather than a

---

[21] Michel de Certeau, "The Look: Nicholas of Cusa," in *The Mystic Fable*, vol. 2, *The Sixteenth and Seventeenth Centuries*, ed. Luce Giard, trans. Michael B. Smith (Chicago: University of Chicago Press, 2015), 41.

[22] Nicholas of Cusa, *De visione Dei*, Praef. (2–3), ed. Riemann, 5; trans. Bond, 235.

[23] Nicholas of Cusa, *De visione Dei*, Praef. (3), ed. Riemann, 5; trans. Bond, 235.

choreographed theatrical dance. The 1630 translation by Lord Golefer, the first French translation of the text, is in this sense more explicit yet: "vous l'attacherès à l'endroit où il vous plaira (par exemple à une muraille du côsté du Septentrion), et vous mettrès tous à l'entour."[24]

What I name here the "revenge of the image," then, bears not only upon Cusanus and the question of the placement of and exercise around a painting, but upon the status of phenomenology and theology as such. I have already investigated this in *God, the Flesh, and the Other*, under the same title, and amid a detour through contemporary philosophy—a pitfall not for contemporary art, but for the artistic references of established phenomenologists.[25] All of them draw from the abstract, and therefore from the invisible, as the other side of the visible: Wassily Kandinsky (whose paintings have been studied by Michel Henry), Kazimir Malevich (Emmanuel Martineau), Mark Rothko (Jean-Luc Marion), among others, with the exception of Paul Cézanne (Maurice Merleau-Ponty). Hence the response of Gilles Deleuze, commenting on Francis Bacon, who in my opinion is even more true to life than the painter Lucian Freud: "the extraordinary work of abstract painting was necessary in order to tear modern art away from figuration. But is there not another path, more direct and more sensible?"[26] Or as Deleuze writes elsewhere, "If the painter keeps to the Figure, if he or she opts for the second path, it will be to oppose the 'figural' to the figurative."[27] In the words of the contemporary artist Wim Delvoye: "with the new positioning of the artist who proclaims himself an *image-maker*, it is perhaps *the revenge of the image against the icon* that is undertaken."[28] In

---

24 "You will affix it at the place where it will please you (for example on a large wall on the northern side), and you will place yourselves all around it." See Gandillac, *Nicolas de Cues*, 376.

25 See Emmanuel Falque, "The Revenge of the Image," in *God, the Flesh, and the Other: From Irenaeus to Duns Scotus*, trans. William Christian Hackett (Evanston, IL: Northwestern University Press, 2014), 132–42.

26 Gilles Deleuze, *Francis Bacon: The Logic of Sensation*, trans. Daniel W. Smith (Minneapolis: University of Minnesota Press, 1981), 12. See Francis Bacon, *L'art de l'impossible: Entretiens avec David Sylvester* (Milan: Skira, 1976).

27 Deleuze, *Francis Bacon*, 6.

28 Catherine Grenier, "La revanche de l'image," *Communio: Revue catholique internationale* 28, no. 4 (July/August 2003): 37. For the complete illustration of this revenge of the image upon the icon in contemporary art performances and installations, see Catherine Grenier, "L'image contre l'icône," in *L'art contemporain est-il chrétien?* (Paris: Éditions Jacqueline Chambon, 1999), 107–15. We find the same reaction, this time from philosophical aesthetics rather than from art criticism, in Geneviève Hébert, "Expérience picturale et phénoménologie française: La dehiscence du visible," in *Subjectivité et transcendance: Hommage à Pierre*

short, the "figural" is perhaps what the Renaissance and even the baroque already anticipated, although it remained attached to the image or the portrait. It is no longer an icon that draws me into the invisibility of God, but an image that returns me to my own human visibility.

Recognition of the Icon

Under this title—"recognition of the icon"—Jean-Luc Marion calls upon the evidence in Nicholas of Cusa's *De icona* against what he names the "misology" or the "obstinate denial" of certain interpreters (among whom I am explicitly named as a sort of leader):

> These two arguments [the textual mention of the painting as icon and the reference to the visage of Veronica] increase the reasons we have to oppose the *unfortunate tendency* among some contemporary interpreters who do not wish to accept the *letter* of the very title *De visione Dei* [*sive de icona liber*], and instead speak only of a "painting." This *obstinate denial* cannot be justified by some worry on the part of Cusanus about keeping his distance from the so-called Byzantine icon—after all, this would be rather strange for someone so dedicated to Christian unity. In fact, this *philological resistance* probably testified to their *reticence* in front of the very usage of *eicona* as a concept. But this misology, far from opening the way to a better understanding of *De visione Dei*, simply results in our *missing its basic intention*.[29]

One sees it clearly now: here we are dealing not simply with an opposition, but a stance taken, feet firmly planted. Coming after my text on Nicholas of Cusa ("The All-Seeing"), Marion ("Seeing, or Seeing Oneself Seen") understands quite well the disagreement with which he is confronted by my thesis, and even highlights the difference between us: namely, my so-called

---

Colin, ed. Philippe Capelle (Paris: Éditions du Cerf, 2001), 189: "Does non-figurative painting bear the exorbitant privilege of being the sole place where the dehiscence of the visible can be enacted? Allow me to think that the price to pay is too steep." Quoted in Falque, *God, the Flesh, and the Other*, 319n69.

29 Marion, "Seeing, or Seeing Oneself Seen," 312 (emphasis added). [Trans.: Marion's and Falque's respective articles on Nicholas of Cusa are quoted here according to the English translations mentioned above. Translations were consulted and are minimally altered in the present translation to maintain consistency.]

"reticence in front of the very usage of *eicona* as a concept." The teacher hits his mark, and sees that his young doctoral student has now cleared his own way forward—for which, I might add, he has never reproached him. If the distinction between image and icon remains operative, and has indeed shaped my thought, it is not or no longer enough, for my part, to designate the whole of phenomenality.

To be sure, one could say with Marion that "the fundamental character of the *icon* . . . [is that] it sees us more than we see it"—although the examples chosen by Nicholas of Cusa have shown that this function did not always belong to icons or representations of God (for example, the "*Sagittarius* of Nuremberg" or "The Justice of Trajan").[30] But the definition of the icon, as it has always been defined by Marion and as he still refers to it, is the "icon of the invisible" or "mirror of the invisible," in that it "indeed renders visible the invisible"—but this invisible is first of all what is aimed at, like the "luminous darkness of silence" that I am called to enter (Dionysius). "Hence this implies that, even presented by the icon," to cite Marion in *God without Being*, "the invisible always remains invisible; it is not invisible because it is omitted by the aim [*invisable*], but because it is a matter of rendering visible this invisible as such—the unenvisageable."[31]

In short, the "icon" allows one to see the entirety only of the invisible and not of visibility; or rather, if there is visibility, it can only refer back directly to invisibility, at the risk, conversely, of idolatry. We understand why, then, this time in *The Idol and Distance*, "depth"—as the fourth dimension after or beyond length, width, and height—constitutes the ground of charity and, Marion says, always gives the "distance" to let God be God: "The fourth dimension, therefore, is indeed revealed as the 'depth' of distance."[32]

Nicholas of Cusa, the Cursor

Icon against image (and not idol), distance against proximity (and not immediacy), such is therefore the true heart of the debate: on the one hand, withdrawal or phenomenology of the unapparent (relying upon Heidegger),

---

30 Marion, "Seeing, or Seeing Oneself Seen," 315.
31 Jean-Luc Marion, *God Without Being: Hors-Texte*, trans. Thomas A. Carlson, 2nd ed. (Chicago: University of Chicago Press, 2012), 17.
32 Jean-Luc Marion, *The Idol and Distance: Five Studies*, trans. Thomas A. Carlson (New York: Fordham University Press, 2001), 249.

on the other hand, chiasm or phenomenology of perception (referring rather to Merleau-Ponty). Nicholas of Cusa—and his *De icona*—therefore serves in some way as a "dividing line" or "cursor" not between two philosophies or two philosophers, but between two ways of seeing or beholding the divine, probably more complementary than opposed, at least with respect to the end of their proposed approaches: drawing us completely toward the divine on the one hand (theocentrism), or referring us back to ourselves on the other (anthropocentrism). Nicholas of Cusa knew, as I have said, that the opposition is unfounded, at least from the vantage of the coincidence of opposites.

Faced with this seeming divide, noted at least once, one can delight in this joust of words that forces each interlocutor to advance unmasked. Yet in the meanwhile one might regret the tone, which is sometimes more in the order of a severe condemnation than of an opening for discussion—as if one side were absolutely correct while the other necessarily wrong. It will suffice here to mention a note by Jean-Luc Marion without commenting on it, so as to make apparent how far his offensive has raised the stakes:

> This disappointing *misinterpretation* [of *eicona* as "image" or "painting" and not as "icon"] was unfortunately orchestrated symphonically, without further explanation, but in a caricatural manner, by Emmanuel Falque: "The novelty of the procedure [namely, attributed to Nicholas of Cusa] *forbids* translating falsely the formula *de icona* in the title (*De visione Dei sive de icona*) by *of the Icon* rather than *of the Painting*, as a number of commentators have sometimes wrongly done" ("L'omnivoyant," 47 n. 4). Forbids? What, and who, forbids it? ... It is the reader, instead, who finds himself *dumbfounded* before so much self-assurance in forbidding the least bit of argumentation.[33]

I have said the attack is severe, and this is why I can only thank the organizers of this volume on Nicholas of Cusa for having boldly invited me to respond to it, hopefully in a way that is well presented and well argued. I am far from having proposed a "non-theological" reading of Nicholas of Cusa, as if falling back from divinity to humanity, contrary to what Marion says when he writes:

---

[33] Marion, "Seeing, or Seeing Oneself Seen," 312n23 (emphasis added). See also Falque, "The All-Seeing," 9.

Aside from its profoundly non-theological character, this *hasty conclusion* [my own, the first citation of Falque in the article] presupposes exactly what has to be demonstrated: how would "brothers" be able to trust one another if they had not already participated in the same filial sighting or aim?[34]

It goes without saying, though it is needless to go on, that for my part I have never spoken of a detached fraternity of filiation in Nicholas of Cusa, or of the human detached from the Trinitarian. My note from *Parcours d'embûches* already noted this and responded there. It suffices to quote it here in order to be convinced:

This does not mean, of course, in a "hasty conclusion," that the "fraternal" is considered "against" the "filial" [J.-L. Marion, note 11], but that, on the contrary, it reveals the filial. It should be enough here to quote the implicated sentence in its entirety: "The filial here gives way to the fraternal [in the vision of God]. Discovering themselves as seen, and intended *by the same Father* and thus constituted as *sons in the Son*, the monks of Tegernsee appear to one another truly as brothers in this 'seeing in common.'" We could not be clearer. Fraternity never dispenses with filiation, but is derived from it, even if it is only afterwards or in retrospect that it is acknowledged, and that the "testimony of the brother" comes to corroborate it.[35]

The Way Out through the Figure

Must we keep to this simple alternative: the "image" or kenotic submersion in the flesh on the one hand, and the "icon" or bedazzling revelation on Mount Horeb on the other? As I have said, if there is a resolution to this it will be found first "in God" in the coincidence of opposites, and so in all likelihood it will be accessible for us only in the final days. Nevertheless, there remains one way forward that can be indicated; a third or simply

---

34 Marion, "Seeing, or Seeing Oneself Seen," 309n11 (emphasis added).
35 This passage from *Parcours d'embûches* is translated in Falque, "The All-Seeing," 28. [Trans.: The words in brackets here do not appear in the original passage in *Parcours d'embûches*, 187n20, but are included in the English translation in "The All-Seeing."]

another way has been proposed. Coming if not as a conciliator then at least as a peacemaker of the "conflict of interpretations" outlined above, the Cusan exegete David Albertson suggests going back "*before* [the image and] the icon," precisely to "the *figural* matrix of *De visione Dei*."[36]

The author is right to point this out: "The centrality of the face in the Cusan Veronica is crucial to both Falque and Marion, but while they connect *facies* to *icona*, they never consider *facies* as *figura*."[37] This would be only a mere suggestion, even a hypothesis, if the famous passage from the Latin text in question in the preface of *De visione Dei sive de icona* did not fully justify this step. It suffices here to quote it in its entirety: *ne tamen deficiatis in praxis, quae sensibilem talem exigit figuram quam habere potui, caritati vestrae mitto tabellam figuram cuncta videntis tenentem, quam eiconam dei appello*. "However, so that you lack nothing in an exercise which requires the *sensible figure* which I was able to acquire, I send to your charity a little painting bearing this *figure of the all-seeing* [*figuram cuncta videntis*], and which I call the painting of God."[38]

Figure (*figura*) here is both the "representation" or "figuration" (the exercise that requires the sensible figure) and the "face" or the "visage" that is its expression (this figure of the all-seeing). *Figura* in Latin, at least in Nicholas of Cusa, but also *figure* in French, says at the same time "figuration" and "face," holding all in one. Everything therefore comes to pass as if the quarrel of the "image" and the "icon," with attention paid to the end of the sentence alone—*quam eiconam dei appello* (that I call the painting of God)—now found its resolution by turning our eyes this time toward the beginning of the formula, that is to say, toward the "figure": *in praxis,*

---

[36] David Albertson, "Before the Icon: The Figural Matrix of *De visione Dei*," in *Nicholas of Cusa and Times of Transition: Essays in Honor of Gerald Christianson*, ed. Thomas M. Izbicki, Jason Aleksander, and Donald F. Duclow (Leiden: Brill, 2019), 266 (emphasis added). I thank the author, my friend, for having provided the text, and in that way for having given the occasion for this possible conciliation—discernible and visible in the text of Nicholas of Cusa himself.

[37] Albertson, "Before the Icon," 283.

[38] Nicholas of Cusa, *De visione Dei*, Praef. (2), ed. Riemann, 5; trans. Bond, 235. From here on I follow the French translation of Agnès Minazzoli, which has the merit of translating literally the term *figura*, which appears twice in the text of this passage from the preface of the *De icona* of Nicholas of Cusa: "Cependant, afin que rien ne vous manqué dans un exercice qui exige la *figure* sensible dont j'ai pu disposer, j'envoie à votre bonté un petit tableau portant cette *figure* de l'omnivoyant et que j'appelle le tableau de Dieu." Nicholas of Cusa, *De visione Dei*, trans. Minazzoli, 32 (emphasis added). One can only regret to see the term *figura* translated by Hervé Pasqua both times with the French word *expression*, which completely misses the point.

quae sensibilem talem exigit figuram ("in an exercise which requires the sensible *figure*"), figuram *cuncta videntis tenentem* ("bearing this *figure* of the all-seeing").

The solution is all the more surprising in that it was not seen by any of the protagonists in this quarrel (neither Marion nor Falque), and had to await a thoroughgoing Cusanian to settle the question (Albertson). This "way out" is all the more elegant in that, far from every invention or false will to pacify, the text itself calls for it. Indeed, the "figure" is *before* the image and the icon, and this is likely the true "matrix of the *De visione Dei*."[39] Nevertheless, we still must have "eyes to see"—or, to speak as Heidegger did regarding Husserl, to "become oneself implanted eyes"—in order to face the facts.

This "resolution through the figure" (*figura*), rather than being confined to the simple opposition of "image" or "icon," is indeed fully justified conceptually in the work of Cusanus himself: from the mathematical point of view (the geometrical figure), and from the theological point of view (the figure of Christ). First, the mathematical reason. The "figure" of the monks of Tegernsee practically *dancing* around the painting quite unequivocally expresses, or better stages [*accomplit*], a "geometrical figure" at first *thought*: hence the "mathematical complements" that precede the "theological complements" in order to constitute the ensemble of the *De icona*. As I quoted Michel de Certeau above: "Nicholas of Cusa conceives as a mathematician the exercise that the monks have to carry out, not with a compass but with their legs."

Second, the theological reason. The very term "figure" (*figura*) will be retrieved by the theologian Hans Urs von Balthasar himself in the "Form" or "Figure of Revelation" (*Gestalt der Offenbarung*). This constitutes the heart of his entire project, or at the very least of his theological aesthetic, and it is directly inspired by Nicholas of Cusa:

> In Jesus Christ God takes possession of both these dimensions [man as the vessel of divine truth and the place of his own misery], not only to lead them beyond themselves to the absolute but also so as to bring together the two divergent extremes, to join them into *one single figure* ... in the union of the infinitely greatest with the infinitely smallest, a union which both *Nicholas of Cusa* and *Pascal* regarded as the *figure*

---

39 See Albertson, "Before the Icon."

defined by Christ, who thus becomes the *figure* [*Gestalt*] that concludes and completes the universe.[40]

By the word "figure" (*Gestalt*), the theologian first means *manifestation*, but probably more in the sense of "image" (visibility) rather than as "icon" (invisibility). For if Christ is the "figure of revelation" for Hans Urs von Balthasar (*Gestalt der Offenbarung*), it is indeed first as "*image* of the invisible God," rather than as "icon of the invisible God," to follow the celebrated formula of Paul (Col 1:15). This matter can certainly surprise us, and yet all languages and all translations agree on it; to contest it would be to think, a little too quickly perhaps, that everyone is mistaken. At least in this Christian context of the hymn of the Colossians, which is also that of Nicholas of Cusa's treatise, *De icona*, εἰκών in the formula εἰκὼν τοῦ θεοῦ τοῦ ἀοράτου is indeed always translated by "image [εἰκὼν] of the invisible God," and never by "icon of the invisible God," whether in French (*l'image*), English (*the image*), German (*das Ebenbild*), Spanish (*la imagen*), or Italian (*l'immagine*).[41] In this sense, to translate the title of Nicholas of Cusa's work, *De visione Dei sive de icona*, as "The Painting (or the Image) of God," remains far from being a heresy; quite the contrary. What is more, Balthasar himself probably would have approved of it, since his concept of "figure" (*Gestalt*) leans more upon "visibility" than upon invisibility, and refers to Christ as the "image of the invisible God" and not "icon of the invisible God" (Col 1:15).

But there is another reason why "figure" resolves the conflict of the image and the icon, or at least "overcomes" it in the Hegelian sense of *aufheben*. "Figure" (*Gestalt*) for Balthasar does not mean *manifestation* alone; it also tends toward *integration*, in this sense avoiding the double pitfall of a phenomenology at once fragmented and ahistorical. Through the "figure," what is manifest comes together at a concentrated point (the all-seeing

---

40 Hans Urs von Balthasar, *The Glory of the Lord*, vol. 1, *Seeing the Form*, trans. Erasmo Leiva-Merikakis (San Francisco: Ignatius Press, 1983), 477 (emphasis added). This passage occurs in part III, "The Objective Evidence," section C, "Christ the Center of the Form of Revelation," sub-section 2, "Measure and Form." [Trans.: The reader will note that in this particular passage Leiva-Merikakis translates *Gestalt* as "figure," otherwise typically translated as "form," as in the passage from *The Glory of the Lord* quoted below.]

41 The phrase εἰκὼν τοῦ θεοῦ τοῦ ἀοράτου (Col 1:15) is translated in all French versions as *l'image du Dieu invisible* (Traduction oecuménique de la Bible; Bible de Jérusalem), in English as *the image of the invisible God*, in German as *das Ebenbild des unsichtbaren Gottes*, in Spanish as *la imagen del Dios invisibile*, and in Italian as *l'immagine dell'invisibile Dio*.

Christ), which the succession of images (the seeing monks) could have forgotten: "the phenomenological approach risks *pointillism* by the *fragmentation of the real*, which can be reduced to a multiplicity of apparitions, by a pure narrative succession *outside of history*. Balthasar responds to it with a theory of *integration*."[42] Therefore, "before the image and the icon," the "figure" (*figura*) finds its ultimate justification in its *theological integration* more than in its phenomenological manifestation or its mathematical variation. By way of the inspiring source of the Swiss theologian, the "coincidence of opposites" in Nicholas of Cusa is likewise fulfilled [*s'accomplit*] in the figure of the God-Man, the theological schema of integration *par excellence*. The "sensible figure" of the little painting (*sensibilem figuram*) is the "figure of the all-seeing" (*figuram cuncta videntis*) who is Christ, as the cardinal emphasizes quite precisely, because the "all-seeing himself" (*figuram cuncta videntis*) who is Christ, *is* a "sensible figure" (*sensibilem figuram*), this time in the sense of the visible and tangible one in the flesh. In the "figure of the God-Man," the dimension of the image (the plasticity of humanity) and the icon (the depths of God) come together—for "*in him* [ἐν αὐτῷ] all things ... have been created" (Col 1:16).

One cannot therefore actually resolve the debate of the image and the icon, despite its phenomenological pertinence, without deriving or finding the solution in theology itself—in the sense of the union of man and God in the "*figure* of Jesus Christ," the unique mediator. Such is the meaning and the evidence of the "objective figure" of revelation in Hans Urs von Balthasar, who takes it from Nicholas of Cusa to boot, namely, that Christ is the "figure of all figures," the coincidence of opposites itself in the union of man and God: "The *figure of revelation* is given not as an independent image of God, facing what is represented, but as a *unique, hypostatic liaison between the model and its reproduction*.... In him (Christ) *God presents himself*, and insofar as this man *is* himself God ... the *figure of Christ* is the *figure of all figures*, the measure of all measures; just as, in the same way, it is the glory of all glories of creation."[43]

---

[42] Henriette Danet, *Gloire et croix de Jésus-Christ: L'analogie chez H. Urs von Balthasar comme introduction à la Christologie* (Paris: Desclée de Brouwer, 1987), 313 (emphasis added).

[43] Balthasar, *La gloire et la croix*, vol. 1 (Paris: Desclée de Brouwer, 1990), 366 (emphasis added). [Trans.: Since Falque's conclusions rely upon the French edition's consistent rendering of *Gestalt* as *figure*, our translation here departs somewhat from Leiva-Merikakis. That English version reads: "[T]he form of revelation does not present itself as an independent image of God, standing over against what is imaged, but as a unique, hypostatic union between

Conclusion

Whether "image" or "icon" prevails, the *De visione Dei sive de icona* of Nicholas of Cusa would probably best be titled, or best be translated from the point of view of its meaning, as "The Figure of God," rather than either "The Painting (or the Image) of God" or "The Icon of God." Admittedly, it is not without some humor that the theologian of Basel (Balthasar) comes to reconcile the philosophers of Paris (Falque and Marion) by way of a Cusan in California (Albertson). Indeed, *Gestalt* in Balthasar approaches at the same time the verticality of manifestation (icon) and the horizontality of integration (image). Belonging neither to phenomenology nor to the ontology of finitude, the author of *The Glory of the Lord* claims neither one nor the other, but somehow holds both the one *and* the other together at an apex in the "figure of the God-Man." The "subjective evidence" in the experience of the spiritual senses (Falque/Bonaventure) and the "objective evidence" in the glory of manifestation (Marion/Dionysius) come together in the cornerstone of the "figure of revelation," insofar as the true resolution, or rather the "recapitulation" (ἀνακεφαλαίωσις) of all things, is found *in* Christ.

There is here, once again, an "amorous struggle." But in the duality of this joust, when a third party or arbitrator comes to intervene, the conflict of the game changes, or rather comes to be pacified. In reality, this never was a war of obliteration (πόλεμος), but at most a conflict of counter-balancing the other (ἀγών). For we exist only in relying upon the other, and the disciple, when he becomes master, begins to combat "on equal terms." This is precisely where "camps" come to be delimited, but also where "recognition" comes to be shared. "I will not let you go, unless you bless me" (Gen 32:26), Jacob whispers in his bout with the angel—in reality less to be knighted, but to exist before the angel as a "man as well." In the locale of Peniel we see "God face to face," but only upon a path taken with difficulty, from which we could not so easily free ourselves: "And there he blessed him. So Jacob called the place Peniel—that is, The Face of God—saying, 'For I have seen God face to face, and yet my life is preserved.' The sun rose upon him as he passed Penuel, limping because of his hip" (Gen 32:29–31).

---

archetype and image. In the form of revelation ... (Christ!) God portrays himself—indeed, in so far as this man himself is God.... [This form] is the form of all forms and the measure of all measures, just as for this reason it is the glory of all glories of creation as well." Balthasar, *The Glory of the Lord*, 1:432.]

15

Cusanus and Heidegger

Multiplying the *Tetractys*

STEPHEN GERSH

Nicholas of Cusa was both a philosopher of singularity and a singular philosopher. His singularity is especially striking within the history of Platonism (or Neoplatonism), which has itself, at least since the end of its dominance as a kind of scholasticism in late antiquity, been a succession of singular thinkers. Considering him as a late medieval writer, it is easy to reveal his singularity by contrasting the originality and creativity of his writing, which, even when it looks back to sources like Pseudo-Dionysius the Areopagite or Hermes Trismegistus, can often modify the latter to the point that they become unrecognizable. At the opposite extreme, one might instance the *non*-singularity of the countless late medieval commentators on the pseudo-Aristotelian *Liber de causis* who follow in the wake of Albert the Great, Thomas Aquinas, and Siger of Brabant and repeat gloss after gloss after gloss. Even though Cusanus's influence on immediate successors was relatively moderate—one thinks here of Jacques Lefèvre d'Étaples, Giordano Bruno, and Athanasius Kircher—it is his singularity that has given and will give him the possibility of speaking to an audience far beyond his own historical milieu.

But in what aspects of Cusanus's work do we find this singularity? It seems to me that it resides in his tentative but significant steps toward formulating a kind of productive-poetic Platonism capable of retaining its value and validity even in abstraction from its original metaphysical and Christian context. I will endeavor to demonstrate this with a thought experiment that juxtaposes Nicholas of Cusa with Martin Heidegger as though juxtaposing a *metaphysical surface* with a *hermeneutical depth*. It will permit the transposition of an analogous structuring from the one dimension to the other, the entire procedure, as it were, leaving Cusanus *placed in the abyss*. More specifically, my thought experiment will juxtapose the similar fourfold structures that each author had derived. I will do so through a complex network of channels that cannot be fully mapped out within the compass of this necessarily brief essay, starting from the famous ancient Pythagorean enigma of the *tetractys*. For convenience, this proposed application of the fourfold structure might be imagined as the projection of a two-dimensional square into the third dimension as a cube: a *quasi*-geometrical procedure that would be not atypical, at the very least, of Nicholas of Cusa.

The Heidegger to be invoked in this essay will not be that of *Being and Time*—a dead end for its author if not for his countless French admirers— but the Heidegger of the *Elucidations of Hölderlin's Poetry* and the lecture courses delivered between 1934 and 1942 on this poet's hymns "Germania," "The Rhine," "Remembrance," and "The Ister."[1] Although it is clear that Heidegger retained some sympathy for medieval thought even after he had ceased to be an overtly "Catholic" thinker, around the time of his association with Edmund Husserl, the generous praise he gives to Meister Eckhart as a founding father of German thought is never conferred by him similarly on the more obviously Latin-speaking cardinal. Therefore, there will be a fruitless search in the works mentioned or indeed elsewhere in the extensive Heideggerian corpus for any real evidence of doctrinal assimilation or even

---

1 In a note attached to the manuscript of his lecture course on the hymn "Der Ister," but not subsequently included in the printed version, Heidegger himself remarks: "It was perhaps inevitable that the poet Hölderlin should become the determining influence on the critical thought of one [i.e., Heidegger himself] who was born at the very time when the 'Ister' hymn was written." Quoted in Rüdiger Safranski, *Martin Heidegger: Between Good and Evil*, trans. Ewalt Overs (Cambridge, MA: Harvard University Press, 1998), 3.

of critical encounter between the twentieth-century writer and his predecessor. Nevertheless, my thought experiment juxtaposing the metaphysical surface of Cusanus's philosophical theology with the hermeneutical depth of Heidegger's path of thinking will be enough to show that the latter was intellectually much closer to the former than perhaps he ever realized.

Cusanus's Fourfold

Nicholas of Cusa makes extensive use of a variety of dialectical classifications based on the combination of semantic elements—understood as metaphysical properties—in order to constitute a fourfold structure. For convenience, the four terms comprised in this structure might be notated as: A/non-B, A/B, non-A/B, non-A/non-B. These terms are semantically stable, although they may be presented in different sequences. Nicholas is clearly following a method definitively formulated in the technical literature of late antiquity with respect to classifications of numbers, propositions, and physical elements and ultimately derived from the Pythagorean notion of the *tetractys*. We may here consider simply the two most important instances of this schematization, the first of which might be termed ontological or objective, and the second, epistemological and subjective. In Book II of *De docta ignorantia*, Cusanus provides a classification of four universal modes of being:[2] "absolute necessity" (*absoluta necessitas*) [non-B/A], or God as Form of forms, Being of beings, reason-principle and quiddity of things; "necessity of complexion" (*necessitas complexionis*) [A/B], or the forms of things in the distinction and order of nature; "determinate possibility" (*possibilitas determinata*) [B/non-A], or the possibility of things existing actually as this or that; and "absolute possibility" (*possibilitas absoluta*) [non-B/non-A], or the possibility of things existing. A careful analysis reveals that the constituent semantic elements here are as follows: A = necessity, non-B = absolute, B = determinate (or: of complexion), and non-A = possibility. In *Idiota de mente*, Nicholas applies the same schematization to four modes of perception:[3] imagination, which applies itself to determinate possibility and produces physical and logical conjectures; reasoning, which deals with

---

[2] Nicholas of Cusa, *De docta ignorantia*, II.7 (127–31), in *Nikolaus von Kues: Philosophisch-Theologische Werke*, vol. 1, ed. Paul Wilpert and Hans Gerhard Senger, rev. ed. (Hamburg: Felix Meiner Verlag, 2002), 48–54.

[3] Nicholas of Cusa, *Idiota de mente*, VII (97–107), in *Nicolai de Cusa Opera Omnia*, vol. V, ed. Renate Steiger (Hamburg: Felix Meiner, 1983), 145–61.

the necessity of complexion and yields mathematical conjectures; intelligence, which applies itself to absolute necessity and produces theological speculations; and sham reasoning, which somehow grapples with absolute possibility.[4]

Heidegger's Fourfold

A dialectical classification based on the combination of semantic elements into a fourfold structure is also derived initially by Heidegger from Friedrich Hölderlin's poetry and then applied quite widely in his later writings.[5] If one were to express them in the kind of technical language that Heidegger himself does not countenance, the constituent terms and implicit semantic properties of what is poetized as a divine and human wedding-festival might be designated in terms of spatial locations and those spaces's inhabitants: heaven (*der Himmel*), that is, location as higher [A/non-B], or world as authentic; earth (*die Erde*), location as lower [A/B], or world as inauthentic; mortals (*die Sterblichen*), inhabitants as lower [non-A/B], or Dasein as inauthentic; and gods (*die Götter*), inhabitants as higher [non-A/non-B], or Dasein as authentic.[6]

Heidegger himself explains these terms not singly but in pairs, as for instance where he cautiously discusses the arrangement of gods and

---

[4] In *De docta ignorantia*, other applications of the fourfold structure reveal the logical structure (A/non-B, A/B, non-A/B, non-A/non-B) more clearly. For example, Nicholas argues that God's truth is either something that is, or both is and is not, or is not, or neither is nor is not. See *De docta ignorantia*, I.6 (15–17), ed. Wilpert and Senger, 24–26. In another passage, Nicholas gives as examples of fourfold the numbers 1, 10, 100, 1000, as four types of universals. See *De docta ignorantia*, II.6 (123–26), ed. Wilpert and Senger, 42–48.

[5] Heidegger associates the structure with Hölderlin throughout his exegesis of the latter, although he admits that the poet presents the entire scheme only in an allusive manner. See the remarks in Martin Heidegger, *Elucidations of Hölderlin's Poetry*, trans. Keith Höller (Amherst: Humanity Books, 2000), 187 (in Heidegger's *Gesamtausgabe* [GA] (Frankfurt am Main: Vittorio Klostermann, 1976–), 4:162–63). In fact, the poet works most frequently with one opposition within the fourfold structure: namely, gods and humans, together with a mediating term, demi-gods. Given his preoccupation with the figure of Empedocles, whose cosmic cycle was one of the earliest extrapolations from the Pythagorean *tetractys*, it is surprising that Hölderlin is not more explicit. The explanation seems to be that he was not familiar with the most relevant Greek fragments preserved in Simplicius.

[6] It would be consistent with Heidegger's general approach to the mutual implication of Dasein and world also to identify—within the expression Dasein itself—the *Da-* with the semantic property of location and the *Sein* with that of inhabitant.

mortals by addition and subtraction of properties.[7] He considers the relation within the duality of gods and mortals primarily with emphasis on the terms of the opposition: thus, the fundamental tonality of the poem "Germania" is said to place us in relation to the gods by turning us toward them or away from them,[8] and likewise this tonality of mourning opens up the flight and the return of the gods with respect to us.[9] The relation itself is constituted by our decision: for instance, with respect to following authentic or inauthentic temporality.[10] By contrast, Heidegger sometimes considers the relation within the duality of heaven and earth by emphasizing the relation itself within the opposition: for instance, the poet both describes and enacts the coming of the "round-dance" (*der Reigen*) to the wedding.[11] Here, the round-dance itself, as the togetherness of the gyrating gods in the heavenly fire, corresponds to one term of the opposition,[12] while the wedding itself, as the celebration of the whole infinite relation considered from below, corresponds to the other term.[13] The prominence of the semantic property of location, that is, spatiality in the fourfold classification as a whole[14]—underlined by the further associations between the gods (heaven) and Greece, and between the mortals (earth) and Germany[15]—must be understood with a complementary emphasis on temporality.

Metaphysical Surface: Cusanus

Now, the "metaphysical surface" of the fourfold in Cusanus can best be understood by considering three aspects of his general dialectical

---

7 Martin Heidegger, *Hölderlin's Hymn "Remembrance"*, trans. William McNeill and Julia Ireland (Bloomington: Indiana University Press, 2018), §12a, 150–51 (GA 52:165). See also ibid., §51, 128 (GA 52:151).

8 Martin Heidegger, *Hölderlin's Hymns "Germania" and "The Rhine"*, trans. William McNeill and Julia Ireland (Bloomington: Indiana University Press, 2014), §16a, 203 (GA 39:223).

9 Heidegger, *Hölderlin's Hymn "Germania"*, §11e, 128 (GA 39:146).

10 Heidegger, *Hölderlin's Hymn "Germania"*, §9e, 102 (GA 39:112).

11 Heidegger, *Elucidations of Hölderlin's Poetry*, 196–97 (GA 4:172–73).

12 Heidegger, *Elucidations of Hölderlin's Poetry*, 198 (GA 4:174).

13 Heidegger, *Elucidations of Hölderlin's Poetry*, 197 (GA 4:173). In the same passage, Heidegger describes the two opposites as the great and the humble respectively.

14 See Heidegger, *Hölderlin's Hymn "Germania"*, §11b, 126 (GA 39:143); and §11e, 128–29 (GA 39:146–47).

15 See Heidegger, *Hölderlin's Hymn "Remembrance"*, §43, 111–12 (GA 52:131).

presentation of the creator God, his created world, and the relation between them. These aspects are opposition, coincidence, and continuity. For this author, reality in both the objective and subjective sense consists of a series of oppositions derived from the traditional Platonic literature and including, in the first instance, unity and multiplicity, sameness and otherness, and rest and motion. The essentially disjunctive structure of the universe that results from the postulation of such oppositions is set out in the objective sense in *De docta ignorantia*, Book II,[16] and in the subjective sense in *Idiota de mente*.[17] In the latter work, Cusanus explains how the enfolding and unfolding of the divine mind can be compared with the enfolding and unfolding of the human mind, and how the series of oppositions mentioned above forms the content of both this divine enfolding and unfolding and the corresponding human mental processes.

But in order to understand more precisely how these oppositions function in Nicholas's work, we need to consider the role of two further teachings: namely, that of the coincidence of opposites and that of certain "non-discursive" contraries. In *De docta ignorantia*, Cusanus applies the coincidence of opposites to various sets of terms in two main contexts: defining God with respect to his various divine names, and defining God with respect to his causal relation to creation.[18] An example of the coincidence of opposites from Nicholas's earlier works would be the epistemological attitude of "learned ignorance" (*docta ignorantia*), which must be taken as a corrective to any discursive argument regarding the infinite deity.[19] An example from the later period would be the theological position whereby God in the sense of "Not-Other" (*non aliud*) can be treated as either unity or non-unity and as either non-relational or relational.[20] Both these examples of coincidence of opposites are treated by the author as representing at the same time an authoritative presentation of the Pseudo-Dionysian

---

16 Nicholas of Cusa, *De docta ignorantia*, II.1–3 (91–111), ed. Wilpert and Senger, 4–30.

17 Nicholas of Cusa, *Idiota de mente*, IV (74–79), ed. Steiger, 112–20.

18 See Nicholas of Cusa, *De docta ignorantia*, I.2 (5–8), I.4 (11–12), I.16–17 (42–51), and I.21 (63–66), ed. Wilpert and Senger, 10–12, 16–18, 58–68, and 84–88.

19 Nicholas of Cusa, *De docta ignorantia*, I.17 (47–51), ed. Wilpert and Senger, 62–68. See also *Apologia doctae ignorantiae*, 21–22, and 31–32, in *Nicolai de Cusa Opera Omnia*, vol. II, ed. Raymond Klibansky (Leipzig: Felix Meiner Verlag, 1932), 14–16, and 21–23.

20 See Nicholas of Cusa, *De non aliud*, XV–XVI (72–79) and XXII (99–103), in *Nicolai de Cusa Opera Omnia*, vol. XIII, ed. Ludwig Baur and Paul Wilpert (Leipzig: Felix Meiner Verlag, 1944), 38–42 and 52–53.

doctrines of divine names and mystical theology[21] and a criticism of the Aristotelian or medieval-Peripatetic assumption regarding the ubiquitous application of the Law of Non-Contradiction.[22]

Because the coincidence of opposites (A/non-B = B/non-A) involves opposed but not mediating terms, it appears at first sight to conflict with the fourfold structure that comprises both opposed and mediating terms (e.g., A/B mediating between A/non-B and B/non-A).[23] However, the implementation of Cusanus's special "conjectural" method provides numerous instances of his readiness to translate the one mode of presentation into the other.[24] In light of this method, we must now consider the initially apparent conflict between certain non-discursive contraries (A/non-B ≠ B/non-A) and the fourfold structure.

Beginning in his earliest works, Cusanus introduces at least two oppositions that—unlike the oppositions of unity and multiplicity, of sameness and otherness, and of motion and rest, traditionally exploited in the Platonic tradition and explicable in conventional logical terms—had not been extensively utilized by earlier thinkers and that in themselves challenged those prevailing logical norms. These are the oppositions of "absolute" (*absolutum*) and "contracted" (*contractum*) and of "infinite" (*infinitum*) and "finite" (*finitum*). There are two important things to note concerning these oppositions. First, although these two pairs of terms are often treated as synonyms in Cusanus's texts,[25] the term "infinite" is sometimes applied to both the absolute and the contracted,[26] and the term "contracted" applied to both infinite and finite. This means that there is a structural ambivalence *between* the two pairs. Second, given that in both these cases there is said to be one term that precludes opposition and another that allows it, we are here

---

21 See Nicholas of Cusa, *De beryllo*, 46, in *Nicolai de Cusa Opera Omnia*, vol. XI/1, ed. Hans Gerhard Senger and Karl Bormann (Hamburg: Felix Meiner Verlag, 1988), 52–53.

22 Nicholas of Cusa, *De non aliud*, XIX (87–89), ed. Baur and Wilpert, 46–47.

23 See Nicholas of Cusa, *De docta ignorantia*, II.4 (112–116), ed. Wilpert and Senger, 30–36.

24 For example, see Nicholas of Cusa, *De docta ignorantia*, II.5 (117–22), ed. Wilpert and Senger, 36–42. Exploration of various combinations of the notions of coincidence of opposites and of fourfold structure is a major preoccupation of *De coniecturis*. See for example the important discussion in *De coniecturis*, I.11 (58–59), in *Nicolai de Cusa Opera Omnia*, vol. III, ed. Karl Bormann and Hans Gerhard Senger (Hamburg: Felix Meiner Verlag, 1972), 59–60.

25 See Nicholas of Cusa, *De docta ignorantia*, I.5 (13–14), ed. Wilpert and Senger, 20–22.

26 At *De docta ignorantia*, II.1 (97), ed. Wilpert and Senger, 12, Nicholas describes the former as "negatively" (*negative*) and the latter as "privatively" (*privative*) infinite. See also *De docta ignorantia*, II.4 (112–16), ed. Wilpert and Senger, 30–36.

presented with two oppositions that have the peculiarity of challenging the nature of opposition itself. In other words, there is a structural ambiguity *within* each pair. Cusanus makes abundant metaphysical use of both these ambivalences.

Finally, it is important to notice that for Cusanus each pair of mutually opposed terms mentioned earlier also represents the poles of a single continuum: something clearly shown by his description of the universe as emanating from God, in which Avicenna's doctrine of a discrete hierarchy of intelligences is specifically criticized.[27] From the objective viewpoint, Cusanus is here underscoring—with respect to a structure that is clearly now conjunctive rather than disjunctive—both the *dynamism* of this structure, by emphasizing the progressive unfolding of the parts of the universe, and also its *simplicity*, by stating that all the universe's parts come into being simultaneously with the whole. From the subjective viewpoint, Cusanus is arguing that this dynamic and simple continuum is reflected in the "assimilative power" (*vis assimilativa*), which permits the human mind to become both a unity in the image of God's unity and also every kind of multiplicity.[28]

Heidegger on Infinite Relation

By comparison, Heidegger's fourfold is a relational structure that is primarily characterized in its unified form as an infinite or whole relation.[29] This structure both approximates to and differs from Cusanus's corresponding formulation, in accordance with the underlying distinction between a relational structure of hermeneutical depth and one of metaphysical surface. Approximation between the respective approaches can be discerned on the basis of Heidegger's references to the opposition between the constituent terms (especially gods and mortals),[30] where he identifies this relation with the πόλεμος ("conflict") mentioned in Heraclitus's fragment,[31] and also on the basis of his references to the continuity between

---

27 Nicholas of Cusa, *De docta ignorantia*, II.4 (112–16), ed. Wilpert and Senger, 30–36.
28 Nicholas of Cusa, *Idiota de mente*, IV (75), ed. Steiger, 114–15; See also *Idiota de mente*, III (72), ed. Steiger, 108–10.
29 See the repeated references in Heidegger, *Elucidations of Hölderlin's Poetry*, 187–204 (GA 4:163–80).
30 Heidegger, *Elucidations of Hölderlin's Poetry*, 76 (GA 4:53).
31 Heidegger, *Elucidations of Hölderlin's Poetry*, 185 (GA 4:160).

the constituent terms,³² where he identifies this relation with the *Innigkeit* ("intimacy") that is a constant motif in Hölderlin's poetry.³³ The main differences between the two thinkers' approaches to the relational structure of the fourfold reside in the facts that Heidegger locates the element of mediation not within the sequence of four terms themselves but between an imagined "center" and one pair of terms (between the demi-gods and the gods/mortals),³⁴ and also that Heidegger envisages a coincidence between the center of the fourfold structure and a term exterior to the structures (between the festival and the Holy).³⁵ However, arguably the most important element in the entire Heideggerian scheme is the role of the demi-god—identifiable with the poet's Dasein—who is said to preserve all the specific relations *as those* specific relations and therefore the infinite structure of the fourfold in its entirety.³⁶

Hermeneutical Depth: Heidegger

Now, the "hermeneutical depth" of the fourfold in Heidegger can best be understood by considering three notions that occur frequently in his writings and that can be translated into one another to varying degrees according to the demands of the context. These three notions are Being, destiny, and *Ereignis*.

For Heidegger, "temporalization" (*zeitigen, die Zeitigung*) is a hermeneutical time, which takes the form of a dynamic oscillation between past and future, eliding presence. It should be contrasted with the empirical time, which is conceptualized as a dynamic flow from past through present to future. In his *Contributions to Philosophy*, Heidegger speaks of the dynamic oscillation as the essential component of Being that represents its temporality and historicity, using the archaic spelling of *Seyn* in order to indicate these features in particular.³⁷ It is Hölderlin's poetry that is one of the foun-

---

32 Heidegger, *Elucidations of Hölderlin's Poetry*, 194–95 (*GA* 4:170–71).
33 Heidegger, *Elucidations of Hölderlin's Poetry*, 195 (*GA* 4:171).
34 Heidegger, *Elucidations of Hölderlin's Poetry*, 185 (*GA* 4:160) and 195 (*GA* 4:171).
35 See Heidegger, *Elucidations of Hölderlin's Poetry*, 90–91 (*GA* 4:68–69), 126–30 (*GA* 4:103–6), and 145 (*GA* 4:123).
36 Heidegger, *Elucidations of Hölderlin's Poetry*, 126–30 (*GA* 4:103–6).
37 Martin Heidegger, *Contributions to Philosophy (From Enowning)*, trans. Parvis Emad and Kenneth Maly (Bloomington: Indiana University Press, 1999), §165, 202 (*GA* 65:287).

dations of this conception of Being as temporalization.³⁸ In commenting on the poem "Remembrance," Heidegger notes that the essential law of Hölderlin's poetic activity is to think with one accord both what *has been* and what *is coming*, instead of sleeping through the time that *now is*.³⁹ In his lecture course on the poem "Germania," he explains Hölderlin's reference to "time that tears" both as an oscillation that tears us away into the future and casts us back into having-been and as an alternation of being torn back and forth between an ever-new preservation of what has been and an ever-new awaiting of that which is to come.⁴⁰

A more complicated form of temporalization is represented by Heidegger's notion of "destiny" (*das Geschick, das Schicksal*). Having defined destiny as the singularity of the historical Dasein,⁴¹ he explains that destiny, in the first place, implies the motions of turning and counter-turning (as in the case of the meandering course of the river Rhine)⁴² and of decision and counter-decision (as in the case of humans turning toward the gods or away from them).⁴³ The fourfold understood as the festival to which Hölderlin refers in the poem "Remembrance" expresses this particular manner of temporalization, which is pre-contained within the essence of destiny and constitutes the origin of history as such.⁴⁴ Therefore, the "sending" (*die Schickung*), which is connected etymologically through its German nomenclature with destiny, can be understood on the one hand as either singular (in the definition of Dasein quoted above) or plural (in the

---

38 Heidegger is undoubtedly pursuing a kind of deconstruction of Hölderlin at this point. It is obvious that the poet himself adopts a kind of Platonist position, at least in the early novella *Hyperion* and in some of his theoretical writings, and Heidegger makes considerable efforts to downplay this element in order to further his own agenda. For example, see the discussions of Hölderlin's treatment of nature and beauty at *Elucidations of Hölderlin's Poetry*, 75–80 (*GA* 4:52–58) and especially his conclusion at *Elucidations of Hölderlin's Poetry*, 80 (*GA* 4:58). At one point, Heidegger justifies his interpretative approach by saying that Hölderlin *thinks* metaphysically but *poetizes* non-metaphysically. See *Hölderlin's Hymn "Remembrance"*, §41, 102 (*GA* 52:119–20). Undoubtedly, if the present essay were concerned with the juxtaposition of Cusanus and Hölderlin alone, the relation between the metaphysical surface and the hermeneutical depth would have to be stated in somewhat different terms.

39 Heidegger, *Elucidations of Hölderlin's Poetry*, 143 (*GA* 4:121).

40 Heidegger, *Hölderlin's Hymn "Germania"*, §9d, 99 (*GA* 39:109).

41 Heidegger, *Hölderlin's Hymn "The Rhine"*, §16b, 208 (*GA* 39:228).

42 Heidegger, *Hölderlin's Hymn "The Rhine"*, §17c, 214 (*GA* 39:234–35).

43 Heidegger, *Elucidations of Hölderlin's Poetry*, 58 (*GA* 4:40).

44 Heidegger, *Elucidations of Hölderlin's Poetry*, 129 (*GA* 4:106).

definition of history as a gathering of such sendings).⁴⁵ On the other hand, the sending can be viewed either in a state of equilibrium (as in the case of the stabilized temporalization of the festival⁴⁶) or in that of disequilibrium (as in the case of the normal flow of historical events).⁴⁷ The various turnings and counter-turnings are often described as the voices of destiny by Heidegger, and the interrelations between these motions as a "jointure" (*die Fuge*).⁴⁸

If temporalization represents a dynamic oscillation between past and future, it equally constitutes a dynamic tension between transition and beginning. This latter forms the first main component of Heidegger's notion of "event" (*Ereignis*), which is illustrated in the Stuttgart preface to the essay "Hölderlin's Earth and Heaven" reprinted in the *Elucidations of Hölderlin's Poetry*. In this passage, Heidegger speaks of the transformation (*Die Umstimmung*: literally, a "re-tuning") of the calculative reflection characteristic of the era of technology—and of the history of metaphysics—into an unprecedented thinking experience, namely, of the self-dissimulating "event of the fourfold" (*das Ereignis des Gevierts*) achievable if we can listen to Hölderlin's poetry in the right manner.⁴⁹ However, the German word *Ereignis* itself combines the sense of "event" with a connotation of "appropriation." This second main component of the notion of "event" emerges clearly in Heidegger's commentary on the poem "Remembrance," where the event is specified as that of the wedding-festival in which gods and humans encounter one another. Here, he notes that the inceptual aspect of what is taking place is vested primarily in the "reciprocal appropriation" (*die wechselweise Übereignung*) of the "[appropriative] event" (*das Er-eignis*) whereby the opposing terms both maintain and remove their *quasi*-spatial distance from one another.⁵⁰

---

45 Heidegger, *Elucidations of Hölderlin's Poetry*, 129–30 (GA 4:106–7).

46 Heidegger, *Hölderlin's Hymn "Remembrance"*, §32, 79 (GA 52:90).

47 Heidegger, *Hölderlin's Hymn "Remembrance"*, §64, 161 (GA 52:188–89).

48 Heidegger, *Elucidations of Hölderlin's Poetry*, 202–3 (GA 4:178–79). With a mixture of the two metaphors and a quotation of Heraclitus's ἁρμονίη ἀφανής, Heidegger adds that it is difficult to hear the silent voice of the joining.

49 Heidegger, *Elucidations of Hölderlin's Poetry*, 176–77 (GA 4:152–53).

50 Heidegger, *Hölderlin's Hymn "Remembrance"*, §27/3, 68–69 (GA 52:77). We have in this paragraph summarized only those aspects of the *Ereignis* that are most relevant to the present context. A fuller account of the matter would especially need to include discussion of the element of "attunement" (*die Stimmung*), which Heidegger introduces immediately after the second passage quoted in our summary.

Cusanus on Being

By comparison, Cusanus treats Being (*esse, ens, essentia*) as a fundamental divine name that has both an existential and an essential sense. This Being approximates to and differs from the Heideggerian notion of *das Sein, das Seyn* in accordance with the underlying distinction between a relational structure of metaphysical surface and hermeneutical depth. Clearly, Cusanus does not practice Heidegger's assimilation of Being to temporalization together with its suppression of presence in favor of the oscillation of past and future. This Cusan difference can be found in many passages but especially the treatise *De non aliud*. Here Cusanus argues that the theologian Dionysius had contrasted the transcendent and immanent forms of the subdivisions of empirical time (eternity, time, day, hour, moment), had shown that these transcendent forms were "not other than" (*non aliud quam*) their immanent correlates, and had argued that God as (transcendent) *eternity* was not other than God as (transcendent) *moment*. After pointing out that "moment" (*momentum*) is identical with "now" (*nunc*) and "present" (*praesentia*), Cusanus concludes that this present is the beginning of the being and the being-known of all the subdivisions of time, and that it is by means of the present that we know past and future things; so that in relation to past things the present is not other than the past, and in relation to future things the present is not other than the future.[51]

The Harmony between Cusanus and Heidegger

Throughout this essay, we have studied the diametrical opposition between the respective fourfold structures of Cusanus and Heidegger, although in juxtaposing the two approaches as metaphysical surface versus hermeneutical depth, we have tended to stress the differences between the two thinkers. As perhaps has become clear from the above discussion, many of these differences hinge upon the two thinkers' respective treatments of time or temporality. In a brief conclusion, I aim to balance the picture by noting the extensive harmony of approach in the two writers. After all, it is precisely because there are fundamental similarities between Cusanus's and Heidegger's thinking regarding the fourfold that the study of the diametrical opposition between them acquires its real philosophical significance.

---

51 Nicholas of Cusa, *De non aliud*, XVI (76–78), ed. Baur and Wilpert, 40–41.

The Cusan doctrine of "conjecture" (*coniectura*) may be taken as the unique starting-point of a fourfold comparison between the two authors. The Latin writer explains in his treatise *De coniecturis* that since ultimate precision of truth is unattainable by human beings—a conclusion already drawn in *De docta ignorantia* from the lack of proportion between truth and the human intellect—any "positive assertion" (*positiva assertio*) about truth must be conjectural.[52] Regarding the conjectural practice implemented in this treatise and various later works, which turns out to be a practice by definition rather than a theory, we will confine ourselves to signaling certain aspects that serve to position Cusanus in the same terrain as Heidegger, who speaks in similar fashion of "poetizing" (*dichten, die Dichtung*) or of the thinking that poetizes. These shared features are:

1. *Productivity*. Cusanus explains the origin of conjecture by comparing the intellectual production of *real* things by the divine mind with the intellectual production of *rational* things by the human mind[53]—these latter corresponding to conjectures—and by identifying the production of rational things or the contemplation of such things with the human mind's participation in or assimilation to the divine.[54] In a gloss on Hölderlin's phrase from "Germania," "dwelling upon this earth," Heidegger defines poetizing as that which sustains the configuration of the being of the human being from the ground up as a historical Dasein in the midst of beings as a whole. Far from being a mode of embellishment, poetizing is rather the fundamental occurrence of the historical Dasein of human being in its exposure to Being.[55]

2. *Singularity*. Cusanus argues that given the same inapprehensible truth, there are "different and graduated" (*diversae . . . graduales*) or "disproportional" (*improportionabiles*) conjectures among different individuals, with the result that no individual will ever perfectly grasp another's meaning, although one individual perhaps comes closer to that meaning

---

[52] Nicholas of Cusa, *De coniecturis*, I. Prol. (2), ed. Bormann and Senger, 4. See also *De docta ignorantia*, I.1 (2–4), ed. Wilpert and Senger, 6–8. On the basics of conjecture, see also Nicholas of Cusa, *Idiota de mente*, V (82), ed. Steiger, 124–25; and *Idiota de mente*, VII (102), ed. Steiger, 153–54.

[53] The argument here should be compared with an analogous one at *De beryllo*, 7, ed. Senger and Bormann, 9–10, where the Hermetic teaching about humanity as second god is quoted as the authority. On the aspect of productivity, see further *Idiota de mente*, II (62), ed. Steiger, 95–96.

[54] Nicholas of Cusa, *De coniecturis*, I.1 (5), ed. Bormann and Senger, 7–8.

[55] Heidegger, *Hölderlin's Hymn "Germania"*, §4f, 34 (*GA* 39:36).

than does another.⁵⁶ For Heidegger, the author of the hymn "The Rhine" is not intent on describing something like destiny in general or attempting a metaphysical treatment of the essence of destiny, but is engaged in the poetizing of that "something singular" (*ein Einziges*) which is the destiny of the Rhine river.⁵⁷

3. *Play*. Cusanus explores the manner in which the "game of bowls" (*ludus globi*) symbolizes the motion of the human soul toward its rest in Christ. He notes that in casting the irregularly curved ball across the surface inscribed with concentric circles we can conjecture with varying degrees of reliability where the ball will come to rest.⁵⁸ Heidegger argues that within the festival dance celebrating the marriage of gods and humans there is a certain freedom within regulation that constitutes "the essence of play" (*das Wesen des Spiels*): namely, the free unfolding of the abundance of possibilities deriving from that original oscillation that is nevertheless controlled within limits.⁵⁹

4. *Enigma*. Cusanus supports with the authority of scripture the notion that his important conjecture of *possest* is also an enigma. He interprets the statements in Romans 1:20 and Exodus 3:14—to the effect that God is almighty, that God is being, and that God is enigmatic for us⁶⁰—as supplying the three components of this invented term: the infinitive verb *posse*, the third-person present indicative *est*, and the compound expression *posse + est*.⁶¹ For Heidegger, the author of the hymn "The Rhine" indicates the enigma regarding the being of the demi-god that is the river itself: it is only in the counter-willing opposed to the originating willing of the river—its current and counter-current—that the origin of the river can come to itself.⁶²

---

56 Nicholas of Cusa, *De coniecturis*, I. Prol. (3), ed. Bormann and Senger, 4–5. See also *De coniecturis*, I.11 (54–60), ed. Bormann and Senger, 55–61.

57 Heidegger, *Hölderlin's Hymn "The Rhine"*, §12d, 169 (*GA* 39:185). See also *Hölderlin's Hymn "The Rhine"*, §16, 208 (*GA* 39:228). For Hölderlin and Heidegger the Rhine is a demi-god; on demi-gods, see above.

58 See Nicholas of Cusa, *Dialogus de ludo globi*, I (1), I (50), and I (58), ed. Senger, 3, 55–56, and 64–66.

59 Heidegger, *Hölderlin's Hymn "Remembrance"*, §25, 59–60 (*GA* 52:66–67).

60 For Romans 1:20, see Nicholas of Cusa, *De possest*, 2–4, ed. Steiger, 3–6; for Exodus 3:14, see *De possest*, 14–15, ed. Steiger, 18–20. However, there are many more explicit and implicit references to scripture scattered through the text.

61 See Nicholas of Cusa, *De possest*, 19, 25, and 58, in *Nicolai de Cusa Opera Omnia*, vol. XI/2, ed. Renata Steiger (Hamburg: Felix Meiner Verlag, 1973), 24–25, 30–32, and 69–70. Cusanus similarly argues that another conjecture, that of the *non aliud*, is also an enigma. See *De non aliud*, V (15–18), ed. Baur and Wilpert, 11–12.

62 Heidegger, *Hölderlin's Hymn "The Rhine"*, §17c, 213–14 (*GA* 39:234); and §19, 223 (*GA* 39:245).

16

Nicholas of Cusa on Infinite Desire

DAVID BENTLEY HART

अयम् आत्मा ब्रह्म

I

In one of the earlier passages in his *Zibaldone*, Leopardi reflects at considerable length upon what he takes to be a sentiment common to all of us: a sense he believes we all share of "the nullity of everything" (*nullità di tutte le cose*), the insufficiency of every pleasure to satisfy the spirit within us, and "our inclination toward an infinite that we do not comprehend" (*la tendenza nostra verso un infinito che non comprendiamo*).[1] It is, taken as a whole, a *tour de force* of psychological phenomenology. It also, however, begins from a logical error; for, according to Leopardi, both this persistent dissatisfaction within us and the infinity of longing that underlie it can probably be ascribed to a cause "more material than

---

1 Giacomo Leopardi, *Zibaldone*, ed. Rolando Damiani (Milan: Mondadori, 2011), §§165–83. For a full English translation, see Giacomo Leopardi, *Zibaldone*, ed. Michael Caesar and Franco D'Intino, trans. Kathleen Baldwin et al., rev. ed. (New York: Farrar, Straus & Giroux, 2015). All translations here are my own.

spiritual" (*più materiale che spirituale*). Which is to say, he begins by assuming a contradiction: that an infinite intention, exceeding every finite object of rational longing, could arise spontaneously from finite physical causes, without any transcendental end to provoke them as, at least, an intentional object and capacity of the rational will. But how, then, could we experience this *tendenza* at all as an actual intelligible volition beyond what lies immediately before us, and arrive at an awareness that it is unfulfilled? An intention without a final intentional horizon can be experienced neither as fulfilled nor as unfulfilled.

And yet Leopardi recognizes that our desire for pleasure is limitless in duration and extent, and that we would not exist as the beings we are without it; it belongs to our substance, he says, not as a longing for this or that, but as a desire for the pleasing as such. And here he is quite correct. One can desire nothing finite as an end wholly in itself, but only "as abstract and limitless pleasure" (*come piacere astratto e illimitato*).[2] "Following on one pleasure," he writes, "the soul does not cease from desire for pleasure, just as it never ceases thinking, because thought and desire for pleasure are two operations equally continuous with and inseparable from our existence."[3] Indeed. But, then, what Leopardi's reflections actually reveal is that our ability to desire anything as a purpose conceived by the willing mind is inexplicable unless we presume that the source of that desire is a transcendental object (real or supposed) to which our rational wills are—at least, again, in intention—wholly adequate. As a matter of simple fact, all purposive human desire is animated at its most primordial level by an unremitting volition toward (for want of a better term) the divine. *Inquietum est cor nostrum donec requiescat in te*, to coin a phrase.

One can see, of course, why as unremittingly dour a godless genius as Leopardi would not be inclined to follow his musings to the conclusion they appear to entail. To grant that the human spirit is capable of a genuinely infinite intentionality is already to grant that the sort of bleak materialism he presumed is at best paradoxical, at worst incoherent. If nothing else, it would mean that even that aspect of human character that seems most irrational—our inability to rest finally content in any proximate and finite

---

2 Leopardi, *Zibaldone*, §165.

3 "Conseguito un piacere, l'anima non cessa di desiderare il piacere, come non cessa mai di pensare, perchè il pensiero e il desiderio del piacere sono due operazioni egualmente continue e inseparabili dalla sua esistenza." Leopardi, *Zibaldone*, §183.

end of longing—is in fact the result of a prior and wholly rational relation between human spirit and the proper end of rational freedom as such. That irrepressible disquiet is not merely the insatiable perversity of aimless appetite, magically positing an ever more exalted end for itself somewhere out there in the nowhere of the will's spontaneous energies, but is rather a constant and cogent longing that apprises us of the true ultimate rationale that prompts the mind and will to seek any end at all, and therefore to be capable of recognition, evaluation, judgment, and choice in regard to proximate ends: a rationale that lies elsewhere, beyond the limits of the finite.

This also, moreover, touches upon an age-old issue within the history of Western metaphysics: the gradual discovery that infinity is not merely a name for unintelligible indeterminate extension—as was the prejudice of early Platonic, Aristotelian, and Stoic thought—nor even merely that infinity is a positive rational category; rather, it is also a proper name for that necessary terminus of all real rational freedom apart from which neither reason nor freedom could exist. Plotinus is perhaps the first Western thinker to have grasped this explicitly. In Christian thought, it was Gregory of Nyssa who first unfolded the principle at length, and with consummate brilliance. But no Christian figure after Gregory, with the possible exception of Maurice Blondel, grasped the principle in all its dimensions as fully as did Nicholas of Cusa. As he writes in *De visione Dei*, "Were God not infinite, he could not be the end for desire."[4] To which, of course, corresponds the reciprocal proposition that nothing desired as a limited quiddity, without any remainder of the "ever greater," can be in itself the sole final cause prompting that desire.[5]

Actually, the sixteenth chapter of *De visione Dei* is oddly similar in some ways to that passage from Leopardi cited above, though of course radically different in intonation.[6] You, God, says Nicholas, "are the form of every desirable thing and are that truth that is desired within every

---

[4] "Quod nisi deus esset infinitus, non foret finis desidere." Nicholas of Cusa, *De visione Dei*, XVI (67), in *Nicolai de Cusa Opera Omnia*, vol. VI, ed. Heide Dorothea Riemann (Hamburg: Felix Meiner Verlag, 2000), 55.

[5] Nicholas of Cusa, *De venatione sapientiae*, XII (32), in *Nicolai de Cusa Opera Omnia*, vol. XII, ed. Raymond Klibansky and Hans Gerhard Senger (Hamburg: Felix Meiner Verlag, 1982), 32–33.

[6] Nicholas of Cusa, *De visione Dei*, XVI (67–70), ed. Riemann, 55–58.

desire."[7] "To taste of your incomprehensible sweetness, which becomes more delightful to me to the very degree that it seems more infinite" is to see that, precisely because the divine is ultimately unknown to all creatures, "they might in holiest ignorance possess a greater contentment, as if amid an incalculable and inexhaustible treasure."[8] Hence, the creature's ignorance of God's full greatness is a "supremely desirable feasting" (*pascentia ... desiderabilissima*) for the intellect.[9] And hence, also, it is God's will both "to be comprehended in my possession and also to remain incomprehensible and infinite," because he is a treasure whose limitation no one can desire.[10] Neither can this rational appetite desire the cessation of its own existence. The *will* may long either to exist or not to exist, but appetite itself cannot desist from itself, for it "is borne into the infinite" (*fertur in infinitum*). He observes: "Indeed, intellectual desire is borne on not into that which is capable of being greater and more desirable, but into that which is incapable of being greater or more desirable.... Therefore, the end of desire is infinite."[11] And so, says Cusanus, with exemplary precision: "Therefore you, God, are infinity itself, which alone I desire in every desire."[12] God shines forth in human longing, and so that longing leads us to God, casting all finite and comprehensible things aside as it does so, for in them it can find no rest; thus it is led ever onward *from* God who is the beginningless beginning *to* God who is the endless end.[13] One sees God, then, under the form of a certain rapture of the mind and thus discovers that the intellect cannot find true satisfaction in anything that it wholly understands, any more than it could in something that it understands not at all; rather, it must always seek "that which it understands through not understanding" (*illud, quod non*

---

[7] "... es forma omnis desiderabilis et veritas illa, quae in omni desiderio desideratur." Nicholas of Cusa, *De visione Dei*, XVI (67), ed. Riemann, 55.

[8] "... degustare incomprehensibilem suavitatem tuam, quae tanto mihi fit gratior, quanto infinitior apparet ... habeant in hac sacratissima ignorantia maiorem quietem, quasi in thesauro innumerabili et inexhauribili." Nicholas of Cusa, *De visione Dei*, XVI (67), ed. Riemann, 55.

[9] Nicholas of Cusa, *De visione Dei*, XVI (67), ed. Riemann, 56.

[10] "... comprehendi possessione mea et manere incomprehensibilis et infinitus." Nicholas of Cusa, *De visione Dei*, XVI (68), ed. Riemann, 56.

[11] "Desiderium enim intellectuale non fertur in id, quod potest esse maius et desiderabilius, sed in id, quod non potest maius esse nec desiderabilius.... Finis igitur desiderii est infinitus." Nicholas of Cusa, *De visione Dei*, XVI (68), ed. Riemann, 56.

[12] "Tu igitur, deus, es ipsa infinitas, quam solum in omni desiderio desidero." Nicholas of Cusa, *De visione Dei*, XVI (68), ed. Riemann, 56.

[13] Nicholas of Cusa, *De visione Dei*, XVI (69), ed. Riemann, 57.

intelligendo intelligit).[14] And so, then, it is only within God's own infinite movement of love that any rational desire exists, coming from and going toward the infinite that gives it being.

"Infinity itself, which alone I desire in every desire," writes Cusanus. And yet for him, quite unlike Leopardi, this very insatiability—this indomitable longing for the infinite within each stirring of finite longing—is also a kind of ecstasy, an eros that finds its highest possible delight precisely in its own perpetual dissatisfaction. Where Leopardi (in his Schopenhauerian way) sees only evidence of the blind, indeterminable striving of idiot will, Cusanus recognizes from the first that nothing could actually prompt an appetite for the infinite that is capable of drawing us toward finite ends except a real intelligible horizon of rational longing, against which the intellect can measure and evaluate any finite object of longing. Every limited terminus of rational desire, then, is recognizable to the intellect only and precisely as a contraction and mediation of that formally limitless terminus. And so Cusanus sees this exquisite state of elated frustration as nothing less than the original intentionality of created spirit toward God's revelation of himself in all things, an openness of created spirit to all things, through which all things are reciprocally opened up to created spirit. God's absolute face or aspect (*facies absoluta*) is the "natural face of every nature," the "art and knowledge of everything knowable," and so the "absolute entity of all Being" (*absoluta entitas omnis esse*).[15] He is the face of all faces, already seen in every face or aspect of any creature, albeit in a veiled and symbolic manner;[16] he is the infinite treasure of delight glimpsed within every delight,[17] manifesting himself in all that is and by every possible means of attracting the rational will to himself.[18] Nor is the mind's ascent beyond every finite end merely a journey into the indeterminate; rather, it is a true engagement with an end at once both infinite *and* rational, because it is nothing less than God's own end, his essence, the only possible determinacy for an infinite nature.[19]

---

14 Nicholas of Cusa, *De visione Dei*, XVI (70), ed. Riemann, 57.
15 Nicholas of Cusa, *De visione Dei*, VII (24), ed. Riemann, 26.
16 Nicholas of Cusa, *De visione Dei*, VI (21), ed. Riemann, 22-23.
17 Nicholas of Cusa, *De visione Dei*, VII (26), ed. Riemann, 27. See also *De visione Dei*, XVI (67-68), ed. Riemann, 55-56.
18 Nicholas of Cusa, *De visione Dei*, XV (66), ed. Riemann, 54-55.
19 Nicholas of Cusa, *De visione Dei*, XIII (52-53), ed. Riemann, 44-46.

We receive the world, therefore, and the world is available to our spiritual overtures, entirely on account of this prior infinite appetite for an infinite end, this desire to know the infinite in a real "infinite mode": that of incomprehensible immediacy, unknowing knowledge. We are capable of knowing anything at all only because the primordial orientation of our nature is the longing to know God as God, to see him as he is, rather than as some limited essence.[20] For that vision to be achieved, however, all finite concepts must be surpassed by the intellect as it ascends to a more direct apprehension. That hunger for the infinite as infinite, which can never come to rest in any finite nature, is also the only possible ground of the mind's capacity for finite realities as objects of rational knowledge or desire. But for our inextinguishable intentionality toward the "Face of all faces," no face would ever appear to us.

II

All of this at times may strike us as more rhapsodic than precise, but it should not. What Cusanus is saying here is not only axiomatic for any coherent theology, but also logically entailed in any truly rigorous phenomenology of the act of rational volition. Theologically speaking, how could God be desired as a determinate quiddity? He would be available to thought and desire, then, only as measured against a more comprehensive realm of rational references, as merely one thing among others, one possible instance of the desirable. But then one would not really be desiring *God* at all. Phenomenologically speaking, Cusanus is clearly correct that every act of finite longing, and hence of finite cognition, is possible only so long as there is, in addition to the thing desired, a deferral of final desire toward a truly ultimate end. The mind attends to any object only to the degree that it is prompted to do so by a prior interest in Being as such. Cusanus, we should always remember, had quite an acute and sophisticated understanding of the relation between the mind's intentional activity and its power of apprehension. Whatever we perceive, he argues, ascends from the confusion of mere sense-knowledge into the intellect only insofar as the intellect actively descends through its rational faculty to inform the senses; even the visible, as an object of rational recognition, is unattainable by the sense of sight if the intellectual power is not directed toward receiving it—as we

---

20 Nicholas of Cusa, *De venatione sapientiae*, XII (31–33), ed. Klibansky and Senger, 31–34.

realize whenever, for instance, we fail to note another person passing us by on the road not because our eyes are averted but because our mind's intentionality is.[21] The same is true of all our faculties of cognition, as we realize whenever, say, many persons are speaking to us simultaneously, but we understand only what one of them is saying because he is the only one to whose words we are paying attention.[22] But Cusanus also recognizes that, even in these simple labors of mental attentiveness, there is already an implicit movement of the intellect beyond any immediate intuition and toward infinity. It is not, he says, our animal powers or "spirits" (in the physical sense of the subtle fluids of the brain and organs of the body) that recognize the things about us, but the "higher spirit" of discrimination;[23] and the more we follow that light of reason up to its source, ascending from mere sense-perception, the more we become conscious of our prior intellectual awareness of the infinite light of God knowing in us and drawing all to himself.[24]

It is worth pausing here to consider the force of Cusanus's reasoning. In one sense, really, he is merely calling attention to a plain fact of experience. It is obvious that the intellectual knowledge of any object involves a kind of attentiveness that is prompted by a more general desire to know "in general." It is equally obvious that no discrete finite end is the original source of this desire, as finite knowledge is by its nature an act of recognition, evaluation, judgment, and choice in light of ends that precede and exceed the particular object of such knowledge. So, any run-of-the-mill Neoplatonist could tell us that all rational desire—as opposed to mere brute impulse, if such a thing exists—is animated by a prior preoccupation of the mind and will with ultimate transcendental indices of identity, meaning, value, and desirability, such as the good, the true, the beautiful, and Being itself in its unity. And even the meanest of modern phenomenologists should be able to see that a rational intentionality isolates the intuitions that fulfill it only as set off against a horizon of much more indeterminate and inexhaustible intentionality. And any of us, when attempting to discover the ultimate source and end of our rational longing—the one terminus in which alone the entire

---

21 Nicholas of Cusa, *De coniecturis*, XVI (157), in *Nicolai de Cusa Opera Omnia*, vol. III, ed. Karl Bormann and Hans Gerhard Senger (Hamburg: Felix Meiner Verlag, 1972), 156–57.
22 Nicholas of Cusa, *De quaerendo Deum*, II (33), in *Nicolai de Cusa Opera Omnia*, vol. IV, ed. Paul Wilpert (Hamburg: Felix Meiner Verlag, 1959), 23–24.
23 Nicholas of Cusa, *De quaerendo Deum*, II (33–35), ed. Wilpert, 23–25.
24 Nicholas of Cusa, *De quaerendo Deum*, II (36–37), ed. Wilpert, 25–27.

energy of the mind and will can come to rest, replete in the good as such or the true as such or the beautiful as such—will find that the interminable deferral of desire can rest only in the infinite as its end. Where Cusanus distinguishes himself, however, is in how clearly he sees that, in unveiling the infinite as reason's final cause, we unveil also a real rational capacity within ourselves for the infinite. Surely, after all, there must be a fairly strict proportionality between what we can actually desire rationally and the natural scope of the power of our intention. I may not be able to make myself a god, for instance, but I can desire to become a god to the precise degree that I grasp what a god is in my intentionality. And if, then, I constantly desire the infinite as the ground of all rational willing, then in some sense my intentionality must be adequate to the infinite. And, as extravagant as such a claim might sound, it entirely accords with our ordinary experience.

Certainly, Cusanus makes much better sense of how we take the world in, even in those moments when it seems unintelligible to us, than does, say, a modern phenomenologist such as Jean-Luc Marion. The latter, after all, in his eagerness to elevate phenomenal givenness beyond the reach of all intentionality (which he often seems to confine to the imaginative and conceptual powers of the psychological subject), has spent much of the last two decades describing what he calls the "saturated phenomenon": that is, the event of a phenomenon—whether ordinary or extraordinary—that overwhelms intentionality with an excess of intuition, beyond the power of the subject to constitute the phenomenon as what it is.[25] And this, supposedly, dissolves the last lingering traces of transcendental subjectivity in phenomenology in favor of an understanding of the human being as *l'adonné*—a pure "immersed" or "devoted" receptivity—forever addressed by a sovereign givenness beyond the limitations even of conceptual "objectivity." In fact, this only preserves the polarity of subject and object, albeit under

---

25 Marion has developed the concept of the saturated phenomenon in a number of texts over a number of years. See especially: *Prologomena to Charity*, trans. Stephen E. Lewis (New York: Fordham University Press, 2002 [first published in French in 1986]); *The Crossing of the Visible*, trans. James K. A. Smith (Stanford, CA: Stanford University Press, 2003 [1996]); *Being Given: Toward a Phenomenology of Givenness*, trans. Jeffrey L. Kosky (Stanford, CA: Stanford University Press, 2002 [1997]); *In Excess: Studies of Saturated Phenomena*, trans. Robyn Horner and Vincent Berraud (New York: Fordham University Press, 2004 [2001]); *The Erotic Phenomenon*, trans. Stephen E. Lewis (Chicago: University of Chicago Press, 2006 [2003]); *The Visible and the Revealed*, trans. Christina M. Geschwandtner (New York: Fordham University Press, 2008 [2005]); *Negative Certainties*, trans. Stephen E. Lewis (Chicago: University of Chicago Press, 2020 [2009]); and *Givenness and Revelation* (Oxford: Oxford University Press, 2016).

the form of a logically incoherent but constant negation of one pole for the sake of the other's hyperbolic supremacy. So concerned is Marion with freeing givenness from the meager conceptual powers of the transcendental subject, as he conceives that subject, that he is willing to embrace the notion of a phenomenon exceeding every intentional capacity of the mind. This is fabulous nonsense.

Cusanus, of course, to the contrary, tells us that: "The seeing that I direct at God is not a visible seeing, but is rather a seeing of the invisible within the visible."[26] But note that this very formulation depends upon the persistence of an intentionality that *exceeds* the occasion of the visible, not one that falls short of it. If, moreover, one considers any of the experiences that Marion describes as instances of saturated phenomenality—especially certain experiences also discussed by Cusanus, such as prayer, love, the eucharist, revelation, or even looking at a painting—what one discovers is that what makes them so mysterious, in those privileged moments of acute awareness when they are mysterious to us, is not a surfeit of intuition over intentionality, but quite the reverse: the poverty of intuition in relation to the richness—the incalculable treasure, as Nicholas says—of intention. Somehow, the mere definable intuitions available to the senses and mind do not yet exhaust what one already knows or expects to be true of the given. And, but for that excessive intentionality, there would be no way of grasping the sheer givenness of the phenomenon at all; one would be fixed forever, and contentedly, in the precise ratio between a finite intention and the objective finitude of what it intends.

Obviously, the finite intentions of the empirical self can be thwarted or overwhelmed in experience. Frankly, though, many of Marion's descriptions of "saturated phenomena," especially those in which one can report a surfeit of qualitative or quantitative intuition, seem scarcely distinguishable from descriptions of cognitive dissonance, such as one's first encounter with what Kant calls the "dynamical sublime," or one's sense of disorientation on taking a sip of wine from a glass that one had thought contained milk. And such dissonances are nothing but corrigible and temporary failures of intentionality. But even when Marion speaks of some extraordinary event, like divine revelation, which may surprise us or overturn our common expectations, he is still providing not an example of what he calls "counter-experience," but

---

[26] Nicholas of Cusa, *De non aliud*, XXII (103), in *Nicolai de Cusa Opera Omnia*, vol. XIII, ed. Ludwig Baur and Paul Wilpert (Leipzig: Felix Meiner Verlag, 1944), 53.

only an example of another kind of cognitive dissonance, one that can be received as given—if at all—only to the degree that it is recuperated into a more capacious intentionality. And when he discusses a sense of meaning or significance that exceeds the merely objectifiable and conceptually limited aspects of a given phenomenon, it seems clear that he is really only calling attention to the inadequacy of intuition as measured against the still-greater extent of the intentionality that has opened it to thought. No phenomenon can give itself if there is no prior realm of rational intentionality where it can show itself. So, yes, no doubt at the level of the empirical, psychological self, with its wandering attention, the limits of intentionality can be reached before experience has been exhausted. But, at the level of what Maximus the Confessor calls the "natural will" and Augustine calls the "unquiet heart" and Cusanus calls that "which alone I desire within every desire," there is only a primordial orientation toward the infinite, one not constituted by, but instead constituting, the psychological self as a phenomenon; and within the full scope of this orientation any phenomenon can make its appearance, and any seeming contradiction can be resolved. This does not mean that that highest intelligibility can be reduced to calculative and quantitative cognition—ultimate knowledge is unitive, not conceptual—but it does mean that, as Cusanus says, the mind can never really extend itself to such a capacity that it is rendered incapable of becoming yet more capacious.[27]

In the end, what certain overwhelming experiences really bring to light is nothing but that same dynamism described above: infinite rational desire seeking its infinite rational end. Rather than speaking of the saturated phenomenon, then, it would be better to adopt Cusanus's language of the "symbolic" or "veiled" phenomenon of the "absolute face" in every face.[28] This is the one "excessive" phenomenal experience to which we are all occasionally admitted, after all, in those rare moments when we become briefly aware of that open interval of the uncanny that stretches out behind every finite thing—that distance that lies between every finite thing and the ultimate horizon of its intelligibility—that difference that exists between the limited reality or fragile contingency of *what* something is and the mysterious fortuity *that* it is. The event of any essence, we find, appears within

---

[27] Nicholas of Cusa, *De theologicis complementis*, 9, in *Nicolai de Cusa Opera Omnia*, vol. X/2a, ed. Heide Dorothea Riemann and Karl Bormann (Hamburg: Felix Meiner Verlag, 1994), 40–48.

[28] Nicholas of Cusa, *De visione Dei*, VI (21), ed. Riemann, 22–23.

the ever-more-embracing horizon of Being's gratuity, a horizon at once intentional and ontological. And the surfeit of intentionality over intuition in such moments turns out to be, not surprisingly, simply an immediate awareness of the infinite and irreducible surfeit of Being over beings, the invisible difference between them. Once again, moreover, this experience apprises us of an intentional range—a deeper natural intentionality—within ourselves capable of that interval, and so capable of going beyond the finite occasion of experience toward the inexhaustible source of its event, the whole horizon of Being's infinite fullness.

III

Another way of saying this, perhaps, is that our natural and irrepressible desire to know the truth of anything and everything is the desire to "see face to face" and thus to "know fully," just as we are "fully known" (1 Cor 13:12), and so "to see him as he is" (1 Jn 3:12). It is the longing to arrive at that place where knowing and the known perfectly coincide, where mind and being achieve so perfect a transparency one to the other that they constitute a single act. The rational will, therefore, can rest content only in that infinite divine simplicity where being and knowing are one event, perfected in the repletion of love. Which brings us to another wholly delightful feature of Nicholas of Cusa's reflections on these matters: that they leave no possible space for the kind of absolute partition between nature and supernature that became so inextirpably rooted in sixteenth-century Thomism and that held so much of Catholic thought in its death-grip up to the middle of the twentieth century, and that even now is enjoying a tragic recrudescence among certain of the more militantly necrophile factions of traditionalist Catholicism. Not that this is the place to elaborate at length on this sad tradition, or on the historical contingencies that spawned it, or even on its many logical deficiencies. But one cannot help but think that, had Cusanus's thought determined the prevailing impulse of the Catholic theology of the next several centuries, it would have produced a far more coherent, orthodox, and beautiful synthesis. Alas, what instead became the increasingly dominant position was that the only way of securing the gratuity of salvation and deification was to insist that, as the formula goes, "grace is extrinsic to the nature of the creature," and to insist also upon the most extreme interpretation of this axiom. Human nature, according to this form of early modern Thomism, has no inherent ordination toward real union with

God, and rational creatures are constitutively incapable even of conceiving a desire for such union if not aided by an infusion of a *lumen gloriae* that is entirely adventitious to everything proper to their creaturehood. There would be no *cor inquietum* within us were it not for a wholly superadded spiritual motive of which our bare nature could never conceive even the faintest agitation. That we do feel such a longing for the supernatural, moreover, is supposedly an entirely contingent fact of the present providential order of this world. It would be perfectly possible, says this tradition, for God to create a world in a state of "pure nature" wherein rational creatures, possessing a human nature identical to our own but one not superelevated by grace, would find that their natural rational wills could rest perfectly satisfied in an entirely natural end. Such creatures would be capable of a kind of intellectual velleity toward God only insofar as he might be the best possible explanatory principle of the world; but this would be no more than an elicited curiosity about the causal history of things, not a true yearning for union with the divine. Nature as such not only has no claim on grace; in itself, it is incapable of desiring grace.

Again, the problems with this way of thinking are too numerous to treat of here. What is worth dwelling upon is how beautifully Cusanus demonstrates that there is no such thing as rational desire that is not a desire for the infinity of God in himself, and so no natural impulse of a truly rational will that is not already—and even more originally—supernatural. "Pure nature" is an atrocity of reason. Even God could not create a rational will not oriented toward deifying union with himself, any more than he could create a square circle. In fact, for Cusanus, the very structure of all finite rational desire is nothing other than a created participation in the infinite movement of the divine life: the Father knowing himself perfectly in his Logos, such that his being and his knowing are one and the same reality, consummated in the love of the Spirit. And the radical implication of this way of seeing things is that the immanent telos of God's own life and the transcendent telos of the life of created spirit are, formally and finally, one and the same telos: the divine essence, understood as the perfect repletion of God's life of love and knowledge. As God is God in the eternal and eternally accomplished movement *of* God *to* God, so we are gods in the process of becoming solely by virtue of always existing within that movement, proceeding from the same source and toward the same end; we do so in the mode of finitude, contingency, and successiveness, and so are not God; but teleologically we are nothing *but* God. There is no "place" other than "in him" where created spirit can live and move and have its being and so seek its ultimate end—which is to say, the fullness of reality that God is. In fact, it might not be wrong to say that, for Cusanus, the difference between God and spiritual creatures is in some sense ontologically modal: it is the difference, that is, of the infinite simplicity of divine being, in whom there is a perfect *identity* of knower and known, from the finite dynamism of created being, which directly participates in that divine reality, but only under the form of a perpetual *synthesis* of knowing and being known. In Cusanus this takes the form not of an identity of essence and existence, but a modal unfolding of difference from enfolded identity.[29]

Certainly Cusanus insists that the rational will can never rest in God as in another thing, an extrinsic end among other extrinsic ends, but must rest in him only as in the *non aliud*, the "Not-Other," desired precisely as Not-Other.[30] For one thing, he notes, God's seeing is also his being—his life is his loving knowledge of his own boundless fullness of being—and hence we exist only because God looks upon us and thereby grants us being: "I am, therefore, because you regard me" (*ideo ego sum quia tu me respicis*).[31] For another, the created intellect truly conceives any finite being as an image of the fullness of the divine simplicity; and the created mind's assimilation of being's boundless diversity is a participatory recapitulation of the divine mind's act of creating beings in knowing them.[32] And then, yet again, this positively requires the complementary formula that, just as God's seeing *of* himself is also his being seen *by* himself, so his seeing *of* all creatures is also his being seen *by* all creatures.[33] And then also, conversely, God is visible insofar as the creature exists, which is in just such degree as the creature sees God.[34] In short, there is no space in which the natural can exist, especially in spiritual creatures, apart from its prior and total constitution by and within the supernatural—by and within, that is, God himself. The very ground of our creaturehood, in its every actuality, is divinity. All

---

[29] See, e.g., Nicholas of Cusa, *De coniecturis*, IX (117-19), ed. Bormann and Senger, 112-15; and Nicholas of Cusa, *Idiota de mente*, VII (97-107), in *Nicolai de Cusa Opera Omnia*, vol. V, ed. Renate Steiger (Hamburg: Felix Meiner Verlag, 1983), 145-61.
[30] Nicholas of Cusa, *De non aliud*, IV (14), ed. Baur and Wilpert, 10.
[31] Nicholas of Cusa, *De visione Dei*, IV (10), ed. Riemann, 14.
[32] Nicholas of Cusa, *Idiota de mente*, III (69-73), ed. Steiger, 105-12.
[33] Nicholas of Cusa, *De theologicis complementis*, 14, ed. Riemann and Bormann, 80-83.
[34] Nicholas of Cusa, *De visione Dei*, XII (47-48), ed. Riemann, 41-42.

natural knowing and desiring is a modality of divine knowledge and love, and nothing else. No absolute ontological caesura is possible between them.

This is what makes the meditations of *De visione Dei* so exhilarating: Cusanus's profound understanding of the shape of every rational nature's necessary relation to God, both insofar as God enfolds creation within himself and insofar also as he unfolds creation from himself. For a finite intellect, everything unfolded and distinct is a created exemplar of what is enfolded in God's boundless actuality and power, never achieving perfection as an image of that power (given every finite thing's mutable and composite nature), but allowing the created intellect to enfold it within thought and thereby ever more to become a mirror of the divine simplicity. By this mirroring, the intellect becomes an ever more luminous icon of the divine act of creating in knowing and knowing in creating, and participates ever more deeply in the identity of thought and being. And there is no other kind of rational knowledge. All things are faces of the one Face of faces, forms of the one Form of forms, and so there is nothing the mind can know or love that is not already a divine disclosure, a supernatural revelation.

It would perhaps be best to leave off here, but I cannot forbear to make one additional observation. To a very great degree, Cusanus's understanding of this delicate interplay of implication and explication—enfolding and unfolding—which, so to speak, interweaves the natural and the supernatural, or the created and the divine, in the single seamless fabric of being and knowing, divine disclosure and human assimilation, is very much shaped by his Christology. For him, it is obvious that what is revealed in Christ is anything but a paradox, much less a merely extrinsic union between essentially incommensurable natures; rather, it is the perfection of an essential unity revealed in its original and ultimate unity. It is only in your human nature, says Cusanus to Christ, that I see what is in your divine nature. "Yet in you, the son of man, I see the Son of God, because you are so the son of man that you are Son of God, and in the finite nature that is drawn I see the infinite nature that is drawing."[35] Just as that image that most perfectly mediates its exemplar is the image that "subsists with the greatest nearness" (*propinquissime subsistit*) within the truth it images forth, "so I see your human nature subsisting within your divine nature" (*sic video naturam*

---

[35] "In te autem filio hominis filium dei video, quia ita es filius hominis quod filius dei, et in natura attracta finita video naturam attrahentem infinitam." Nicholas of Cusa, *De visione Dei*, XX (88), ed. Riemann, 69.

tuam humanam in divina natura subsistentem).[36] Of course, one thus sees the divine nature in a human way; but then, conversely, one also sees the image joined immediately to its exemplar. In Christ's human—which is to say rational—nature, we see the rational human spirit in its most intimate and most natural unity with divine Spirit, which is absolute reason, and the most intimate and natural unity of human intellect with divine intellect.[37] And so on.

One should not let the sheer grandiloquence of these apostrophes to the God-man distract one from their deepest import. Because what Cusanus is also saying here, simply enough, is that in Christ the fullness of human nature is revealed precisely to the degree that it perfectly reveals the divine nature of which it is the image, and that human spirit achieves the highest expression of its nature only to the degree that it is perfectly united with divine Spirit. That is, in Christ we see that the only possible end for any rational nature is divine, because such also is its ground; apart from God drawing us into ever more perfect union with himself, we do not exist at all. We are nothing but created gods coming to be, becoming God in God, able to become divine only because, in some sense, we are divine from the very first.

---

[36] Nicholas of Cusa, *De visione Dei*, XX (88), ed. Riemann, 70.
[37] Nicholas of Cusa, *De visione Dei*, XX (89), ed. Riemann, 70–71.

17

Coincident Unities

Nicholas of Cusa in Radical Orthodox Tradition

JOHN MILBANK

Nicholas of Cusa can be situated in a loose tradition of radicalized orthodoxy that has at once hovered on the margins of the officially acceptable and yet remained disconcertingly near the core transmission of Christian thought.[1] This tradition runs mainly from John Scottus Eriugena's blending of Maximus's metaphysics with the liberal arts techniques of Augustine and Boethius, up through Albert the Great and his German Dominican successors, including Meister Eckhart, as well as the heavily Boethian School of Chartres (and to a degree, also, the School of St. Victor) with important outliers in Robert Grosseteste, and at times Albert's more conventionally orthodox pupil, Thomas Aquinas. It is throughout marked by the Roman

---

[1] A longer version of this essay was previously published in *Why We Need Cusanus / Warum wir Cusanus brauchen*, ed. Enrico Peroli and Marco Moschini (Münster: Aschendorff Verlag, 2022), 43–90.

lay thinker Boethius's humanism and his readiness to express a Christian philosophy in an "anonymous" Platonic guise.²

Boethius is the key link between patristic and Scholastic theology, who conveyed a Platonic metaphysical legacy that both preceded and survived the huge influence of Arabic Aristotelianism, after the latter had fallen under some ecclesiastical suspicion. Eriugena, like his later disciples Amalric of Bena and David of Dinant (the latter, though not the former, half-exonerated at one point by Cusanus³), may have received official condemnation in the thirteenth century, but he was also the most important late synthesizer of patristic traditions; the most considerable mediator between Greek patristic thought and that of Augustine and Boethius; the most sophisticated theorist of realism regarding universals in relation to doctrine, logic, grammar, and ontology; and the most important Christian contributor to the Neoplatonic tradition.⁴ Albert was the most central initial thinker in the Christian absorption of Arabic philosophy, even though some of his later pupils fell under various degrees of suspicion and the relationship of the whole Albertist tradition to suspect Averroism was complex.⁵ As for Nicholas of Cusa himself, who blended all these currents with the ecumenical thought of the Catalan Ramon Llull, as mediated to him by the Flemish Albertist, Heymericus de Campo, he was a cardinal of the Church and, in the dawning Renaissance, managed to survive the imputations of heresy made against him by Johannes Wenck and others.⁶

---

2 See Claudio Moreschini, *A Christian in Toga. Boethius: Interpreter of Antiquity and Christian Theologian* (Göttingen: Vandenhoeck & Ruprecht, 2014).

3 Nicholas of Cusa, *Apologia doctae ignorantiae*, 29–30, in *Nicolai de Cusa Opera Omnia*, vol. II, ed. Raymond Klibansky (Leipzig: Felix Meiner Verlag, 1932), 19–21; and Nicholas of Cusa, *De non aliud*, XVII (81), in *Nicolai de Cusa Opera Omnia*, vol. XIII, ed. Ludwig Baur and Paul Wilpert (Leipzig: Felix Meiner Verlag, 1944), 42–43. Nicholas suggests in the *Apologia* that the works of David of Dinant (like those of Pseudo-Dionysius, Victorinus, Eriugena, and Berthold of Moosburg) should not be read by novices, who might misread their intentions. See further Matthew T. Gaetano, "Nicholas of Cusa and Pantheism in Early Modern Catholic Theology," in *Nicholas of Cusa and the Making of the Early Modern World*, ed. Simon J. G. Burton, Joshua Hollmann, and Eric M. Parker (Leiden: Brill, 2019), 199–228, who shows that Cusanus himself was not read as a "pantheist" before the nineteenth century.

4 See Christoph Erismann, *L'Homme Commune: La genèse du réalisme ontologique durant le haut Moyen Âge* (Paris: J. Vrin, 2011), 193–282; and John Marenbon, *From the Circle of Alcuin to the School of Auxerre: Logic, Theology and Philosophy in the Early Middle Ages* (Cambridge: Cambridge University Press, 1981), 67–115.

5 See Alain de Libera, *Métaphysique et noétique: Albert le Grand* (Paris: J. Vrin, 2005).

6 See Ramon Llull, *Ars Brevis*, in *Doctor Illuminatus: A Ramon Llull Reader*, trans. Anthony Bonner (Princeton, NJ: Princeton University Press, 1985), 297–364; Florian Hamann, *Das*

What most of all characterizes this loose but linked tradition? One could say that it is a determination to think through Christian doctrine in such a way that does not compromise divine unity and simplicity. In this respect a simultaneous fidelity was maintained to Neoplatonism as well as to Christianity; yet, by the same token, an equal fidelity was sustained to the biblical tradition of strict monotheism, philosophically regarded, in accordance with some impulses of the scriptures themselves. Given these commitments, specifically Christian doctrines of the Creation, the Fall, grace, the Trinity, and the Incarnation were never seen as qualifications of the divine unity and simplicity, any more than of monotheism. Instead, they were seen as intensifications of monotheism and a deepening of henology in such a way that the inherent paradoxes of the thought of ultimate unity are drawn to the fore.

In this tradition, the divine actions of creating, on the one hand, and of redeeming and elevating, on the other, are not separated; no distinction is made between metaphysical and "revealed" theology, the thinking of reason and the thinking of faith. God is to be understood from the outset as three-in-one, not just as philosophically "One" in a preliminary fashion that faith will later elaborate. The wisdom of reason and the wisdom of faith are held to coincide, along with the inspiration of oracular disclosures to prophets and visionaries of whatever tradition. The disclosure of Christ fulfills all other theophanies, and Christian teaching consummates all philosophy. It was only later, mainly under Islamic Arabic influence, that the notion of a distinction between "the theology of philosophy" and *sacra doctrina* started to intrude.[7]

Aquinas imposed this alien division in his early (and notably unfinished) commentary on Boethius's *De Trinitate* and even seems to have been largely responsible for the very notion of "revelation" as something contrasting with "reason," as opposed to earlier ideas of a theophanic and

---

Siegel der Ewigkeit: Universalwissenschaft und Konziliarismus bei Heymericus de Campo (Münster: Aschendorff Verlag, 2006), 129–46; and Johannes Wenck, *De ignota litteratura*, in *Complete Philosophical and Theological Writings of Nicholas of Cusa*, vol. 1, trans. Jasper Hopkins (Minneapolis: Arthur J. Banning Press, 2001), 425–56.

7 See Andreas Speer, "The Hidden Heritage: Boethian Metaphysics and Its Medieval Tradition," *Quaestio* 5 (2005): 163–81; and Andreas Speer, "The Division of Metaphysical Discourses: Boethius, Thomas Aquinas and Meister Eckhart," in *Philosophy and Theology in the Long Middle Ages*, ed. Kent Emery, Jr. (Leiden: Brill, 2011), 91–115. More integral and mystical traditions within Islam, like those within Judaism prior to the Renaissance reception, had little influence within the Latin West.

apocalyptic "making known" in various records of inspired disclosure that include pagan philosophical wisdom.[8] In practice, Aquinas did not pursue metaphysics in isolation from revealed theology and understood the dependence of this theology upon the self-knowledge of God and the participatory beatific vision of the blessed.[9] Nevertheless, his departure from Boethian integralism eventually allowed an extrinsicist view of revelation to arise, along with notions of a doubled beatitude, supernatural and purely natural. Both of these combined with an increasing marginalization of the philosophical significance of the Incarnation and Trinity that largely prevailed in the mainstream (despite Boehme, Comenius, and Leibniz) up until the time of Schelling and Hegel. Albert the Great, with greater loyalty to Pseudo-Dionysius, made it clear that the subject matter of Christian doctrine is the *sigillatio*, the symbolic enigma, which is divinely disclosed at once externally in things and inwardly to human minds.[10]

By contrast, across the long tradition of a "radicalized orthodoxy," the divine Trinity had been regarded as comprehensible in terms of a deeper understanding of the divine unity. Equally, the Incarnation had been regarded not as the result of a contingent divine decision, nor as occasioned by human sin, but rather as a perfection required by divine goodness and a necessary resolution of the apparent problem that finitude lies outside God. In this regard the case of Nicholas of Cusa is highly telling and remains vital today. For Cusanus, the drastic unity of all things is an integration or enfolding of Neoplatonist henology, Trinity, and Incarnation, all as modalities of the singular divine unity. Cusanus's ability to accomplish this is largely due to his novel approach to the arts of the trivium and quadrivium and particularly the relevance of mathematical thinking to Christian theology (another venerable Boethian legacy), which he absorbed mainly from Thierry of Chartres's recapitulation of Boethius and Augustine into the mathematical Trinity of *unitas, aequalitas,* and *connexio*.[11] Parts of this

---

[8] Thomas Aquinas, *In Boethiam de Trinitate*, q. 5, a. 4, quoted in Jean-Luc Marion, *D'ailleurs, la révélation* (Paris: Grasset, 2020), 72 (see 65–84 generally).

[9] John Milbank, "Manifestation and Procedure: Trinitarian Metaphysics after Albert the Great and Thomas Aquinas," in *Tomismo Creativo: Letture Contemporanee del "Doctor Communis"*, ed. Marco Salvioli, OP (Bologna: Edizioni Studio Domenicano, 2015), 41–117.

[10] Albertus Magnus, *Summa Theologiae*, I, Prol., S. 1, quoted in Hamann, *Das Siegel der Ewigkeit*, 69.

[11] On the sources of the mathematical Trinity, see especially: Augustine, *De doctrina christiana*, I.12 (V.5), ed. R. P. H. Green (Oxford: Clarendon, 1995), 16–17; Boethius, *De Trinitate*, III.6, in *De consolatione philosophiae. Opuscula theologica*, ed. Claudio Moreschini (Munich:

story I have already treated elsewhere.[12] Here I show how Nicholas on his own terms uses the *coincidentia oppositorum* to intensify and deepen the divine unity manifested in the Trinity and the Incarnation.

The Trinitarian Unity of Opposites

The mathematicization of Trinitarian doctrine in Cusanus and its connection with numerical repetition was first developed by the Chartrians. Following Boethius, they linked the latter's Trinitarian theology with mathematical reflections, and then both with the Augustinian mathematical triad. If Thierry spoke in more affective terms of a mutual *appetitio* between unity and equality, Cusanus significantly underscored the linkage between the figure of numerical repetition on the one hand and the figure of substantive interpersonal relation on the other.[13] In other words, unity is unthinkable without its reflective self-sustaining through iteration, although the pure reflection of absolute unity is no "doubling" that would compromise its simplicity. In this way, even though infinite repetition in God is uniquely an identical one, it remains the case for Cusanus that only the supplement of repetition paradoxically establishes the original unity; in this regard he anticipates Hegel, Kierkegaard, and Péguy. The multiplication of the divine One is not an incidental doubling of the self-sufficient, since reflection takes place only through a co-original substantive generation and

---

K. G. Saur, 2005), 179–81; Thierry of Chartres, *Tractatus de sex dierum operibus*, 36–47, in *Commentaries on Boethius by Thierry of Chartres and His School*, ed. Nikolaus M. Häring (Toronto: Pontifical Institute of Mediaeval Studies, 1971), 570–75; and Pseudo-Bede, *Commentarius Victorinus*, 81, in *Commentaries on Boethius*, ed. Häring, 498. For studies, see Rudolf Haubst, *Das Bild des Einen und Dreieinen Gottes in der Welt nach Nikolaus von Kues* (Trier: Paulinus Verlag, 1952), 203–54; and David Albertson, *Mathematical Theologies: Nicholas of Cusa and the Legacy of Thierry of Chartres* (New York: Oxford University Press, 2014), 93–139.

12 See John Milbank, "From *Mathesis* to *Methexis*: Nicholas of Cusa's Post-Nominalist Realism," in *Participation et vision de Dieu chez Nicolas de Cues*, ed. Isabelle Moulin (Paris: J. Vrin, 2017), 143–69; and John Milbank, "Writing and the Order of Learning," *Philosophy, Theology and the Sciences* 4, no. 1 (2017): 46–73.

13 Thierry of Chartres, *Lectiones in Boethii Librum De Trinitate*, VII.7, in *Commentaries on Boethius*, ed. Häring, 225. Cf. Nicholas of Cusa, *De docta ignorantia*, I.8–9 (22–26), in *Nikolaus von Kues: Philosophisch-Theologische Werke*, vol. 1, ed. Paul Wilpert and Hans Gerhard Senger, rev. ed. (Hamburg: Felix Meiner Verlag, 2002), 30–36; and Nicholas of Cusa, *De aequalitate*, 24, in *Nicolai de Cusa Opera Omnia*, vol. X/1, ed. Hans Gerhard Senger (Hamburg: Felix Meiner Verlag, 2001), 31–33.

procession. Nicholas of Cusa's Trinitarian metaphysics is able to think a supplement at the origin that is not a betrayal.

At the same time, the addition of Boethian-Chartrian repetition to Augustinian relation serves to convey Cusanus's striking insistence on the divine *Tri-Unity*, as opposed to any excessively orthodox insistence that God is one only in essence, and three only in person or hypostasis. He does not, of course, deny this orthodoxy, but, like Aquinas, insists that these distinctions are only according to our limited, for him "conjectural," mode of finite understanding.[14] In an incomprehensible way, God is "united," in excess of our contrast of threefold substantive diversity and essential unity.

Nicholas's mathematical (but also grammatical and categorial) theology of the divine Tri-Unity is articulated in full keeping with his doctrine of the coincident unity of opposites. The latter is for him a development of Dionysian teaching in *Divine Names* and other works, besides being a Christianization of the alternative Hermetic logic of the *Asclepius*.[15] Any affirmative statement about God implies logically an exclusion of both opposite and incompatible terms. For this reason, no affirmation is adequate to God: even "true" and "good" are false in relation to him as implying automatically "not good" and "not true," or excellences other than good or true. Negations are in this sense more adequate: because God is simple, they necessarily imply the negation of logical exclusions as well. Even as Being, God cannot be thought of as not not-being; he is beyond the contrast of being and nothingness, potency and act, unity and multiplicity. For this reason, a higher name for him even than Unity (which can comprise non-being as well as Being) is *non aliud*, by which Cusanus does not just offer a synonym for "the same," but implies that even difference in God is also "not difference" at all.

From this perspective one can see, first, that most Cusan accounts of the Trinity and Trinitarian ontology are *variants* of the mathematical Trinity; second, that the thesis of the mathematical Trinity is not really *different* from the thesis of the coincidence of opposites; and third, that both in turn are not really *different* from the thesis that God is self-generating life (a kind of eminent "self-creation"—with all due apophatic

---

14 Nicholas of Cusa, *De pace fidei*, VII (19–21), in *Nicolai de Cusa Opera Omnia*, vol. VII, ed. Raymond Klibansky and Hildebrand Bascour, 2nd ed. (Hamburg: Felix Meiner Verlag, 1970), 18–21. It is of course striking that Cusanus says this in the context of interreligious dialogue.

15 See Florian Ebeling, *The Secret History of Hermes Trismegistus: Hermeticism from Ancient to Modern Times*, trans. David Lorton (Ithaca, NY: Cornell University Press, 2007), 139–41.

qualification—as Nicholas explicitly declares) more than that he is pure unity or pure actuality.[16]

First, just as God as Not-Other encompasses God as both paternal One and filial "Other" as equality, so likewise God as *possest* involves the thought that nothing actual can exist unless it is possible, and yet only the actual can actualize the possible.[17] The entire field of possibility is the ultimate "One," and yet it is only more than nothing (which it "is" in itself) insofar as it is always already actualized, or in other words repeated or equalized in its very possibility. The *posse ipsum* of Cusanus's final writings is really a vital, active power that describes the divine essence, but as such is also the Trinitarian "possibility of making" and "possibility of being made" and their necessary union.[18] These relatively active and passive possibilities are variously ascribed by Nicholas either to the Father or the Son respectively; in either case one sees that an active power is involved, which must be thought as a relational equality of unity lest divine simplicity be compromised.

Second, Nicholas is able to think "Tri-Unity" beyond the sheer dislocation of the personal and essential registers because he takes "deifying" essence as totally coinciding with its instantiation as three divine persons (in contrast to Gilbert of Poitiers's "particularizing" of essence, even in the case of God).[19] Universal and particular are contraries that coincide, and yet (one can extrapolate) this is, for Cusanus, not just a static coincidence. They coincide as dynamic life, since God transcends the opposition of rest and motion, and therefore coincidence is found in the "moving" life of the three persons who repeat the unity of the essence, which is also the

---

16 "It is no more absurd to say that God creates Himself and all other things than [it is to say that] God sees himself and all other things." Nicholas of Cusa, *De theologicis complementis*, 14, in *Nicolai de Cusa Opera Omnia*, vol. X/2a, ed. Heide Dorothea Riemann and Karl Bormann (Hamburg: Felix Meiner Verlag, 1994), 82; trans. Jasper Hopkins, *Nicholas of Cusa: Metaphysical Speculations* (Minneapolis: Arthur J. Banning Press, 1998), 772.

17 Nicholas of Cusa, *Trialogus de possest*, 6, in *Nicolai de Cusa Opera Omnia*, vol. XI/2, ed. Renata Steiger (Hamburg: Felix Meiner Verlag, 1973), 6–8.

18 Nicholas of Cusa, *Compendium*, X (29–31), in *Nicolai de Cusa Opera Omnia*, vol. XI/3, ed. Bruno Decker and Karl Bormann (Hamburg: Felix Meiner Verlag, 1964), 23–25; and Nicholas of Cusa, *De apice theoriae*, 26, in *Nicolai de Cusa Opera Omnia*, vol. XII, ed. Raymond Klibansky and Hans Gerhard Senger (Hamburg: Felix Meiner Verlag, 1982), 135.

19 See John Marenbon, "Gilbert of Poitiers," in *A History of Twelfth-Century Western Philosophy*, ed. Peter Dronke (Cambridge: Cambridge University Press, 1992), 328–52. One can think of Gilbert as the opposite of "radically orthodox," namely "conservatively heterodox," in his threatening of divine simplicity, as noted by William of St. Thierry. The technical radicalism of the Chartrians restored a rigorous orthodoxy against Gilbert's distortions of Boethius.

originating unity of the Father. The Son cannot be "other" to the Father, or the Spirit to either, since the Son is equal to the Father's unity and the Spirit is the equality of the equal with the unity; their respective "otherness" is also Not-Other. This dynamic conception of the Trinity implies that rather than being eternally without duration, God is rather an eminent and paradoxical duration. As eternal repetition and generative life, God cannot be simply "without beginning," but instead is an eternal "beginning without beginning," besides a "beginning that is begun" and "that which is begun from both of these beginnings."[20] Only the paradoxical coincidence of the eternal with its commencements beyond the sway of the Law of Non-Contradiction (LNC) allows us to think of God as both eminently eventful life and yet also simply unchanging.

Third, the mathematical Trinity and the coincidence of opposites both coincide with the view of God as "self-creating," which grounds Nicholas of Cusa's entire and entirely novel (but proto-Bergsonian) metaphysics of *creativity*, rather than unity, being, modal possibility, or existential actuality. Both concepts involve the repetitive-relational coincidence of making with makeability, which in created imaging may imply either the action of shaping form on passive matter, or of a subjective maker of artifacts or signs out of already given material. God is at once, beyond the LNC, equally artist and artifact, a Trinitarian contradictoriness.

Everything else, from pure matter up to spiritual beings, is a dynamic sharing in what for finitude is an impossibility of such coincidence, keeping everything in tensional motion. Despite the full operation of the LNC in the finite realm, finite things still encounter and to a degree transgress these bounds of sense in order to be coherently articulated. Fire does not itself burn, says Cusanus, just as heat is not of itself hot, and the essences of things have nothing apparently in common with their accidents by which alone we recognize their presence, even though these essences are required to explain the coherence of the things we encounter.[21] The unburning somehow is the burning; accidents are somehow modes of substance, identical with

---

20 Nicholas of Cusa, *De principio [Tu quis es]*, 11, in *Nicolai de Cusa Opera Omnia*, vol. X/2b, ed. Karl Bormann and Heide Dorothea Riemann (Hamburg: Felix Meiner Verlag, 1988), 13–14; trans. Hopkins, *Metaphysical Speculations*, 883.

21 Nicholas of Cusa, *De venatione sapientiae*, XXXIX (118–22), in *Nicolai de Cusa Opera Omnia*, vol. XII, ed. Raymond Klibansky and Hans Gerhard Senger (Hamburg: Felix Meiner Verlag, 1982), 109–12.

substance, even though they are by definition opposite, just as all effects *are* their causes, even though they cannot be.

Similarly, when I imagine or think "fire," I do not get any hotter, even though (as for Aristotle) the form of fire in my imagination and mind is the same as the form in reality.[22] Cusanus agrees with Eckhart that we can know anything only through the (Keatsian) negative capability of *not* being that thing, rendering knowledge a mode of non-being and nothingness. Yet this nothing and non-embodied form is *none other* than the actuality of embodied form (or else thought would be merely the "encounter" that is sensation, as Plotinus and Augustine showed).[23] In the same way, the intended spoon in the spoon-maker's mind is the entire causal reality of the physically formed spoon, and yet the latter is, as Nicholas famously declares in *Idiota de mente*, an entirely *new* thing, as much emergent from "nothing" (in the sense that no such "thing" was present before) as any other finitely created, and immanently co-created, reality.[24] For Nicholas, to sense, imagine, understand, intuit, and create all involve paradoxical leaps between incommensurate and yet mutually dependent realms.[25]

Precisely because the intellectual work of God himself is "contradictory," he creates multiplicity entirely through the "non-otherness" of unity, equality, and their union. For this reason, Nicholas denies that alterity constitutes any positive reality at work in bringing about created divergences: "otherness is not anything. That the sky is not the earth is because the sky is

---

[22] Nicholas of Cusa, *Compendium*, IV (9), ed. Decker and Bormann, 8; cf. *Compendium*, VII (19), ed. Decker and Bormann, 14–16.

[23] See, e.g., Augustine of Hippo, *De Genesi ad litteram*, VII.1–21, in Corpus Scriptorum Ecclesiasticorum Latinorum [CSEL] 28, ed. Joseph Zycha (Vienna: Hölder-Pichler-Tempsky, 1894), 200–219; trans. John Hammond Taylor, SJ, *The Literal Meaning of Genesis*, vol. 2 (New York: Newman Press, 1982), 3–23.

[24] Nicholas of Cusa, *Idiota de mente*, II (59–65), in *Nicolai de Cusa Opera Omnia*, vol. V, ed. Renate Steiger (Hamburg: Felix Meiner Verlag, 1983), 93–101.

[25] One recalls how the twelfth-century Boethians attached psychic degrees to the same modes of being that Cusanus explicitly and frequently invokes: imagination to the fluidity of prime matter, sometimes named *sylva*; sense to the everyday realm of formed things; reason (or with Thierry himself the lower aspect of intellect) to the shaping power of the formation of things, named by Thierry *necessitas complexionis*; and intellect to the knowledge of the absolute necessity, which is God. See Alan of Lille, "Sermon on the Intelligible Sphere," in *Literary Works*, ed. and trans. Winthrop Wetherbee (Cambridge, MA: Harvard University Press, 2013), 1–19; and Thierry of Chartres, *Lectiones*, II.6–14, in *Commentaries on Boethius*, ed. Häring, 156–59.

not infinity itself, which embraces all being."[26] Trinitarian contradictoriness also appears in the way the real point without space is "not other" than the geometric point that the geometer requires in order to think it.[27] The difference between things is only a negative contrast, and so no positive creative force of othering is at work. The latter is rather a merely negative mark of created limitation or "contraction": *omnis determinatio est negatio*.

There might seem to be a real resemblance to Hegel here, but Cusanus is not saying that logical negativity as such generates the positive content of each thing. Negation on its own does no perversely positive work (as for Hegel); rather, positive content proceeds immediately as an expression of divine plenitude, limited only by the negativity of contraction manifested as variegated difference (as in Spinoza). Indeed, beyond the *via negativa*, says Cusanus in his later work, and even beyond "unknowing," we must declare most of all that God is the "affirmativeness of the affirmation."[28] If, within the contracted or explicated finite domain, otherness is therefore negation, in God, inversely, negation is "not other," and yet not "the same," insofar as the Father is not the Son is not the Holy Spirit. Here also these personal differences are produced, not by a dialectical unfolding, but by repetition, (quasi-) reflection, relation, and development, ensuring that one thinks entirely in terms of Tri-Unity rather than merely "Trinity."

In this way, the Tri-Unity involves a coincidence of opposites. God is internally both different and not-different, one and many, existence and essence: somehow at the same time and in the same way both single essence and diverse persons, even though these ontological "levels" must be distinguished by our affirmative discourse and are for that discourse incompatible. By the same token, God is the coincidence of essential indistinctness and personal distinctness. God is also "uncontracted," yet supremely

---

26 Nicholas of Cusa, *De visione Dei*, XIV (58), in *Nicolai de Cusa Opera Omnia*, vol. VI, ed. Heide Dorothea Riemann (Hamburg: Felix Meiner Verlag, 2000), 49; trans. Jasper Hopkins, *Nicholas of Cusa's Dialectical Mysticism: Text, Translation, and Interpretive Study of "De Visione Dei"*, 2nd ed. (Minneapolis: Arthur J. Banning Press, 1988), 707 (caveat: Hopkins's chapter numbers differ).

27 Thierry of Chartres, *Lectiones*, II.52–53, in *Commentaries on Boethius*, ed. Häring, 171–72. Cf. Dronke, "Thierry of Chartres," in *A History of Twelfth-Century Western Philosophy*, 358–85.

28 Nicholas of Cusa, *De non aliud*, Prop. 13 (119), ed. Baur and Wilpert, 63. One is reminded of Achard of St. Victor and his dream-like sense that the realm of God is but our world seen as it really is. Achard came to the famous Abbey of St. Victor in Paris directly from the obscurity of Bridlington Priory and was almost certainly English, perhaps a native of the East Riding of Yorkshire.

contracted or distinct. Nor, if we follow Eckhart, can God as the infinite really be "bounded" from the finite: according to Dionysius, he must be the coincidence of the infinite with the finite and so, says Eriugena, also of the negative with the affirmative.[29]

The long tradition of naming God, commenced by Dionysius and radicalized by Eriugena, had a far more ontological bearing than often is allowed by modern commentators. The affirmative names are not primarily the names *we* give, but the names God gives himself by "uttering" creatures, names that therefore fully belong to him. Just for this reason, as Cusanus says, each creature exists by praising God and re-uttering its own name, and human beings do this most intensely, though exploratively.[30] Equally, negation is less our despairing gesture of failure than it is in part the real character of the infinite God, who *lacks* bounds and is as much potential as actuality.[31]

This raises the question of how the ontologically negative God who creates relates to the ontologically affirmative one who is created, according to Cusanus (following Eriugena), since God is one and simple. For the most part, the coincidence of opposites in Nicholas of Cusa appears to mark the difference of the infinite from the finite. It is true that the finite, including the universe itself, is seen as aporetically running out into the infinite at its extreme and problematically self-defining *termini*—thus, for example, we can define the real ideal triangle (a figure of the Trinity) only as an infinite triangle, which is by that token an infinite straight line and also every other geometrical figure.[32] Nonetheless, as we have seen, Cusanus typically upholds the LNC as delimiting finite definition itself and sees it as mysteriously and apophatically violated only in the case of the infinite, which is also, significantly, said to be "above" the coincidence of contraries.[33] Despite the ways in which the coincidence of opposites appears to intrude at the outer and inner borders of the finite when the finite reaches

---

29 See Milbank, "From *Mathesis* to *Methexis*."

30 Nicholas of Cusa, *De venatione sapientiae*, XVIII-XIX (52–55), ed. Klibansky and Senger, 49–53. Nicholas says that doxology is one of the ten primary "fields of wisdom," the others being *docta ignorantia*, *possest*, *non aliud*, light, oneness, equality, union, delimitation, and order.

31 Negative theology originally *derived* from mathematical considerations in Alcinous: see Albertson, *Mathematical Theologies*, 49–50.

32 Nicholas of Cusa, *De docta ignorantia*, I.14–15 (37–41), ed. Wilpert and Senger, 52–56.

33 Nicholas of Cusa, *De visione Dei*, XIII (53), ed. Riemann, 46.

the indefinite margin or crosses indefinite gulfs of the incommensurable, Nicholas is frequently at pains to insist on the absolute and unbridgeable gulf fixed between the finite and the absolute infinite, the creation and the Creator.

Christology is certainly absent from *De coniecturis*, so it can be tempting to suppose that here Cusanus adopts a more Platonic and Chartrian account of metaphysical mediation, in contrast to the Christological mediation of *De docta ignorantia*.[34] Yet much later on, in *Dialogus de ludo globi*, he combines both modes of mediation and yet clearly indicates he has not abandoned Thierry's radicalism, especially as he now explicitly names

---

34 Albertson thinks that these were two alternative theses about mediation, even if they were later blended in *Dialogus de ludo globi*: see *Mathematical Theologies*, 217–35. This seems to be because he himself reads Thierry of Chartres's second mode (*necessitas complexionis*) as compromising the reach of divine omnipotence and thinks it is eventually embraced by Cusanus only when translated from ontological terms into epistemological ones of degrees of ascent of the mathematicizing human mind (230). Yet this would appear to involve a still somewhat Kantian reading of the later Cusanus, after Kurt Flasch and many others, despite Albertson's general and admirable refusal of this view. Such an overall construal is linked to an apparent tendency to ascribe a "literal," as it were pre-Platonic Pythagoreanism to both Thierry and Nicholas, such that the "pagan" element removed by Nicholas is taken to be the Platonic rather than the Pythagorean one. Correspondingly, in either case—but in Nicholas eventually post-*De coniecturis*—it is supposed that both authors link mathematics to *intellectus* rather than to *ratio*. Albertson contends that in *De coniecturis*, Nicholas cannot exalt the second mode without reducing the theological role of mathematics, confined to *ratio* (216). Instead, I would argue that both writers see the second mode as ontological and cosmic, but that neither thinks that our numbers literally rather than symbolically reach God. Thus, for both authors, once more (as with the whole Boethian tradition and as with Alan of Lille), it is *theology* alone that is fully associated with the intellect, and mathematics is only hyper-rationally intellectual to the degree that it ventures onto the symbolic but really and genuinely paradoxical margins of the mathematical realm. See Thierry of Chartres, *Glosa Victoriana*, II.16, in *Commentaries on Boethius*, ed. Häring, 543, which rather clarifies *Commentum super Boethii librum de Trinitate*, II.9, in *Commentaries on Boethius*, ed. Häring, 71. See also Dronke, "Thierry of Chartres," in *A History of Twelfth-Century Western Philosophy*, 370–71. Thus at *Glosa supra Boethii librum de Trinitate*, II.27, in *Commentaries on Boethius*, ed. Häring, 274, Thierry distinguishes between the true *intelligibilitas* (his coinage) of God, or "absolute necessity," as studied by theology and the "less dignified" *intelligentia* or *disciplina* of mathematics, which considers "the necessity of connexion" (*necessitas complexionis*), which is the generative confinement of things and categories to number in the created world, as similarly understood by Cusanus. Then physics, along with sense and imagination, deals with both determinate and absolute possibility. By contrast, Alan of Lille ("Sermon on the Intelligible Sphere," in *Literary Works*, 10–14) more schematically links physics to sense, mathematics to reason, and theology to intellect—and imagination, as with Thierry, to matter.

the second mode *necessitas complexionis*.³⁵ But this had never consisted, for Thierry himself, in any denial of the absolute gulf between God and creation, nor of the total and unmediated reach of divine power. Rather, it merely suggested that the four modes are four perspectives on the same *rerum universitas*, in a way that clearly recalls the radicalism of Eriugena's fourfold division of one "Nature," which includes God himself.³⁶

In the case of both the twelfth- and the fifteenth-century philosopher, one should understand this as an attempt to reckon with the contradiction that nothing outside God can really be outside God. It follows that from one ultimate perspective, *complicatio* asymmetrically governs *explicatio* much as Boethian Providence governs Boethian fate; yet from another, equally ultimate perspective, there is indeed a reciprocal involvement of enfolding in unfolding as much as vice-versa, this being yet another Trinitarian and paradoxical truth.³⁷ What is not God is fully real, and yet as such it cannot be simply "other" to the omnipotent and omnipresent God, who is all in all. Eventually we will see how for Cusanus the Christological mode of mediation fits with the mediations carried through by the modes.

At the same time, Nicholas *relies* on the LNC, following Zeno, to oppose the idea that there could be a plural absolute: "it is evident that there is not a plurality of *beings* that exist utterly apart from the One. For since they would not partake of the One, they would at one and the same time, and in the same respect, be *like* and *unlike*."³⁸ Similarly, "if heat were *per se* what it is, then it would make itself hot. And thus it would be both hot and

---

35 Nicholas of Cusa, *Dialogus de ludo globi*, I (40), in *Nicolai de Cusa Opera Omnia*, vol. IX, ed. Hans Gerhard Senger (Hamburg: Felix Meiner Verlag, 1998), 45–46. Nicholas had already used Thierry's term for the second mode: see Nicholas of Cusa, *Idiota de mente*, XIII (146), ed. Steiger, 199.

36 "In God all things are God, in an intelligence all things are intellect; in a soul all things are soul; in a body all things are body." Nicholas of Cusa, *De coniecturis*, I.4 (15), in *Nicolai de Cusa Opera Omnia*, vol. III, ed. Karl Bormann and Hans Gerhard Senger (Hamburg: Felix Meiner Verlag, 1972), 20; trans. Hopkins, *Metaphysical Speculations*, 169. These four divisions are ontological as well as cognitive ones: "the world is threefold: a small world, that is *man*, a maximum world that is *God*, and a large world that is called *universe*." Nicholas of Cusa, *Dialogus de ludo globi*, I (42), ed. Senger, 47; trans. Hopkins, *Metaphysical Speculations*, 1201.

37 See Albertson, *Mathematical Theologies*, 126–39, 228–35.

38 Nicholas of Cusa, *De principio [Tu quis es]*, 7, ed. Bormann and Riemann, 6; trans. Hopkins, 881. One could argue, as does Alain Badiou, that an ontology of the multiple beyond unity suppresses its violation of the LNC and renders impossible an *apophasis* beyond both violation and non-violation. Qualified transcendent monism that allows difference, ever since Plato's *Parmenides*, has preserved such *apophasis*.

not-hot."[39] The violation of the LNC here is absurd since it remains within the finite, and yet any absolutizing of the limited involves just such an absurdity. The exceeding of the LNC in the infinite is, by comparison, not absurd, and this includes the "contradictory" identity of "making hot" with "heat" already considered, just because this is a making hot of finite heat by the form of heat, which has its ultimate identity in the infinite and eternal. Nonetheless, the linkage here of the LNC to the ultimate One reveals that what Cusanus really teaches is the entirely apophatic "coincidence of opposites with their non-coincidence."

On account of this unbridgeable *apophasis*, there is no coincidence of infinite with finite for Cusanus, any more than there is coincidence purely within the finite. Nor is there any coincidence of the infinite realm, where opposition and difference diminish to the point of collapse, with the finite realm, where they hold uncontested tenure. Or at least, on a first reading of Cusanus, that *seems* to be the case. The coincidence of opposites applies fully only to the infinite and especially to the Tri-Unity. But a closer reading reveals that there is, after all, a second coincidence between the infinite and the finite, or between opposition and non-opposition, between the *non aliud* and negative difference, between the divine original and the created theophanic image. This coincidence is inseparable from Nicholas of Cusa's Christology, which turns out to be the ultimate core of his philosophy.

The Christological Unity of Opposites

We can speak of a Trinitarian unity of opposites in Cusanus, and then of a Christological one. The first is the coincidence of one essence with three hypostases or persons; the second is the coincidence of two essences, despite their absolutely incommensurable separation, only through a single hypostasis or substance, in strict accordance with orthodox dogma. But a coincidence of the infinite with the finite in Cusanus has already been intimated in the previous section. The coincidence of opposites impinges not just at the margins of the finite but within its constitutive gaps. It is subject to degrees insofar as the senses absolutely adhere to the LNC, but reason can think at least two opposites at once, while the intellect already glimpses their coincidence, even while remaining baffled: only in God is

---

[39] Nicholas of Cusa, *De principio [Tu quis es]*, 4, ed. Bormann and Riemann, 4; trans. Hopkins, 880.

the coincidence fully realized and transparent. What is more, in *De docta ignorantia*, Cusanus invokes a coincidence of complication with explication and of the divine descent with the human ascent.[40]

In *De visione Dei*, Nicholas goes further, and now speaks of God as hidden behind the wall of Paradise, which is impenetrably composed of the coincidence of opposites.[41] Behind this wall, there not only lies the negative infinite, wherein everything collapses into everything else, there also lies the mystery of how God is both negatively within himself and yet goes affirmatively out of himself. Thus Cusanus explicitly states that on the outskirts of this Paradise and not just externally, the divine *complicatio* or enfolding within himself is at one with the divine *explicatio*, or unfolding, which is the emanative process of Creation: "Trusting in your help O Lord, I turn once again in order to find you beyond the wall of the coincidence of enfolding and unfolding."[42] But as this quotation implies, he goes further and follows Eriugena in saying that within Paradise God exceeds even the coincidence of the creating God and the "created God" which is all finite things: "when I see You-who-are-God in Paradise, which this wall of the coincidence of opposites surrounds, I see that you neither fold nor unfold.... For both separating and conjoining are the wall of coincidence, beyond which you dwell, free of whatever can be either spoken of or thought of."[43] In Eriugena this contrast is mediated by the "creating and created" powers of the primordial causes, what Thierry and Nicholas call the "necessity of connection," or world-soul. What Cusanus adds, especially in *Idiota de mente*, is that humanity as the very image of God brings this work to fruition by finitely repeating, as the human production of signs, numbers, art, technology, religion, and the whole of culture, the divine capacity for origination itself.[44]

---

40 Nicholas of Cusa, *De coniecturis*, II.1 (78), ed. Bormann and Senger, 76–77. See also Nicholas of Cusa, *Dialogus de genesi*, I (149), in *Nicolai de Cusa Opera Omnia*, vol. IV, ed. Paul Wilpert (Hamburg: Felix Meiner Verlag, 1959), 108–9.

41 Nicholas of Cusa, *De visione Dei*, X-XII (38–50), ed. Riemann, 35–43.

42 Nicholas of Cusa, *De visione Dei*, XI (45), ed. Riemann, 40; trans. Hopkins, 701.

43 Nicholas of Cusa, *De visione Dei*, XI (45), ed. Riemann, 40; trans. Hopkins, 701.

44 See Milbank, "From *Mathesis* to *Methexis*." This intensifies the "ontological turn to the subject" ever since Socrates, which has nothing to do with the "epistemological turn to the subject" in Kant. The former, in its intensified, Cusan version, is about a human external addition to reality under the lure of teleology intrinsic to our true emerging works themselves; the latter is about a supposedly narcissistic confinement within our own fated internal construal of the outer world, which can never appear to us as it is in itself.

But this new coincidence of the infinite with the finite, and its surpassing, is introduced by him in a specifically Christological context in this treatise, *De visione Dei*, concerning the face of God, which is always taken to be the face of Christ. It is especially Christ who dwells serenely behind the wall of Paradise, and it is said that the eye of faith and of love can see *beyond* the work even of the intuitive intellect (never mind the discursive reason), somehow over or through this wall.[45] When Nicholas states in *De coniecturis* that the intellect can grasp without grasping (alone possible for God) the union of opposites—being more satisfied by the ever-yet-to-be-comprehended than by either the totally comprehended or the sheerly incomprehensible—he implies that faith intensifies intellectual life toward a greater unity with the divine perspective itself.[46] Alluding to John's gospel, Cusanus speaks of Christ as the door into Paradise by which one goes constantly in and out, thereby revealing that it is specifically Christ who secures the coincidence of explication and complication.[47]

This securing, however, has for Nicholas a prior ground in the Trinity, since he sometimes speaks of the Son and the Spirit as "explicating" or unfolding what is enfolded or complicated within the Father. More commonly the entire Godhead is spoken of as a *complicatio*, and *explicatio* is normally reserved for the aeonic-temporal and the spatial laying-out of the creation by degrees.[48] Thereby a certain anticipation of this sequence and diversity is involved in the eternal generation of the Son and the procession of the Spirit. Indeed, unless one realizes that for Nicholas there is also an infinite *explicatio* in God and that there cannot be, even in God, a pure *contractio* without it, one will fail to see that his metaphysics is fully Trinitarian precisely because modal or hypostatic unfolding is not literally an unravelling, as if of a ball of wool, but rather (as for Neoplatonism in

---

[45] Nicholas of Cusa, *De visione Dei*, XVII (75), ed. Riemann, 83. See also Nicholas's Sermons *Mutifarie Multisque Modis*, 7–14; in *Nicholas of Cusa's Didactic Sermons: A Selection*, trans. Jasper Hopkins (Loveland, CO: Arthur J. Banning Press, 2008), 22–26; and *Fides autem Catholica*, 5–16; in *Nicholas of Cusa's Didactic Sermons*, trans. Hopkins, 96–100. I cite by title and paragraph using Hopkins's translations.

[46] See Nicholas of Cusa, *De coniecturis*, II.1 (78), ed. Bormann and Senger, 76–77.

[47] Nicholas of Cusa, *De visione Dei*, XX (88–89), ed. Riemann, 69–70.

[48] "In eternity the center eternally begets, or unfolds, from its own unfolding power a consubstantial begotten thing, viz. the line, and the center with the line eternally unfolds the union, or circumference." Nicholas of Cusa, *De theologicis complementis*, 6, ed. Riemann and Bormann, 30; trans. Hopkins, 756.

general, though for its pagan versions beneath the level of the absolute One) an unanticipated creative and novel development.[49]

This particular fluidity in the habitual technical vocabulary of Cusanus can be matched with the fluidity already referenced in relation to *contractio*: normally this seems to imply the finite limitation of the infinite and so to be coterminous with explication. Yet *contractio* is also something of a mediating term: the relatively more "complicated" seminal reasons or immanent creative powers are also said to be more "contracted," in the sense of being more concentrated than the unfolded individual works to which they give rise. For this reason, the supreme divine complication itself can also be understood as the supreme contraction.

The fluctuating usage of the latter term suggests a still more mysterious coincidence of enfolding with unfolding, and a surpassing of even this coincidence, beyond the mystery of the singular enfolding of all the unfolded. It also suggests that this coincidence is, to a degree, Trinitarian before it is Christological. There *is* no original inclusion without elaboration first as an artistic, making power, and then as the fully realized artistic work of the Spirit. In the eternal beginning stands not just the lone potential artist, but the artist with his unfolding vision and his accomplished operation. The Trinity is the spiritual unity of *posse* with *aequalitas* or of active power with form, which for Nicholas develops the Boethian account of God as *forma essendi*.[50]

In this account, God is not just supreme Being, participation in which ensures for Boethius (as for Aquinas after him) that creatures "are" good in themselves, since existence, as much as goodness, is only borrowed and shared.[51] God is also supreme form and essence, which guarantees that

---

49 One could argue that the number 1, though transcendent to all later numbers, does not as the mere number 1 in the number line pre-contain all later numbers and arithmetic results. This is why, for Wittgenstein, the reduction of mathematics to logic fails: 2 + 2 = 4 is absolutely true only when it "occurs" and becomes apparent: nothing logically prior determines its ineluctability.

50 Nicholas of Cusa, *Compendium*, X-XI (34–35), ed. Decker and Bormann, 26–28.

51 See Boethius, *Quomodo Substantiae [De Hebdomadibus]*, in *De consolatione philosophiae. Opuscula theologica*, ed. Moreschini, 186–94. Cf. Thomas Aquinas, *An Exposition of the "On the Hebdomads" of Boethius*, trans. James L. Schultz and Edward A. Synan (Washington, DC: The Catholic University of America Press, 1992). Moreschini rightly rejects any "Thomist existentialist" reading of Boethian *esse* as entirely lacking in form (*A Christian in Toga*, 74–76). Yet he supports John Marenbon's historically implausible view, given the Platonic framework and how Boethius was later read, that it involves no inherent divine transcendence, rendering it more like Aquinas's immanent *ens commune*. The point is rather that God as *esse* is not a

creaturely participation cannot be merely existential, as if the essential qualities of creatures were not also taken from God. In this way, the Boethian metaphysics clearly forbids any idea that created essences are "purely natural."[52] Thus Cusanus writes that "in every existing thing the form *is* the being, so that the very form that gives being *is* the being which is given to the thing."[53] But for Nicholas this participation at once in divine Being and divine Form is also "horizontally" dynamic and Trinitarian: "the True Being, by means of a likeness to itself, bestows being on all things." He elaborates with a quotation from Albert the Great's commentary on Dionysius: "from the First, one Form flows into all things. This Form is the likeness of the essence of the First, and through it all things partake of being that is derived from the First."[54]

This sharing in the existentially potent genesis of form in God is also a matter of sharing in supreme *life*: "a true and living oneness which enfolds all things." All life, infinite and finite, "without which there is no joy and no eternal perfection," is declared to be "triune," and the most perfect life, "most perfectly triune." Thus in God "the Possibility-to-live is so omnipotent that from itself it begets a Life of its own. From these [two] proceeds Eternal Joy, the spirit of Love."[55] Alternatively put: "in God generation and procession ... [are] a movement of infinite fecundity, whose measuring standard is eternity," rather than time.[56]

---

quod est, like all created things, but is still the supreme *forma essendi*, source of all their particularity and so himself hyper-formal. This is how Boethius is read by Thierry and Nicholas.

52 It is possible to read Aquinas as still adhering to this full Boethian account of participation (for example, he speaks of *forma dat esse*), but in the Chartrians and Cusanus it is clearer. One can argue that although the core of Aquinas's metaphysics of *esse* is Boethian, he does not sufficiently embrace the full dimensions of this metaphysics in the way that Eckhart and Cusanus do.

53 Nicholas of Cusa, *De dato patris luminum*, II (98), in *Nicolai de Cusa Opera Omnia*, vol. IV, ed. Paul Wilpert (Hamburg: Felix Meiner Verlag, 1959), 72–73. See also Nicholas of Cusa, *Trialogus de possest*, 12–14, ed. Steiger, 14–18; and Sermon *Ubi es qui Natus est?*, 17, in *Nicholas of Cusa's Didactic Sermons*, trans. Hopkins, 253.

54 Nicholas of Cusa, *De beryllo*, 18, in *Nicolai de Cusa Opera Omnia*, vol. XI/1, ed. Hans Gerhard Senger and Karl Bormann (Hamburg: Felix Meiner Verlag, 1988), 21–22; trans. Hopkins, *Metaphysical Speculations*, 799.

55 Nicholas of Cusa, *Trialogus de possest*, 50, ed. Steiger, 62; trans. Hopkins, *A Concise Introduction to the Philosophy of Nicholas of Cusa*, 940.

56 Nicholas of Cusa, *De theologicis complementis*, 8, ed. Riemann and Bormann, 40; trans. Hopkins, 759.

These theoretical elaborations suggest a particularly Cusan fulfilment of the whole Neoplatonic problematic regarding the relationship between the One and what "emerges" from it. For this emergence had never been for Neoplatonism *simply* a copying, since the One was taken in some way to give rise to finite structures that it did not in itself "have" as such. Nor was it taken to be merely a deduction, whether of a Leibnizian or a Hegelian kind. The notion of an artistic expression, of a creative impulse toward the elaboration of an inspiration in the mode of formed beauty or as the spontaneity of a dance, appeared more apt, just as for Plotinus a preceding "life" gives rise to the formation of intellect from the One.[57] Only to a degree with Porphyry (who significantly influenced Victorinus), and then much more emphatically with the Christian idea of the Trinity, was the Neoplatonic *aporia* of the inherent self-giving of the nonetheless all-sufficient One really resolved. This sufficiency now became paradoxically and entirely a self-giving, and a modal self-forming of vitality, just as for Thierry and Nicholas singular unity is established only as repetition.

The Cusan suggestion of a hyper-contracted coincidence of complication with explication fully forbids any notion that the Son is *just* a later identical copy of the Father (even though he is indeed that) or a merely ineluctable and logical expression of his nature or "thought." The Logos is instead an unfathomably original, perfect, verbal and actual willed "expression" of the Father's unified potency (beyond necessity, as Nicholas insists), fully interpreted and realized in the Spirit. One requires the imagery of language, rather than simply the imagery of number, in order to conceive them, however "proper" and more than "appropriated" both symbolic registers may be.

Equivalently, even though the more exact and maximal reality of every created thing resides in the Logos, it is nonetheless the case that, because things that are fully present there are ontologically and not just epistemologically "unknown," they are fully *known* only in the sense of being "comprehended" in their finite instances. As with Eriugena (himself after Gregory of Nyssa), Cusanus implies that God adds a certain positive and affirmative knowing of himself by creating, whereas in himself he has no

---

57 Pierre Hadot, "Être, vie, pensée," in *Plotin, Porphyre. Études neoplatoniciennes* (Paris: Les Belles Lettres, 2010), 127–81.

self-knowledge in the sense of "comprehension" that implies boundaries.[58] For both thinkers, finitude retains thereby a certain irreplaceable integrity, even though it is clearly stated (as with Eckhart) to be analogically or "proportionally" dependent, not univocally self-situated in being (as with Scotus).[59] The creation is not simply a copy of God, much less a *deduction* from him. It is rather his chosen finite self-expression of his infinitude. Its symbols in one dimension only *point to* God, and yet in another they also *realize* God in various unique theophanic enigmas.

It is partly on account of the twin integrities of the infinite and the finite that Cusanus, following Dionysius and Eckhart, denies commensurability between the two. He emphasizes that we can never be sure of our success in naming God and insists (especially in his sermons) that Catholic truths are reached only by faith.[60] What he has to say about the divine names in different places is various and complicated, but includes the notion found also in Aquinas of an "eminent" validity of affirmation, such that God is hyper-good, hyper-beautiful, and so forth.[61] Nonetheless, Cusanus does seem to deny, more than Aquinas does, that this projection of meaning into the sublime can ever be more than "conjectural." In the same way, sheer negation does not capture God as he is in himself with any surety: to negate is still to conceptualize, and, following Eckhart, we must negate even negation.[62]

---

58 "Properly speaking, God does not 'understand'; rather, he 'imparts Being.'" Nicholas of Cusa, *De venatione sapientiae*, XXIX (87), ed. Klibansky and Senger, 83; trans. Hopkins, *Metaphysical Speculations*, 1332.

59 Nicholas very rarely uses the word "analogy," but he does use the language of "proportion" in an equivalent sense and consistently uses "participation" and "participation in being," which is inseparable from analogy. See Nicholas of Cusa, *De docta ignorantia*, I.1 (2) and I.18 (52–54), ed. Wilpert and Senger, 6 and 68–72. The same goes for his elaboration of the Dionysian tradition of "naming God" (Haubst, *Das Bild*, 84–86). To read Cusanus as in any way Scotist is simply baffling. The only real hint of Franciscan influence, apart from some occasional echoes of Bonaventure or the eccentric Llull, comes when he once contrasts the "natural" generation of the Son with the "willed" generation of the Spirit—which is surprising, given his general ascription of Trinitarian personal difference to relationality. See Nicholas of Cusa, Sermon *Fides autem Catholica*, 35; in *Nicholas of Cusa's Didactic Sermons*, trans. Hopkins, 110–11.

60 Nicholas of Cusa, Sermon *Fides autem Catholica*, 4–16; in *Nicholas of Cusa's Didactic Sermons*, trans. Hopkins, 96–100.

61 Nicholas of Cusa, Sermon *Fides autem Catholica*, 33; in *Nicholas of Cusa's Didactic Sermons*, trans. Hopkins, 108–9.

62 Nicholas of Cusa, Sermon *Ubi est qui Natus est?*, 16; in *Nicholas of Cusa's Didactic Sermons*, trans. Hopkins, 252–53.

Yet Nicholas also states in his sermon "On Many Occasions and in Many Ways" that given the inadequacy of both affirmations ("names for our spirit's desires" and "not, in a proper sense, names of God") and "mystical" negation ("which indicates what he is not ... and falls short of face-to-face manifestation"), we require the divine disclosure of more certain names. Even an absolute divine theophany that we can literally see with greater certainty would be only the certainty of faith, which is able to behold in Christ the absolute coincidence of the invisible with the visible, the uncreated with the created.[63] Through the mystical seeing of Christ, we realize that we exist only as seen by him, and yet that this seeing of us is only our seeing of him.[64] Equally, we realize that God's seeing in Christ is his "working" or making of all things, through that coincidence of knowing with making that Cusanus greatly elaborates from Eriugena.[65] It is also true for him that all of our own seeings and makings, our discoveries and inventions, tend toward coincidence, insofar as whatever we truly make or see is God both seeing and continuously making in and through us. Nevertheless, in our case the coincidence is imperfect: some things precede us as already given to be discovered; others proceed from us as invented by us.

This partial human coincidence of vision with construction tends, all the same, to prevent any reading of *De visione Dei* in purely phenomenological terms: even though we now have faith with which to see, through Christ, a speculative reach is not just abandoned. Indeed, the theorizations of God as perfect, maximally creative glance, in which our lookings and makings participate, depend upon speculation or "conjecture." Only by faith are we able reliably to "see through" our metaphysical speculations, but they remain speculative insofar as they are expressions of faith. Faith is in the unseen, for all that it enables us in some sense to "see already"—for speculation is already a heightening of sight, through the wearing of "spectacles," the mystical *beryllus*.[66] This sense of a speculative "seeing beyond the seen" connects faith with conjecture and disallows any dualism of the two. In neither case is this "seeing beyond" simply a saturated encounter with the sublime, à la Jean-Luc Marion, or an intuitive registering of the absolute

---

[63] See Nicholas of Cusa, Sermon *Multifarie Multisque Modis*, 7–14; in *Nicholas of Cusa's Didactic Sermons*, trans. Hopkins, 22–26.

[64] Nicholas of Cusa, *De visione Dei*, XXII (94–100), ed. Riemann, 74–78.

[65] Nicholas of Cusa, *De visione Dei*, V (16), ed. Riemann, 19; cf. *De visione Dei*, VIII (27–31), ed. Riemann, 28–31.

[66] Nicholas of Cusa, *De beryllo*, 8, ed. Senger and Bormann, 10–11.

limit of intuition. For Nicholas, a real and positive transgressing of the finite boundary is involved, such that we intellectually intimate something of the content of the infinite.[67]

The discourse of faith in the sheer historical singularity of the Incarnation at once provides the lynchpin to Cusanus's highly intellectual metaphysics and even requires this kind of metaphysics for its own coherence. Since there can be no mediation between infinite and finite, their coincidence in Christ is absolutely necessary, as can be made speculatively apparent, even if this requirement, a need both cognitive and ontological, has been supplied only contingently and historically. In cognitive terms, Cusanus regards the entirety of human culture and technology as a conjecture as to how to live well within this world. In the same way, he views all of human religion as a conjecture about how to live well eternally. Both conjectures, at once of nature and of grace, shift toward certainty only through the event of the Incarnation. This assertion reveals that for Cusanus the *analogia entis*—or the analogy of Unity or Form or Intellect—can operate only on the ground of the *analogia Christi*, just as it operates only on the equally "contradictory" ground of the *analogia Trinitatis*.

This is not merely because even reason (in a mode beyond Aquinas's treatment)[68] requires revelation in order to surpass sheer speculation, but also—one can infer—because analogy of attribution, in order not to sink back into univocity or equivocity, requires the *coincidence* of identity with difference, in the same way, at the same time, and in the same respect. Analogy, or *proportio*, in other words, must be a full-scale paradox, or else it evaporates into a banal notion of "like in some respects, unlike in others." There is a Trinitarian analogy to the God who resides beyond the sway of the logic of identity, and there is a Christological analogy to this God by virtue of the coincidence of his infinitude with the finite, within which the logic of identity necessarily holds. For Cusanus, only the *absolute* instance of this paradox can guarantee its reality and non-dilution. If the infinite and the finite are able to meet in speech, such that we can after all speak of God, then they must have done so once and absolutely, if all other speaking instances are able to share in that coinciding in whatever degree. Hence the

---

67 On this point, see the essay by David Bentley Hart in chapter 16.
68 But see John Milbank and Catherine Pickstock, *Truth in Aquinas* (London: Routledge, 2001), 60–61.

unified hypostasis, involving after all the full coincidence of the infinite with the finite plane.

Mathematicized Christology

Once more Cusanus deploys mathematics in order to express more precisely just how the two natures of Christ are hypostatically fused without either merging or hybridity. Theoretically, he says, any finite thing, such as heat, might be brought to its maximum, although this never occurs without an immeasurable metamorphosis into something else. In ordinary reality this can happen only when the finite thing has ceased to be finite and become finitely infinite, either by vanishing, as when heat evaporates moisture or water turns to ice, or through indefinite extension, as with space and time.[76] Today, we might say that any transfinite quantity is only a possible projection, or else is hypothetically actualized as a "set."

However, in the case of Christ, hypostasization by the infinite Logos is able to bring even the finite human nature to what we might call its transfinite, ontologically actualized perfection.[77] Cusanus expresses this by explaining that since Christ is the absolute contracted Maximum, we have in him uniquely a sheerly finite, realized human maximum, unlike the cases of metamorphosis or indefinite extension. It is as if a polygon has been infinitely expanded such as to perfectly match an infinite circle, and yet remains nonetheless a polygon.[78] The difference between the two has become imperceptible and yet it *remains* ontologically in place. Similarly, water remains as water at its maximum (or rather minimum) in ice, even though it has become something else. In the case of the Incarnation, it is as if ice arrives before water, establishing water at its minimum without the usual progression to freezing of preexistent water—even though the full

---

[76] Nicholas of Cusa, Sermon *Puer Crescebat*, 7; in *Nicholas of Cusa's Didactic Sermons*, trans. Hopkins, 34.

[77] Nicholas of Cusa, Sermon *Puer Crescebat*, 3; in *Nicholas of Cusa's Didactic Sermons*, trans. Hopkins, 33. The point of my invoking transfinites is not to suppress paradox, to which Cusanus cleaves, but instead to bring out the difference between indefinite finite infinites and the genuine absolute infinite. This difference was also allowed by the Platonizing inventor of transfinites, Georg Cantor, and arguably the deployment of set theory to suppress the paradoxes of the infinite is subsequent to his endeavors. Christ as *maximum contractum* is then like an absolutely ontologically realized actual transfinite set, otherwise impossible.

[78] Nicholas of Cusa, *De docta ignorantia*, III.4 (203–7), ed. Wilpert and Senger, 26–32; cf. *De docta ignorantia*, I.3 (10), ed. Wilpert and Senger, 14–15.

continuity with water, or the humanity inherited from Mary, is also present. Thus, when the freezing wind of the Spirit arrived to Mary (Nicholas cites Job 37: "when God blows there comes frost"), it "congealed the pure blood of the Virgin fount and by means of the infused Word of God formed Jesus in [her], from whose womb came the ice."[79]

By way of this bizarre trope, Nicholas suggests that just as a maximum line would incorporate every possible figure, so the contracted maximum-minimum of any individual member of a species would be equivalent to the form and essence of that species and so to the totality of all its other members (and in the human, microcosmic case, of every other thing). The absolute opposition between particular and universal, despite their reciprocal linkage, is thereby breached. The infinite polygon who is Christ is all of human nature in one human individual, through the divine person. Such a Christological metaphysics explicitly fits with Cusanus's Eckhartian modalist view that "the part [is not reduced to] nothing by virtue of the fact that the being of the part is completely from the being of the whole,"[80] just as "the fertility of the species is unfolded through individuals ... and that considered in and of itself is uncontracted as to *mode*."[81]

In wider metaphysical terms, the Incarnation is held by Cusanus to be necessary for the very holding together of reality, the very existence of anything, not just necessary for the certainty of our cognition. Without Christ's mediation, the entire cosmos would fall apart, such that all things literally hold together in Christ (Col 1:17). This is in part, as we have seen, because for Nicholas humanity is a microcosm, a unique blend of all aspects of the created order, and also the being through and for which everything was created. For this reason, God could become incarnate only as a human being. This had to occur because of the need for an ontological mediator between the infinite and the finite, besides it being appropriate to God's perfection

---

[79] Nicholas of Cusa, Sermon *Puer Crescebat*, 5–12; in *Nicholas of Cusa's Didactic Sermons*, trans. Hopkins, 34–36.

[80] Nicholas of Cusa, *Apologia doctae ignorantiae*, 26, ed. Klibansky, 18. One can note that Aquinas had a similarly modalist view of the inherence of accidents and qualities in substance and of parts in wholes, just as he also had a strongly Cyrilline Christology, whereby the entire being of Christ was from his divine Personhood.

[81] Nicholas of Cusa, Sermon *Loquere et Exhortare*, 24; in *Nicholas of Cusa's Didactic Sermons*, trans. Hopkins, 50–51.

(as argued by Robert Grosseteste),[82] not to leave undone the most perfect and remarkable work imaginable.

In terms of a requisite cosmic mediator, one can gloss Nicholas, in accordance with his embrace of Thierry's four modes, as meaning that the "created God" cannot be truly divided from the "Creating God" without breaking God and all order apart, even though the "created God" has of its very nature departed from the simple, infinite, and unified nature that God in himself possesses. In that case, the Incarnation becomes necessary as the resolution of a kind of lived-out metaphysical *aporia*: the creation must and yet cannot stand outside God. In and through the hypostatic union it stands at once and paradoxically outside and within: unified both substantively and "characterfully," yet not essentially, although here the distance of finite from infinite is paradoxically abolished in accord with a deeper mystery of ultimate reality.

As the "maximum" of finite human experience, Christ's humanity, for Cusanus, is able to assume, through enhypostasization, all the attributes of the divine nature; inversely, by virtue of the substantive blending of the finite and infinite *maxima*, Christ's divine nature is able actively to take on the experience and sufferings of human nature, including the ultimate suffering of hell, which, as Cusanus affirms with some novelty, Christ redemptively undergoes.[83] In this manner, the infinitesimal merging of the *maxima* mathematizes the communication of idioms: "Jesus's humanity is like a middle point between the purely absolute and the purely contracted.... [I]t was corruptible ... according to temporality ... and incorruptible according to the fact that it was free from time...."[84]

Eschatology and Unity

Although all of these reflections by Cusanus are orthodox, he has effectively pushed orthodoxy itself to the limit and reached quite radical conclusions. Behind the wall of Paradise, glimpsed only by the eyes of faith, it is no longer the case that the eternal union of the Tri-Unity according to

---

[82] See Robert Grosseteste, *On the Cessation of the Laws*, trans. Stephen M. Hildebrand (Washington, DC: The Catholic University of America Press, 2012).

[83] Nicholas of Cusa, *De docta ignorantia*, III.7 (223), ed. Wilpert and Senger, 48–50.

[84] Nicholas of Cusa, *De docta ignorantia*, III.7 (225), ed. Wilpert and Senger, 50–52; trans. H. Lawrence Bond, *Nicholas of Cusa: Selected Spiritual Writings* (New York: Paulist Press, 1997), 188.

infinite coincidence stands in any sense higher or beyond the hypostatic union of divine with human nature, which for Nicholas's inherited realism about universals brings all of humanity along with it, and then all finite nature as such, since humanity is the microcosm. How could it possibly stand higher, if God is simple and eternal?

Beyond the wall, the divine nature and the divine persons are somehow one, though they are also equally many. If that is the case, then beyond the wall the divine person and natures of Christ must also somehow be one. And since Christ's person hypostasizes the human nature, and behind the wall explication coincides with complication, his human and divine natures have also somehow become one, for all their radical division, in a way that our grasp *in via* of the hypostatic union of two natures can only intimate.

What is more, our cleaving to Christ in the Church ensures that we all reach, in our various degrees, through faith and filiation or birth in the Son, a coincidence of all our finite *maxima* with the infinite Maximum of Christ, the Church being, according to Cusanus, the one maximum human society in its ultimate and impermeable nature.[85] Thus at one crucial point in the *De docta ignorantia*, Nicholas says that the unity of God, the unity of Christ, and the unity of the Church are all absolutely one eternal unity, without any priority whatsoever.[86]

This drastic Christological monism follows through on Eriugena's eschatology, where in the end we are to be united with that God who is "neither created nor creating." And this God at the end is of course the God who is also at the beginning and continues to be for always, since the Trinitarian figure of God as beginning, middle, and end (a temporal figure of the Trinity for Nicholas)[87] really applies only economically. At the end, indeed, we meet the God who is sufficient in himself and does not need to create. In the end the political image of God as divine governor, on which Nicholas frequently insists,[88] is somehow deactivated: God as king includes all subordinate roles of mediating rule, but their very identity within his

---

[85] Nicholas of Cusa, *De docta ignorantia*, III.12 (254–62), ed. Wilpert and Senger, 86–98.

[86] Nicholas of Cusa, *De docta ignorantia*, III.12 (262), ed. Wilpert and Senger, 96–98.

[87] Nicholas of Cusa, *Apologia doctae ignorantiae*, 9, ed. Klibansky, 7.

[88] For example, see Nicholas of Cusa, *De beryllo*, 16, ed. Senger and Bormann, 19–20; Nicholas of Cusa, *De quaerendo Deum*, V (49), in *Nicolai de Cusa Opera Omnia*, vol. IV, ed. Paul Wilpert (Hamburg: Felix Meiner Verlag, 1959), 33–34; and Sermon *Multifarie Modisque Nobis*, 19–21; trans. Jasper Hopkins, *A Miscellany on Nicholas of Cusa* (Minneapolis: Arthur J. Banning Press, 1994), 27–29.

eternity ultimately collapses even the distinction between ruler and ruled and so, it would seem, the ontologically political as such—which has both personal (political) and ontological dimensions.

But since God is the God who eternally in the Logos and the Spirit did in fact create, this God who does not create is also the God who is not created as something *aliud*: the God who entirely within himself and from always includes also the creation through Christ and through the eternal Church. The apolitical God *remains* the political God, the divine governor, and Trinitarian metaphysics enshrines this mystery of an ultimate ontological democracy that *remains* an eminent affirmation of ontological hierarchy.[89] Indeed, the democracy is attained only via Christ's personal and therefore "political" and governing enhypostasization of finite nature, which at once sustains its governed subordination and yet manifests the end of such subordination as total educative transfiguration or deifying filiation, which achieves the equalizing of the finite with the infinite and of creation with Creator.[90]

For behind the mystical wall of Paradise, the "essential" unity of God (sophianically) coincides with the "personal" unity of God with the creation, just as divine essence coincides with divine persons, and human person coincides with divine and human essences. The distinctions are not abolished, because the *non aliud* of infinite definition is not sameness, yet they are not "other" to an absolute unity that exceeds (beyond Neoplatonism, save perhaps that of Damascius) the contrast of infinite with finite. Behind the wall there is but one triadic infinite-finite being-essence, and yet this is also, as it were, a unique infinite-finite individual person (thus Cusanus could speak of the "icon of God")[91] by virtue of Christ's assumption of humanity and the communication of idioms. What Christ supremely reveals, one might say, is that even the universal, even reality as such, has its

---

[89] This coincidence of deactivation with cosmic political activity can obviously be contrasted with Giorgio Agamben's metaphysical quietist anarchism in his *Homo Sacer* sequence. Similarly, though this cannot be fully explained here, it seems to me that the Chartrian tradition is much more genuinely "modalist" than the Franciscan and Aegidian formal and modal distinctions that Agamben invokes in *The Use of Bodies*, trans. Adam Kotsko (Stanford, CA: Stanford University Press, 2016), which really tend toward division, dissolution, and negative ending rather than intrinsic elaboration.

[90] See Nicholas of Cusa, *De filiatione Dei*, in *Nicolai de Cusa Opera Omnia*, vol. IV, ed. Paul Wilpert (Hamburg: Felix Meiner Verlag, 1959), *passim*.

[91] Perhaps this is in part why Cusanus could consider Islamic monotheism sympathetically, despite offering a Trinitarian and Christological critique.

own distinctive flavor, albeit a savor without contrast. But of what else have mystics of all traditions ultimately spoken?

Is this pantheism or acosmism? It is both, in one sense, and yet in a deeper sense neither and the refusal of both as premature resolutions. Because the entire going out from and going in through the gate of Paradise, which is Christ, has not been abolished. It is simply that we cannot as yet see or understand how the going out is also a remaining and returning, how God lies beyond the contrast between God and not God, without thereby merely abolishing this difference. No doubt this is the ultimate "taking leave of God in the name of God" of which Meister Eckhart spoke. God as the creation is kenotically "more than God" in the Trinity, passing forever "downward," but he is also "more than God" insofar as all of created reality abides with God as uncreating, as eschatologically and eternally itself uncreated, passing mystically "upward."

The long if intermittent theological tradition of radicalized orthodoxy, which Nicholas of Cusa in a sense consummates, is curiously at once very particularist and very universalist. We see this most of all with Cusanus. In his sermons especially, it is clear that the exclusive way to God lies through faith in Christ and the body of Christ: through specific words, rituals, and codes of practice long inherited and developed. God turns out to have a particular face within this world, with a particular, recognizable glance and expression, even though in the light of the incarnate Christ and in the one name of Jesus (already insisted upon, by Dionysius, as the one, truly reliable, ultimate name), it is now seen to shine forth everywhere.[92]

Yet at the same time, it is well known that Cusanus had a new and generous respect for all human and religious traditions. There was, for him, some truth in all their conjectures and all of them are taken to point toward the Trinity and the God-Man and to assist irreplaceably in elucidating his nature.[93] What is more, the ultimate failure of these conjectures has to do with their attempted theoretical universality that turns out to be too constraining. It is rather and with a supreme height of paradox, a very particular if endlessly ramifying tradition, a particular style and idiom, founded in a complex narrative and set of symbols, metaphors, and

---

[92] See Dionysius the Areopagite, *The Divine Names*, XIII.3 (980B–980C), in *Corpus Dionysiacum*, vol. 1, *De divinis nominibus*, ed. Beate Regina Suchla (Berlin: Walter de Gruyter, 1990), 228–29.

[93] See Nicholas of Cusa, *De pace fidei*, ed. Klibansky and Bascour, *passim*.

performances, expressive of but one (extra)ordinary human life that opens the way to something truly universal and all-inclusive. If God is truly God and absolutely One, then the entire cosmos is eternally at one with him through human love and in a human society constituted by love alone. By thinking monotheism and henology more radically in Christian terms of grace, Trinity, and Incarnation, Cusanus was thereby loyal not only to a wider-than-Christian monotheism but even to a current of perennial monism, common to both East and West. The event of the Incarnation, which discloses God's Tri-Unity, finally allows humanity to think both monism and monotheism with more coherence.

Ultimate reality, as Cusanus shows, is subjective-objective unity that can be unity only insofar as it transcends unity and is equally all difference: the One-Many, person-essence, existence-essence, potentiality-actuality, nothing-being, political-ontological, or ultimate "There" (Achard of St. Victor). It can only "be" insofar as it modally repeats, reflects, and relates itself as that "equality" with the original that is the perfect "artistic" expression realized with further equality as perfect intellectual understanding. A Trinitarian ontology is a modal one from the patristic outset, insofar as the Trinitarian notion of hypostasis, taken (at least in part) from Middle Platonism and Neoplatonism, is a particular mode of expression of absolute unity or substance, which for the pagan Neoplatonists occurred beneath the level of the One as the emanation of the spheres of Intellect and Soul. To project these hypostases into the ultimate itself is to elevate the modal to an equal share in this ultimacy.

The Absolute, modally conceived, must then emanate modally outward all the diverse and particular realities it eminently contains, and each of these is necessarily an echo of modal ultimacy, or of the Trinity. This echoing is manifested in the way that they consist both individually and connectedly in the ineffable and constantly re-realized and re-interpreted (or modally expressed) linkage of unity with plurality. Nicholas illustrates this in multifarious ways.

One might gloss him as indicating that an oscillating co-primacy of internally-related finite unities with external relational links among different unities (in either case both creatively in time and contemplatively in space) itself serves to witness to a finite lack of Trinitarian perfection while inevitably echoing it. As Cusanus writes in a late work, "an invisible spirit-of-union pervades all things. All the parts of the world are conserved within themselves by this spirit and these parts are united to the world as a whole."[94]

And yet this very lack does not lack its own ultimate reality, as the oscillation implies. An apparent lack that has been the occasion for spiritual sin is both ontologically and redemptively healed by Christ as the *maximum contractum* insofar as his internal relational binding is sustained by the person of the Son-Logos, who is necessarily the totality of all relational connections, both within the divine Trinity and among creatures—at once as the internal consistency of substances and their harmonious, musical, and beautiful linkages, creatively sustained through time and across space. It follows, as for Augustine, that Christ is the *totus Christus*: his internal coherence uniquely coincides with all his external relations to everything else (a coherence that constrains what every substance is in itself), such that the coherence of Christ is the coherence of all creatures who are through humanity the members of his body. Their very fragility, with its hierarchical dependence and interplay of integral substance with relational process, is not thereby abolished, but rather united to a final, infinite glory.

---

[94] Nicholas of Cusa, *De venatione sapientiae*, XXV (73), ed. Klibansky and Senger, 70; trans. Hopkins, 1324.

18

(Con)figuring Cusanus

CYRIL O'REGAN

In terms of difficulty, my task is at once the easiest and hardest, thus itself an illustration of the *coincidentia oppositorum* that is a pivotal concept and operator in Nicholas of Cusa's discourse. My task is easier, since, unlike the wonderful scholars who come before me in the present volume, I am not responsible for interpreting particular texts or the relation between texts, not responsible for providing the general context for Cusanus's work and outlining and discussing his relation to his more heterodox as well as more orthodox predecessors. Nor do I take on the responsibility of providing an in-depth analysis of one of his major contributions, whether philosophy, theology, the relation between both and mathematics, his take on authority in the Church, or his probing of the relationship between Christianity and other faiths. Relatively speaking then, compared with the incisive and detailed essays that make up this volume, my contribution is impressionistic, at once recapitulative, crystallizing, and hortatory. Recapitulative, in that I intend to evoke and put into relief lines of inquiry, historical and analytic excavation, comparison, and conflict of interpretation that crisscross the contributions. Crystallizing, in that I intend to offer a gestalt of Nicholas of Cusa through the production of a very general likeness that does not assume the responsibility of the nuances and textures of a portrait. Hortatory, given the desire to conclude the volume by recommending Cusanus to our contemporary attention, whatever the particular field we work in, and by suggesting some confidence that the Cusan oeuvre will behave like a classic in that it will have a future, indeed, multiple futures. Of course, what makes my task easy is precisely what makes it difficult. If I do not recapitulate copiously, I do want to recapitulate meaningfully; if I beg off providing a portrait, I still want the gestalt to be sharp and individuated enough that it picks out Cusanus uniquely rather than making him a member of a class, whether that class is Neoplatonic philosopher, negative theologian, nominalist, or Renaissance humanist. With these three tasks in mind, I want to speak of Nicholas of Cusa under the three auspices: singularity, liminality, and iconicity. I hope the meaning of each will become clear in what I say.

Singularity and Exemplarity

I would like to suggest that when it comes to intellectual, spiritual, and practical performance in philosophical and theological discourse, Nicholas of Cusa represents a singularity. This is not a hyperbole. I want to provide warrant for the claim in and through adducing two sets of marks as to how this singularity is illustrated in the Cusan corpus. If roughly speaking the first group of marks concerns general features visible at the surface level of his oeuvre, the second group of marks are less visible and are interpretively generated. They concern Cusanus's never-ending attempt at rendering different poles of philosophical and theological thought with a view to their reconciliation or synthesis. With regard to the first group it is responsible to claim the following: (1) no philosophical or theological thinker between the thirteenth and seventeenth centuries was quite so versatile in terms of approach to reality, quite so constructive and speculative, yet so compendiously recollective of the philosophical and theological traditions; (2) during the same time span it is difficult to come across a mainline philosopher or theologian who is quite so willing to invent and to neologize (e.g., *coincidentia oppositorum, non aliud, possest*, etc.), yet so disinclined toward adopting the character of an author; and (3) no figure during the same time period is so at ease in dealing with the different demands of the discourses of both philosophy and theology, while being so committed to tracking their imbrication, allowing trespasses across borders that are—in any event—always temporary and moveable. Or otherwise put, there is no mainline Western philosophical and theological thinker between the thirteenth and seventeenth centuries so disposed to allowing theology to supplement philosophy and vice versa; (4) no philosophical or theological figure during the period demonstrates the same capacity to elide the "inside" and "outside" in elevating a discourse for the Church (e.g., *De visione Dei*) that, nonetheless, has apologetic weight outside, and constructing a discourse for outside the Church that has transformative capacity within (e.g., *De pace fidei*); (5) no mainline philosophical and theological figure between the thirteenth and seventeenth centuries so clearly wanted to stretch and challenge the truths of the philosophical and theological tradition by means of other disciplines, especially that of mathematics (*De transmutationibus geometricis*; *De arithmetricis complementis*), while using that tradition to discipline the experimental thrust of his extra-theological and extra-philosophical "conjectures" (*De coniecturis*).

The above set of marks, intended to explicate what is complicated in the idea of Cusanus as a singularity, can be complemented by a second set, in which the emphasis falls on dynamic polarities. The following can be claimed: (6) there is no philosophical or theological figure between the thirteenth and seventeenth centuries who talked so much about the infinite—invented or at least reinvented it as a category—and who so counterintuitively lodged it in a devastated Christ divested of all glory and in solidarity with the nothings that humans have made of themselves (e.g., *De docta ignorantia*); (7) there is no philosophical or theological figure during this period who so clearly commanded the mainline philosophical and theological traditions (e.g., Augustine, Pseudo-Dionysius, Albert the Great), yet was so inclined to invest in the margins (e.g., Ramon Llull, John Scottus Eriugena, Meister Eckhart, and even nominalism to a certain extent), and thus staged the tension between centripetal and centrifugal force in their discourse or discourses; (8) there was no philosopher or theologian between the thirteenth and seventeenth centuries who so clearly grasped the movement of speech that intends all reality and gives it voice, but who insists at the same time that all speech is an expression of the inexhaustible Word who expresses reality as well as meaning (*De docta ignorantia*); and relatedly no figure so demonstrative in his repeated attempts to get a vision of reality through new apertures and through the minting of new vocabularies and new lines of inquiry[1]; (9) there was no philosophical or theological figure who during this time span showed more capability in using the linguistic protocols of the cataphatic and apophatic, while never forgetting that the goal is the presence of the hyperousiological Other who is beyond negation as well as affirmation and who can be met in silence as well as in the well-aimed speech; (10) there is no philosopher or theologian between the thirteenth and seventeenth centuries, given to elevating reason, who is quite so affirming of the idiot (e.g., *Idiota de sapientia, Idiota de mente, Idiota de staticis experimentis*), who is at once more whole than the rationalist limited to discursive thought and not taken in by its spurious claims.[2] Foolishness, stepping outside regimes of discourses whose purpose is to contain a divine in principle uncontainable, is a requirement if we are really to approach God rather than an idol (*De docta ignorantia*).

By contrast, worldly wisdom and its advanced protocols amount to foolishness insofar as encountering the Godhead is the aim. (11) There is no philosopher or theologian from the thirteenth to the seventeenth centuries who so elevates the subjective approach toward reality, while pushing the constraints on this subjectivity by the phenomenon of Christ, whose solicitous regard is the condition of a subject's seeing. As the revelation of the hyperousiological Godhead, this means that the Godhead not only infiltrates subjectivity, but maddens it, so that its greatest accomplishment is a never-ending search; in short, there is no philosopher or theologian within Western thought during this time period who generates a Western analogue to the Greek cipher of *epektasis* or "eternal becoming."[3] (12) There is no thinker between the thirteenth and seventeenth centuries who so squares the inquiry of philosophy and the articulation of theology with the practical demands of the administration of the Church (*De concordantia catholica*) and its humane relation to others, especially adherents to other faiths (*De pace fidei*).

These two shorthand sets of marks, which, incidentally, overlap and represent more nearly pragmatic than theoretical unities, are as much expressive of the singularity of Nicholas of Cusa's work as arguments for

---

[1] On learned ignorance and the limits of language, see Jean-Marie Nicolle's essay on Jacques Lacan in chapter 9.

[2] On the reception of Cusanus's *idiota*, see Alexia Schmitt's essay on Gilles Deleuze in chapter 8.

[3] On the infinite desire for God in Cusanus, see David Bentley Hart's essay in chapter 16.

it. For with regard to Cusanus, as with any singularity one wants to underscore, while the intellectual, discursive, and social-political conditions throw light on his work, they cannot finally explain it. Or, to put it in more technical language, Cusanus is excessive or "supernumerary" with respect to conditions that, indeed, do make his discourse or discourses possible, and to the philosophical and theological discourses that he seems to faithfully repeat. Needless to say, this is an extraordinary claim. It suggests that with respect to those features of the Cusan oeuvre to which I have brought attention, I am suggesting that when the likes of Alain Badiou assign singularity to the discourses of Paul, by extension one can make the same hyperbolic claim with regard to Cusanus, who, it turns out, as our second set of marks indicate more than the first, is an extraordinary generator of hyperbole, of language being roughed up but stretching across an infinite divide where there is no guarantee of fully securing what is aimed at. Still, even if the attribution of singularity were not dismissed as excessive, and if the marks I provided of it in Cusanus's case were accepted, it would still be necessary to make a distinction between importance and singularity. On pain of being a *flatus vocis*, every claim to singularity is a claim to importance. Crucially, however, every claim to importance may not necessarily imply a claim to singularity.

Although one could imagine different answers to the question of whether Thomas Aquinas is a singularity, I take it that no one interested in the history of Western thought or more particularly in the history of Catholic theology would deny the extraordinary nature of his synthetic intellectual achievement and his equally extraordinary influence in philosophy, theology, and their relation. If the standard line of interpretation is pushed, namely, that Aquinas represents the great adjudicator of the Christian tradition across philosophical discourse, the discourse of method, and doctrinal conjugation, then one underscores Aquinas's continuity with these traditions and suggests that the extent to which he surpasses the tradition is a matter of degree rather than kind. This line of interpretation would tend to suggest either that Aquinas is an extraordinarily important thinker, but not a singularity (weaker thesis); or that the extraordinary nature of Aquinas's importance is predicated upon his not being singular (stronger thesis). This is not to deny, however, that an interpreter of medieval thought or a commentator on Aquinas might refuse the distinction. A commentator on Aquinas or a medieval historian might claim the consensus position that Aquinas is a master of at least three discourses and their relation, but that at the same time he is highly original, for example, that he is responsible for constructing a Christian philosophy (Étienne Gilson, et al.), or that he is an original metaphysical thinker, and the formulator of the analogy of being. A historian of the medieval period or a commentator on Aquinas, disdaining the route of originality, might want to claim that his mastery of those three discourses, and especially their synthesis, is such that we are necessarily talking about a difference in kind.

When it comes to Aquinas I myself am open to being persuaded by those who would link rather than delink importance and singularity. My simple point is that in Aquinas's case, while his importance is a given, singularity is not. Logically, of course, one could decide so much the worse for singularity. If the distinction between importance and singularity holds despite the obvious complications, what can one say about exemplary thinkers at all, when it comes to those who are either important or singular? If one of them is exemplary, what would imitation or repetition look like? I am sure that while just about any follower of Aquinas would consider his thought to be exemplary, it is not evident that they would agree about why it is so. Still, a considerable number would tend to opt for the following features: (i) real knowledge of the history of philosophy and theology, but also (ii) the ability to use both of these traditions of discourse forensically and speculatively in light of questions that philosophy and theology have bequeathed to us; (iii) analytic rigor and logical consistency in argument together with a keen sense of what is at stake in an argument; (iv) systematic ability—matched up with fidelity to Church doctrine—that valorizes both comprehensiveness and the ability to see the relations among parts and wholes; and finally and conclusively (v) the general conviction that the exemplarity of Aquinas self-consciously lies in a pedagogy that is repeatable in principle and such that a disciple of Aquinas can more or less approximate it. Exemplarity in the case of Nicholas of Cusa, whom I am suggesting is a singularity, would necessarily look very different.

Now, while it can safely be said that Cusanus's work displays in some measure the first three features mentioned above, the differences come out with respect to the fourth and fifth features. First, in comparison with what we see in Aquinas, in the work of Cusanus comprehensiveness and the ability to relate part to whole and part to part are less an accomplishment than a task, more in the order of indication of categorical synthesis than its realization. The comprehensiveness is indicated or "contracted" in just about every text, but indicated differently: it can be Christ as the coincidence of the maximum and the minimum, or the Trinity as Not-Other. The relation might be between part and part, whether in doctrine (for example, the view of Christ and the view of human being; or the view of human being and that of God in speaking to participation) or in discourse (for example, the resonance between the discourse of mathematics and its preoccupation with the infinite and the discourses of Neoplatonic metaphysics and theology). But with respect to the relation of part to whole, or part to part, the circle can never be entirely closed. Structurally speaking, incompletion is built into a Cusan form of inquiry. The explications of the human person and Christ overlap but are not fully coincident; *a fortiori* there is no ultimate gateway from theological anthropology to the doctrine of the Trinity. Similarly, the discourse of mathematics turns out to be a surprising analogue of a deeply Neoplatonic metaphysics and theology. Yet—to use an image made popular by Paul Ricoeur—once again one is talking about discourses that are "elliptical" with respect to each other. Nicholas of Cusa insists throughout his work on the difference between the privative infinity of mathematics and a positive, metaphysically and theologically specified, infinity.[4] Finally, one should draw attention to the Cusan notion of "conjecture," in the text of the same name, but also the use of "conjecture" throughout. Conjecture represents the human mind's attempt to reach beyond toward a knowing and participation that is the object of its aim. It is a declaration that it cannot fully incorporate the unknown that it would know, and yet despite this it is not simply a matter of guessing or merely alleviating one's skepticism.

Second, what is exemplary in Cusanus's work is not simply a set of newly minted concepts such as *non aliud*, *coincidentia oppositorum*, or *possest*, but the continued attempt to achieve synthesis across tensions and polarities within and between discursive fields. Thus the attractiveness of Nicholas of Cusa to a twentieth-century Catholic thinker such as Erich Przywara.[5] We are talking about a complex process of equilibration within and across intellectual and discursive fields. While this process of equilibration might remind one of Immanuel Kant's articulation of "architectonic" near the end of the *Critique of Pure Reason*, in the case of Cusanus the process does not depend entirely on iteration. Nor is it merely heuristic. And again, while comparison with Jacques Derrida is more justified in the case of Cusanus than in that of any other Christian thinker who performs

---

4 On mathematics and the Trinity in Cusanus, see John Milbank's essay in chapter 17.
5 On Erich Przywara and Cusanus, see John Betz's essay in chapter 1.

as well as speaks to the limits of language, his performance of incompetence is more restrained than Derrida's dissemination. This is so given the constraints provided both by the Neoplatonic metaphysics that frames Cusan exploration and by the Christian beliefs that undergird them and function as ineluctable. None of this means that Nicholas of Cusa is not advancing a pedagogy or that his work fails to perform a kind of exemplarity that calls for emulation. The point is that in contrast to Aquinas's thought, which is less multiverse and more given to stable conclusion, there is considerably less prospect of repetition. There are ways of knowing that do not answer to the protocols of philosophy and theology and the in-built pressures in both discourses that expose them to irradicable incompleteness.

Liminality in Two Registers

Nicholas of Cusa is a figure of the limen or threshold in the *epochal sense* insofar as he can be cast as a transitional figure in what Louis Dupré calls the "passage to modernity."[6] Creativity, novelty, the power of mathematics, and the splendor of the cosmos are elevated, along with the commitment to Neoplatonic metaphysics, to a Neopythagorean and Hermetic view of the arcane power of number, as well as an interest in marginal forms of the Catholic theological tradition that seemed to upset Catholic dogmas about *creatio ex nihilo*, the possibility of equally affirming the humanity as well as the divinity of Christ, and the hypostatic understanding of the Trinity.[7] Cusanus is a thinker in a century of passage in which whatever side of a polarity seems to be ascendant, whether the subject or object, transcendent reality or worldliness, univocity or equivocity, will be undone, and whatever there is of real synthesis or approximation to synthesis will be subject to extraordinary negative pressure threatening the undoing of what has been achieved. The liminality of Cusanus in the epochal sense gains specification in the work of Karsten Harries, among others, who reflects on perspective as a privileged site of transition from the medieval way of construing the world, in which human being is not only heteronomous but whose subjectivity refers to God, Christ, and the Church, to a world that in its disenchantment is no longer world in the original sense of cosmos

---

6 On Louis Dupré and Cusanus, see Peter Casarella's essay in chapter 11.
7 On Hermetic sources in Cusanus, see José González Ríos's essay on Peter Sloterdijk in chapter 6.

as given, but a world that precisely in its objectivity is subject to figuration and construction, where the individual begins to assume more and more the role of mediator.[8]

This liminality is further specified epochally in the attempt to account for the continuum of transition that reaches from Nicholas of Cusa to Giordano Bruno. The latter then becomes, on a Blumenbergian model, either the threshold of thresholds (1600) or a threshold after the fact, a kind of legitimation of the new that has already emerged in Cusan philosophy.[9] Yet, this continuum of transition also concerns a shift in emphasis in the Neoplatonic register that affects the understanding of the infinite, the relation of the infinite to the world, and the nature of the self. The movement in the transitional continuum between Cusanus and Bruno might be described as univocalizing what is analogical in Nicholas of Cusa (although Nicholas exhibits a less sanguine type of analogy than that found in Aquinas). This transition demonstrates two different kinds of pull: (i) first, the pull of nominalism, perspectivalism, conjecturalism, constructivism, and notions of contraction, which suggest that the power of untamable equivocity shadows Cusan discourse; (ii) second, the pull toward unity illustrated from time to time in Cusanus, in his analyses of the transcendent triune God through the category of *possest* and of the God-world relation articulated in the conceptual pair *non aliud* and *complicatio-explicatio*. This second pull is the ground of the recurring interpretive debate as to whether Cusanus supports analogy or does not, or, in the German language version of the conflict of interpretation, whether at last Cusanus exhibits a *Seinsmetaphysik* or an *Einheitsmetaphysik*. This conflict of interpretation can be seen, for example, in the different construals of Nicholas of Cusa in Przywara and Hans Urs von Balthasar. With appropriate caveats Przywara subscribes to the former, Balthasar to the latter. Przywara thinks that Cusanus is more an answer to Hegel than an anticipator of him; Balthasar thinks that Cusanus recalls Eckhart and anticipates Hegel via Bruno.[10]

Still, even those critics of the Cusan tendency toward an *Einheitsmetaphyik* of the sort one sees illustrated in Eckhart would agree that there are orthodox reserves in Nicholas of Cusa, whose discourses stretch rather than break with the Christian tradition. The probity of this judgment

---

8 On Karsten Harries and Cusanus, see Il Kim's essay in chapter 12.
9 On Hans Blumenberg and Cusanus, see Elizabeth Brient's essay in chapter 4.
10 On Hegel and Cusanus, see Valentina Zaffino's essay on Werner Beierwaltes in chapter 5.

becomes fairly evident in the two texts that perhaps most tax the analogy of being as a bulwark of divine transcendence. I am speaking of *De possest* and *De non aliud*. Despite making God correlative to the world in a way that departs from or at least stretches the standard Christian model (if not necessarily as far as Eriugena and Eckhart), Cusanus in general, and in particular his category of *possest* in the text of the same name, constructs a concept of God whose otherness is absolute. Similarly, in *De non aliud* there is a distinction between Not-Other and all others. I am here making a minimal claim. I allow that Cusanus might be orthodox without remainder on this point. I simply want to register that his category, or, better, meta-category of Not-Other, which formalizes the kind of non-contrastive relation between God and the world that is typical of the Neoplatonic tradition and has different inflections in Augustine, Albert the Great, Aquinas, and Bonaventure, functions as a hyperbole that brings the divine and the world so close together as to make them appear to be the same. For while, as already indicated, the Not-Other is distinguished from all others, in a reverse move Cusanus says that all others are in the end Not-Other. Still, even if finally there is only an infinitesimal difference between Not-Other and all others, this difference makes all the difference, indeed, infinite difference, since it is nothing less than that between nothing and being.

Similarly with *complicatio-explicatio*. This categorial is the summary of the *exitus-reditus* dynamic and accordingly the productive account of the relation between the divine and the world borrowed by early Christian thinkers from the classical Neoplatonism of Plotinus and Proclus and recycled in Christian thinkers from Eriugena to Eckhart, but found also in Aquinas and Bonaventure. Perhaps the figure that needs to be highlighted is the ninth-century Irish thinker John Scottus Eriugena, whose *De divisione naturae* arguably provides the most complete, and certainly the most lustrous, Christian example of the model, as well as the Christian adaptation before Cusanus that most equivocates concerning the inequality and equality of divine ground and what is expressive of the ground and thus consequent to it. Of course, as Reiner Schürmann has pointed out, Eckhart sets the standard here for the subversion of analogy, indeed, testing it in both directions of univocity and equivocity. And neither Eriugena nor Cusanus quite reach Eckhart's level. Furthermore, the tension in the Cusan account of the divine-world relation between an explanation that allows God's transcendence of the world, on the one hand, and an explanation that makes them entirely correlative, on the other, is relieved in the case of

Giordano Bruno. For the Nolan the divine and the world are commensurate, if not qualitatively, at least insofar as the explication of the divine is without reserve; there is no excess of possibility over expression, and no excess of divine freedom over necessity. Thus, we find in Bruno's case a particular interpretation of *complicatio-explicatio* that ushers in the claim of an infinity of worlds. Not for Bruno either are the distinctions between the qualitatively absolute infinity of God and infinity as a mathematical construct or spatial infinity that one finds in Nicholas of Cusa's mature texts. It is this Brunian view that directly funds German Idealism, even if something of Cusanus is also forwarded and redeployed. In terms of actual transmission, it is Schelling who is the main conduit of Bruno, although some knowledge of Bruno is to be found in the likes of Herder and Goethe. And it is Schelling—at least the middle and later Schelling—who pushes back in the qualified fashion of Cusanus against the kind of blatant univocity that one finds in Bruno's more philosophical texts (e.g., *De la causa, principio, et uno* and *De l'infinito universi et mondi*).

The philosophical and theological anthropology of Cusanus also illustrates significant tension as well as complication. He seems to have a particularly dynamic view of human being as in-between, which, plausibly, can be traced back to Eriugena. When it comes to human being, there seems to be an almost infinite register from height to depth, from godlikeness to a creature that is barely above nothing. On the high side we have the emphasis on human beings as genuinely creative, insofar as they are the source of conjectures and pedagogies of learning and equally, and even more importantly, the source of pedagogies of unlearning and breaking convention. Karl Jaspers thinks that the latter pedagogy represents Nicholas of Cusa's main contribution to a philosophical anthropology. Still, even Jaspers would not ignore human beings's elevation as they ascend the epistemic register and specifically leave behind sense and that form of dianoetic knowing that operates in terms of the principle of contradiction.[11] Of course, human beings reach their apogee when they experience a presence of the Trinity in a trans-dianoetic or sapiential form of knowledge that provokes silent participation but also elicits forms of hyperbole and speech in which contraries coincide.

Yet the anthropological register is not solely concerned with the limit-capacities of human being, especially regarding their creativity. Cusanus

---

11 On Karl Jaspers and Cusanus, see Tamara Albertini's essay in chapter 2.

does not forget to underscore the way in which human beings have the capacity to move toward degree zero, which is enabled by our being created from nothing and exacerbated in our physical or spiritual death. As *De docta ignorantia*, Book III, reveals, this is overcome in and by Christ, who is at once the supreme instance and principle of coincidence of opposites and the reason why we can communicate with the hyperousiological Godhead, the basis of being, life, and intelligence. As Cusanus says in *De non aliud*, we are other to the Not-Other; in *De possest*, we are possibilized, but we are not possibility itself. And in *De visione Dei*, our very seeing of God is not a human capacity, but is capacitated by God seeing us in Christ. This derelict side of human subjectivity as the other pole to the genuine deification of human being is found neither in Giordano Bruno, nor in Italian Renaissance figures such as Marsilio Ficino and Pico della Mirandola who precede that controversial Dominican, who in 1600 was a casualty of an auto-da-fé. Human being is not unilaterally Ficino's erotic madness, Pico's *magnum miraculum* of human creativity, or Bruno's "heroic fury." Cusanus—it should be said—not only appears to have a sense of the lessness as well as greatness of human being, but also a real sense of the analogical structure of human being, which finds its paradigm in Christ. From both a metaphysical and theological point of view human beings are tensional betweens. It may well be that the metaxic character of human being displays itself existentially. But if it does so, it is because in the first instance it is intimated as a reality constituted metaphysically by the poles of superabundant being and nothingness, and theologically by being a created being that emerges from nothing and does not subsist in itself. Yet paradoxically human beings are capacitated to creatively conjecture, philosophize, and theologize and thereby express gloriously their status as *imago Dei*.

For good reasons I have limited myself to speaking of the epochal form of liminality as an index of Cusan singularity. Nevertheless, this is just one of the two registers of liminality expressed in and by Cusanus's discourse. We can and should also speak to his liminality in a more contemporary *non-epochal* register. What most needs to be said has already been implied in our discussion of Nicholas of Cusa's liminality in the epochal mode. Essentially all that remains is to filter out the historical markers and permit Cusan discourse to reveal itself as constitutively a discourse of dynamic, maybe even oscillating, betweens: between the poles of subject and object; between unity and plurality; between sign and symbol; between radical plurality and equally radical unity. Perhaps Cusanus is the one major Catholic thinker on whom one can hang the hat of "undecidability" without embarrassment, even if the discursive environment we are still dealing with has not disposed of what Derrida calls the "transcendental signified."

Yet by way of reminder, let me draw three lessons from what can be seen in Cusanus. First, in philosophical and especially theological discourse the apprehension of radical alterity and unknowability of the divine needs to be secured again and again. The protocols of cataphasis and apophasis—especially the latter—are only relatively adept with respect to this task. Over time even apophatic constructs lose the counter-force intended to prevent God or the Trinity from becoming part of a universal semantic system. Although privileged within a discourse that wants to say as much about the divine as possible, but no more than necessary, too often apophatic language ceases to disrupt and destabilize and comes to name and behave in a cataphatic manner. Thus the need for constant refreshing in order for the transcendental signified to remain out of reach of language and concept; thus the need also for many names and new names. One might even say that that the neologistic tendency of Cusanus is a requirement, since the obvious artifice shown in terms such as *non aliud* and *possest* is indicative of the difficulty of naming with the desired effect of destabilizing the semantic field while, nonetheless, keeping it relatively intact.

The second major Cusan contribution to liminality in general, and thus to us moderns and postmoderns in particular, is what I would call—neologizing after the manner of Nicholas himself—the operation of hyperbolization, with respect both to God's non-contrastive transcendence with regard to the world, and to the intermediate character of human being vouchsafed in Christian theology and Neoplatonic metaphysics. In the case of the first of these, it is a given within Scholasticism (e.g., Aquinas) and Christian as well as classical Neoplatonism that divine transcendence is not opposed to divine immanence in the world. To a certain extent, God's non-contrastive relation to the world functions as a general rule intended to inhibit the natural tendency of the mind to spatialize transcendence and thus contrast a transcendent beyond with an immanent here. The pervasiveness of that contrastive view has been the object of continual complaint in modern thought, which has found expressions in objections to Christianity as various as Hegel, Feuerbach, and in a different form in Heidegger (ontological difference).[12] It would be all too easy to say that modern philosophy is

---

[12] On Martin Heidegger and Cusanus, see Stephen Gersh's essay in chapter 15.

therefore tilting at windmills insofar as that general rule against spatialized contrast is a relative constant in the Christian tradition. For a rule is only as effective as the freshness and power of its expressions. Hyperboles, or the verbal form of hyperbolization, of precisely the non-contrast between God and the world despite or because of ontological difference, are necessary to prevent the entropic tendency toward contrast in philosophical and theological systems. The cipher of *non aliud* is exemplary here in that it provides at once an envelope for the rule of non-contrastive transcendence. The particular formulation "all others are precisely Not-Other" brings to mind transcendence in the most exaggerated form possible, that is, its proximity to the point almost of coincidence with the order of the world and its teeming plurality. Not an absolute coincidence, however, since Not-Other is in a class of its own, being not simply another other, even if the biggest or highest one. That is, in the cipher of "Not-Other," Cusanus forces us to attend to a form of transcendence that refuses merely to be a transcendent distance that repels nearness.[13]

The activation of hyperbolization permits Nicholas of Cusa to be our contemporary in the way few philosophical and theological figures can. Obviously, hyperbolization allows us to continually pry the divine away from our conceptual entrapments and misprisions. Moreover, it encourages us not simply to repeat Cusanus, but, having learned from him, to create our own hyperboles that serve the same function. Perhaps hyperbolizations also allow Christian theologians to radicalize apophatic theology further without ceding to postmodern deconstruction and semiosis. The second contribution that the Cusan mode of hyperbolization can make concerns the metaxic character of human beings. The between-character of human being is now intuited to be more verb than noun, less a site equidistant from what is highest and lowest in the order of creation, and more a dynamic swing between poles of absolute inertia and creativity that point toward, but do not in fact realize, an actual synthesis.

Iconicity: Possible Futures and the Future of the Possible

Thus far our discussion of Nicholas of Cusa has proceeded under the guidance of the predicates of singularity and liminality. Under both aspects,

---

13 On spatialization and proximity in Cusanus, see David Albertson's essay on Michel de Certeau in chapter 10.

scholarly judgements about Cusanus's historical importance and excellence as a thinker were ratified, and along the way I made independent judgments to the same effect. Scholarly judgments were reported and rendered with the confidence that they will be sustained well into the future, despite questions in the contemporary world concerning the criteria of what counts as excellence in any discourse—here philosophical and theological—who counts as judges, and finally, in the shadow of the "barbarism of reflection" (Vico), whether we should think of intellectual excellence as a value at all. My confidence remains unshaken, and I remain unmoved by reductively historicist explanations of the discourses of the past and present and more or less immune to the apotropaic power of the concept of "undecidability."

Nonetheless, I think it appropriate to expand further our gestalt of Cusanus developed in significant part through reading and listening to the essays in this volume. The expansion proceeds under the auspices of the predicate of "iconicity." Of course, this is a peculiarly appropriate way of figuring Nicholas of Cusa, given his own reflections on the icon (*De visione Dei*).[14] Some of what I want to say has already been anticipated by the discussion of Cusanus under the aspects of singularity and liminality, especially in my tentative profile of him in the mode of exemplarity. I would, however, like to add some final reflections that are considerably more speculative and have to do with plurality of perspective within and without Christianity and the question about the possible futures of Nicholas of Cusa, which in turn lift up the question of the future of the possible.

When the goal is approximating as far as possible to the reality of realities that resists naming, the conceptual engineering afoot in Cusanus's work organizes an economy of failure that paradoxically is the vehicle for success. Relative to the philosophical and theological traditions he presupposes, Cusanus deploys a larger and more heterogeneous vocabulary of naming, along with more extreme forms of hyperbole, all with the aim of interfering with and disrupting the semantic system so that the divine remains out of reach. Of course, this is to say neither more nor less than that Nicholas of Cusa offers a variant of mystical theology more amenable than most to our own more strained and plural linguistic and conceptual environments. Undoubtedly, especially in light of Cusanus's own mathematical predilections, one thinks of analogies with Kurt Gödel's system, in which we are allowed consistency but not completeness and vice versa. Or the paradoxes

---

14 On iconicity in Cusanus, see Emmanuel Falque's essay in chapter 14.

of set theory (Cantor, Hilbert, Russell), specifically the paradox concerning a set of sets not members of themselves: if the set is a member of itself, it contradicts the definition, and if it is not a member of itself, the definition dictates that it is. The mathematical analogy may not fully illuminate the Cusan task that, for all the use of mathematics, is essentially philosophical and theological in nature. Yet I think it does make more clear what success in language and naming looks like when it comes to the hyperousiological divine. Absolute success is ruled out; the linguistic or conceptual system does not have the capacity to describe or explain the superessential Trinitarian divine. Ruled out also, however, is a kind of total semantic and alethic failure that would suggest there is no positive connection between the linguistic or conceptual system and the transcendental signified, such that we are left with semiosis on the linguistic level and agnosticism on the epistemological.

The kind of philosophy and theology practiced by Cusanus enacts a form of apophasis that acknowledges change, plurality, and contestation. It makes clear that a linguistic and conceptual economy that would name the ultimate is one of programmed failure, and not a failure that simply happens. Moreover, the failure is not total. Cusan apophasis is the central feature or operator of an economy of failure that is limited. It can be said, therefore, that not only does Cusanus make the icon a theme in his work (*De visione Dei*), but his entire system is iconic, in that it is intended to scuttle any attempted mastery over the Other who is precisely Not-Other. All linguistic and conceptual systems are by the nature of the case forms of idolatry. The icon is the presence of the Other who cannot be made present and necessarily turns the tables on the vocabulary and grammar that would make the Other as totally Other hostage. Analogously, "Nicholas of Cusa" is the proper name for a linguistic-conceptual implosion that invites emulation, but rules out the prospect of strict repetition. For Cusanus, arguably, unlike many practitioners of apophatic theology, the emphasis is far more on function and process than on the terms themselves and also far more on finding analogies for this process wherever we might find them—in mathematics certainly, but potentially in any of the sciences and, given the weave of "conjecture," any of the arts. Nicholas of Cusa's being an icon means that we cannot replicate, but we can, as the Wittgenstein of *Philosophical Investigations* says of the true student, "go on."

Here I pivot to more speculative reflections on Nicholas of Cusa's iconicity. One of the glories of Cusan thought is how he maintains the tension between unity and plurality at the philosophical, theological, ecclesial, and theology of religions level. In the case of philosophy, there can be no doubt there exists a serious gravitational pull in Cusanus toward unity as foundational of reality. Simultaneously, however, there is the attempt to value the plurality of things as in the form of contracted infinites or irreducibly perspectival points of view. Preservation of the tension is calculated to avoid a henological metaphysics and non-perspectival point of view, on the one hand, and a flaccid metaphysical plurality with no integrity and an incipient monadology, on the other. Furthermore, the tension is irreducible: any movement toward either of the poles is necessarily going to generate a counterpull, because the evidence is insufficient to validate either a unitary or a pluralist position. With regard to theology, the tension is between a unitive source with regard to which the teeming plurality of the world is not an accident, and a unitive—even if paradoxical—Christ, whose look figures each person as irreducible and intrinsically perspectival. To complete the inventory, but without further expatiation, one can extrapolate from the tension left intact by Cusanus between the claims of papal supremacy and the authority of the council to the tension between the magisterium and the college of bishops. The reduction of the bipolar tension to one or other of the poles does an injustice to catholicity. One might also note the tension between the claim that Christianity is the unsurpassed religion and the sanctioning of other religions, which can be resolved only on pain of either a dangerous triumphalism or a saccharine pluralism.[15]

Finally, with respect to the iconicity of Nicholas Cusa that makes possible a Cusan future, I would like to speculate awhile on the prospects of the future of possibility that Cusanus brings to our attention: neither exhaustively modal, in that it distinguishes adequately between possibility and reality or even possibility and necessity, nor exhaustively temporal, as is the case with Heidegger. In speaking of *posse*, Cusanus wants to point to a power of being that not only grounds but enables, and not only enables but refreshes, inspires, and respires, and while giving time never lets itself be clogged or sedimented.[16] Perhaps it is not going too far to say that possibility is precisely the transformative reality that gives a future to all things,

---

15 On Cusanus and non-Christian religious and philosophical traditions, see the essays by Kazuhiko Yamaki in chapter 7 and João Maria André in chapter 13.

16 On possibility in Cusanus, see Michael Edward Moore's essay on Hans-Georg Gadamer in chapter 3.

without itself being that future anticipated in the present and the past. There are tantalizing lines of connection between Nicholas of Cusa's understanding of possibility and Schelling's experimental and cryptic *Die Weltalter*. The absolute future is the ultimate mark of a dynamic divine that will continue to elude all linguistic and conceptual systems, even while compelling them to intimate and pursue precisely such a naming.

Bibliography

Works of Nicholas of Cusa

Apologia doctae ignorantiae (1449). *Nicolai de Cusa Opera Omnia.* Vol. II. Edited by Raymond Klibansky. Leipzig: Felix Meiner Verlag, 1932. Translated by Jasper Hopkins as *Nicholas of Cusa's Debate with John Wenck. A Translation and an Appraisal of "De Ignota Litteratura" and "Apologia Doctae Ignorantiae"* (Minneapolis: Arthur J. Banning Press, 1981). Reprinted in *Complete Philosophical and Theological Treatises of Nicholas of Cusa*, vol. 1, 459–92 (Minneapolis: Arthur J. Banning Press, 2001).

Compendium (1464). *Nicolai de Cusa Opera Omnia.* Vol. XI/3. Edited by Bruno Decker and Karl Bormann. Hamburg: Felix Meiner Verlag, 1964. Translated by Jasper Hopkins as *Nicholas of Cusa on Wisdom and Knowledge* (Minneapolis: Arthur J. Banning Press, 1996). Reprinted in *Complete Philosophical and Theological Treatises of Nicholas of Cusa*, vol. 2, 1386–1419 (Minneapolis: Arthur J. Banning Press, 2001).

De aequalitate (1459). *Nicolai de Cusa Opera Omnia.* Vol. X/1. Edited by Hans Gerhard Senger. Hamburg: Felix Meiner Verlag, 2001. Translated by Jasper Hopkins as *Nicholas of Cusa: Metaphysical Speculations* (Minneapolis: Arthur J. Banning Press, 1998). Reprinted in *Complete Philosophical and Theological Treatises of Nicholas of Cusa*, vol. 2, 842–76 (Minneapolis: Arthur J. Banning Press, 2001).

De apice theoriae (1464). *Nicolai de Cusa Opera Omnia.* Vol. XII. Edited by Raymond Klibansky and Hans Gerhard Senger. Hamburg: Felix Meiner Verlag, 1982. Translated by H. Lawrence Bond as *Nicholas of Cusa: Selected Spiritual Writings*, 293–303 (New York: Paulist Press, 1997). Translated by Jasper Hopkins in *Nicholas of Cusa: Metaphysical Speculations* (Minneapolis: Arthur J. Banning Press, 1998). Reprinted in *Complete Philosophical and Theological Treatises of Nicholas of Cusa*, vol. 2, 1423–42 (Minneapolis: Arthur J. Banning Press, 2001).

De beryllo (1458). *Nicolai de Cusa Opera Omnia.* Vol. XI/1. Edited by Hans Gerhard Senger and Karl Bormann. Hamburg: Felix Meiner Verlag, 1988. Translated by Jasper Hopkins in *Nicholas of Cusa: Metaphysical Speculations* (Minneapolis: Arthur J. Banning Press,

1998). Reprinted in *Complete Philosophical and Theological Treatises of Nicholas of Cusa*, vol. 2, 792–838 (Minneapolis: Arthur J. Banning Press, 2001).

De caesarea circuli quadratura (1457). *Nicolai de Cusa Opera Omnia.* Vol. XX. *Scripta Mathematica.* Edited by Menso Folkerts. Hamburg: Felix Meiner Verlag, 2010. Translated by Jean-Marie Nicolle in *Nicolas de Cues: Écrits mathématiques* (Paris: Honoré Champion, 2007), 406–27.

De coniecturis (1440–42). *Nicolai de Cusa Opera Omnia.* Vol. III. Edited by Karl Bormann and Hans Gerhard Senger. Hamburg: Felix Meiner Verlag, 1972. Translated by Jasper Hopkins in *Nicholas of Cusa: Metaphysical Speculations*, vol. 2 (Minneapolis: Arthur J. Banning Press, 2000). Reprinted in *Complete Philosophical and Theological Treatises of Nicholas of Cusa*, vol. 1, 163–297 (Minneapolis: Arthur J. Banning Press, 2001).

De dato patris luminum (1445–46). *Nicolai de Cusa Opera Omnia.* Vol. IV. Edited by Paul Wilpert. Hamburg: Felix Meiner Verlag, 1959. Translated by Jasper Hopkins in *Nicholas of Cusa's Metaphysic of Contraction* (Minneapolis: Arthur J. Banning Press, 1983). Reprinted in *Complete Philosophical and Theological Treatises of Nicholas of Cusa*, vol. 1, 372–90 (Minneapolis: Arthur J. Banning Press, 2001).

De docta ignorantia (1440). *Nikolaus von Kues: Philosophisch-Theologische Werke.* Vol. 1. Edited by Paul Wilpert and Hans Gerhard Senger, rev. ed. Hamburg: Felix Meiner Verlag, 2002. Translated by Jasper Hopkins as *Nicholas of Cusa on Learned Ignorance* (Minneapolis: Arthur J. Banning Press, 1985). Reprinted in *Complete Theological and Philosophical Treatises of Nicholas of Cusa*, vol. 1, 3–159 (Minneapolis: Arthur J. Banning Press, 2001). Translated by H. Lawrence Bond in *Nicholas of Cusa: Selected Spiritual Writings*, 87–206 (New York: Paulist Press, 1997).

De filiatione Dei (1445). *Nicolai de Cusa Opera Omnia.* Vol. IV. Edited by Paul Wilpert. Hamburg: Felix Meiner Verlag, 1959. Translated by Jasper Hopkins in *A Miscellany on Nicholas of Cusa* (Minneapolis: Arthur J. Banning Press, 1994). Reprinted in *Complete Philosophical and Theological Treatises of Nicholas of Cusa*, vol. 1, 341–69 (Minneapolis: Arthur J. Banning Press, 2001).

De non aliud (1462). *Nicolai de Cusa Opera Omnia.* Vol. XIII. Edited by Ludwig Baur and Paul Wilpert. Leipzig: Felix Meiner Verlag, 1944. Translated by Jasper Hopkins as *Nicholas of Cusa on God as Not-Other*, 3rd ed. (Minneapolis: Arthur J. Banning Press, 1987). Reprinted in *Complete Theological and Philosophical Treatises of Nicholas of Cusa*, vol. 2, 1106–78 (Minneapolis: Arthur J. Banning Press, 2001).

De pace fidei (1454). *Nicolai de Cusa Opera Omnia.* Vol. VII. Edited by Raymond Klibansky and Hildebrand Bascour. 2nd ed. Hamburg: Felix Meiner Verlag, 1970. Translated by Jasper Hopkins in *Nicholas of Cusa's "De pace fidei" and "Cribatio Alkorani": Translation and Analysis*, 2nd ed. (Minneapolis: Arthur J. Banning Press, 1994). Reprinted in *Complete Philosophical and Theological Treatises of Nicholas of Cusa*, vol. 1, 633–76 (Minneapolis: Arthur J. Banning Press, 2001).

De principio [Tu quis es] (1459). *Nicolai de Cusa Opera Omnia.* Vol. X/2b. Edited by Karl Bormann and Heide Dorothea Riemann. Hamburg: Felix Meiner Verlag, 1988. Translated by Jasper Hopkins in *Nicholas of Cusa: Metaphysical Speculations*

(Minneapolis: Arthur J. Banning Press, 1998). Reprinted in *Complete Philosophical and Theological Treatises of Nicholas of Cusa*, vol. 2, 880–911 (Minneapolis: Arthur J. Banning Press, 2001).

De quaerendo Deum (1445). *Nicolai de Cusa Opera Omnia*. Vol. IV. Edited by Paul Wilpert. Hamburg: Felix Meiner Verlag, 1959. Translated by Jasper Hopkins in *A Miscellany on Nicholas of Cusa* (Minneapolis: Arthur J. Banning Press, 1994). Reprinted in *Complete Philosophical and Theological Treatises of Nicholas of Cusa*, vol. 1, 314–38 (Minneapolis: Arthur J. Banning Press, 2001). Translated by H. Lawrence Bond in *Nicholas of Cusa: Selected Spiritual Writings*, 217–31 (New York: Paulist Press, 1997).

De theologicis complementis (1453). *Nicolai de Cusa Opera Omnia*. Vol. X/2a. Edited by Heide Dorothea Riemann and Karl Bormann. Hamburg: Felix Meiner Verlag, 1994. Translated by Jasper Hopkins in *Nicholas of Cusa: Metaphysical Speculations* (Minneapolis: Arthur J. Banning Press, 1998). Reprinted in *Complete Philosophical and Theological Treatises of Nicholas of Cusa*, vol. 2, 747–88 (Minneapolis: Arthur J. Banning Press, 2001).

De venatione sapientiae (1463). *Nicolai de Cusa Opera Omnia*. Vol. XII. Edited by Raymond Klibansky and Hans Gerhard Senger. Hamburg: Felix Meiner Verlag, 1982. Translated by Jasper Hopkins in *Nicholas of Cusa: Metaphysical Speculations* (Minneapolis: Arthur J. Banning Press, 1998). Reprinted in *Complete Philosophical and Theological Treatises of Nicholas of Cusa*, vol. 2, 1278–1381 (Minneapolis: Arthur J. Banning Press, 2001).

De visione Dei (1453). *Nicolai de Cusa Opera Omnia*. Vol. VI. Edited by Heide Dorothea Riemann. Hamburg: Felix Meiner Verlag, 2000. Translated by Agnès Minazzoli as *Le tableau ou la vision de Dieu* (Paris: Les Éditions du Cerf, 1986). Translated by Jasper Hopkins as *Nicholas of Cusa's Dialectical Mysticism: Text, Translation, and Interpretive Study of "De Visione Dei"*, 2nd ed. (Minneapolis: Arthur J. Banning Press, 1988). Reprinted in *Complete Philosophical and Theological Treatises of Nicholas of Cusa*, vol. 2, 679–743 (Minneapolis: Arthur J. Banning Press, 2001). Translated by H. Lawrence Bond in *Nicholas of Cusa: Selected Spiritual Writings*, 235–89 (New York: Paulist Press, 1997). Translated by Hervé Pasqua as *L'icône ou la vision de Dieu* (Paris: Presses Universitaires de France, 2016).

Dialogus de Deo abscondito (1444). *Nicolai de Cusa Opera Omnia*. Vol. IV. Edited by Paul Wilpert. Hamburg: Felix Meiner Verlag, 1959. Translated by Jasper Hopkins in *A Miscellany on Nicholas of Cusa* (Minneapolis: Arthur J. Banning Press, 1994). Reprinted in *Complete Philosophical and Theological Treatises of Nicholas of Cusa*, vol. 1, 300–311 (Minneapolis: Arthur J. Banning Press, 2001). Translated by H. Lawrence Bond in *Nicholas of Cusa: Selected Spiritual Writings*, 209–13 (New York: Paulist Press, 1997).

Dialogus de genesi (1447). *Nicolai de Cusa Opera Omnia*. Vol. IV. Edited by Paul Wilpert. Hamburg: Felix Meiner Verlag, 1959. Translated by Jasper Hopkins in *A Miscellany on Nicholas of Cusa* (Minneapolis: Arthur J. Banning Press, 1994). Reprinted in

Complete Philosophical and Theological Treatises of Nicholas of Cusa, vol. 1, 393–422 (Minneapolis: Arthur J. Banning Press, 2001).

Dialogus de ludo globi (1463). *Nicolai de Cusa Opera Omnia*. Vol. IX. Edited by Hans Gerhard Senger. Hamburg: Felix Meiner Verlag, 1998. Translated by Jasper Hopkins in *Nicholas of Cusa: Metaphysical Speculations*, vol. 2, 1182–1274 (Minneapolis: Arthur J. Banning Press, 2000). Reprinted in *Complete Philosophical and Theological Treatises of Nicholas of Cusa*, vol. 2, 1182–1274 (Minneapolis: Arthur J. Banning Press, 2001).

Idiota de mente (1450). *Nicolai de Cusa Opera Omnia*. Vol. V. Edited by Renate Steiger. Hamburg: Felix Meiner Verlag, 1983. Translated by Jasper Hopkins in *Nicholas of Cusa on Wisdom and Knowledge* (Minneapolis: Arthur J. Banning Press, 1996). Reprinted in *Complete Philosophical and Theological Treatises of Nicholas of Cusa*, vol. 1, 531–601 (Minneapolis: Arthur J. Banning Press, 2001).

Idiota de sapientia (1450). *Nicolai de Cusa Opera Omnia*. Vol. V. Edited by Ludwig Baur and Renata Steiger. Hamburg: Felix Meiner Verlag, 1983. Translated by Jasper Hopkins in *Nicholas of Cusa on Wisdom and Knowledge* (Minneapolis: Arthur J. Banning Press, 1996). Reprinted in *Complete Philosophical and Theological Treatises of Nicholas of Cusa*, vol. 1, 497–526 (Minneapolis: Arthur J. Banning Press, 2001).

Sermons (selected). *Nicolai de Cusa Opera Omnia*. Vol. XVIII, *Sermones III (1452–1455), Fasc. 2*. Edited by Heinrich Pauli. Hamburg: Felix Meiner Verlag, 2001. Vol. XVIII, *Sermones III (1452–1455), Fasc. 3*. Edited by Silvia Donati, Isabella Mandrella, and Harald Schwaetzer. Hamburg: Felix Meiner Verlag, 2003. Vol. XIX/2, *Sermones IV (1455–1463), Fasc. 2*. Edited by Marc-Aeilko Aris, Silvia Donati, et al. Hamburg: Felix Meiner Verlag, 2001. Translated by Jasper Hopkins in *Nicholas of Cusa's Didactic Sermons: A Selection* (Loveland, CO: Arthur J. Banning Press, 2008). Additional sermons are translated in Thomas M. Izbicki, *Nicholas of Cusa: Writings on Church and Reform* (Cambridge, MA: Harvard University Press, 2008).

Trialogus de possest (1460). *Nicolai de Cusa Opera Omnia*. Vol. XI/2. Edited by Renata Steiger. Hamburg: Felix Meiner Verlag, 1973. Translated by Jasper Hopkins in *A Concise Introduction to the Philosophy of Nicholas of Cusa* (Minneapolis: University of Minnesota Press, 1978). Reprinted in *Complete Theological and Philosophical Treatises of Nicholas of Cusa*, vol. 2, 912–62 (Minneapolis: Arthur J. Banning Press, 2001).

Other Works

Agamben, Giorgio. *The Use of Bodies*. Translated by Adam Kotsko. Stanford, CA: Stanford University Press, 2016.

Aikin, Scott F., and Jason Aleksander. "Nicholas of Cusa's *De pace fidei* and the Meta-exclusivism of Religious Pluralism." *International Journal for Philosophy of Religion* 74 (2013): 219–235.

Alan of Lille. "Sermon sur le thème: Deus est sphaera intelligibilis." In *Alain de Lille: Textes inédits*, edited by Marie-Thérèse D'Alverny, 297–306. Paris: J. Vrin, 1965.

———. "Magister Alanus de Insulis Regulae Caelestis Iuris." Edited by Nikolaus M. Häring. *Archives d'histoire doctrinale et littéraire du Moyen Âge* 48 (1981): 97–226.

———. *Literary Works*. Edited and translated by Winthrop Wetherbee. Cambridge, MA: Harvard University Press, 2013.

Alberti, Leon Battista. *On Painting: A New Translation and Critical Edition*. Edited and translated by Rocco Sinisgalli. Cambridge: Cambridge University Press, 2011.

Albertini, Tamara. "Nicholas of Cusa's Mathematics and Astronomy." In Bellito, Izbicki and Christianson, *Introducing Nicholas of Cusa*, 373–406.

———. "'Clarity Is What I Seek First.' Interview with Prof. Tamara Albertini." By Piotr Pietrzak. In *Statu Nascendi* 3, no. 2 (2020): 20–37.

Albertson, David. *Mathematical Theologies: Nicholas of Cusa and the Legacy of Thierry of Chartres*. New York: Oxford University Press, 2014.

———. "*Boethius Noster*: Thierry of Chartres's *Arithmetica* Commentary as a Missing Source of Nicholas of Cusa's *De docta ignorantia*." *Recherches de théologie et philosophie médiévales* 83, no. 1 (2016): 143–99.

———. "Before the Icon: The Figural Matrix of *De visione Dei*." In *Nicholas of Cusa and Times of Transition: Essays in Honor of Gerald Christianson*, edited by Thomas M. Izbicki, Jason Aleksander, and Donald F. Duclow, 262–85. Leiden: Brill, 2019.

———. "Cataphasis, Visualization, and Mystical Space." In *The Oxford Handbook of Mystical Theology*, edited by Edward Howells and Mark A. McIntosh, 347–68. Oxford: Oxford University Press, 2020.

———. "Inside the Fold: Gilles Deleuze and the Christian Neoplatonist Tradition." In *Mystical Theology and Platonism in the Time of Cusanus: Essays in Honor of Donald F. Duclow*, edited by Jason Aleksander, Sean Hannan, Joshua Hollmann, and Michael Edward Moore, 347–83. Leiden: Brill, 2023.

Álvarez-Gómez, Mariano. *Die verborgene Gegenwart des Unendlichen bei Nikolaus von Kues*. Munich: Anton Pustet, 1968.

———. "Hacia los fundamentos de la paz perpetua en la religión según Nicolás de Cusa." *La Ciudad de Dios* 212, no. 2 (1999): 299–340.

Anderson, Lisa Marie, ed. *Hamann and the Tradition*. Evanston, IL: Northwestern University Press, 2012.

André, João Maria. "Conocer es dialogar: Las metáforas del conocimiento y su dimensión dialógica en el pensamiento de Nicolás de Cusa." In *El problema del conocimiento en Nicolás de Cusa*, edited by Jorge M. Machetta and Claudia D'Amico, 15–38. Buenos Aires: Editorial Biblos, 2005.

———. *Nikolaus von Kues und die Kraft des Wortes*. Trier: Paulinus Verlag, 2006.

———. "Dimensões antropológicas da douta ignorância." In *Manuductiones. Festschrift zu Ehren von Jorge M. Machetta und Claudia D'Amico*, edited by Cecilia Rusconi and Klaus Reinhardt, 93–121. Münster: Aschendorff Verlag, 2014.

———. "Sehen ist auch Hören und Sprechen: Dialogische dimensionen in *De visione Dei*." In *Nikolaus von Kues—Denken im Dialog*, edited by Walter Andreas Euler, 27–42. Münster: LIT Verlag, 2019.

Arendt, Hannah. *The Human Condition*. 2nd ed. Chicago: University of Chicago Press, 1998.

Aristotle. *Aristotle's Metaphysics: A Revised Text with Introduction and Commentary*. Edited by W. David Ross. 2 vols. Oxford: Clarendon Press, 1924.

———. *Nicomachean Ethics*. Translated by Christopher Rowe. Oxford: Oxford University Press, 2002.

Aubenque, Pierre. *Le problème de l'être chez Aristote*. Paris: Presses Universitaires de France, 1962.

Augustine of Hippo. *De Genesi ad litteram*. CSEL 28. Edited by Joseph Zycha. Vienna: Hölder-Pichler-Tempsky, 1894.

———. *The Literal Meaning of Genesis*. Vol. 2. Translated by John Hammond Taylor, SJ. New York: Newman Press, 1982.

———. *De doctrina christiana*. Edited by R. P. H. Green. Oxford: Clarendon, 1995.

———. *The City of God against the Pagans*. Edited and translated by R. W. Dyson. Cambridge: Cambridge University Press, 1998.

Bachelard, Gaston. *The Poetics of Space*. Translated by Maria Jolas. Boston: Beacon Press, 1994.

Bacon, Francis. *L'art de l'impossible: Entretiens avec David Sylvester*. Milan: Skira, 1976.

Badiou, Alain. *Being and Event*. Translated by Oliver Feltham. New York: Continuum, 2005.

Balthasar, Hans Urs von. *The Glory of the Lord*. Vol. 1, *Seeing the Form*. Translated by Erasmo Leiva-Merikakis. San Francisco: Ignatius Press, 1983.

———. *La gloire et la croix*. Vol. 1. Paris: Desclée de Brouwer, 1990.

———. *Mysterium Paschale: The Mystery of Easter*. Translated by Aidan Nichols. San Francisco: Ignatius Press, 2000.

———. *Herrlichkeit. Eine theologische Ästhetik*. Bd. III, 1: Im Raum der Metaphysik. Teil II: Neuzeit. 3rd ed. Einsiedeln: Johannes Verlag, 2009.

Bauerschmidt, Frederick Christian. "The Abrahamic Voyage: Michel de Certeau and Theology." *Modern Theology* 12, no. 1 (1996): 1–26.

———. "The Otherness of God." *South Atlantic Quarterly* 100, no. 2 (Spring 2001): 349–64.

Baum, Matthias. *Die Hermeneutik Hans-Georg Gadamers als philosophia christiana: Eine Interpretation von "Wahrheit und Methode" in christlich-theologischer Perspektive.* Tübingen: Mohr Siebeck, 2002.

Bayer, Oswald. "Die Geschichten der Vernunft sind die Kritik ihrer Reinheit: Hamanns Weg zur Metakritik Kants." In *Hamann—Kant—Herder: Acta des vierten Internationalen Hamann-Kolloquiums*, edited by Bernhard Gajek, 9–87. Frankfurt am Main: Peter Lang, 1987.

Beccarisi, Alessandra. "Deus est sphaera intellectualis infinita: Eckhart interprete del *Liber XXIV philosophorum*." In Totaro and Valente, *Sphaera* 167–92.

———. "'nich sint ez allez heidenischer meister wort, die niht enbekanten dan in einem natiurlîchen liehte': Eckhart e il *Liber vigintiquattuor philosophorum*." In *Studi sulle fonti di Meister Eckhart II*, edited by Loris Sturlese, 73–96. Fribourg: Academic Press Fribourg, 2012.

Beierwaltes, Werner. "*Deus oppositio oppositorum*: Nicolaus Cusanus, *De visione Dei* XIII." *Salzburger Jahrbuch für Philosophie* 8, no. 1 (1964): 175–85.

———. *Platonismus und Idealismus.* Frankfurt am Main: Vittorio Klostermann, 1972.

———. *Identität und Differenz: Zum Prinzip cusanischen Denkens. 219. Sitzung am 16. Februar 1977 in Düsseldorf.* Opladen: Westdeutscher Verlag, 1977.

———. *Identität und Differenz.* Frankfurt am Main: Vittorio Klostermann, 1980.

———. *Denken des Einen: Studien zur neuplatonischen Philosophie.* Frankfurt am Main: Vittorio Klostermann, 1985.

———. "*Liber XXIV philosophorum*." In *Die deutsche Literatur des Mittelalters: Verfasserlexikon*, edited by Kurt Ruh et al., 767–70. Berlin: De Gruyter, 1985.

———. "*Visio Absoluta*": *Reflexion als Grundzug des göttlichen Prinzips bei Nicolaus Cusanus.* Heidelberg: Sitzungsberichte der Heidelberger Akademie der Wissenschaften, Philosophisch-historische Klasse 1, 1989.

———. "*Visio Facialis*—Sehen ins Angesicht. Zur Coinzidenz des endlichen und unendlichen Blicks bei Cusanus." In *Das Sehen Gottes nach Nikolaus von Kues. Akten des Symposions in Trier vom 25. bis 27. September 1986*, MFCG 18, edited by Rudolf Haubst, 91–124. Trier: Paulinus Verlag, 1989.

———. *Platonismus im Christentum.* Frankfurt am Main: Vittorio Klostermann, 1998.

———. "Das Verhältnis von Philosophie und Theologie bei Nicolaus Cusanus." In *Nikolaus von Kues: 1401–2001. Akten des Symposiums in Bernkastel-Kues vom 23.–26. Mai 2001*, MFCG 28, edited by Klaus Kremer and Klaus Reinhardt, 65–102. Trier: Paulinus Verlag, 2003.

———. *Cusanus: Reflexión metafísica y espiritualidad.* Translated by Joaquín Alberto Ciria Cosculluela. Pamplona: Ediciones Universidad de Navarra, S.A., 2005.

———. *"Catena Aurea": Plotin, Augustinus, Eriugena, Thomas, Cusanus*. Frankfurt am Main: Vittorio Klostermann, 2017.

Bellito, Christopher M., Thomas M. Izbicki, and Gerald Christianson, eds. *Introducing Nicholas of Cusa: A Guide to a Renaissance Man*. Mahwah, NJ: Paulist Press, 2004.

Bendon Davis, Carmel. *Mysticism and Space: Space and Spatiality in the Works of Richard Rolle, The Cloud of Unknowing Author, and Julian of Norwich*. Washington, DC: The Catholic University of America Press, 2008.

Benedict XVI. *Jesus of Nazareth*. Vol. 1. New York: Doubleday, 2007.

Benz, Hubert. *Individualität und Subjektivität: Interpretationstendenzen in der Cusanus-Forschung und das Selbstverständnis des Nikolaus von Kues*. Münster: Aschendorff Verlag, 1999.

Betz, John R. *After Enlightenment: The Post-Secular Vision of J. G. Hamann*. Oxford: Wiley-Blackwell, 2009.

———. "Reading Sibylline Leaves: Hamann in the History of Ideas." *Journal of the History of Ideas* 70 (January 2009): 93–118.

Biechler, James E. "Interreligious Dialogue." In Bellito, Izbicki, and Christianson, *Introducing Nicholas of Cusa*, 270–96.

Bieler, Martin. "*Analogia Entis* as an Expression of Love according to Ferdinand Ulrich." In *The Analogy of Being: Invention of the Antichrist or the Wisdom of God?*, edited by Thomas Joseph White, OP, 314–37. Grand Rapids, MI: Eerdmans, 2011.

Blumenberg, Hans, ed. *Nikolaus von Cues: Die Kunst der Vermutung. Auswahl aus den Schriften*. Bremen: Carl Schünemann Verlag, 1957.

———. *Die Legitimität der Neuzeit: Erneuerte Ausgabe*. Frankfurt am Main: Suhrkamp Verlag, 1966.

———. *Die Legitimität der Neuzeit (erweiterte und überarbeitete Neuausgabe)*. Frankfurt am Main: Suhrkamp Verlag, 1973–1976.

———. *The Legitimacy of the Modern Age*. Translated by Robert M. Wallace. Cambridge, MA: MIT Press, 1983.

Bocken, Inigo. "Der Kampf um Kommunikation: Karl Jaspers' existentielle Cusanus-Lektüre." In Reinhardt and Schwaetzer, *Cusanus-Rezeption in der Philosophie des 20. Jahrhunderts*, 51–66.

———. "Nirgendwo zu Hause? Die Rhetorik des Wohnens nach Michel de Certeau." In *Wohnen*, vol. 3 of *Felderkundungen Laienspiritualität*, edited by Ulrich Dickmann and Wolfgang Christian Schneider, 33–58. Schwerte: Katholische Akademie, 2011.

———. "Nomad and Layman: Spiritual Spaces in Modernity—Mysticism and Everyday Life in Michel de Certeau." In Bocken, *Spiritual Spaces*, 111–23.

———, ed. *Spiritual Spaces: History and Mysticism in Michel de Certeau*. Leuven: Peeters, 2013.

Boethius. *Anicii Manlii Severini Boethii Philosophiae consolatio*. CCSL 94. Edited by Ludwig Bieler. Turnhout: Brepols, 1957.

———. *De consolatione philosophiae. Opuscula theologica*. Edited by Claudio Moreschini. Munich: K. G. Saur, 2005.

Böhlandt, Marco. *Verborgene Zahl—Verborgener Gott: Mathematik und Naturwissen im Denken des Nicolaus Cusanus (1401–1464)*. Stuttgart: Franz Steiner Verlag, 2009.

Bond, H. Lawrence. "Nicholas of Cusa from Constantinople to 'Learned Ignorance': The Historical Matrix for the Formation of the *De docta ignorantia*." In *Nicholas of Cusa on Christ and the Church: Essays in Memory of Chandler McCuskey Brooks for the American Cusanus Society*, edited by Gerald Christianson and Thomas M. Izbicki, 107–26. Leiden: Brill, 1996.

Borges, Jorge L. "Pascal's Sphere." In *Other Inquisitions (1937–1952)*. Translated by Ruth L. C. Simms. Austin: University of Texas Press, 1964.

Boulnois, Olivier. *Métaphysiques rebelles: Genèse et structures d'une science au Môyen Age*. Paris: Presses Universitaires de France, 2013.

Bredow, Gerda von, ed. *Cusanus-Texte IV. Briefwechsel des Nikolaus von Kues. Dritte Sammlung: Das Vermächtnis des Nikolaus von Kues. Der Brief an Nikolaus Albergati nebst der Predigt in Montoliveto (1463)*. Heidelberg: Carl Winter Verlag, 1955.

———. *Im Gespräch mit Nikolaus von Kues: Gesammelte Aufsätze 1948–1993*. Edited by Hermann Schnarr. Münster: Aschendorff Verlag, 1995.

Brient, Elizabeth. "Transitions to a Modern Cosmology: Meister Eckhart and Nicholas of Cusa on the Intensive Infinite." *Journal of the History of Philosophy* 37, no. 4 (1999): 575–600.

———. *The Immanence of the Infinite: Hans Blumenberg and the Threshold to Modernity*. Washington, DC: The Catholic University of America Press, 2002.

———. "Blumenberg Reading Cusanus: Metaphor and Modernity." In *Erinnerung an das Humane: Beiträge zur phänomenologischen Anthropologie Hans Blumenbergs*, edited by Michael Moxter, 122–44. Tübingen: Mohr Siebeck, 2011.

———. "Epochenschwelle." In *Blumenberg lesen: Ein Glossar*, edited by Robert Buch and Daniel Weidner, 72–86. Berlin: Suhrkamp Verlag, 2014.

Bruford, W. H. *Culture and Society in Classical Weimar, 1775–1806*. Cambridge: Cambridge University Press, 1962.

Buchanan, Ian. "Heterophenomenology, or de Certeau's Theory of Space." *Social Semiotics* 6, no. 1 (1996): 111–32.

Caiazzo, Irene, ed. *Thierry of Chartres: The Commentary on the "De arithmetica" of Boethius*. Toronto: Pontifical Institute of Mediaeval Studies, 2015.

Carman, Charles H. *Leon Battista Alberti and Nicholas Cusanus: Towards an Epistemology of Vision for Italian Renaissance Art and Culture*. Burlington, VT: Ashgate, 2014.

Casarella, Peter. "Nicholas of Cusa and the Power of the Possible." *American Catholic Philosophical Quarterly* 64, no. 1 (1990): 7–34.

———. "'Modern Forms Filled with Traditional Spiritual Content': On Louis Dupré's Contribution to Christian Theology." In *Christian Spirituality and the Culture of Modernity: The Thought of Louis Dupré*, edited by Peter J. Casarella and George P. Schner, SJ, 275–310. Grand Rapids, MI: Eerdmans, 1998.

———. "Cusanus on Dionysius: The Turn to Speculative Theology." In *Re-Thinking Dionysius the Areopagite*, edited by Sarah Coakley and Charles M. Stang, 137–48. Malden, MA: Wiley Blackwell, 2009.

———. *Word as Bread: Language and Theology in Nicholas of Cusa*. Münster: Aschendorff Verlag, 2017.

Casey, Edward S. *The Fate of Place: A Philosophical History*. Berkeley: University of California Press, 1997.

Certeau, Michel de. "Nicolas de Cues: Le secret d'un regard." *Traverses* 30–31 (1984): 70–85.

———. *The Practice of Everyday Life*. Translated by Steven Rendall. Berkeley: University of California Press, 1984.

———. "What We Do When We Believe." In *On Signs*, edited by Marshall Blonsky, 193–202. Baltimore: Johns Hopkins University Press, 1985.

———. "The Gaze: Nicholas of Cusa." *Diacritics* 17 (1987): 2–38.

———. *The Writing of History*. Translated by Tom Conley. New York: Columbia University Press, 1988.

———. *The Mystic Fable*. Vol. 1, *The Sixteenth and Seventeenth Centuries*. Edited by Luce Giard. Translated by Michael B. Smith. Chicago: University of Chicago Press, 1992.

———. "How is Christianity Thinkable Today?" In *The Postmodern God: A Theological Reader*, edited by Graham Ward, 142–55. London: Wiley Blackwell, 1997.

———. "White Ecstasy." In *The Postmodern God: A Theological Reader*. Edited by Graham Ward, 155–58. London: Wiley Blackwell, 1997.

———. "The Weakness of Believing: From the Body to Writing, A Christian Transit." Translated by Saskia Brown. In *The Certeau Reader*, edited by Graham Ward, 214–43. Oxford: Blackwell, 2000.

———. *La Fable mystique. XVIe-XVIIe Siècle, tome II*. Edited by Luce Giard. Paris: Éditions Gallimard, 2013.

———. *The Mystic Fable*. Vol. 2, *The Sixteenth and Seventeenth Centuries*. Translated by Michael B. Smith. Chicago: University of Chicago Press, 2015.

Colomer, Eusebio. "Nicolau de Cusa (1401–1464): Um pensador na fronteira de dois mundos." *Revista portuguesa de filosofia* 20 (1964): 5–62.

Counet, Jean-Michel. "Philosopher, c'est faire l'idiot: Le Cusain en filigrane dans l'oeuvre de Gilles Deleuze." *Noesis* 26/27 (2015–2016): 247–63.

D'Alverny, Marie-Thérèse, ed. *Alain de Lille: Textes inédits*. Paris: J. Vrin, 1965.

D'Amico, Claudia, ed. *Todo y nada de todo*. Buenos Aires: Ediciones Winograd, 2008.

Danet, Henriette. *Gloire et croix de Jésus-Christ: L'analogie chez H. Urs von Balthasar comme introduction à la Christologie*. Paris: Desclée de Brouwer, 1987.

Daniélou, Jean. *Origen*. Translated by Walter Mitchell. New York: Sheed & Ward, 1955.

Dante Alighieri. *The Convivio*. Translated by Philip Henry Wickstool. London: J. M. Dent, 1903.

Darwin, Charles. *The Origin of Species*. New York: John D. Morris & Co., 1900.

De Lubac, Henri. *The Mystery of the Supernatural*. Translated by Rosemary Sheed. New York: Crossroad, 1998.

De Sousa Santos, Boaventura. *A gramática do tempo: Para uma nova cultura política*. Porto: Afrontamento, 2006.

———. "Toward a Multicultural Conception of Human Rights." In *International Human Rights Law in a Global Context*, edited by Felipe Gómez Isa and Koen de Feyter, 97–122. Bilbao: University of Deusto, 2009.

Deissmann, Adolf. *St. Paul: A Study in Social and Religious History*. Translated by Lionel R. M. Strachan. New York: Hodder & Stoughton, 1912.

Deleuze, Gilles. *Francis Bacon: The Logic of Sensation*. Translated by Daniel W. Smith. Minneapolis: University of Minnesota Press, 1981.

———. *Qu'est-ce que la philosophie?* Paris: Éditions de Minuit, 1991.

———. "Una entrevista, ¿qué es?, ¿para qué sirve?" In *Confesiones filosóficas*, ed. José González Ríos, 165–69. Buenos Aires: Editorial quadrata, 2006.

Demacopoulos, George E. *Gregory the Great: Ascetic, Pastor, and First Man of Rome*. Notre Dame, IN: University of Notre Dame Press, 2015.

Denys the Carthusian. *Doctoris ecstatici D. Dionysii Cartusiani Opera omnia in unum corpus digesta ad fidem editionum Coloniensium, cura et labore monachorum sacri ordinis Cartusiensis favente Pont. Max. Leone XIII*. Monstrolii: Typis Cartusiae S. M. de Pratis, 1896–1935.

Denzinger, Heinrich. *Enchiridion symbolorum definitionum et declarationum de rebus fidei et morum: Compendium of Creeds, Definitions and Declarations on Matters of Faith and Morals*, edited by Peter Hünermann, Robert Fastiggi, and Anne Englund Nash. 43rd ed. San Francisco: Ignatius Press, 2012.

Derman, Joshua. "Philosophy Beyond the Bounds of Reason: The Influence of Max Weber on the Development of Karl Jaspers' *Existenzphilosophie*, 1909–1932." In *Max Weber Matters: Interweaving Past and Present*, edited by Daniel Chalcraft et al., 55–71. Aldershot: Ashgate, 2008.

Derrida, Jacques. "On How Not to Speak: Denials." In *Languages of the Unsayable: The Play of Negativity in Literature and Literary Theory*, edited by Sanford Budick and Wolfgang Iser, 3–70. New York: Columbia University Press, 1989.

Descartes, René. *Regulae ad directionem ingenii*. In *Oeuvres de Descartes*, vol. 10, edited by Charles Adam and Paul Tannery, 349–488. Paris: Léopold Cerf, 1908.

———. *The Philosophical Writings of Descartes*. Edited by John Cottingham, Robert Stoothoff, and Dugald Murdoch. Cambridge: Cambridge University Press, 1985–1991.

Diels, Hermann, ed. *Die Fragmente der Vorsokratiker*. Berlin: Weidmannsche Verlagsbuchhandlung, 1952.

Dionysius the Areopagite. *Corpus Dionysiacum*. Vol. 1, *De divinis nominibus*. Edited by Beate Regina Suchla. Berlin: Walter de Gruyter, 1990.

Doyle, John P. "Suarez on the Analogy of Being." *The Modern Schoolman* 46 (1969): 219–49, 323–41.

Dronke, Peter, ed. *A History of Twelfth-Century Western Philosophy*. Cambridge: Cambridge University Press, 1992.

Duclow, Donald F. "Nicholas of Cusa in the Margins of Meister Eckhart: *Codex Cusanus* 21." In *Nicholas of Cusa in Search of God and Wisdom*, edited by Gerald Christianson and Thomas M. Izbicki, 57–69. Leiden: Brill, 1991.

———. "Life and Works." In Bellito, Izbicki, and Christianson, *Introducing Nicholas of Cusa*, 25–56.

———. "Cusanus' Clock: Time and Eternity in *De visione Dei*." In *Akten des Forschungskolloquiums in Freising vom 8. bis 11. November 2012*, MFCG 34, edited by Walter Andreas Euler, 135–46. Trier: Paulinus Verlag, 2016.

Duportail, Guy-Félix. "Le moment topologique de la phénoménologie française: Merleau-Ponty et Derrida." *Archives de philosophie* 73, no. 1 (2010): 47–65.

Dupré, Louis. "Transcendence and Immanence as Theological Categories." In *Proceedings of the Thirty-First Annual Convention of The Catholic Theological Society of America*, 1–10. New York: Catholic Theological Society of America, 1976.

———. *A Dubious Heritage: Studies in the Philosophy of Religion after Kant*. New York: Paulist Press, 1977.

———. *The Deeper Life: An Introduction to Christian Mysticism*. New York: Crossroad, 1981.

———. "Nature and Grace in Nicholas of Cusa's Mystical Philosophy." *American Catholic Philosophical Quarterly* 64, no. 1 (1990): 153–70.

———. "Ignatian Humanism and Its Mystical Origins." *Communio: International Catholic Review* 18, no. 2 (1991): 164–82.

———. *The Passage to Modernity: An Essay in the Hermeneutics of Nature and Culture*. New Haven, CT: Yale University Press, 1993.

———. *Metaphysics and Culture*. Milwaukee: Marquette University Press, 1994.

———. "The Mystical Theology of Nicholas of Cusa's *De visione Dei*." In *Nicholas of Cusa on Christ and the Church: Essays in Memory of Chandler McCuskey Brooks for the American Cusanus Society*, edited by Gerald Christianson and Thomas M. Izbicki, 205–20. Leiden: Brill, 1996.

———. "The Question of Pantheism from Eckhart to Cusanus." In *Cusanus: The Legacy of Learned Ignorance*, edited by Peter J. Casarella, 74–88. Washington, DC: The Catholic University of America Press, 2006.

———. *Religion and the Rise of Modern Culture*. Notre Dame, IN: University of Notre Dame Press, 2008.

———. "On the Natural Desire of Seeing God." *Radical Orthodoxy: Theology, Philosophy, Politics* 1, nos. 1–2 (August 2012): 81–94.

———. *Thinking the Unknowable*. Notre Dame, IN: University of Notre Dame Press, forthcoming.

Dupré, Louis, and James A. Wiseman, OSB, eds. *Light from Light: An Anthology of Christian Mysticism*. 2nd ed. Mahwah, NJ: Paulist Press, 2001.

Dupré, Wilhelm. "Von der dreifachen Bedeutung der 'docta ignorantia' bei Nikolaus von Kues." *Wissenschaft und Weltbild* 15 (1962): 264–76.

———. "Menschsein und Mensch als Wahrheit im Werden." In *Der Friede unter den Religionen nach Nikolaus von Kues: Akten des Symposions in Trier vom 13. bis 15. Oktober 1982*, MFCG 16, edited by Rudolf Haubst, 313–24. Mainz: Matthias-Grünewald-Verlag, 1984.

———. "Liebe als Grundbestandteil allen Seins und 'Form oder Leben aller Tugenden.'" In *Sein und Sollen: Die Ethik des Nikolaus von Kues*, MFCG 26, edited by Klaus Kremer and Klaus Reinhardt, 65–91. Trier: Paulinus Verlag, 2000.

Ebeling, Florian. *The Secret History of Hermes Trismegistus: Hermeticism from Ancient to Modern Times*. Translated by David Lorton. Ithaca, NY: Cornell University Press, 2007.

Eickhoff, Georg. "Geschichte und Mystik bei Michel de Certeau." *Stimmen der Zeit* 126, Bd. 219 (2001): 248–60.

El-Bizri, Nader. "Being at Home among Things: Heidegger's Reflections on Dwelling." *Environment, Space, Place* 3, no. 1 (Spring 2011): 45–69.

Erismann, Christoph. *L'Homme Commune: La genèse du réalisme ontologique durant le haut Moyen Âge*. Paris: J. Vrin, 2011.

Falque, Emmanuel. "Le Pouvoir-Est (*De Possest*) ou le 'Dieu im-possible' (Nicolas de Cues)." *Archivio di filosofia* 78, no. 1 (2010): 131–42.

———. *God, the Flesh, and the Other: From Irenaeus to Duns Scotus*. Translated by William Christian Hackett. Evanston, IL: Northwestern University Press, 2014.

———. "L'omnivoyant: Fraternité et vision de Dieu chez Nicolas de Cues." *Revue des sciences philosophiques et théologiques* 98, no. 1 (January/March 2014): 37–73.

———. *Parcours d'embûches: S'expliquer*. Paris: Éditions franciscaines, 2016.

———. "Un Dieu ineffable? La querelle de la docte ignorance chez Nicolas de Cues." In *L'Unique seul importe: Hommage à Pierre Magnard*, edited by Alain Galonnier, 103–19. Leuven: Peeters, 2019.

———. "The All-Seeing: Fraternity and Vision of God in Nicholas of Cusa." Translated by Kyle H. Kavanaugh and Barnabas Aspray. *Modern Theology* 35, no. 4 (September 2019): 1–28.

Ferrari, G. R. F. *Listening to the Cicadas: A Study of Plato's "Phaedrus."* Cambridge: Cambridge University Press, 1987.

Ferrer, Diogo. "A Dupla Negação em Nicolau de Cusa e Hegel." In *Coincidência dos opostos e concórdia: Caminhos do pensamento em Nicolau de Cusa*, edited by João Maria André and Mariano Álvarez-Gómez, 187–200. Coimbra: Faculdade de Letras, 2001.

Flasch, Kurt. *Nikolaus von Kues: Geschichte einer Entwicklung*. Frankfurt am Main: Vittorio Klostermann, 1998.

———. *Das philosophische Denken im Mittelalter vom Augustin zu Machavelli*. Stuttgart: Reclam, 2001.

———. *Was ist Gott? Das Buch der 24 Philosophen*. Munich: Beck, 2011.

Fletcher, Angus. *The Topological Imagination: Spheres, Edges, and Islands*. Cambridge, MA: Harvard University Press, 2016.

Foucault, Michel. "Lacan, le libérateur de la psychanalyse." In *Dits et écrits, tome II: 1976–1988*, edited by Daniel Defert and François Ewald, 1023–24. Paris: Gallimard, 2001.

Fox, Robin Lane. *The Classical World*. New York: Basic Books, 2005.

Fränkel, Hermann. *Early Greek Poetry and Philosophy*. Translated by Moses Hadas and James Willis. New York: Harcourt Brace Jovanovich, 1975.

Freeman, Kathleen. *Ancilla to the Pre-Socratic Philosophers: A Complete Translation of the Fragments in Diels, "Fragmente der Vorsokratiker."* Cambridge, MA: Harvard University Press, 1977.

Friedman, Maurice, ed. *The Worlds of Existentialism: A Critical Reader*. New York: Random House, 1964.

Frijhoff, Willem. "Michel de Certeau (1925–1986)—A Multifaceted Intellectual." In Bocken, *Spiritual Spaces*, 5–23.

Füssel, Marian. "Writing the Otherness: The Historiography of Michel de Certeau SJ." In Bocken, *Spiritual Spaces*, 25–44.

Gadamer, Hans-Georg. "Nikolaus von Kues im modernen Denken." In *Nicoló Cusano agli inizi del mondo moderno*, 39–48. Florence: G. C. Sansoni Editore, 1964.

———. "Praise of Theory." In *Praise of Theory: Speeches and Essays*. Translated by Chris Dawson, 16–36. New Haven, CT: Yale University Press, 1998.

———. *Truth and Method*. Translated by Joel Weinsheimer and Donald G. Marshall. New York: Continuum, 1998.

———. "On the Possibility of a Philosophical Ethics (1963)." In *Hermeneutics, Religion, and Ethics*, translated by Joel Weinsheimer, 18–36. New Haven, CT: Yale University Press, 1999.

———. "Nicolaus Cusanus and the Present." *Epoché* 7 (2002): 71–79.

Gadamer, Hans-Georg, et al. *Gadamer in Conversation: Reflections and Commentary*. Edited and translated by Richard E. Palmer. New Haven, CT: Yale University Press, 2001.

Gaetano, Matthew T. "Nicholas of Cusa and Pantheism in Early Modern Catholic Theology." In *Nicholas of Cusa and the Making of the Early Modern World*, edited by Simon J. G. Burton, Joshua Hollmann, and Eric M. Parker, 199–228. Leiden: Brill, 2019.

Gandillac, Maurice de. "Nicolas de Cues, précurseur de la Méthode cartésienne." In *Travaux du IXe Congrès international de philosophie, Congrès Descartes*, vol. 5, edited by Raymond Bayer, 127–33. Paris: Hermann et cie, 1937.

———. *La philosophie de Nicolas de Cues*. Paris: Aubier, 1941.

———, ed. *Oeuvres choisies de Nicolas de Cues*. Paris: Aubier-Montaigne, 1942.

———. "Nicolas de Cues." In *Dictionnaire de spiritualité: Ascétique et mystique, doctrine et histoire*, vol. 11, 262–69. Paris: Beauchesne, 1942.

———. "Denys l'Aréopagite." In *Dictionnaire de spiritualité: Ascétique et mystique, doctrine et histoire*, vol. 3, 375–78. Paris: Beauchesne, 1942.

———. "Sur la sphere infinie de Pascal." *Revue d'histoire de la philosophie et d'histoire générale de la civilisation* 33 (1943): 32–44.

———. "El problema de la comprensión entre los pueblos según los principios teóricos y las sugerencias de orden práctico del Cardenal Nicolás de Cusa." *Folia humanistica* 2, no. 23 (November 1964): 939–52.

———. "Die aristotelische erste Philosophie nach *De venatione sapientiae*." In MFCG 6, edited by Rudolf Haubst, 30–34. Mainz: Matthias-Grünewald-Verlag, 1968.

———. "Nikolaus von Kues zwischen Platon und Hegel." In *Nikolaus von Kues in der Geschichte des Erkenntnisproblems. Akten des Symposions in Trier vom 18. bis 20. Oktober 1973*, MFCG 11, edited by Rudolf Haubst, 21–38. Mainz: Matthias-Grünewald-Verlag, 1975.

———. *Gêneses da modernidade*. São Paulo: Editora 34, 1995.

———. *Le siècle traversé: Souvenirs de neuf décennies*. Paris: Albin Michel, 1998.

———. "Du Cusain à Descartes." *Enrahonar: An International Journal of Theoretical and Practical Reason* [Special issue] (1999): 359–62.

———. *Nicolas de Cues*. Paris: Ellipses, 2001.

———, ed. *Historia de la filosofía*. Vol. 5, *La filosofía del Renacimiento*. Mexico City: Siglo XXI Editores, 2006.

Geldof, Koenraad. "Ökonomie, Exzess, Grenze: Michel de Certeaus Genealogie der Moderne." In *Michel de Certeau: Geschichte—Kultur—Religion*, edited by Marian Füssel, 91–151. Konstanz: UVK Verlagsgesellschaft, 2007.

Giard, Luce, ed. *Michel de Certeau: Le voyage de l'oeuvre*. Paris: Éditions Facultés Jésuites de Paris, 2017.

González Ríos, José, ed. *Confesiones filosóficas*. Buenos Aires: Editorial Quadrata, 2006.

———. "Die zeichentheoretische Bedeutung des 'non aliud'." In *Nikolaus von Kues: De non aliud / Nichts anderes*, edited by Klaus Reinhardt, Jorge M. Machetta, and Harald Schwaetzer, 211–24. Münster: Aschendorff Verlag, 2011.

———. "Los nombres enigmáticos como manuductiones en el pensamiento cusano de senectud." In *Manuductiones*, edited by Klaus Reinhardt and Cecilia Rusconi, 169–90. Münster: Aschendorff Verlag, 2014.

Gougaud, Louis. "La *theoria* dans la spiritualité médiévale." *Revue ascétique et de mystique* 3 (1922): 381–94.

Grenier, Catherine. *L'art contemporain est-il chrétien?* Paris: Éditions Jacqueline Chambon, 1999.

———. "La revanche de l'image." *Communio: Revue catholique internationale* 28, no. 4 (July/August 2003): 37–53.

Grotz, Stephan. *Negationen des Absoluten: Meister Eckhart, Cusanus, Hegel*. Hamburg: Felix Meiner Verlag, 2009.

Hadot, Pierre. *Plotinus, or the Simplicity of Vision*. Translated by Michael Chase. Chicago: University of Chicago Press, 1993.

———. *What Is Ancient Philosophy?* Translated by Michael Chase. Cambridge, MA: Belknap Press, 2002.

———. *Plotin, Porphyre. Études neoplatoniciennes*. Paris: Les Belles Lettres, 2010.

Halfwassen, Jens. *Auf den Spuren des Einen: Studien zur Metaphysik und ihrer Geschichte*. Tübingen: Mohr Siebeck, 2015.

Hamann, Florian. *Das Siegel der Ewigkeit: Universalwissenschaft und Konziliarismus bei Heymericus de Campo*. Münster: Aschendorff Verlag, 2006.

Hamann, Johann Georg. *Sämtliche Werke*. Edited by Josef Nadler. 6 vols. Vienna: Herder, 1949–57.

———. *Briefwechsel*. Edited by Walther Ziesemer and Arthur Henkel. 7 vols. Wiesbaden: Insel-Verlag, 1955–75.

Hamburger, Jeffrey F. *Color in Cusanus*. Stuttgart: Hiersemann Verlag, 2021.

Häring, Nikolaus M., ed. *Commentaries on Boethius by Thierry of Chartres and His School*. Toronto: Pontifical Institute of Mediaeval Studies, 1971.

Harries, Karsten. "Hegel on the Future of Art." *The Review of Metaphysics* 27, no. 4 (1974): 677–96.

———. "The Infinite Sphere: Comments on the History of a Metaphor." *Journal of the History of Philosophy* 13 (1975): 5–15.

———. "The Dream of the Complete Building." *Perspecta: The Yale Architectural Journal* 17 (1980): 36–43.

———. *The Bavarian Rococo Church: Between Faith and Aestheticism*. New Haven, CT: Yale University Press, 1983.

Bibliography

———. "Problems of the Infinite: Cusanus and Descartes." *American Catholic Philosophical Quarterly* 64, no. 1 (Winter 1990): 89–110.

———. *The Ethical Function of Architecture*. Cambridge, MA: MIT Press, 1998.

———. *Infinity and Perspective*. Cambridge, MA: MIT Press, 2001.

———. "Journeys into the Wilderness of Artifice." In *Lebbeus Woods: Experimental Architecture*, edited by Tracy Myers, Lebbeus Woods, and Karsten Harries, 38–51. Pittsburgh: Carnegie Museum of Art, 2004.

———. *Wahrheit: Die Architektur der Welt*. Munich: Wilhelm Fink Verlag, 2012.

Haubst, Rudolf. *Das Bild des Einen und Dreieinen Gottes in der Welt nach Nikolaus von Kues*. Trier: Paulinus Verlag, 1952.

———. *Nikolaus von Kues—Pförtner der neuen Zeit*. Kleine Schriften der Cusanus-Gesellschaft. Trier: Paulinus Verlag, 1988.

———. *Streifzüge in die cusanische Theologie*. Münster: Aschendorff Verlag, 1991.

Hébert, Geneviève. "Expérience picturale et phénoménologie française: La dehiscence du visible." In *Subjectivité et transcendance: Hommage à Pierre Colin*, edited by Philippe Capelle, 169–94. Paris: Éditions du Cerf, 2001.

Hegel, G. W. F. *Wissenschaft der Logik*. Edited by Georg Lasson. 2 Vols. Hamburg: Felix Meiner Verlag, 1951.

———. *Werke*. Vol. 11, *Berliner Schriften 1818–1831*. Edited by Eva Moldenhauer and Karl Markus Michel. Frankfurt am Main: Suhrkamp Verlag, 1970.

———. *Sämtliche Werke*. Vol. 12, *Vorlesungen über die Aesthetik*. Jubiläumsausgabe. Edited by Hermann Glockner. Stuttgart: Fromann Verlag, 1937.

Heidegger, Martin. *Poetry, Language, Thought*. Translated by Albert Hofstadter. New York: Harper & Row, 1971.

———. "Anmerkungen zu Karl Jaspers' 'Psychologie der Weltanschauungen' (1919/21)." In *Karl Jaspers in der Diskussion*, edited by Hans Saner, 70–100. Munich: R. Piper Verlag, 1973.

———. "Art and Space." Translated by Charles H. Seibert. In *Man and World*, vol. 6, no. 1, 3–8. The Hague: Nijhoff, 1973.

———. *Basic Writings*. Edited by David Farrell Krell. 2nd ed. New York: HarperCollins, 1993.

———. *Contributions to Philosophy (From Enowning)*. Translated by Parvis Emad and Kenneth Maly. Bloomington: Indiana University Press, 1999.

———. *Elucidations of Hölderlin's Poetry*. Translated by Keith Höller. Amherst: Humanity Books, 2000.

———. *Vorträge und Aufsätze*. Vol 7 of *Gesamtausgabe*. Edited by Friedrich-Wilhelm von Herrmann. Frankfurt am Main: Vittorio Klostermann, 2000.

———. *Off the Beaten Track*. Edited and translated by Julian Young and Kenneth Haynes. Cambridge: Cambridge University Press, 2002.

———. *Hölderlin's Hymns "Germania" and "The Rhine"*. Translated by William McNeill and Julia Ireland. Bloomington: Indiana University Press, 2014.

———. *Hölderlin's Hymn "Remembrance"*. Translated by William McNeill and Julia Ireland. Bloomington: Indiana University Press, 2018.

Herodotus. *The Histories*. Translated by George Rawlinson. New York: Alfred A. Knopf, 1997.

Hoff, Johannes. "Philosophie als performative Praktik: Spuren cusanischen Denkens bei Jacques Derrida und Michel de Certeau." In Reinhardt and Schwaetzer, *Cusanus-Rezeption in der Philosophie des 20. Jahrhunderts*, 93–119.

———. *Kontingenz, Berührung, Überschreitung: Zur philosophischen Propädeutik christlicher Mystik nach Nikolaus von Kues*. Freiburg: Verlag Karl Alber, 2007.

———. *The Analogical Turn: Rethinking Modernity with Nicholas of Cusa*. Grand Rapids, MI: Eerdmans, 2013.

Hollywood, Amy. "Love Speaks Here: Michel de Certeau's *Mystic Fable*." *Spiritus: A Journal of Christian Spirituality* 12, no. 2 (2012): 198–206.

Hopkins, Jasper. *Nicholas of Cusa: Metaphysical Speculations*. Minneapolis: The Arthur J. Banning Press, 1998.

Hudry, Françoise, ed. *Le livre des XXIV philosophes*. Grenoble: Millon, 1989.

———, ed. *Liber viginti quattuor philosophorum*. CCCM 143A. Turnhout: Brepols, 1997.

———. *Le livre des XXIV philosophes: Résurgence d'un texte du IVe siècle*. 2nd ed. Paris: J. Vrin, 2015.

Husserl, Edmund. *The Crisis of the European Sciences and Transcendental Phenomenology*. Translated by David Carr. Evanston, IL: Northwestern University Press, 1970.

Izbicki, Thomas M., ed. *Nicholas of Cusa: Writings on Church and Reform*. Cambridge, MA: Harvard University Press, 2008.

Jacobi, Klaus. *Die Methode der cusanischen Philosophie*. Freiburg: Karl Alber Verlag, 1969.

Jaeger, Werner. *Paideia: The Ideals of Greek Culture*. Translated by Gilbert Highet. 2nd ed. 3 vols. New York: Oxford University Press, 1945.

Jaspers, Karl. *Psychologie der Weltanschauungen*. Berlin: Springer Verlag, 1919.

———. *Von der Wahrheit*. Munich: R. Piper Verlag, 1947.

———. "On My Philosophy (1941)." Translated by Felix Kaufmann. In *Existentialism from Dostoyevsky to Sartre*, edited by Walter Kaufmann, 131–205. Cleveland/New York: Meridian Books, 1956.

———. *The Great Philosophers*. Vol. 2. Edited by Hannah Arendt. Translated by Ralph Manheim. New York: Harcourt, Brace & World, 1962.

———. *Der philosophische Glaube angesichts der Offenbarung*. Munich: R. Piper Verlag, 1962.

———. *Nikolaus Cusanus*. Munich: R. Piper Verlag, 1964.

———. *Philosophical Faith and Revelation.* Translated by E. B. Ashton. London: Collins, 1967.

———. *Philosophy.* Translated by E. B. Ashton. 3 vols. Chicago: University of Chicago Press, 1970.

———. *Anselm and Nicholas of Cusa.* Edited by Hannah Arendt. New York: Harcourt Brace Jovanovich, 1974.

Jerphagnon, Lucien. *Á l'école des Anciens: Portraits et préférences.* Paris: Perrin, 2014.

Jolivet, Jean. "Situation de l'histoire de la philosophie médiévale en France." *Cahiers de civilisation médiévale* 39, nos. 153–54 (1996): 85–95.

Julianus Pomerius. *De vita contemplativa.* PL 59:415–520.

Kaegi, Dominic, and Reiner Wiehl, eds. *Karl Jaspers Korrespondenzen: Philosophie.* Göttingen: Wallstein Verlag, 2016.

Kaluza, Zénon. "Besprechung: 'Liber viginti quattuor philosophorum', ed. Françoise Hudry (Corpus Christianorum, Continuatio Mediaevalis 143/A, Hermes Latinus III.1), Turnhout 1997." *Mittellateinisches Jahrbuch* 35 (2000): 161–66.

———. "Comme une branche d'amandier en fleurs: Dieu dans le *Liber viginti quattor philosophorum.*" In *Hermetism from Late Antiquity to Humanism*, edited by Paolo Lucentini, Ilaria Parri, and Vittoria Perrone Compagni, 99–127. Turnhout: Brepols, 2003.

Kant, Immanuel. "On the Failure of All Attempted Philosophical Theodicies (1791)." In *Kant on History and Religion: With a Translation of Kant's "On the Failure of All Attempted Philosophical Theodicies,"* edited and translated by Michel Despland, 283–97. Montreal: McGill-Queen's University Press, 1973.

Keefer, Michael. "The World Turned Inside Out: Revolutions of the Infinite Sphere from Hermes to Pascal." *Renaissance and Reformation* 12 (1988): 303–13.

Kelsen, Hans. *Pure Theory of Law.* Translated by Max Knight. Clark, NJ: The Lawbook Exchange, 2009.

Kelter, Irving A. "The Refusal to Accommodate: Jesuit Exegetes and the Copernican System." *The Sixteenth Century Journal* 26, no. 2 (1995): 273–83.

Kosaka, Kunitsugu. *Nishida-tetsugaku no Kisoh* 西田哲学の基層 [The basic layers of Nishida's philosophy]. Tokyo: Iwanami Shoten, 2011.

Koyré, Alexandre. *From the Closed World to the Infinite Universe.* Baltimore, MD: Johns Hopkins University Press, 1968.

Kremer, Klaus. *Praegustatio naturalis sapientiae: Gott suchen mit Nikolaus von Kues.* Münster: Aschendorff Verlag, 2004.

Küng, Hans. *Projekt Weltethos.* Munich: Pieper, 1990.

Lacan, Jacques. *Écrits.* Paris: Seuil, 1966.

———. "Proposition du 9 octobre 1967 sur le psychanalyste de l'école." *Scilicet* 1 (1968): 14–30.

———. *Séminaire.* Vol. 1, *Les écrits techniques de Freud (1953–1954).* Paris: Seuil, 1975.

———. "Note italienne." In *Ornicar? Bulletin periodique du champ Freudien*, no. 25. Paris: Seuil, 1982. Reprinted in *Autres écrits* (Paris: Seuil, 2001).

Ladner, Gerhart B. *The Idea of Reform: Its Impact on Christian Thought and Action in the Age of the Fathers*. Cambridge, MA: Harvard University Press, 1959.

Lash, Scott. "Deforming the Figure: Topology and the Social Imaginary." *Theory, Culture & Society* 29, nos. 4–5 (2012): 261–87.

Latham, R. E. *Revised Medieval Latin Word-List from British and Irish Sources*. London: The British Academy & Oxford University Press, 1994.

Le Goff, Jacques. *Time, Work, and Culture in the Middle Ages*. Translated by Arthur Goldhammer. Chicago: University of Chicago Press, 1980.

Leclercq, Jean. *The Love of Learning and the Desire for God: A Study of Monastic Culture*. Translated by Catherine Misrahi. New York: Fordham University Press, 1977.

Lefebvre, Henri. *The Production of Space*. Translated by Donald Nicholson-Smith. Oxford: Blackwell, 1991.

Leopardi, Giacomo. *Zibaldone*. Edited by Rolando Damiani. Milan: Mondadori, 2011.

———. *Zibaldone*. Edited by Michael Caesar and Franco D'Intino. Translated by Kathleen Baldwin et al. Rev. ed. New York: Farrar, Straus & Giroux, 2015.

Levesque, Paul. "Symbol as the Primary Religious Category in the Thought of Louis Dupré: Foundations for Contemporary Sacramentology." PhD diss., Katholieke Universitaeit Leuven, 1995.

Lévi-Strauss, Claude. *Tristes tropiques*. Translated by John Weightman and Doreen Weightman. New York: Athenaeum, 1975.

Libera, Alain de. *Métaphysique et noétique: Albert le Grand*. Paris: J. Vrin, 2005.

Long, Stephen A. *Analogia Entis*. Notre Dame, IN: University of Notre Dame Press, 2011.

Lucentini, Paolo. *Il libro dei ventiquattro filosofi*. Milan: Adelphi, 1999.

———. "Il *Liber viginti quattuor philosophorum* nella *Commedia* dantesca e nei suoi primi commentator." In *Platonismo, ermetismo, eresia nel Medioevo*, edited by Paolo Lucentini, 235–64. Textes et Études du Moyen Âge 41. Louvain: Fédération internationale des instituts d'études médiévales, 2007.

Machetta, Jorge M. "'Sé tú tuyo y yo seré tuyo': síntesis cusana de antropología y mística." In *Memoria y silencio en la filosofía medieval*, edited by Carlos Ruta, 203–14. Buenos Aires: Jorge Baudino Ediciones, 2006.

Magnard, Pierre. *La couleur du matin profonde: Dialogue avec Eric Fiat*. Paris: Les Petits Platons, 2013.

Mahnke, Dietrich. *Unendliche Sphäre und Allmittelpunkt: Beiträge zur Genealogie der mathematischen Mystik*. Halle: Max Niemeyer Verlag, 1937.

Mancini, Sandro. *Congetture su Dio: Singolarità, finalismo, potenza nella teologia razionale di Nicola Cusano*. Milan: Mimesis, 2014.

Marenbon, John. *From the Circle of Alcuin to the School of Auxerre: Logic, Theology and Philosophy in the Early Middle Ages.* Cambridge: Cambridge University Press, 1981.

Marinho Nogueira, Maria Simone. "Amor, caritas e dilectio—Elementos para uma hermenêutica do amor em Nicolau de Cusa." PhD diss., University of Coimbra, 2008.

Marion, Jean-Luc. *The Idol and Distance: Five Studies.* Translated by Thomas A. Carlson. New York: Fordham University Press, 2001.

———. *Being Given: Toward a Phenomenology of Givenness.* Translated by Jeffrey L. Kosky. Stanford, CA: Stanford University Press, 2002.

———. *Prologomena to Charity.* Translated by Stephen E. Lewis. New York: Fordham University Press, 2002.

———. *The Crossing of the Visible.* Translated by James K. A. Smith. Stanford, CA: Stanford University Press, 2003.

———. *In Excess: Studies of Saturated Phenomena.* Translated by Robyn Horner and Vincent Berraud. New York: Fordham University Press, 2004.

———. *The Erotic Phenomenon.* Translated by Stephen E. Lewis. Chicago: University of Chicago Press, 2006.

———. *The Visible and the Revealed.* Translated by Christina M. Geschwandtner. New York: Fordham University Press, 2008.

———. *God Without Being: Hors-Texte.* Translated by Thomas A. Carlson. 2nd ed. Chicago: University of Chicago Press, 2012.

———. *Givenness and Revelation.* Oxford: Oxford University Press, 2016.

———. "Voir, se voir vu: L'apport de Nicolas de Cues dans le *De visione Dei*." *Bulletin de littérature ecclésiastique* 117, no. 2 (April/June 2016): 7–37.

———. "Seeing, or Seeing Oneself Seen: Nicholas of Cusa's Contribution in *De visione Dei*." Translated by Stephen E. Lewis. *The Journal of Religion* 96, no. 3 (July 2016): 305–31.

———. *Negative Certainties.* Translated by Stephen E. Lewis. Chicago: University of Chicago Press, 2020.

———. *D'ailleurs, la révélation.* Paris: Grasset, 2020.

Markus, R. A. *Gregory the Great and His World.* Cambridge: Cambridge University Press, 1997.

Maurizi, Marco. "La dialettica dell'altro: Cusano e Hegel a confronto." *Rivista di filosofia neo-scolastica* 98, no. 1 (2006): 99–120.

Meekins, Angela G. "Contemplative Life." In *The Dante Encyclopedia*, edited Richard Lansing, 216–18. London: Routledge, 2010.

Meier-Oeser, Stephan. *Die Präsenz des Vergessenen: Zur Rezeption der Philosophie des Nicolaus Cusanus vom 15. bis zum 18. Jahrhundert.* Münster: Aschendorff Verlag, 1989.

———. "Symbol (Antike, Mittelalter, Neuzeit)." In *Historisches Wörterbuch der Philosophie*, vol. 10, edited by Joachim Ritter and Karlfried Gründer, 710–23. Basel: Schwabe & Co., 1998.

Meinhardt, Helmut. "Konjekturale Erkenntnis und religiöse Toleranz." In *Der Friede unter den Religionen nach Nikolaus von Kues. Akten des Symposions in Trier vom 13. bis 15. Oktober 1982*, MFCG 16, edited by Rudolf Haubst, 325–32. Mainz: Matthias-Grünewald-Verlag, 1984.

Meister Eckhart. *Die deutschen und lateinischen Werke*. Stuttgart & Berlin: W. Kohlhammer, 1936–.

Merleau-Ponty, Maurice. *Phenomenology of Perception*. Translated by Donald A. Landes. New York: Routledge, 2012.

Milbank, John. *Theology and Social Theory: Beyond Secular Reason*. 2nd ed. Oxford: Blackwell, 2006.

———. "Manifestation and Procedure: Trinitarian Metaphysics after Albert the Great and Thomas Aquinas." In *Tomismo Creativo: Letture Contemporanee del "Doctor Communis*," edited by Marco Salvioli, OP, 41–117. Bologna: Edizioni Studio Domenicano, 2015.

———. "From *Mathesis* to *Methexis*: Nicholas of Cusa's Post-Nominalist Realism." In *Participation et vision de Dieu chez Nicolas de Cues*, edited by Isabelle Moulin, 143–69. Paris: J. Vrin, 2017.

———. "Writing and the Order of Learning." *Philosophy, Theology and the Sciences* 4, no. 1 (2017): 46–73.

Milbank, John, and Catherine Pickstock. *Truth in Aquinas*. London: Routledge, 2001.

Miller, Clyde Lee. "A Road Not Taken: Nicholas of Cusa and Today's Intellectual World." *Proceedings of the American Catholic Philosophical Association* 57 (1983): 68–77.

Miroy, Jovino. *Tracing Nicholas of Cusa's Early Development*. Leuven: Peeters, 2009.

Mitchell, W. J. T. "Spatial Form in Literature: Toward a General Theory." *Critical Inquiry* 6, no. 3 (Spring 1980): 539–67.

Mommaers, Paul. *Jan van Ruusbroec: Mystical Union with God*. Leuven: Peeters, 2009.

Monaco, Davide. "Pensare l'Uno con Cusano: L'interpretazione di Werner Beierwaltes." *Il Pensiero* 48, no. 1–2 (2009): 115–27.

———. *Nicholas of Cusa: Trinity, Freedom and Dialogue*. Münster: Aschendorff Verlag, 2016.

Moore, Brenna. "How to Awaken the Dead: Michel de Certeau, Henri de Lubac, and the Instabilities between the Past and the Present." *Spiritus: A Journal of Christian Spirituality* 12, no. 2 (2012): 172–79.

Moore, Michael Edward. *Nicholas of Cusa and the Kairos of Modernity: Cassirer, Gadamer, Blumenberg*. Brooklyn, NY: Punctum Books, 2013.

———. "Epilogue: Ernst Cassirer and Renaissance Cultural Studies: The Figure of Nicholas of Cusa." In *Nicholas of Cusa and the Making of the Early Modern World*, edited by Simon J. G. Burton, Joshua Hollman, and Eric M. Parker, 485–506. Leiden: Brill, 2019.

Moran, Dermot. "Pantheism from John Scottus Eriugena to Nicholas of Cusa." *American Catholic Philosophical Quarterly* 64, no. 1 (1990): 131–52.

Moreschini, Claudio. *A Christian in Toga. Boethius: Interpreter of Antiquity and Christian Theologian*. Göttingen: Vandenhoeck & Ruprecht, 2014.

Morin, Edgar. *O método*. Vol. 3, *O conhecimento do conhecimento/1*. Translated by M. G. Bragança. Mem Martins: Publicações Europa-América, 1987.

Müller, Tom. *Perspektivität und Unendlichkeit: Mathematik und ihre Anwendung in der Frührenaissance am Beispiel von Alberti und Cusanus*. Regensburg: S. Roderer-Verlag, 2010.

Müller, Tom, and Matthias Vollet, eds. *Die Modernitäten des Nikolaus von Kues: Debatten und Rezeptionen*. Bielefeld: Transcript Verlag, 2013.

Mykhailova, Iryna. "Paul Oskar Kristeller und Karl Jaspers: ein Dialog, der nie stattgefunden hat." *Freiburger Zeitschrift für Philosophie und Theologie* 62 (2015): 337–49.

Nemo, Philippe. *A History of Political Ideas from Antiquity to the Middle Ages*. Translated by Kenneth Casler. Pittsburgh, PA: Duquesne University Press, 2013.

Nicolle, Jean-Marie. *Mathématiques et métaphysique dans l'oeuvre de Nicolas de Cues*. Villeneuve d'Ascq: Presses Universitaires du Septentrion, 2001.

———. "Hommage à Maurice de Gandillac." In *Die Sermones des Nikolaus von Kues. Merkmale und ihre Stellung innerhalb der mittelalterlichen Predigtkultur*, MFCG 30, edited by Klaus Kremer and Klaus Reinhardt, xxix-xxxiii. Trier: Paulinus Verlag, 2005.

———. *Nicolas de Cues: Écrits mathématiques*. Paris: Honoré Champion, 2007.

———. *Le laboratoire mathématique de Nicolas de Cues*. Paris: Éditions Beauchesne, 2020.

Nightingale, Andrea Wilson. *Spectacles of Truth in Classical Greek Philosophy: Theoria in its Cultural Context*. Cambridge: Cambridge University Press, 2004.

Nishida Kitaro. *Last Writings: Nothingness and the Religious Worldview*. Translated by David A. Dilworth. Honolulu: University of Hawaii Press, 1987.

———. *Nishida Kitaro Zenshu* 西田幾多郎全集 [The complete works of Nishida Kitaro]. Tokyo: Iwanami Shoten, 2002–2009.

O'Flaherty, James C. *Unity and Language: A Study in the Philosophy of Johann Georg Hamann*. Chapel Hill: University of North Carolina Press, 1952.

Oliva, Mirela. "Gadamer and Cusanus on Creation." *Philosophy Today* 55 (2011): 184–91.

———. "The Metaphysics of Language in Cusanus and Gadamer." *Anuario Filosofico* 49 (2016): 401–22.

Olson, Alan M. "Jaspers's Critique of Mysticism." *Journal of the American Academy of Religion* 51, no. 2 (1983): 251–66.

Osmaston, F. P. B. "Selections from *The Philosophy of Fine Art*." In *Philosophies of Art and Beauty: Selected Readings in Aesthetics from Plato to Heidegger*, edited by Albert Hofstadter and Richard Kuhns, 382–445. Chicago: University of Chicago Press, 1964.

Panikkar, Raimon. *Mito, fe y hermenéutica*. Barcelona: Herder, 2007.

———. *Pluralisme et interculturalité*. In *Oeuvres*, 6/1. Paris: Éditions du Cerf, 2012.

Panofsky, Erwin. *Perspective as Symbolic Form*. Translated by Christopher S. Wood. New York: Zone Books, 1991.

Paprotny, Thorsten. *Karl Jaspers' Philosophie interkulturell gelesen*. Nordhausen: Traugott Bautz, 2006.

Paredes Martín, María del Carmen. "El concepto de 'sabiduría' en *Idiota de sapientia*." *Anuario filosófico* 28, no. 3 (1995): 671–94.

———. "Sabiduría y mística en Nicolás de Cusa: El *Idiota de sapientia*." In *Filosofía, arte y mística*, edited by María del Carmen Paredes Martín and Enrique Bonete Perales, 159–72. Salamanca: Ediciones Universidad Salamanca, 2017.

Pascal, Blaise. *Pascal's Pensées*. Translated by W. F. Trotter. New York: E. P. Dutton & Co., 1958.

Peroli, Enrico, and Marco Moschini, eds. *Why We Need Cusanus / Warum wir Cusanus brauchen*. Münster: Aschendorff Verlag, 2022.

Pickstock, Catherine. *After Writing: On the Liturgical Consummation of Philosophy*. Oxford: Blackwell, 1997.

Pieper, Josef. *Happiness and Contemplation*. Translated by Richard Winston and Clara Winston. South Bend, IN: St. Augustine's Press, 1998.

Plato. *The Dialogues of Plato*. Translated by Benjamin Jowett. 2 vols. New York: Random House, 1937.

Plotinus. *Ennead IV*. Translated by A. H. Armstrong. Loeb Classical Library 443. Cambridge, MA: Harvard University Press, 1984.

Poblete, Rodrigo Núñez. *Metafísica de la singularidad*. Buenos Aires: Editorial Biblos, 2015.

Pöggeler, Otto. "Heidegger on Art." In *Martin Heidegger: Politics, Art, and Technology*, edited by Karsten Harries and Christoph Jamme, 106–24. New York: Holmes & Meier, 1994.

Poulet, George. "Le symbole du cercle infini dans la literature et la philosophie." *Revue de métaphysique et de morale* 64, no. 3 (1959): 257–75.

———. *Les métamorphoses du cercle*. Paris: Flammarion, 1975.

Preus, Anthony. *Historical Dictionary of Ancient Greek Philosophy*. Lanham, MD: Rowman & Littlefield, 2015.

Przywara, Erich. "Thomas oder Hegel? Zum Sinn der 'Wende zum Objekt.'" *Logos: Zeitschrift für systematische Philosophie* 15 (1926): 1–20.

———. Review of *Nicholas von Cues und der deutsche Geist*, by Rudolf Odebrecht. *Deutsche Literaturzeitung* 55 (1934): 680–82.

———. "Plotin und Nikolaus von Cues." *Stimmen der Zeit* 134 (1938): 263–65.

———. *Humanitas: Der Mensch Gestern und Morgen*. Nuremberg: Glock und Lutz, 1952.

———. *Christentum gemäß Johannes*. Nuremberg: Glock und Lutz, 1954.

———. "Der späte Jünger des Nikolaus von Kues." Review of *Eine Untersuchung zur Vorgeschichte der modernen Existenz*, by H.-J. Heydorn. *Die Österreichische Furche* 11, no. 1 (January 1, 1955): 11.

———. Review of *Nicolaus Cusanus*, by K.-H. Volkmann. *Les Études philosophiques* 12 (1957): 432.

———. "Philosophisches Denken." *Die Furche* 14 (March 8, 1958).

———. *Schriften*. 3 vols. Einsiedeln: Johannes Verlag, 1962.

———. *Analogia Entis*. Translated by John R. Betz and David Bentley Hart. Grand Rapids, MI: Eerdmans, 2014.

Rahner, Karl. *Gnade als Freiheit: Kleine theologische Beiträge*. Freiburg: Herder, 1968.

———. *Hearer of the Word*. Translated by Joseph Donceel. New York: Continuum, 1994.

Ramon Llull. *Doctor Illuminatus: A Ramon Llull Reader*. Translated by Anthony Bonner. Princeton, NJ: Princeton University Press, 1985.

Rausch, Hannelore. *Theoria von ihrer sakralen zur philosophischen Bedeutung*. Munich: Wilhelm Fink Verlag, 1982.

Reibe, Nicole. "Reconsidering the *Homo Assumptus* Position." In *Achard de Saint-Victor métaphysicien: Le "De Unitate Dei" et pluralitate creaturam*, edited by Vincent Carraud et al., 149–67. Turnhout: Brepols, 2009.

Reinhardt, Klaus, and Harald Schwaetzer, eds. *Cusanus-Rezeption in der Philosophie des 20. Jahrhunderts*. Regensburg: S. Roderer-Verlag, 2005.

Remes, Pauliina. *Neoplatonism*. Berkeley: University of California Press, 2008.

Riedweg, Christoph. *Pythagoras: His Life, Teaching, and Influence*. Translated by Steven Rendall. Ithaca, NY: Cornell University Press, 2005.

Robert Grosseteste. *On the Cessation of the Laws*. Translated by Stephen M. Hildebrand. Washington, DC: The Catholic University of America Press, 2012.

Safranski, Rüdiger. *Martin Heidegger: Between Good and Evil*. Translated by Ewalt Overs. Cambridge, MA: Harvard University Press, 1998.

Sannino, Antonella. "The Hermetical Sources in Berthold von Moosburg." *Journal of the Warburg and Courtauld Institutes* 63 (2000): 243–58.

———. "*Il Liber viginti quattuor philosophorum* nella metafisica di Bertoldo di Moosburg." In *Per perscrutationem philosophicam: Neue Perspektiven der mittelalterlichen Forschung*, edited by Alessandra Beccarisi, Ruedi Imbach, and Pasquale Porro, 252–72. Hamburg: Felix Meiner Verlag, 2008.

Santinello, Giovanni. "L'Ermeneutica scritturale nel 'De genesi' del Cusano." *Archivio di filosofia* 3 (1963): 81–90.

Scharpff, Franz Anton von. *Des Cardinals und Bischofs Nicolaus von Cusa wichtigste Schriften in deutscher Übersetzung*. Freiburg in Breisgau: Herder, 1862.

Schelling, F. W. J. *Sämtliche Werke*. Edited by K. F. A. Schelling. Stuttgart/Augsburg: J. G. Cotta'scher Verlag, 1856–61.

Schmitt, Alexia. *Interioridad y trascendencia. Asimilación de la interioridad agustiniana en el pensamiento Cusano: hacia la subjectividad moderna*. Buenos Aires: Editorial Biblos, 2017.

Schuhl, Pierre-Maxime. "Remarques sur Platon et la technologie." *Revue des études grecques* 66 (1953): 465–72.

Schwaetzer, Harald. "Viva similitudo: Zur Genese der cusanischen Anthropologie in den Schriften 'Responsio de intellectu evangelii Iohannis', 'De filiatione Dei' und 'De genesi.'" In *Nicolaus Cusanus: Perspektiven seiner Geistphilosophie. Internationale Tagung junger Cusanus-ForscherInnen von 24.-26. Mai 2002*, edited by Harald Schwaetzer, 79–94. Regensburg: S. Roderer-Verlag, 2003.

Secchi, Pietro. "Declinazioni della sfera in Niccolò Cusano." In Totaro and Valente, *Sphaera*, 245–60.

Senger, Hans Gerhard. "Gerechtigkeit und Gleichheit und ihre Bedeutung für die Tugendlehre des Nikolaus von Kues." In *Sein und Sollen: Die Ethik des Nikolaus von Kues*, MFCG 26, edited by Klaus Kremer and Klaus Reinhardt, 39–63. Trier: Paulinus Verlag, 2000.

———. "Warum es bei Nikolaus von Kues keine Transzendentalien gibt und wie sie kompensiert werden." In *Die Logik des Transzendentalen: Festschrift für Jan A. Aertsen*, edited by Martin Pickavé, 554–77. Miscellanea Medievalia 30. Berlin: De Gruyter, 2003.

———. *Nikolaus von Kues: Leben—Lehre—Wirkungsgeschichte*. Heidelberg: Universitätsverlag Carl Winter, 2017.

Sfez, Jocelyne. "Michel de Certeau, lecteur de Nicolas de Cues: Nicolas de Cues était-il un mystique?" *Archives de sciences sociales des religions* 172 (October/December 2015): 67–79.

Sheldrake, Philip. "Michel de Certeau: Spirituality and the Practice of Everyday Life." *Spiritus: A Journal of Christian Spirituality* 12, no. 2 (2012): 207–16.

Sloterdijk, Peter. *Spheres*. Vol. 1, *Bubbles: Microspherology*. Translated by Wieland Hoban. Los Angeles: Semiotext(e), 2011.

———. *Spheres*. Vol. 2, *Globes: Macrospherology*. Translated by Wieland Hoban. Los Angeles: Semiotext(e), 2014.

———. *Spheres*. Vol. 3, *Foams: Plural Spherology*. Translated by Wieland Hoban. Los Angeles: Semiotext(e), 2016.

Smith, Adam. *Theory of Moral Sentiments*. Edited by D. D. Raphael and A. L. Macfie. Indianapolis, IN: Liberty Fund, 1982.

Snell, Bruno. *The Discovery of the Mind: The Greek Origins of European Thought*. Translated by T. G. Rosenmeyer. New York: Harper Torchbook, 1960.

Souter, Alexander. *A Glossary of Later Latin to 600 A.D.* Oxford: Clarendon Press, 1949.

Spee, Meinholf von. "'*Donum Dei*' bei Nikolaus von Kues: Zum Verständnis von Natur und Gnade nach den Schriften *De quaerendo Deum*, *De filiatione Dei* und *De dato patris luminum*." In MFCG 22, edited by Klaus Kremer and Klaus Reinhardt, 69–120. Trier: Paulinus Verlag, 1995.

Speer, Andreas. "*Ethica sive theologia*: Wissenschaftseinteilung und Philosophieverständnis bei Meister Eckhart." In *Was ist Philosophie im Mittelalter?*, Miscellanea Mediaevalia 26, edited by Jan A. Aertsen and Andreas Speer, 683–93. Berlin: De Gruyter, 1998.

———. "The Hidden Heritage: Boethian Metaphysics and Its Medieval Tradition." *Quaestio* 5 (2005): 163–81.

———. "The Division of Metaphysical Discourses: Boethius, Thomas Aquinas and Meister Eckhart." In *Philosophy and Theology in the Long Middle Ages*, edited by Kent Emery, Jr., 91–115. Leiden: Brill, 2011.

Stallmach, Josef. "Einheit der Religion—Friede unter den Religionen. Zum Ziel der Gedankenführung im Dialog 'Der Friede im Glauben'." In *Der Friede unter den Religionen nach Nikolaus von Kues. Akten des Symposions in Trier vom 13. bis 15. Oktober 1982*, MFCG 16, edited by Rudolf Haubst, 61–81. Mainz: Matthias-Grünewald-Verlag, 1984.

Starr, Chester G. *A History of the Ancient World*. New York: Oxford University Press, 1991.

Stewart, Columba. *Cassian the Monk*. New York: Oxford University Press, 1998.

Sturlese, Loris. "Saints et magiciens: Albert le Grand en face d'Hermès Trismégiste." *Archives de Philosophie* 43 (1980): 615–34.

———. "Proclo e Ermete in Germania da Alberto Magno a Bertoldo di Moosburg." In *Von Meister Dietrich zu Meister Eckhart*, edited by Kurt Flasch, 22–33. Hamburg: Felix Meiner Verlag, 1984.

Taylor, Charles. "Comparison, History, Truth." In *Myth and Philosophy*, edited by Frank Reynolds and David Tracy, 37–55. Albany: State University of New York Press, 1990.

Terán-Dutari, Julio. "Die Geschichte des Terminus 'Analogia Entis' und das Werk Erich Przywaras." *Philosophisches Jahrbuch der Görres-Gesellschaft* 77 (1970): 163–79.

Thomas Aquinas. *Summa Theologiae. Divi Thomae Aquinatis ordinis Praedicatorum Doctoris Angelici a Leone XIII P.M. . . . Summa theologica*. Rome: Ex Typographia Forzani et S., 1894. Translated by the Fathers of the English Dominican Province. New York: Benziger Brothers, 1947.

———. *Summa Theologiae*. Vol. 2, *Existence and Nature of God*. Translated by Timothy McDermott, OP. New York: McGraw-Hill, 1964.

———. *An Exposition of the "On the Hebdomads" of Boethius*. Translated by James L. Schultz and Edward A. Synan. Washington, DC: The Catholic University of America Press: 1992.

———. *Commentary on Aristotle's Nicomachean Ethics*. Translated by C. I. Litzinger, OP. Notre Dame, IN: Dumb Ox Books, 1993.

Thornhill, Chris. *Karl Jaspers: Politics and Metaphysics*. London: Routledge, 2002.

Thurner, Martin. "Die Philosophie der Gabe bei Meister Eckhart und Nikolaus Cusanus." In *Nicolaus Cusanus zwischen Deutschland und Italien*, edited Martin Thurner, 153–84. Veröffentlichungen des Grabmann-Institutes 48. Berlin: De Gruyter, 2002.

Thurneysen, Rudolf. *A Grammar of Old Irish*. Rev. ed. Dublin: School of Celtic Studies, 1975.

Tiles, Mary. "Technology, Science, and Inexact Knowledge: Bachelard's Non-Cartesian Epistemology." In *Continental Philosophy of Science*, edited by Gary Gutting, 157–75. London: Wiley Blackwell, 2005.

Totaro, Pina, and Luisa Valente, eds. *Sphaera: Forma, immagine e metafora tra Medioevo e età moderna*. Florence: Leo Olschki Editore, 2012.

Tracy, David. "Fragments of a Synthesis? The Hopeful Paradox of Dupré's Modernity." In *Christian Spirituality and the Culture of Modernity: The Thought of Louis Dupré*, edited by Peter J. Casarella and George P. Schner, SJ, 9–24. Grand Rapids, MI: Eerdmans, 1998.

Tuan, Yi-Fu. *Space and Place: The Perspective of Experience*. Minneapolis: University of Minnesota Press, 1977.

Varnhagen, Stefan. *Ehrung eines grossen Denkers: Zwiegespräch zwischen Autor und Verleger anlässlich des 65. Geburtstags Erich Przywaras am 12. Oktober 1954*. Nuremberg: Glock und Lutz, 1954.

Vernant, Jean-Pierre, and Pierre Vidal-Naquet. *Myth and Tragedy in Ancient Greece*. Translated by Janet Lloyd. New York: Zone Books, 1990.

Vescovini, Graziella Federici. "Les Métamorphoses de quelques propositions hermétiques après le *De docta ignorantia* (1440)." In *Identité et différence dans l'oeuvre de Nicolas de Cues*, edited by Hervé Pasqua, 1–13. Louvain: Éditions Peeters, 2011.

Vimercati, Emmanuele, and Valentina Zaffino, eds. *Nicholas of Cusa and the Aristotelian Tradition: A Philosophical and Theological Survey*. Berlin: De Gruyter, 2020.

Volkmann-Schluck, Karl-Heinz. "La filosofía de Nicolás de Cusa: Una forma previa de la metafísica moderna." *Revista de filosofía* 17 (1958): 437–58.

Wackerzapp, Herbert. *Der Einfluss Meister Eckharts auf die ersten philosophischen Schriften des Nikolaus von Kues (1440–1450)*. Münster: Aschendorff Verlag, 1962.

Ward, Graham. "Michel de Certeau's 'Spiritual Spaces.'" *South Atlantic Quarterly* 100, no. 2 (Spring 2001): 501–17.

Wasserschleben, Hermann, ed. *Die irische Kanonensammlung*. 2nd ed. Aalen: Scientia Verlag, 1966.

Watanabe, Morimichi. "The Origins of Modern Cusanus Research in Germany and the Foundation of the Heidelberg *Opera omnia*." In *Nicholas of Cusa in Search of God and Wisdom: Essays in Honor of Morimichi Watanabe by the American Cusanus Society*, edited by Gerald Christianson and Thomas M. Izbicki, 17–42. Leiden: Brill, 1991.

Wenck, Johannes. *De ignota litteratura*. Translated by Jasper Hopkins. In *Complete Philosophical and Theological Writings of Nicholas of Cusa*, vol. 1, 425–56. Minneapolis: Arthur J. Banning Press, 2001.

Williams, Rowan. *Christ the Heart of Creation*. London: Bloomsbury, 2018.

Wisser, Richard. "Nikolaus Cusanus im 'lebendigen Spiegel' der Philosophie von Karl Jaspers." *Zeitschrift für philosophische Forschung* 19 (1965): 528–40.

Wittgenstein, Ludwig. *Philosophical Investigations*. Translated by G. E. M. Anscombe. 2nd ed. Oxford: Basil Blackwell, 1958.

Yusa, Michiko. "Nishida Kitarō and 'Coincidentia oppositorum': An Introduction." In Reinhardt and Schwaetzer, *Cusanus-Rezeption in der Philosophie des 20. Jahrhunderts*, 211–26.

Ziebart, K. Meredith. *Nicolaus Cusanus on Faith and the Intellect: A Case Study in 15th-Century Fides-Ratio Controversy*. Leiden: Brill, 2014.

Žitko, Pavao. "Karl Jaspers lettore di Cusano: Presupposti Interpretativi ed esiti teoretici." PhD diss., University of Zagreb and University of Perugia, 2017.

Contributors

Tamara Albertini is professor and chair of philosophy at the University of Hawai'i at Manoa and the author of books on Marsilio Ficino and Charles de Bovelles, as well as many other publications in Islamic philosophy and Renaissance philosophy. She is the founding president of the International Charles de Bovelles Society.

David Albertson is associate professor of religion at the University of Southern California and Executive Director of the Nova Forum for Catholic Thought. He is the author of *Mathematical Theologies: Nicholas of Cusa and the Legacy of Thierry of Chartres* (2014) and co-editor with Cabell King of *Without Nature? A New Condition for Theology* (2009).

João Maria André is professor of philosophy at the Universidade de Coimbra, where he teaches philosophy and theater. In addition to having published several volumes of poetry and criticism, he is most recently the author of *Renascimento e Modernidade: Releituras filosóficas* (2022) and *Douta ignorância, linguagem e dialog: O poder e os limites da palavra em Nicolau de Cusa* (2019). He has translated several works of Nicholas of Cusa into Portuguese.

John R. Betz is associate professor of theology at the University of Notre Dame. He is the author of *After Enlightenment: The Post-Secular Vision of J. G. Hamann* (2009) and with David Bentley Hart has translated the magnum opus of Erich Przywara, SJ, *Analogia Entis* (2014).

Elizabeth Brient is associate professor of philosophy at the University of Georgia. A scholar of continental philosophy, late medieval mysticism, and Neoplatonism, she is author of *The Immanence of the Infinite: Hans Blumenberg and the Threshold to Modernity* (2002).

Peter Casarella is professor of theology at Duke Divinity School. He is the author of *Word as Bread: Language and Theology in Nicholas of Cusa* (2017) and most recently co-editor of *Pope Francis and the Search for God in America* (2021) with Maria Clara Bingemer, and of *The Whole Is Greater Than Its Parts* (2020) with Gabriel Said Reynolds.

Emmanuel Falque is professor and honorary dean of the Faculty of Philosophy at the Institut Catholique de Paris and the founder of the International Network in Philosophy of Religion. His many works in medieval theology and modern phenomenology recently include *Hors phénomène: Essai aux confins de la phénoménalité* (2021) and, in translation, *Nothing to It: Reading Freud As a Philosopher* (2020) and *By Way of Obstacles: A Pathway through a Work* (2022).

Stephen Gersh is professor emeritus of medieval studies in the Medieval Institute at the University of Notre Dame. The author of numerous books and articles, he has recently published a collection of essays, *Metaphysics and Hermeneutics in the Medieval Platonic Tradition* (2023), as well as a translation of Marsilio Ficino's *Commentary on Plotinus* (2018).

David Bentley Hart is a theologian, critic, translator, and novelist. His most recent works include *Roland in Moonlight* (2021), *Kenogaia (A Gnostic Tale)* (2021), *Tradition and Apocalypse: An Essay on the Future of Christian Belief* (2022), *You Are Gods: On Nature and Supernature* (2022), and *The New Testament: A Translation* (2023).

Il Kim is associate professor and program chair of architecture at Auburn University. A practicing architect and historian of art, he is the author of articles on Nicholas of Cusa, Renaissance culture, and Japanese design. He currently serves as president of the American Cusanus Society.

Jean-Luc Marion is a member of the Académie Française and emeritus professor of philosophy at the Université Paris-Sorbonne (Paris IV). For many years he held the Andrew Thomas Greeley and Grace McNichols

Greeley Chair in Catholic Studies at the University of Chicago and the Dominique Dubarle Chair at the Institut Catholique de Paris. In 2020 he was awarded the Ratzinger Prize. His most recent books are *La métaphysique et après: Essai sur l'historicité et sur les époques de la philosophie* (2023) and *D'ailleurs, la révélation* (2020).

John Milbank is emeritus professor in the Department of Theology and Religious Studies at the University of Nottingham, where he is president of the Centre of Theology and Philosophy. He is the author of many books in theology and two volumes of poetry. His most recent works are *After Science and Religion: Fresh Perspectives from Philosophy and Theology* (2022) with Peter Harrison, and *The Politics of Virtue: Post-Liberalism and the Human Future* (2016) with Adrian Pabst.

Michael Edward Moore is associate professor of history at the University of Iowa. He is the author of *Nicholas of Cusa and the* Kairos *of Modernity: Cassirer, Gadamer, Blumenberg* (2013) and *A Sacred Kingdom: Bishops and the Rise of Frankish Kingship* (2011).

Jean-Marie Nicolle is professor of philosophy at Le lycée Jeanne-d'Arc in Rouen. He is a leading authority on Nicholas of Cusa's mathematics and the author of many works in philosophy. His most recent books are *Le laboratoire mathématique de Nicolas de Cues* (2020) and *Les trois fenêtres* (2021).

Cyril O'Regan is Catherine F. Huisking Professor of Theology at the University of Notre Dame. He has written several works on Hegel, modern theology, Gnosticism, and continental philosophy. His most recent book is *The Anatomy of Misremembering: Balthasar's Response to Philosophical Modernity, vol. 1, Hegel* (2014).

José González Ríos is associate professor of the history of modern philosophy at the Universidad de Buenos Aires and a member of the National Scientific and Technical Research Council (CONICET). He is author of *Metafísica de la Palabra: Una investigación sobre el problema del lenguaje en el pensamiento de Nicolás de Cusa* (2014) and most recently the editor of *Verbum et imago coincidunt: Il linguaggio come specchio vivo in Cusano* (2018).

Alexia Schmitt is associate professor of the history of medieval philosophy at the Universidad del Salvador. A member of the Círculo de Estudios Cusanos in Buenos Aires, she is the author of *Interioridad y Trascendencia. Asimilación de la interioridad agustiniana en el pensamiento Cusano: hacia la subjetividad moderna* (2017).

Kazuhiko Yamaki is professor of philosophy at Waseda University in Tokyo and president of the Japanese Cusanus Society. His recent publications include *Anregung und Übung: Zur Laienphilosophie des Nikolaus von Kues* (2017) and *Der Zusammenhang von Ort und Person bei Nikolaus von Kues* (2017).

Valentina Zaffino was for many years professor of the history of modern philosophy at the Pontifical Lateran University in Vatican State. She is now based at the University of Calabria and is Rome Associate at the Rome Global Gateway of the University of Notre Dame. She is the author of *Totum et unum: Giordano Bruno e il pensiero antico* (2020) and co-editor with Emmanuele Vimercati of *Nicholas of Cusa and the Aristotelian Tradition* (2020).

Index

A

absolute, 30, 35, 41–42, 77–80, 82–83, 97, 101, 179, 247, 257, 297. *See also* contractio

Achard of St. Victor, 290n28, 304n73, 311

aenigma (enigma), 79–80, 80n15, 252, 264, 284

aequalitas (equality), 146, 219, 226, 285, 289, 291n30, 297, 311, 322; as divine Son, 223, 284, 287–88

aesthetics, 140, 189, 193–94, 237–38, 241n28, 247. *See also* architecture, art

Agamben, Giorgio, 309n89

Alan of Lille, 97n30, 289n25, 292n34

Albergati, Nicholas, 220–21

Albert the Great, 251, 281–82, 284, 298

Alberti, Leon Battista, 179, 198–200

Albertson, David, 232, 246–47, 250, 292n34

Alexander of Hales, 178

Alighieri, Dante, 50

alterity, xxii, 78, 81, 101, 130, 153, 199–200, 204, 289, 325

Althusser, Louis, 132

Álvarez-Gómez, Mariano, 141, 208, 211n29

Amalric of Bena, 282

Ambrose of Milan, 49

anachronism, xiv–xvi

analogy, xvi, 36, 64, 124, 133, 147, 152, 178, 184, 300n59, 321, 328; *analogia entis* (analogy of being), xvi–xvii, 11, 13–17, 19–20, 125, 167, 302, 318, 322

Anselm of Canterbury, 44, 181

apophasis, xvii, xxii, 4, 14, 15n35, 17, 80, 159, 166, 181, 183, 186, 230, 233, 286, 293n38, 294, 316, 325, 328. *See also* cataphasis, *docta ignorantia*, negation, *via negativa*

Aquinas, Thomas, xvii, 13, 50, 174, 176–77, 180, 184n58, 251, 281, 283–84, 286, 297, 298n52, 300, 302, 306n80; compared to Cusanus, 317–18, 320–22, 325. *See also* Thomism

architecture, xiv, 141, 155, 160, 189–96, 200

Aristotelianism, xvi, 40n54, 79, 82, 88, 92, 121, 123, 174, 180, 251, 257, 267, 282, 303n71

Aristotle, 16, 17, 24, 44, 47, 50–51, 55, 81–84, 122–23, 133, 136, 174, 289

art, 189–96, 200, 235–39, 241, 295

Augustine of Hippo, 12–13, 21, 44, 49–50, 121, 172, 183, 186–87, 235, 274, 281–282, 284, 289, 303, 312, 315

Augustinianism, xiv–xv, 169, 172, 183, 185–87, 285–86

Avicenna (Ibn Sina), 258

B

Baader, Franz Xaver von, 17

Bachelard, Gaston, 154, 162n99

Bacon, Francis (painter), 241

Bacon, Francis (philosopher), 62

Badiou, Alain, xxii, 154, 165, 293n38, 317

Balthasar, Hans Urs von, xxii, 11, 20, 184, 247–50, 321

Barth, Karl, 14

Bauhaus, 192–93

Baxandall, Michael, 141

Beierwaltes, Werner, xxii, 75–88, 130

Benedict of Nursia, 50

Berthold of Moosburg, 95, 282n3

Blondel, Maurice, 175, 185, 267

Blumenberg, Hans, 54, 59–74, 170, 173, 321

body, 57, 143, 149n43, 161, 271, 293n36, 310, 312

Boehme, Jacob, 284

Boethius, xx, 49, 281–82, 284–85, 287n19, 297, 298n51

Bonaventure, 178, 230, 250, 300n59, 322

Bond, H. Lawrence, 180

Borges, Jorge Luis, 89

Bourdieu, Pierre, 141

Brixen, xiv, 4, 182, 239

Bruno, Giordano, xiv, xx, 4, 8, 19n45, 25, 39, 66–70, 72, 74, 120, 173, 251, 321, 323–24

Buber, Martin, xxi, 23n1

Buddhism, 114, 116–17, 135

Byzantine, 233, 236, 238, 242

C

Cajetan, Thomas, 13–14

Calcidius, 123

Campanella, Tommaso, 39

Campo, Heymericus de, 282

Cantor, Georg, 305n77, 328

Carlson, Thomas, 232

cartography, xx, 153

Casarella, Peter, 79

Casey, Edward, 154

Cassian, John, 48, 50

Cassirer, Ernst, xx, 23n1, 54, 120, 123, 141, 170, 180

cataphasis, xvii, xxii, 159, 230, 233, 316, 325. *See also* apophasis

causality, 37, 61, 93, 114–15, 176–77, 213, 219, 256, 266–67, 272, 276, 295; four Aristotelian causes, xvi, 173–74, 180, 289. *See also* Aristotelianism

Certeau, Michel de, xvi, xxi, xxiii, 132, 139–53, 159–67, 240, 247

Cézanne, Paul, 241

Chartres, School of, 44, 281, 286, 292, 309n89. *See also* Thierry of Chartres

Christology, 94, 181, 238n16, 278, 304n73, 305–6, 308; as *coincidentia oppositorum*, 9–10, 19–20, 292–97, 302, 309. *See also* Incarnation

circle, 30, 34, 99, 102, 212, 239–40, 264, 276, 303, 319; infinite, 97, 109, 115, 305; polygon inscribed in a, 206–207; squaring the, 141, 161–62. *See also* geometry, sphere

circumference, 30, 92–94, 98, 101–3, 109, 113, 127, 296n48; infinite, 99. *See also* circle, geometry

Claudel, Paul, 135

Clement of Alexandria, 44, 48

clock, 36. *See also* eternity, time

Cohen, Hermann, xx–xxi

coincidentia oppositorum (coincidence of opposites), xvi, xx, 3, 8, 11, 13–20, 26, 35, 38, 78–79, 86, 88, 96, 108, 110n4, 115–16, 137, 141, 162, 165, 167, 174n16, 179, 230, 244–45, 256–57, 275, 283, 285–86, 301–3, 305, 308, 313–14, 318–19, 323–24,

326; as apophatic, 4, 32, 80, 87, 125, 294; as Christological, 9–10, 249; of *complicatio* and *explicatio*, 37, 295–97, 299; of love and knowledge, 220–21; and Trinity, 287–91; and wall of paradise, 27, 32, 34, 36, 42. *See also* paradox

Comenius, John Amos, 284

complicatio (enfolding), 15, 36–37, 101, 103, 113, 127–28, 208, 277, 297–99, 303, 308, 321–23; of God, 293, 295–96; of mind, 98, 207, 256, 278, 284. *See also explicatio*

coniectura (conjecture), 59, 67, 79, 102, 122, 124, 127, 167, 197–98, 200, 209–11, 253–54, 257, 263–64, 286, 300–302, 310, 315, 319, 321, 323–24, 328. *See also* epistemology, truth

contractio (contraction), 33, 42, 53, 75, 78, 97, 101–3, 145, 207–10, 212, 214, 218, 227, 257, 269, 290–91, 296–97, 299, 305–7, 318, 321, 329; of the world, 41, 98–99, 290; of sight, 83, 217, 224. *See also* absolute

Copernicus, Nicolaus, 62–63

creation, 10, 14–17, 20, 36–37, 127, 172, 174, 178, 180, 223, 249, 256, 278, 283, 286, 292–93, 295–96, 300, 307, 309–10, 326

Creator, 14, 17, 37, 117, 125, 127, 177–79, 223, 256, 292, 295, 307, 309

D

Da Vinci, Leonardo, 239

Damascius, 309

Dasein, 195, 254, 259–60, 263

David of Dinant, 282

De Lubac, Henri, 142, 174–75, 185

deification, 212, 275–76, 279, 287, 309, 324

deity, 32, 49, 256. *See also* gods

Deleuze, Gilles, xxii, 121, 126–30, 141, 241

Denys the Carthusian, 51

Derrida, Jacques, xxi, 130, 165n112, 319, 325

Descartes, René, xvii, xx, 18, 24, 35, 62–63, 67, 119–20, 125, 128–29, 147–49, 151–55, 160, 175, 195, 231

dialectic, xx, 18–19, 77–79, 81, 84–87, 121, 123, 125, 142, 174n16, 178, 253–55, 290. *See also* paradox

dialogue, interreligious, xx, xxiii, 203–27, 286n14, 329

Dilthey, Wilhelm, 8

Dionysius. *See* Pseudo-Dionysius the Areopagite

docta ignorantia (learned ignorance), xvi–xvii, 3–5, 7–8, 10–11, 19, 91, 95, 103, 129, 132, 135–37, 141, 183, 205–207, 210–11, 223–24, 256. *See also* apophasis, *via negativa*

Duméry, Henry, 185

Duns Scotus, John, xvii, 300

Dupré, Louis, xxiii, 169–87, 320

E

Eckhart, Meister, xiv, xxi–xxii, 44, 68, 80, 90–91, 95, 100, 110n5, 121–22, 150, 170, 178, 180, 186, 252, 281, 289, 291, 298n52, 300, 304, 306, 310, 315, 321–22

ecstasy, 147, 155, 269. *See also* rapture

empiricism, 9n13, 174, 259, 262, 273–74

Enlightenment, 4–5, 8, 10, 173, 176, 190. *See also* modernity

epektasis, 316

epistemology, xx, 9n13, 18n42, 35, 67, 77, 179, 205, 208, 253, 256, 292n34, 295n44, 299, 323, 328; of scientific disciplines, 146, 150–54, 161–62

epoch, xvi–xvii, 59–73, 173, 184, 320, 324. *See also* modernity

Erasmus, Desiderius, xiv

Eriugena, John Scottus, 14–15, 121, 281–82, 291, 293, 295, 299, 301, 308, 315, 322–23

eros, 161, 269, 324. *See also* love

eschatology, 212, 308, 310

eternity, 16, 36, 38–39, 108, 113, 219, 262, 276, 288, 294, 296n48, 298, 302–4, 307–11. *See also* time

ethics, 19, 47, 50, 135, 183, 190, 194–95, 200, 208, 216, 218–19, 226, 304

eucharist, 147, 273, 303

Euripides, 6

explicatio (unfolding), 15, 36–37, 87, 101, 103, 128, 144–145, 154, 161, 179, 198, 207–8, 214–15, 258, 264, 277–78, 290, 293, 297, 299, 303, 306, 308, 321–22; of God, 14, 77, 86, 295–96, 304, 323; of human mind, 82–83, 196–97, 224, 256. *See also complicatio*

eyes, 6, 33–34, 41, 99, 114–15, 143, 145, 198–200, 209, 217, 229, 247, 271, 296, 307

F

face, 33, 136, 164, 179, 209, 238, 246, 250, 269–70, 274–75, 278, 296, 301, 304, 310

Falque, Emmanuel, xxi–xxiii, 143, 186

Fénelon François, 140, 150

Feuerbach, Ludwig, 325

Fichte, Johann Gottlieb, 45, 90

Ficino, Marsilio, 23, 197, 324

figure, of Cusanus, xiii, xx, xxiii, 12, 16, 25, 54, 59–60, 67, 69, 73, 167, 230, 314–16, 320; Figure P, 199–200, 210; geometrical, 97, 145, 162, 165, 247, 291, 306; painted, 33, 42, 235, 239, 241, 246–49; of revelation, 247–50. *See also* form, geometry, painting

Flasch, Kurt, 27, 93, 223n68, 292n34

Florensky, Pavel, xxi

form: divine, 97, 114, 208, 215, 226, 247, 248n40, 249n43, 253, 267, 278, 297–98, 302, 304; and matter, 8, 171, 208, 288–89, 294, 298, 306. *See also* causality

Foucault, Michel, 137, 144, 154

Franciscans, 178, 230, 233, 300n59, 309n89

freedom, 29, 31–33, 39, 42, 55–56, 136, 150, 164, 179, 185n59, 267, 323. *See also* liberation

Freud, Lucian, 241

Freud, Sigmund, 131, 136

future, xxiii, 30, 60, 108, 113, 146, 161, 185, 200, 203, 227, 259–62, 314, 327, 329–30. *See also* temporality, time

G

Gadamer, Hans Georg, xxii, 44–45, 47, 54–58, 170

Galilei, Galileo, 39, 56, 151, 153

Gandillac, Maurice de, xxii, 119–30, 132n2, 141, 165n112

Gasset, Ortega y, xxi

geometry, 97, 140, 143–46, 149, 152–54, 157–58, 160–67, 247, 252, 291. *See also* circle, figure, line, point, polygon, sphere, triangle

Gilbert of Poitiers, 287

Gilson, Étienne, 119–20, 318

gods, 133, 254–55, 258–61, 264, 276, 279. *See also* deity

Gödel, Kurt, 327

Görres, Johann Joseph von, 17

Goethe, Johann Wolfgang von, 55, 323

Gothic, 53, 192–93

Gregory of Nyssa, 50, 267, 299

Gregory the Great, 49

Grosseteste, Robert, 281, 307

Guyon, Madame Jeanne, 150

H

Habermas, Jürgen, 45
Hadewijch of Brabant, 150
Hamann, Johann Georg, 4–11
Harries, Karsten, xx, xxiii, 170, 189–98, 200, 320
Haubst, Rudolf, 14, 141, 169, 182, 184
Hegel, Georg Wilhelm Friedrich, xiv, xv, xx, 8, 10–11, 15–19, 45, 56, 75–77, 79, 81–88, 121, 123, 132, 172–74, 185, 187, 189–90, 194–95, 200, 248, 284–85, 290, 299, 321, 325
Heidegger, Martin, 19, 57, 148, 155–60, 162n99, 164, 167, 175, 186, 190, 194–96, 200, 232, 243, 247, 252–55, 258–64, 325, 329
Heidelberg, xiv, 119, 121
henology, 283–84, 311, 329. *See also* One
Henry, Michel, 241
Heraclitus, 12, 258
Herder, Johann Gottfried, 8, 55, 323
hermeneutics, xv, 9, 54–55, 144, 149, 160, 167, 170, 173, 184–85, 205–207, 210, 213, 216, 222–23, 252–53, 258–59, 262
Hermes Trismegistus, 91, 251
Hermeticism, 95, 263n53, 286, 320
Herodotus, 45, 48, 57
historicity, 62, 90, 259, 327. *See also* temporality
Hoff, Johannes, 165n112, 184
Hölderlin, Friedrich, 55, 157, 252, 254, 259–61, 263
Hugh of St. Victor, 50
humanism, 55, 81, 170, 179, 232, 282
Husserl, Edmund, xvi–xvii, 143, 152–55, 162, 185, 232, 247, 252

I

icon, xxii, 36, 42, 140, 143, 145, 164, 166, 217–18, 229–250, 278, 309, 327–28. *See also* idol, image
iconicity, 314, 327–29
iconology, 142, 144
Idealism, German, 3, 56, 75–76, 79, 88, 90, 323
idem (same), 87, 213–14, 223
identity, xvi, 10n17, 13–14, 16, 18, 19, 65, 76–82, 84–85, 87–88, 101, 116, 167, 178, 277–78, 294, 302, 308; self-identity, xvii, 107–13
idiota (layman), 39, 56, 120, 128–30, 133, 214
idol, 243, 316, 328. *See also* image, icon
Ignatius of Loyola, 128, 145, 172–73
imagination, 152, 208, 233, 253, 289, 292n34
impossibility, xvii, 92, 94n22, 98, 150–51, 166, 206, 288, 305n77. *See also posse ipsum*
Incarnation, 10, 177, 180, 283–85, 302, 304–7, 310–11. *See also* Christology
infinity, xv, xvii, xxii, 26, 28, 32–33, 68, 74, 92–94, 120, 126, 166, 205, 208, 213, 215, 274, 290–91, 294, 296–97, 300, 302–4, 305n77, 309, 315, 321, 323; of desire, 265, 267–72; divine, 78–79, 175, 268–69, 276; negative or privative, 97–98, 101, 257n26, 295, 319; perspectival, 200. *See also* sphere
intellect, 32, 34–36, 41–42, 53, 95–96, 98, 100n49, 107, 123, 174–75, 181, 208, 215, 221, 225, 263, 268–71, 278–79, 289n25, 292n34, 294, 296, 299, 302, 311
intentionality, 266, 269–75
intuition, 40, 271–75, 302
invisibility, xxii, 53, 57, 122, 144, 147, 159, 164, 233, 237, 241–43, 248, 273, 275, 301, 311. *See also* visibility
Islam, xxii, 38, 211, 283n7

J

Jacobi, Friedrich Heinrich, 8, 11
Jaspers, Karl, xxii, 23–42, 175, 185n59, 323
Jerome, 49
John of St. Thomas, 13
John of the Cross, 140
Judaism, 10, 211, 283n7
Jung, Carl, xxi
justice, 46, 182

K

Kandinsky, Wassily, 241
Kant, Immanuel, xvii, xx, 4, 8–11, 19, 24, 64, 67, 111, 132, 179, 194, 226–27, 233, 273, 292n34, 295n44, 319
Kierkegaard, Søren, 8, 24, 285
Kircher, Athanasius, 251
Klibansky, Raymond, 119
Koyré, Alexandre, 119
Küng, Hans, 226–27

L

Lacan, Jacques, xxii, 131–37, 141
Lautman, Albert, xxii
law, xiv, 40, 45–46, 226, 260. *See also* non-contradiction, law of
Lebenswelt, xvi
Lefebvre, Henri, 144, 154
Lefèvre d'Étaples, Jacques, xx, 199, 200n27, 251
Leibniz, Gottfried Wilhelm, 25, 68, 72, 90, 108, 111–13, 117, 284, 299
Leopardi, Giacomo, 265–67, 269
Levinas, Emmanuel, xxii
Lewis, Stephen, 232
Liber de causis, 251
liberation, 24, 42, 127. *See also* freedom
line, 127, 145–46, 161, 165, 199, 296n48; infinite 97, 291, 303, 306. *See also* figure, geometry
liturgy, 20–21, 145, 147, 240
Llull, Ramon, 282, 300n59, 315
logic, xvi, 8, 19, 24, 42, 77–79, 83–84, 88, 111–13, 115, 145, 167, 205, 210, 215, 221, 253, 254n4, 257, 265, 275, 282, 286, 290, 297n49, 299, 302, 318
Logos, 9–10, 276, 299, 304n73, 305, 309, 312. *See also* Incarnation, Trinity, Word
Lorenzetti, Ambrogio, 179, 237
love, 7, 21, 34, 46, 50, 133–37, 181, 187, 215–22, 225–26, 269, 273, 275–76, 278, 296, 311. *See also* eros
Luhmann, Niklas, xxi

M

magnitude, xvii, 115, 156–57. *See also* quantity
Mahnke, Dietrich, 89–90, 110, 115
Malevich, Kazimir, 241
Maréchal, Joseph, 175
Marion, Jean-Luc, xx–xxii, 143, 229, 231–32, 234, 241–47, 250, 272–73, 301
Martineau, Emmanuel, 241
Marx, Karl, 178
materialism, 11, 266
mathematics, xv–xvii, xx, xxii, 40n54, 120, 135, 141, 144–45, 146n32, 151–52, 154, 156–58, 161, 162n99, 165–66, 181, 196, 239, 247, 249, 254, 284–86, 288, 292n34, 297n49, 305, 313, 315, 319–20, 323, 327–28. *See also* geometry
mathesis universalis, 151–52, 154, 160–61, 163, 165
maximum, 7, 15, 96–103, 181, 211, 305–308, 319. *See also* absolute, *contractio*
Maximus the Confessor, 9, 274, 281
Meier-Oeser, Stephan, xx–xxi

Meister Eckhart. *See* Eckhart, Meister

Mendelssohn, Moses, 10

Merleau-Ponty, Maurice, xxii, 143, 154, 163, 241, 244

Mersenne, Marin, xx

metaphysics, 13, 20, 24, 27, 36, 38–39, 42, 47, 51, 53, 79, 83–84, 88, 90, 99, 102, 174, 179, 184–85, 198, 213, 218, 223, 252–53, 255, 258, 261–62, 264, 267, 281–84, 288, 292, 298, 301–2, 306–7, 318, 324, 329; Aristotelian, 81–82; beyond, xv–xvii, 155; Neoplatonic, 87, 124, 180, 319–20, 325; Trinitarian, 286, 296, 309. *See also* Neoplatonism

Milbank, John, xxi, xxiii

mirror, 101, 113–16, 136, 179, 198, 212, 243, 278

modernity, xiii, xv, xx–xxi, 16, 18–19, 54, 56, 59, 61–62, 66, 69, 72–74, 90, 95, 146–47, 151, 155, 169–71, 173, 176, 182, 184, 187, 204, 320. *See also* Enlightenment, epoch

modes of being, 253, 288, 289n25, 293, 307

monad, 96, 111–12, 329

Montaigne, Michel de, xiv

mysticism, 12, 33, 42, 139–42, 148–50, 153, 160–61, 165–66, 172–73, 176, 181, 183–87

N

names, divine, 79, 127, 166, 207, 211, 213, 223, 256–57, 291, 300–301, 325. *See also* apophasis, cataphasis

nearness, 156, 160, 166–67, 278, 326

necessitas complexionis (necessity of connection), 253, 289n25, 292n34, 293. *See also* modes of being

negation, xxii, 84, 87, 116, 135, 165–66, 171, 176, 185, 273, 286, 290–91, 300–301, 316. *See also* apophasis, *docta ignorantia*, *via negativa*

Neo-Kantianism, xx–xxi

Neoplatonism, xiii, xv, 14, 52n58, 76, 78–79, 81–83, 85–88, 91, 121, 124, 129, 180, 182, 251, 271, 282–84, 296, 299, 309, 311, 314, 319–22, 325. *See also* henology, One

Newman, John Henry, 21

Newton, Isaac, 56, 151

Nietzsche, Friedrich, xvii, xxi, 24, 57, 93, 147

nihilism, 146–147

nominalism, 65, 70, 170, 173–74, 177, 314–15, 321

non aliud (not-other), xvi, 76, 79–81, 87, 127, 147, 256, 262, 277, 309, 314, 319, 321, 325–26

non-contradiction, law of, 257, 288, 291, 293–94

nothingness, 87, 112, 116, 136, 146, 286, 289, 324

Novalis, 90

number, 37, 99, 113, 116, 156–59, 164, 166, 197, 207, 292n34, 297n49, 299, 303, 320

O

One, xvi, 14, 76n3, 78, 84, 86–87, 101, 103, 293, 299, 311. *See also* henology

ontology, 77–79, 88, 108, 111, 114, 127, 144, 148, 167, 205, 208, 215, 250, 253, 275, 277–78, 282, 290–91, 292n34, 293n38, 294n36, 295n44, 299, 302, 304–6, 309; ontological difference, 19, 194, 325–26; Trinitarian, 286, 311. *See also* metaphysics

optics, xx, 114, 144, 164

Origen of Alexandria, 48

P

painting, xx, 33, 231, 233, 235–42, 244, 246–47, 249, 273

Panikkar, Raimon, 210, 222

Panofsky, Erwin, 141, 233, 237

pantheism, xv, 14–15, 173, 174n16, 178, 282n3, 304, 310

paradox, xvii, 80, 96, 129, 185, 266, 278, 283, 288–89, 292n34, 293, 302–4, 305n77, 310, 327–29. *See also* coincidentia oppositorum

Paris, xx, 119, 132, 199, 231, 250, 290n28

Pascal, Blaise, xvii, 132, 140, 166, 247

Patocka, Jan, xxi

Paul, 7, 52, 136, 182–83, 223, 225, 248, 317

Péguy, Charles, 285

perspective, 33, 73–74, 84, 143, 145, 177, 179, 185, 198–200, 237, 239, 296, 303, 320, 327, 329. *See also* optics

phenomenology, xvi, xxii, 142–43, 148, 153, 169, 174–75, 185, 232, 241, 243–44, 248–50, 265, 270–71, 301; limited phenomenon, 186, 229–30; saturated phenomenon, 229–30, 272–74

physics, xv, 140, 151–52, 154, 180, 292n34

Pico della Mirandola, Giovanni, 324

Pius II, Pope, 204

Plato, 24, 44, 46, 51, 54–55, 123–24, 132–33, 174, 197

Platonism, 76, 82, 87, 121, 123, 167, 180n40, 184n58, 251–52, 256–57, 267, 282, 292, 297n51, 303, 311. *See also* Neoplatonism

Plotinus, 25, 110n5, 178, 184n58, 267, 289, 299, 322

poetry, 150, 155, 157–59, 252, 254, 259, 261

point, 68–69, 93–94, 113–15, 127, 145–46, 165, 199–200, 248, 290, 303, 307. *See also* geometry

polygon, 162, 206–7, 305–6. *See also* figure

Porphyry, 299

posse ipsum (possibility itself), 52–53, 287, 324

possest (actualized possibility), xvi, 53, 79, 87, 127, 264, 287, 291n30, 314, 319, 321–22, 324–25

prayer, 157, 240, 273

present, xx, xxiii, 12n21, 27–28, 36, 57, 61, 83, 108, 195, 259, 262, 264, 276, 327, 330; absolute, 108–17. *See also* temporality, time

Proclus, 44, 123–24, 322

proportion, xvi, 17, 78, 96, 161, 206, 215, 263, 272, 300n59, 302. *See also* analogy

Protagoras, 197–98

Przywara, Erich, xxii, 4, 11–21, 319–21

Pseudo-Dionysius the Areopagite, xx, xxii, 12, 50, 121–22, 124, 166, 183, 230, 233, 243, 250–51, 256, 262, 282n3, 284, 291, 298, 300, 310, 315

psychoanalysis, 131–37, 161–62

Pythagoreanism, 121, 252–53, 254n5, 292n34, 320

Q

quantity, 101, 144, 146, 148, 151–53, 157–60, 162n99, 163, 165–67, 273–74, 305. *See also* magnitude

quiddity, 52–53, 101, 198, 253, 267, 270

R

Rahner, Karl, xxi, 11, 12n21, 174–75, 185

rapture, 33, 52, 268, 303. *See also* ecstasy

Renaissance, 23, 26, 36, 54, 81, 122–24, 161, 166, 200, 231, 233, 236–38, 240, 242, 282, 314, 324

revelation, 8, 26, 35, 135, 170, 173, 245, 247–50, 269, 273, 278, 283–84, 302, 316

Richard of St. Victor, 50

Ricoeur, Paul, 132, 185n59, 319

Rococo, 193–94

Rome, xix, 195

Rothko, Mark, 241

roundness, 33, 102, 255. *See also* circle, sphere

Rufinus, 49

Index   373

Ruusbroec, Jan van, 50, 172–73, 178

S
Sartre, Jean-Paul, 179
Scheler, Max, 175
Schelling, Friedrich Wilhelm Joseph von, xvii, xx, 8, 10–11, 25, 90, 284, 323, 330
Schleiermacher, Friedrich, xxi, 174n16
Schmitt, Alexia, 186
Scholasticism, xv, 51, 102, 120, 124, 171, 174, 185, 251, 282, 325. *See also* Thomism
Shakespeare, William, 135
Siger of Brabant, 251
silence, 160, 164n105, 166, 243, 316
Simmel, Georg, 28
simplicity, 13, 16, 83, 258, 275, 277–78, 283, 285, 287
singularity, 100n50, 102–3, 123, 130, 145, 165, 204, 212, 217–20, 224, 251–52, 260, 302, 314–18, 324, 326–27
Skepticism, xvi, xxi, 5, 137, 205, 319
Sloterdijk, Peter, xxii, 90–96, 100, 102–103, 154–55
Socrates, 5–7, 46, 101, 133–35, 295n44
Sophocles, 6, 135
space, 37–38, 42, 50, 60, 65–66, 69–72, 86, 93, 108–11, 144–49, 152–61, 162n99, 163–67, 189, 193, 197–98, 200, 210, 227, 237, 254–55, 290, 305, 311–12, 325. *See also* topology
sphere, 34, 89–103, 110–17, 127. *See also* geometry
Spinoza, Baruch, xx, 24, 128, 290
Spirit, Holy, 187, 207, 223, 276, 279, 288, 290, 296–97, 299, 300n59, 306, 309. *See also* Trinity
Stein, Edith, 11
Stoicism, 267
Suárez, Francisco, xv, xvii

sublime, 192, 273, 300–301. *See also* aesthetics
sufficient reason, principle of, xvi
supernatural, 175, 180, 185, 276–78

T
Taylor, Charles, 19, 171
technology, xxii, 56–57, 152, 154–55, 190, 261, 295, 302
Tegernsee monastery, 33, 42, 141, 220, 235–36, 238n14, 239–40, 245, 247
temporality, 150n47, 212, 255, 259, 262, 307. *See also* historicity, time
Teresa of Ávila, 140
Thierry of Chartres, 146n32, 284–85, 289n25, 292–93, 295, 299, 307. *See also* Chartres, School of
Thomas Aquinas. *See* Aquinas, Thomas
Thomism, 11, 14–16, 173–76, 180, 182, 275, 297n51. *See also* Aquinas, Thomas
time, 15–16, 26, 36–37, 42, 61–62, 66, 68–72, 74, 86, 108–11, 158, 193, 227, 259–62, 298, 303, 305, 307, 311–12. *See also* temporality
topology, xvi, 143–49, 152–53, 159–61, 163–66. *See also* space
totalitarianism, 28, 30, 33
triangle, 97, 200, 291
Trinity, 85n36, 97, 125, 127, 172–73, 181, 186, 207, 223, 225, 245, 283–88, 290–91, 293–94, 296–99, 300n59, 302, 307–12, 319–20, 323, 325, 328
truth, 5, 8, 15, 25, 30, 35, 39–40, 48, 50, 80, 85, 112, 120–23, 125, 129, 131–32, 136–37, 147, 171, 173, 179, 192–95, 204–14, 216, 247, 254n4, 263, 267, 275, 278, 293, 303, 310, 328. *See also coniectura*, epistemology
Tuan, Yi Fu, 154

U
Uccello, Paolo, 237

V

Veronica, 242, 246

via negativa, xvi, 137, 165n112, 166, 183, 207, 216, 290–91, 314. *See also* apophasis, *docta ignorantia*, negation

Vico, Giambattista, 327

Victorinus, Marius, 92, 282n3, 299

Virgin Mary, 306

visibility, 60, 66, 68, 71–74, 80, 114, 143–44, 147, 154, 158–59, 164–65, 230, 233, 237, 241–43, 248–49, 270, 273, 277, 301, 314. *See also* invisibility

vision, xxii, 33, 48, 74, 83–84, 143, 164, 198, 217, 219, 229, 232–35, 239, 245, 270, 284, 297, 301. *See also* optics, perspective

W

wall, 27, 31–38, 240, 295–96, 307–9

Weber, Max, 28

Wenck, Johannes, 282

Weyden, Rogier van der, 237–39

Whitehead, Alfred North, 185

William of Moerbeke, 123

Williams, Rowan, 304

wisdom, xix–xx, xxii, 6–7, 44–45, 48, 114, 124, 137, 165, 214–17, 224–25, 227, 233, 283–84, 291n30, 316

Wittgenstein, Ludwig von, 43, 297n49, 328

Word, 37, 54n67, 101, 173, 175, 180–81, 185, 212, 223, 306, 315. *See also* Logos, Trinity

Z

Zeno, 293